Don't
Touch
That Dial!

Radio Programming
in American Life,
1920–1960

Don't Touch That Dial!

Radio Programming in American Life, 1920–1960

J. Fred MacDonald

Nelson-Hall nh *Chicago*

LIBRARY OF CONGRESS CATALOGING IN PUBLICATION DATA

MacDonald, J. Fred.
   Don't touch that dial!

   Bibliography: p.   412 pp.
   Includes index.
   1. Radio broadcasting—United States—History.
2. United States—Popular culture. I. Title.
PN1991.3.U6M3   791.44'0973   79-87700
ISBN 0-88229-528-4

Manufactured in the United States of America

10 9 8 7 6 5 4 3 2 1

For my parents
whose understanding made it all possible

Contents

Preface

For most Americans in the mid-twentieth century, radio was an amazing invention. With just a twist of the dial a listener could tune in the greatest personalities in world affairs and show business. Radio brought current events and entertainment directly into the home, and it required little of a listener except time and imagination. It was often called a "theater of the mind" because broadcasting, as an audio-only medium, was fully realized only in the mind of the listener. Each person in the audience provided his own mental imagery of friendliness and sincerity when the pleasant voice of President Roosevelt began chatting with him from in front of an imaginary fireplace. It was the individual listener, too, who mentally provided the props and stage effects for the broadcast of a Shakespearian drama, and the substance that spoken words only suggested in an adventure or mystery program.

The physical principles of radio were not important to the average radio user. He cared little, and knew even less, about the way the vacuum tubes in the receiver actually worked. As long as they began to glow when he turned the knob and heard a familiar click—that was all he generally understood about broadcasting. The average listener was not really concerned with how the "air" or the "ether" carried sound waves, or about the way in which a station could transmit electrical impulses and have them received by a million radio sets simultaneously. What he did care about, however, was the programming he heard once he turned on his receiver.

For the vast majority of the citizenry, radio and the programs it carried were synonymous. To enjoy good programming, the typical listener was willing to endure static, transmission interference, commercials, shows he did not care for, and a certain amount of control over the receiver by other members of the family. But when he enjoyed a series, he enjoyed it loyally for two or three decades. Whether it was the adventurous *Lone Ranger* (twenty-two years), the heart-wrenching *Ma Perkins* (twenty-seven years), the uproarious *Jack Benny Program* (twenty-five years), or the soberly factual *Lowell Thomas and the News* (forty-six years), when a radio listener fell in love with a program, it was for keeps.

While scholars have produced substantial studies of the history of broadcasting, and encyclopedic compilations of program descriptions, little has been done to relate programming and program content to the life of the average listener. As a study in popular culture, this present book attempts to tie together the loose ends. It seeks to relate, within a historical context, the importance of broadcasting in the lives of most Americans. By bringing together the content of radio and the evolution of national life from 1920 to 1960, this book offers a perspective which sees culture—and especially the commercialized mass culture of the United States in the twentieth century—as a reflector and creator of popular values, attitudes, fantasies, and realities.

To accomplish this, it has been necessary to turn to new sources of information. Certainly, I have utilized authoritative works by past scholars, as well as the traditional, accepted newspaper sources. But this book exploits relatively untouched materials. From my private collection of more than eight thousand hours of tape-recorded vintage radio shows, it was possible to make extensive use of actual programs. Because this is a private collection with an unpublished system of classification, I have quoted from these shows without footnoting the source. Wherever possible, however, I have cited the date of the broadcast in the text. Further, this book is the first such study to make extensive use of radio fan magazines.

These monthly publications often published interviews with celebrities or articles written by them. The book also makes extensive use of the most important publication in the entertainment world, *Variety*, a weekly tabloid which offers valuable information and insights on the evolution of programming.

The book is divided into two complementary sections. The first traces the history of radio and its programs, seeking to understand the ways in which broadcasting arose and collapsed during the period 1920–1960. The second section looks more closely at distinct types of programs or social themes within radio during this time span. In this manner, merging the historical overview with in-depth genre and thematic considerations, the fullest comprehension of the significance of radio in popular culture can be gained.

In acknowledging the many whose support made possible a book such as this, it is necessary to begin at the beginning— with those collectors of recordings of old-time radio who first infected me with the spirit and importance of preserving such materials: Paul Gremley, Bill Schurk, and Don Pellow. There are also those who opened their collections and archives to me, thereby presenting the widest range of programs from which to sample the cultural past: Martin Maloney, Chuck Schaden, John Edwards, Dick Judge, and Roger Rittner. A special note of thanks must go to Jay K. Springman of Xavier University in New Orleans whose backing in terms of recordings and advice was always abundant. And Eli Segal spent time and energy in reading the manuscript and offering valuable ideas—much gratitude is due him.

Without a sabbatical leave from Northeastern Illinois University, or the encouragement from my colleagues in the Department of History, June Sochen and C. David Tompkins, this study might not have been possible.

A great deal of appreciation goes also to John Wright who offered criticism without being discouraging, and to Stuart Kaminsky of Northwestern University whose personal and professional suggestions were crucial.

In a more general vein, but strategic nonetheless, was the

support I have gained in the study of American popular culture from those academicians who have done, and are still doing, much to show the worth of its preservation and study: Ray Browne, Russel Nye, John Cawelti, Lew Carlson, Maurie Crane, and Robert Ferguson.

Appreciation is also expressed to the secretarial assistance so important to the preparation of this book: Noreen Ciesielczyk Jones, Jan Majka Hansen, and Mary Hamilton.

Finally, I would like to express a special thanks to my wife, Leslie MacDonald, who offered ideas, advice, assistance, and endurance throughout the months of research and composition.

1

The History of Broadcasting, 1920–1960

Somewhere between vaudeville with its travelling troupes and live stage shows, and television with its audio-visual forms of amusement, America was in love with radio. It was not the news-and-music sameness of contemporary programming, which may be popular and lucrative, but is lacking in creative imagination. Instead, America was enamored of an entertainment medium which showcased everything from fine drama, mundane soap operas, and sports action, to formulaic detective stories, lavish comedy-variety shows, and the latest developments in world news. Regardless of age, taste, wealth, or sex, there was much in broadcasting to please everyone. Daily tens of millions of Americans were so pleased. And by the 1940s almost every home in the nation was equipped with a receiving set through which to hear and enjoy this programming.

Radio was criticized. In the minds of many, radio was too banal, too concerned with the unspectacular vanities of commonness and not involved enough with uplifting subjects like fine music and intellectual discussion. For others, it was too commercial. The advertisements that were sandwiched within and between programs not only interfered with the artistic aspects of broadcasting, they also insulted the intelligence of listeners. Moreover, it was alleged, the stations and networks airing shows lost their integrity and independence when they sold themselves to the makers of laxatives, automobiles, shortening, and the like. Instead of being a great moral force,

1

radio had become an audial peddler to which program content was less important than the commercial announcements. Culture reflects the environment in which it grows. One could not have expected to transplant the values and content of another historical period or of a privileged few to the mass audience of twentieth-century America. The culture of the United States must reflect the commercial and democratic populace. Although modified by governmental regulations and subsidies, the American economic system was primarily one of free enterprise. This system abhorred governmental interference and stressed the importance of selling. To have excluded commercialism from radio would have demanded either independent wealth on the part of each station, or financial dependence upon government.

Seeking to please an audience of millions of relatively free-and-equal, middle-class citizens, radio inevitably reflected the democratic environment which it served. It played to their tastes and it mirrored their values. The critics were in part correct. Radio, overall, never reached the high esthetic plane many felt it should have attained. It also never escaped the commercialism others felt hampered its sophistication. Yet, radio could not have done otherwise and still retained the mass following it had. It was an instrument of electrical entertainment aimed at a commercial democracy—a world of independent, average people who preferred an occasional advertising announcement to the implications of a broadcasting system fully regulated by governmental bureaucrats.

The Emergence of Radio Programming to 1925

American radio programming was born in a shack atop a six-story building in East Pittsburgh, Pennsylvania. The date was November 2, 1920; the shack housed the 100-watt transmitter of station KDKA; and the first scheduled, non-experimental, public program was an evening broadcast of results from the Presidential election that day between Warren G. Harding and James M. Cox. It was an inauspicious beginning for radio—a medium which in a few years would be a daily indulgence for millions—as no more than a few hundred listeners had the proper equipment to hear that program. Nonetheless, technicians and executives of Westinghouse Electric company, the owners of KDKA, were convinced that radio was commercially and scientifically feasible. Their faith in the medium would soon be rewarded.

Within eighteen months of that first recognizable radio program, public and commercial interest in broadcasting became a national fad. Newspaper and magazine accounts of the achievement in East Pittsburgh spread the message of radio's potential. Whatever it was called—"wireless telephone," "wireless musicbox," "radio telephone," or simply "radio"— the new invention encouraged hundreds of thousands of people throughout the nation to jam electrical shops and department stores to purchase receivers. Those who lacked the technical skill to assemble the simple and inexpensive crystal sets that were so popular turned often to friends, relatives, or the prospering new businessman, the radio repairman. By 1921, however, stores were selling ready-made radios. Most of these were vacuum-tube models, more powerful than crystal sets. But, regardless of model, most required headphones; few, indeed, were equipped with speakers. Despite inconveniences, listeners were fascinated with this new form of amusement which brought music and the human voice into the home. Reception of radio emissions was not always clear. Listeners had to endure static, weak signals, and other forms of interference. But the allure of the novelty even made tolerable the crackling and popping noises of primitive reception.

The financial potential in owning a radio station led many businesses, institutions, and wealthy individuals to acquire federal licenses and establish their own broadcasting facilities. Since licenses and stations were easy to acquire, by the end of 1922 they were owned by such disparate entities as Gimbel's Department Store (WIP, Philadelphia), the Ford Motor Company (WWI, Detroit), the Omaha Grain Exchange (WAAW, Omaha), St. Matthew's Cathedral (KFBU, Laramie), the Alabama Power Company (WSY, Birmingham), and Packard dealer Earl C. Anthony (KFI, Los Angeles). The Westinghouse company did not rest idly while other commercial interests exploited the broadcasting boom. As well as KDKA, that company established WJZ (Newark), KYW (Chicago), and WBZ (Springfield, Mass.). Colleges and universities recognized the importance of radio as an academic subject, and at the end of 1922 a total of seventy-four institutions of higher education had their own stations. Newspapers also established broadcasting outlets. WWJ was the "voice" of the *Detroit News*; KWH was owned by the *Los Angeles Examiner;* KSD by the *Des Moines Register and Tribune;* WHAF by the *Kansas City Star*; and WSB by the *Atlanta Journal.* By December 1922, sixty-nine newspapers owned stations. That radio had struck a responsive chord within the American citizenry was obvious. Two years after the KDKA inaugural broadcast, there were 1.5 million sets in the country; there were more than 550 stations; and there was at least one station in every state—ranging from California with sixty-nine, to several states with only one.

Given the quality of programming in its earliest years, it is a miraculous achievement that radio flourished. In contrast to the breadth and technical sophistication of later broadcasting, the earliest programs were austere. Stations only broadcast at specific times of the day. Most programs were filled with recorded music. And talk shows were usually lectures on domestic topics, or news and sports announcements. Typical of such programming is the radio log for the Bamberger's Department Store station, WOR (Newark), as it appeared in the *New York Times* on May 29, 1922:

> 10:30 A.M.—"Packing the Week-End Bag," by Vanity Fair
> 11:30 A.M.—"Smiles," by J.E.K.
> 12:30 P.M.—A period of song selections from the recordings of Alma Gluck and Homer Rodeheaver
> 1:30 P.M.—During this period the numbers requested by our radio audience will be played
> 2:30 P.M.—Richter String Quartet: Beethoven Quartet, op. 18, No. IV, first and second movements, and "Andante Cantabile."
> 3:30 P.M.—Carl Bannwart, Superintendent of Olivet Sunday School, ex-President of the Presbyterian Union, will speak on "The Man with a Handicap."

4:30 P.M.—Ruth Dale, soprano: "The Awakening,"
"The Morning-Glory Song," "There Are
Fairies at the Bottom of the Garden."
5:30 P.M.—A talk to Boy Scouts
5:40 P.M.—A talk on timely vegetable garden topics,
by Charles H. Nissley, Extension Specialist
in Vegetable Gardening from the Agricultural
and Extension College at New Brunswick, N.J.
6:30 P.M.—Sky pictures for the kiddies, by Mr. Radiobug.
6:45 P.M.—Good-night stories for the children by
Uncle George of The Newark Ledger.

Missing from this programming was the diversity of dramatic series, the various types of audience participation shows, and the array of comedy programs that later came to typify radio. Absent, too, was the adept use of sound effects by which broadcast engineers made believable the images that spoken words alone could only propose.

Because of the newness of the art, and because of the primitive quality of the equipment, mistakes often occurred in these early broadcasts. Harold Arlin, an early announcer with KDKA, recalled pitch-black smoke from a passing locomotive engulfing the studio and covering everything with soot, including a renowned and elegantly-dressed soprano in the midst of a broadcast. He also related how one hot summer evening, filled with moths and other flying bugs, proved unsettling for a tenor who, in the middle of his aria, inhaled an insect and began choking.[1] Less startling, however, were the common mistakes that were invariably met with innovation. Thus, if a program lasted more than its allotted time, it was not considered bad form to follow it with the regularly scheduled, but now late, show. And if a program ran short, the time gap might be filled with the announcer telling stories or with recorded music.

Despite shortcomings, radio in its first years was a spectacular invention which continued to explore new dimensions. On Thanksgiving Day, November 25, 1920, the Texas A & M University station, WTAW (then operating experimentally with the call-letters 5XB), aired the first collegiate football game; in January 1921, directly from the Calvary Episcopal

Church in Pittsburgh, KDKA transmitted the first church service in radio history; the first debate in radio was broadcast in May 1922, on WJH (Washington, D.C.) on the subject, "That Daylight Saving Is an Advantage"; and in 1922, station WJZ broadcast a theatrical production directly from the stage. One of the most important types of programming began at WGY (Schenectady) in October 1922, when the first radio drama, "The Wolf," by Eugene Walter, was produced by the WGY Players. This dramatic unit continued to air radio plays—and by the end of its second radio season had produced eighty-three dramas. Importantly, the success of WGY was imitated by other stations. Professional theatrical troupes, such as the Provincetown Players, the Washington Square College Players, and the Cherry Lane Players, were regularly airing plays by early 1924. Other stations, such as KGO (Oakland), developed their own dramatic units, and soon stations like WGBS (Astoria, New York) were producing several dramas weekly.

The appearance of radio drama was responsible for the great advancements made at this time in the field of sound effects. Without sound effects, drama would have been little more than recitation. Since sound alone was the device that created the mental pictures in the mind of the listener, sound effects were as important to effective broadcasting as the words of the play. Sound effects "lend color and realism," wrote the radio producer and personality Samuel L. "Roxy" Rothafel. "A performance unaccompanied by noises that indicate actions on the part of the actors and actresses," he continued, "would result in a bare and somewhat unreal presentation."[2] While sound effects would not be perfected until the 1930s, innovative engineers at this early date developed convincing ways to produce common noises. Forest fires were duplicated with the roar of a blowtorch and the breaking of wooden match sticks near the microphone. Rain on a roof was accomplished by rolling dried peas down a paper tube, and thunder was reproduced by waving a thin sheet of metal. Other standard devices included doorbells, alarms, telephone bells, locks and dummy doors that could be opened and shut to indicate the coming and going of a character.

If the development of drama broadened creativity within radio, the heavy usage of radio by politicians made broadcasting an influential medium within American society. Because of its ability to reach millions of voters simultaneously, political office-holders and candidates quickly adopted radio. President Harding was most supportive of it. The fact that he owned a 25,000-meter receiver—with its antenna prominently attached to a tall tree on the south side of the White House—helped to popularize and legitimize broadcasting. Although Woodrow Wilson had been the first President to have his voice carried by radio,[3] Harding's Armistice Day speech in 1921 was the first address by a Chief Executive that was transmitted by commercial radio. This event was heralded by the editors of the *New York Times,* who remarked:

> When the very voice of the President of the Republic can be heard by tens of thousands of people, in hall and park and street, at the selfsame moment in New York and San Francisco, and when a wireless message from the President can be heard almost in the same instant, as it was a few days earlier by the heads of twenty-eight different Governments before it returned, within the space of seven seconds, from its circuit of the earth, one's imagination leaps to the political, social and moral consequences of these physical achievements.[4]

Even more a "radio" President was Harding's successor, Calvin Coolidge. Within three months of his taking office, he had made three separate radio speeches including a eulogy for Harding on December 10, 1923, and addresses on Lincoln's and Washington's birthdays. When he ran for election in 1924, Coolidge utilized the radio, concluding with a dramatic election-evening broadcast heard on a network of stations running from coast to coast. At his inauguration in March, 1925, President Coolidge spoke to a radio audience estimated at twenty-three million. While he had earned the nickname "Silent Cal" for his less than loquacious style in public,

Coolidge found early radio flattering to his flat, soft voice, and effective in reaching a maximized audience with a minimum of effort. One contemporary observer, Charles Michelson of the *New York World*, suggested that given Coolidge's weak physical appearance, it was his voice that actually carried him to election victory.[5]

Radio expanded the implications of democracy in America. Political personalities now began to appeal directly to the public. The words in 1925 of Governor Alfred E. Smith of New York summarized the potential which politicians saw in broadcasting:

> The American democracy covers so vast a territory that we must heartily welcome an art that brings its Executives and Legislators into the most immediate contact with the public that they have been elected to serve.[6]

Foreign statesmen, such as David Lloyd George of Great Britain and Georges Clemenceau of France, now explained their intentions to a listening American public. Even the Presidential nominating conventions, once the private domain of party bosses and deal-makers, now became national events heard and understood by voters. During those held in the summer of 1924, for instance, radio showed the American political process as never before. Millions of listeners could not help but be struck by a comparison of the smooth-running Republican convention which nominated incumbent Coolidge on the first ballot, and the lengthy and quarrelsome Democratic meeting which, after fifteen days of smoke-filled-room conferences and over one hundred ballots, finally settled on the obscure John W. Davis as its compromise nominee. Throughout the ensuing Presidential campaign the Republicans continued to demonstrate their understanding of radio as a form of communication. To ensure listeners, they effectively mixed speeches by Coolidge and administration spokesmen with appearances by entertainers such as Al Jolson. While Davis spoke over a six-station hook-up, Coolidge addressed the nation over a chain of twenty-two stations. In later Presidential elections both parties would make greater, more efficient use of broadcasting. But even in the campaign of 1924, the future of radio as an informational and democratizing influence was clearly established. According to one critic at the time:

> Hundreds of thousands of voters, otherwise uninfluenced, will cast their ballots for the candidate with whom they feel acquainted, because they "like his voice" and his ideas and the planks of his party which they picked up on the radio.[7]

As limited as radio was in its programming during this formative period, in two areas it made significantly popular achievements: sports and music. As a vehicle for the dissemination of sports information, radio had always been effective by relaying scores and related information. This was especially the case during the baseball season when several times a day regularly-scheduled programs reported the results of ball games. By the fall of 1922, football was being broadcast on a regular basis. WOR, for example, aired a game every Saturday; and WGI (Medford Hillside, Massachusetts) transmitted all football games played in Harvard Stadium.

Boxing was also a popular attraction with listeners. One of the first technical achievements of commercial radio, in fact, had been the broadcast of the heavyweight championship bout between Jack Dempsey and Georges Carpentier on July 2, 1921. Here the ringside "announcer" telephoned his "blow by blow" description as the match progressed; a technician sitting in a transmitting station received the phone call, wrote down the information, and then relayed the description to his audience of thousands. In this same manner WJZ aired a "running description" of the World Series in the fall of 1921.

Within a year, however, sporting events would be broadcast directly from the stadium or ball park, and sportscasters like Graham MacNamee and Ted Husing would become early radio celebrities. The excitement of sports contests, especially to male listeners, was always attractive. Interestingly, when television began to replace radio a quarter-century later, televised sports was one of the most alluring features of that medium.

Radio was most effective as a purveyor of music in all its forms. For a nation of music listeners, if not music-makers, the new instrument provided inexpensive and well-produced musical entertainment. According to an early radio scholar, one reason for radio's initial adoption was its musical potential and its superiority to the phonograph in reproducing music.[8] E. C. Millis, the president of the American Society of Composers, Authors and Publishers (ASCAP), went so far as to suggest that "Music is the foundation upon which the structure of radio in its popular aspects rests."[9] Early polls by radio stations and trade journals confirmed the fact that music—whether classical or popular—was the favored type of programming with the public. Well over sixty percent of all broadcasting time in the 1920s was music.

Classical music was especially prominent in early radio. In the minds of many pioneers of the radio business, the new device was to be used for uplifting and upgrading the tastes of the American masses. As an educational medium, it was envisioned as a means through which the most acclaimed singers and instrumentalists could demonstrate their talents to listeners hungry for culture and aesthetics. Although the concept was somewhat simplistic and failed to foresee a commercialized future for radio in which popular music would find greater acceptance with a mass audience, early broadcasting presented outstanding musicians. In 1921 station KYW (Chicago) was formed for the purpose of broadcasting the Chicago opera season. By 1925 stations like WGBS were transmitting live performances by virtuosi such as violinist Efram Zimbalist and conductor Josef Stansky.

Light classical music was heard regularly on programs featuring groups such as the A & P Gypsies, the Victor Salon Orchestra, the Goodrich Silver Cord Orchestra. The most ambitious musical undertaking in radio at this time was the *Victor Hour* (later called the *RCA Victor Hour*) which premiered in 1925 on WEAF (New York City), the station owned by the American Telephone and Telegraph Company. The program featured the finest in classical music provided by the reputed Victor Salon Orchestra and regular performers John

McCormack and Lucrezia Bori of the New York Metropolitan Opera Company. The weekly program also presented performances by singers like Frances Alda, Reinald Werrenrath, and Emilio DeGogorza, and violinist René Chemet. The popularity of this series soon led to other classical music "Hours," such as those sponsored by Cities Service, Philco, Brunswick, and the Edison Company.

By the middle of the 1920s radio was developing the types of programs and the personalities that would flourish for the next three decades. Radio was already demonstrating its potential as an electrical communicator of news and information, much to the consternation of slower-paced newspapers. The variety show was born in December 1923, when WEAF inaugurated *The Eveready Hour,* a broadcasting extravaganza which throughout the decade presented a wide spectrum of entertainment, from minstrel shows and drama to comedy and classical music. On this program, which became a model for later variety shows, listeners also encountered celebrities from motion pictures, vaudeville, musical comedy, and the legitimate stage.[10]

Radio was also making its first attempts at regular comedy programming. The success in 1922 of Ed Wynn's appearance on WEAF in his play, "The Perfect Fool," illustrated early that verbal humor—if not the wild physical antics of slapstick comedy—was easily adaptable to broadcasting. By late 1925, several comedy series had already appeared including *The Smith Family* with Jim and Marian Jordan (later known as Fibber McGee and Molly) ; comedy patter was amply mixed in the musical fare of Billy Jones and Ernie Hare (*The Happiness Boys*) , Trade and Mark (*The Smith Brothers*) , and Goldy and Dusty (*The Gold Dust Twins*) ; and the broad comedic styles of minstrelsy and vaudeville found their models in the success of comedians like Sam and Henry (Freeman Gosden and Charles Correll, later known as Amos 'n' Andy) and novelty-singer, Wendell Hall. Radio even produced at this time its own nationally known personalities in the likes of announcer Milton Cross and popular singer Vaughn de Leath.

Radio was healthy and prospering by the end of its first

five years. While this era might have been "the Jazz Age" or "the Roaring Twenties" to many urban, middle-class Americans, for the overwhelming majority of the citizenry it was the Radio Era. By 1925 there were millions of radio receivers in American homes, and that year citizens spent $430 million on radio products. This represented more than twice as much money as was spent on all sporting goods, and about seventy-five cents for each dollar spent on phonographs, pianos, and all other musical instruments. It is no wonder that in 1924 Dr. Lee De Forest could announce that radio was now out of the laboratory stage, and a noted economist could proclaim that "radio has passed through the fad stage and has become a utility. It has rightly achieved its proper permanent status among the important industries of the country."[11]

Not only had radio "arrived" in terms of economic importance, but it was definitely a part of American popular culture. Radio aerials now began to clutter the skyline, and people shopping for new homes began looking for locales with good reception. Since early 1922, a daily radio log listing programs for the day became a regular feature of most newspapers, and by the end of the year twenty-seven fan magazines were being published in the United States. Christmas of 1922 was the first Yule season in which a new radio was suggested by newspaper advertisements as "the perfect gift," and the first National Radio Week was proclaimed for the last week of November 1923. Radio began to influence daily routines. Thousands religiously did their morning exercises to the cadence of physical culturists broadcasting calisthenic routines. In 1924, a prominent lexicographer revealed that because of radio at least five thousand new words had entered the English language.

Major cities began observing a "Silent Night" one evening per week in which all local stations ceased broadcasting about 6 P.M. to allow distant signals—sometimes from the East or West Coast, from the South and Midwest, and even from Havana or London—to be heard by local listeners. More than ten million people listened to radio each night, and in a spirit of optimism, General David Sarnoff, later the president of the

Radio Corporation of America, proclaimed in 1924 that before the end of the decade there would be fifty million listeners. Radio was affecting even popular music, providing material for novelty songs like "I Wish There Was a Wireless to Heaven (Then Mama Would Not Seem So Far Away)," "Mister Radio Man (Tell My Mammy to Come Back Home)," "Tune in On L-O-V-E," and "Love Her by Radio."[12] One of the more revealing reflections of the penetration of radio into the daily lives of Americans was the sentiment which prefaced a radio scrapbook published in 1925:

> Memories—like firelit flames
> Will quickly fade—so write their names
> Within this book—and keep the glow—
> Heart of the home—the Radio![13]

The emergence and flourishing of radio programming in the United States was the result of four strategic developments: (1) technological achievements in the producing of radio; (2) commercial interest in the medium; (3) governmental concerns about radio; and (4) the generally-optimistic spirit of the times. From the interaction of these trends, broadcasting evolved from a faddist national craze to a mass medium of communication and entertainment integral to American civilization.

Ultimately, broadcasting was one more technological contribution to American society from scientific investigation. In an age that saw the popularity of the telephone, electric lights, phonographs, automobiles, motion pictures, and countless other electrical devices, the radio receiver was another achievement serving to confirm the faith of Americans in technology.

But radio did not appear suddenly. For several decades it had been the focus of scientific research and development. In 1896, the Italian researcher Guglielmo Marconi improved upon the older telegraph system, with its reliance on electrical wires and underseas cables, by transmitting a "wireless" coded message through the air. Five years later he demonstrated the advancement of wireless telegraphy by sending an intercontinental transmission from Europe to Canada.

It was the development of the oscillating vacuum tube, the "Audion," by the American scientist, Dr. Lee De Forest, however, that made it possible to transmit the human voice instead of the dots and dashes of telegraphic codes. The invention of this vacuum tube in 1906 made it possible to conduct a "telephone" conversation through a wireless transmitter, hence the early name for radio, the wireless telephone. Experimenting broadcasters throughout the country soon discovered that rather than a monotonous single voice, those people equipped with receivers preferred to hear recorded music on the air. A pioneer in this respect was Charles D. Herrold of San Jose, California. In 1909 he began regular transmissions of musical programs from his small 15-watt station. Although his listeners at first were confined to students at his College of Engineering, Herrold's station later became KQW and eventually KCBS, the Columbia Broadcasting System outlet in San Francisco.[14]

The requirements of the World War caused the United States government in 1917 to seal or confiscate all wireless equipment in the country. Full power to develop broadcasting was given to the Department of the Navy. Professional and amateur radio experimenters, however, were not thwarted by such developments. Under the control of the Navy, radio made great strides. Improvements in transmission equipment and output soon enabled consistent and clear radio communication from the Navy's station NNF, in New Brunswick, New Jersey, to the Allied forces in Europe. Importantly, too, the Navy's dictatorial control effectively ended patent suits, business rivalries, and other factors that were retarding the development of a streamlined, standardized radio industry. By the end of the war, the Navy had forged a rationalized industry able to mass-produce receiving and transmitting components. Amateur radiophiles were also not abandoned. Throughout the war, hobbyist magazines, such as *The Electrical Experimenter*, reported on new advancements in wireless techniques. The magazine's editor, Hugo Gernsbach, was quick to dispel fears that his publication was violating governmental wartime controls.

As most of our radio readers are undoubtedly aware, the U.S. Government had decided that all Amateur Wireless Stations, whether licensed or unlicensed, or equipt [*sic*] for receiving or transmitting, shall be closed. This is a very important consideration, especially for those who are readers of THE ELECTRICAL EXPERIMENTER, for the reason that we desire to continue to publish valuable articles on the wireless art from time to time, and which may treat on both transmitting and receiving apparatus. In the first place, there are a great many students among our readers who will demand and expect a continuation of the usual class of Radio subjects which we have publisht [*sic*] in the past four years, and secondly, there will be hundreds and even thousands of new radio pupils in the various naval and civilian schools throughout the country, who will be benefitted by up-to-date wireless articles treating on both transmitting as well as receiving equipment. Remember that you must not connect up radio apparatus to any form of antenna.[15]

The election-night broadcast on KDKA in 1920 may have capped two decades of experimentation by those who saw a great potential in radio, but it did not diminish scientific investigation and innovation. In the next several years radio was improved. This was accomplished by advancements made in station apparatus, microphones, tubes, and speakers. In 1923, manufacturers introduced an all-electric radio model that could operate without the cumbersome storage batteries that were needed for the earliest models. One of the most significant innovations at this time was the utilization of telephone lines to broadcast across great distances. Broadcasters in early 1921 were limited in the range of their signal. On a clear night, when there was a minimum of atmospheric interference, it was possible for a radio signal to travel long distances. But during the day, and on most evenings, especially in the summer when the sun dissipated the strength of radio signals, such coverage was not possible. The use of long-lines telephone equipment, however, enabled a transmission to travel anywhere in the country—much like a long-distance telephone call—then to be fed directly to radio stations in other cities. Here the signal would be amplified to its original strength and sent on to another city, and/or broadcast from that station. Although it appeared to be a lengthy operation, the radio signal actually travelled at the speed of light, 186,000 miles per second.

This type of broadcasting allowed the creation of a "chain" or network of stations, simultaneously broadcasting the same program. In this manner, the first network broadcast was made January 4, 1923, when a concert was broadcast in New York City on WEAF, and simultaneously in Boston on WNAC. Within two years, the future of chain broadcasting seemed bright. When President Coolidge spoke before the United States Chamber of Commerce on October 23, 1924, his words were carried live on the largest chain to date. Twenty-two stations, from WEAF and WCAP (Washington), to KFI and KFOA (Seattle) broadcast the address. In the words of one historian, it was a technical feat of "amazing proportions."[16] It also set the stage for the next logical step: the establishment of permanent radio networks.

If radio was made possible because of technological innovations, it was rendered viable because of commercial interest. From its inception broadcasting was envisioned by American business as a commercial vehicle through which to make profits. The ownership of early stations by specific businesses and corporations clearly illustrates the future anticipated for radio. In this regard, by 1922 several major American corporations—General Electric, American Telephone and Telegraph, Westinghouse, Radio Corporation of America, and United Fruit—conspired to create a monopoly over high-powered radio broadcasting in the United States. Although the monopoly never was successfully achieved, out of the effort would emerge the first radio network, the National Broadcasting Company.

Despite the ownership of radio by wealthy business interests, the first years of commercial radio were filled with the problems of finance: how to pay for a station and its personnel, how to obtain good and popular talent for programs. In its earliest days radio programming was free. Since most broadcasters and listeners abhorred the idea of filling the air with commercial messages, radio did not generate revenue from advertisers. Yet, a lack of income prevented stations from offering a fee to those who appeared before their microphones. Those who did broadcast were offered only the free publicity which their appearances created. Compounding this problem concerning live talent, by 1922 lawyers for ASCAP demanded an annual fee for the right to air phonograph recordings of music composed or recorded by ASCAP members. Since this included most of the popular music of the day, stations had to pay annual fees ranging in 1925 from $250 to $2500. It should not be a surprise that many early stations went bankrupt. In the period from 1922 to 1925, for example, although there were 1079 new stations established, 626 were closed.

The debate over methods of financing radio was intense by late 1922. Some looked to European methods which relied upon taxing owners of radios with the revenue allotted to radio stations by the government. Others, averring governmental interference, suggested answers that ranged from reliance upon philanthropy or the sale to the public of subscriptions and/or memberships, to a two-percent tax on manufacturers for each receiver built, or the sale by each station of electrical devices needed to unscramble programs intentionally garbled in their transmission.

The debate brought forth prominent voices on the varying positions. Martin Rice, Director of Broadcasting for General Electric, felt that the public should be made to pay for radio programs by subscriptions or by a tax. Secretary of Commerce Herbert Hoover argued for the creation of six or seven national networks that would air "simultaneous broadcasts" and thereby lessen costs. But David Sarnoff of RCA stridently opposed commercializing radio. In 1923 he eloquently stated his position against taxing listeners for owning and using their radios.

> It is my firm conviction that broadcasting can be made commercially practicable without any means being found

for collecting from the consumer, that the greatest advantage for broadcasting lies in its universality, in its ability
to reach everybody, everywhere, anywhere, in giving free
entertainment, culture, instruction, and all the items
which constitute a program, in doing that which no other
agency has yet been able to do, and it is up to us, of the
radio art and industry . . . to preserve that most delightful
element in the whole situation—the freedom of radio. Just
as soon as we destroy that freedom and universality of
radio and confine it to only those who pay for it . . . we
destroy the fundamental of the whole situation.[17]

The most important breakthrough in this quandary was
the broadcasting of paid commercials by station WEAF. The
first such announcement was aired August 28, 1922, and concerned Hawthorne Court, a complex of tenant-owned apart-
ment homes in Jackson Heights in New York City. Long and
verbose by later standards, this commercial announcement
earned $100 for WEAF and provided a model for other sta-
tions. The courage and success of WEAF were soon emulated
by others. Within three years these so-called toll stations were
prevalent throughout the country. With them came the first
appearance of the rhetoric that advertisers would develop
throughout the history of radio. Thus, as at KGW (Portland,
Oregon) businesses were informed that sponsorship should be
considered "the contribution to home entertainment which
the firm makes for the public good-will and friendship to be
derived."[18] In a sense, the air was becoming a magazine—
filled with stories, features, and now, advertisements. As with
commercialized publications, the success of toll radio signified
that public approval of the entertainment more than offset
public annoyance with interruptions and commercial messages.

By the middle of the decade, the effects of commercialized
broadcasting were obvious. Many shows were now named
after the sponsor. Guests on the *Eveready Hour* cost the
Eveready Battery Company up to $1000 per performance.
From toothpaste companies (*The Ipana Troubadours*) to tire
manufacturers (*The Goodrich Zippers*), radio programs be-

came integrally linked to business enterprises. Yet, given the traditional distaste for governmental interference by free enterprise, given the inability of radio to finance itself with public donations, and given the necessity of finding sources of revenue to survive, the development of American radio as a commercialized medium was inevitable. Proof of this rested in the conversion of David Sarnoff. Long an opponent of advertisements on the air, by 1925 he had changed his thinking and now paved the way for the leadership of RCA in forging the commercialized NBC radio network.

A few statistics demonstrate the rapid growth of radio in its first years. Government figures indicate that in the period 1921–1922, ownership of radio receivers rose by a rate somewhere between 1100 and 1900 percent. Where in early 1921 there were less than fifty thousand radios in the United States, within a year figures suggested anywhere from 600,000 to one million sets in circulation. The opening of new stations became popular. In the ten months between August 1921, and May 1922, a total of 286 new facilities were opened. Underscoring such statistics was the fact that between 1922 and 1924, public investment in radio equipment leaped from $60 million to $358 million.

With its sudden expansion, the radio industry quickly developed problems. Some stations complained of infringements on their assigned wavelengths by more powerful stations. Others feared that those stations with more powerful wattage would eventually monopolize all broadcasting. A good number of broadcasters resented the commercialization of the air by toll stations. And there were many legal altercations involving stations, manufacturers, equipment distributors, and other components of the new industry. It was in this atmosphere of growth and consternation that Secretary of Commerce Herbert Hoover convened the first Washington Radio Conference in 1922. The conference signalled to all parties that the United States government was taking an alert, arbitrational role in the development of radio. As Hoover told the conferees:

It is the purpose of this conference to inquire into the
critical situation that has now arisen through the aston-
ishing development of the wireless telephone; to advise
the Department of Commerce as to the application of its
present powers of regulation, and further to formulate
such recommendations to Congress as to the legislation
necessary.[19]

Even before this conference, the federal government had
established a regulatory role for itself in the nascent radio
industry. The Radio Law of 1912 assigned to the Department
of Commerce the task of licensing experimental radio stations.
During the Great War, the Department of the Navy controlled all transmitting equipment in the United States, and
exercised its monopolistic options to establish by late 1918 a
rationalized industry capable of meeting the demands of a
mass market. The government had also been indirectly involved with the development of radio through federal court
decisions, contracts for large-scale purchases of radio equipment, and its refusal to allow the Navy Department to maintain its control of broadcasting beyond the end of the war.
When Secretary Hoover convened the leaders of the industry
at the Radio Conference, therefore, it was not an unfamiliar
role that the government was playing.

During the conference of 1922—and in the Radio Conferences of the three following years—Hoover and the government maintained their fundamental Republican principles
concerning the role of government in the realm of free enterprise. Hoover felt that government at best was an arbiter. Its
function was to enforce laws and work at the will of the industry to ensure a healthy situation. When the representatives at
the conference recommended to Congress that the secretary of
commerce should be given "adequate legal authority" to act
effectively as an arbitrator, they knew that Hoover would be
sympathetic to their demands for respect of private interests
and corporate independence.

The striking defect in the role of the government in regu-
lating the new industry was the lack of suitable legislation.
Until 1927 the only regulatory legislation under which the

Department of Commerce could act was the Radio Law of 1912. Written with no idea of radio as a multi-million-dollar enterprise touching the lives of most Americans, that law lacked specifics for dealing with the problems besetting radio in the 1920s. Such simple problems as denying an application for a radio license, or actions to be taken when the broadcast spectrum was filled and no more stations could be created, were not envisioned by the law. Further, the Department of Commerce was not given power to enforce its decisions.

Under Hoover, however, the department did play an active role in the radio industry. It attempted to overcome problems of broadcast interference by reassigning all wavelengths, trying to separate on the radio dial those powerful regional stations from the weaker local transmitters. Hoover also deplored the notion of monopolistic control of radio. He cooperated with the Federal Trade Commission in its investigation of the trust established between GE, RCA, Westinghouse, United Fruit, and AT&T. He also operated his department as an "honest broker" between various radio interests, acting to encourage development, improvement, and expansion of broadcasting.

Although he lacked substantial power and legislative direction, Hoover was greatly responsible for the direction in which the radio industry developed. He assiduously left its control in the hands of businessmen and entrepreneurs, reserving for the government the nebulous right to interfere to protect the public interst. Even had he so desired, Hoover lacked the specific right to exercise strong control. Not until passage of the Radio Law of 1927 in which Congress established the Federal Radio Commission (replaced in 1934 by the Federal Communications Commission) was there a regulatory body with specified powers to settle the problems of modern broadcasting.

Hoover never allowed personal prejudices to compromise his *laissez-faire* economic ideals. Although he deplored cluttering the air with commercial announcements, he never acted to prevent stations from charging tolls. Although he favored the creation of several national networks, he did not compel stations to create such arrangements. If radio in America later became a healthy, vital, and entertaining medium aiming its programming at the so-called "common man" instead of a more discriminating and esthetic audience, it was in great part because the government refused to thwart radio's early growth toward becoming a commercialized communication form seeking to sell its various programs to mass consumers.

An invention like radio, bringing free entertainment directly into the home, fit the spirit of the time in which it was born. Postwar America—the society into which broadcasting was introduced as a commercial item—was entering one of its most exciting eras. The 1920s has been called a time of normalcy. This was not only incorrect grammar, it was a misnomer. It was a decade generally typified by prosperity, self-confidence, isolationism, and a relative wealth of leisure time. Coming as it did after World War I with its austerity and self-sacrifice, the new decade was an experimentive time in which new values and new patterns emerged.

One mark of the 1920s was its faddist nature. Flagpole sitters, miniature golf, mahjong, dance crazes, flapper dresses, real estate booms, and autosuggestive health cures all enjoyed popularity for a while. This was the era of the celebrity faith healers from fundamentalists Billy Sunday and Aimee Semple McPherson, to Frank Buchman of Moral Rearmament and Jiddu Krishnamurti, a Hindu visitor heralded as the New Messiah. Even radio was destined to produce its own faith healer, Dr. John Brinkley of KFKB in Milford, Kansas, who for years sold patent medicines to people throughout the nation. While followers of such fads may have been gullible, their credulity should not be taken as a sign of mental aberration. According to Dr. Emory S. Bogardus, founder of the University of Southern California journal, *Sociology and Social Research,* fads are a healthy sign, for "they flourish only in social environments in which people are looking forward and seeking progress by trying out new things and ideas."[20]

The 1920s also witnessed the emergence of mass spectator sports. Sports such as horse racing had been attracting large crowds for many decades, but now the throngs came to football, baseball, golf, boxing, and tennis. Annual attendance at professional sporting events doubled during the decade; gigantic concrete stadiums were erected to house such spectator sports. America also lionized its heroes of sport. Red Grange, Knute Rockne, Bobby Jones, Helen Wills, Babe Ruth, and Jack Dempsey all became readily-recognized personalities. The writer who said of football in 1928, "It is at present a religion . . . sometimes it seems to be almost our national religion,"[21] could well have made such a statement about sports in general.

American society in the 1920s was also in love with technology. Never had so many enjoyed the fruits of so much technology in so short a time. Automobile registration rose from 9.3 million in 1921 to 23.1 million in 1929; telephone ownership rose from 14.3 million in 1922 to 20.3 million by the end of 1930; and the domestic use of electricity increased 135 percent during the decade. In 1926 the first scheduled air service was inaugurated and 5782 passengers utilized it that year. By 1930—just three years after Col. Charles A. Lindbergh had become the most renowned man of the decade because of his solo non-stop flight across the Atlantic—the number of people utilizing air service had risen to 417,505.

The new technology of the 1920s gave Americans innovative forms of entertainment. During that decade motion pictures soared to new heights of popularity, becoming by 1930 an industry worth over $2 billion, employing 325,000 people, and weekly entertaining up to 15 million Americans. Technological developments were visible in other areas. From the development of rayon and the irradiation of food to increase vitamin content, to the mass production of typewriters (one million by 1929) and the development of the electric refrigerator, Americans were inundated with modern technological products. The fervent faith in science created by such inventions was evidenced by a writer in January 1925, who noted that if Coolidge's voice could be broadcast throughout the nation at this inauguration, surely the next such ceremony in four years should be televised—perhaps even in Europe.[22]

Radio's Early Network Years, 1926–1932

In the middle of the 1920s American radio entered a new phase of importance and influence. The emergence of the National Broadcasting Company in 1926, and of the Columbia Broadcasting System the next year, launched an era in which programming became national in scope. In previous years, entertainers or speakers might be heard at best on small, regional chains of stations, some of which were contractually bound together, others of which were hastily put together for a specific broadcast. To air the 1923 World Series, for example, WEAF and WGY were joined by a special wire and only listeners in New York City and Schenectady were able to hear the broadcasts. The *Atwater Kent Program,* a program of classical music which premiered in late 1925, was heard on Sunday afternoons on a chain of thirteen stations covering many of the major cities from the East coast to the Midwest: WEAF, WCAP, WWJ, WJAR (Providence), WEEI (Boston), WCAE (Pittsburgh), WSAI (Cincinnati), WOC (Ames, Iowa), WCCO (Minneapolis), WGR (Buffalo), WOO (Philadelphia), KSD (St. Louis), and WTAC (Worcester, Massachusetts). When Coolidge delivered his Inaugural Address in March 1925, the speech was carried on two webs of twenty-one and three stations, respectively. With no effective means of recording programs and replaying them on distant stations, only through such networks could listeners in one locale hear broadcasts made in far-away cities. Although radio as an instrument was affecting all parts of the nation, programming remained overwhelmingly local in orientation, its national force yet to be registered.

National network radio developed rapidly. While few people envisioned such arrangements at the beginning of the decade, by the late 1920s both NBC and CBS were sizable businesses broadcasting simultaneously throughout the country. The history of the rise of NBC is the story of corporate rivalries, governmental litigation, brilliant business leadership, and an understanding of the potential of radio. Under the command of David Sarnoff, since 1926 the president of

NBC's parent company, the Radio Corporation of America, the network became the leading communications-entertainment organization in the world.

NBC was actually two networks, called "Red" and "Blue" because of colored lines with which affiliated stations were linked on company maps. The Red Network (NBC-Red) emanated from WEAF (eventually renamed WRCA and later WNBC), which RCA had purchased from AT&T in 1926. It was the smaller, more prestigious chain of stations at NBC. The Blue Network (NBC-Blue) was based on the RCA station, WJZ, which had moved from Newark to New York City. NBC had commenced broadcasting with twenty-four stations, but by 1931 had expanded to sixty-one stations for each of its networks. The success of NBC, however, had one important, but unanticipated effect: the creation of a rival network, CBS, with the capital, management, and scope capable of challenging the broadcasting leadership exercised by the older web.

Above all, the emergence of CBS is the story of the leadership of William S. Paley, who assumed the presidency of the year-old network in 1928. With Paley's business and programming acumen, the struggling, nearly-bankrupt network of forty-seven stations—with the key station being WABC (later WCBS) in New York City—was by 1931 a prospering organization with seventy-nine affiliates.

The creation and expansion of national radio networks would alter national listening patterns. No longer did local stations—especially those situated in small cities—have monopolistic control over programming. Instead, network affiliates throughout the nation were contractually obliged to broadcast the more sophisticated and technically-advanced programs emanating from WEAF, WJZ, or WABC. Rather than local musicians and entertainers, network radio presented nationally-known figures like Walter Damrosch, Paul Whiteman, Jessica Dragonette, Will Rogers, Major Bowes, and Billy Jones and Ernie Hare. In entertaining an audience that spread from coast to coast, network radio was compelled to air programs that had broad appeal and top-flight talent. The formula apparently worked, for a survey conducted in

1935 showed that 88 percent of American listeners preferred network to local programming. [23]

The state of radio programming was epitomized on November 15, 1926, when NBC in its premier broadcast presented not only some of the nation's most famous talent, but an adequate representation of the dimensions of types of shows heard on radio at that time. The broadcast was an elaborate affair that cost the fledgling network an exorbitant $50,000 and reached an estimated audience of twelve million people. Yet the program lacked originality. It was, predictably, a musical affair with the New York Symphony, New York Oratorio Society, Titta Ruffo, and Mary Garden providing classical selections; and popular dance music coming from the orchestras of Vincent Lopez, George Olsen, Ben Bernie, and B. A. Rolfe. Except for speeches from NBC officials, the only alternative was vaudeville humor from Will Rogers and the comedy team of Weber and Fields. This was, however, an accurate cross-section of radio in the middle of the decade: music, talk, and an occasional celebrity. Certainly, this was entertainment, but it would continue for years to be the scope of regularly-scheduled programs.

American radio by the late 1920s was filled with pleasant, but unspectacular, shows. Poets such as Tony Wons and spreaders of good cheer like Cheerio (Eugene Field) blended soft music and inspirational words for their many listeners. American women received recipes and household hints from Betty Crocker, Ida Bailey Allen, and Josephine Gibson; and beauty hints from Barbara Gould, Edna Wallace Hopper, and Nell Vinick. *The Voice of Experience* offered troubled listeners a sympathetic Marion Sayle Taylor answering their personal problems. And *The American School of the Air* was a daily CBS attempt to teach children history, current events, geography, economics, and music through the use of radio dramas. Indicative of the course of programming, one source asserts that the heaviest fan mail for any program in 1931 was received by astrologist Evangeline Adams whose horoscope show "took the country by storm."[24] The appearance in

August 1929 of *Amos 'n' Andy,* however, would set in motion
a series of events that would change the format of radio
programming.

Freeman Gosden and Charles Correll began developing
their blackface characters, Amos Jones and Andy Brown—plus
more than one hundred minor personalities—in Chicago in
the latter half of the 1920s. First as Sam and Henry, and then
Amos 'n' Andy, these two white dialecticians created in their
black characterizations sympathetic figures whose trials and
tribulations would soon become the concern of the nation.
Broadcasting first at WEBH and then at WGN, Gosden and
Correll eventually brought their minstrel comedy to WMAQ
and the NBC-Red network. As a quarter-hour, serialized program it was aired Monday through Saturday at 7:00 P.M. By
the end of 1929, *Amos 'n' Andy* had become the most popular
show in radio. It appealed to most Americans, capturing about
sixty percent of all listeners. The *Amos 'n' Andy* craze was responsible for the surge in sales that set manufacturers experienced in 1929 as 4.4 million receivers were sold, and sales
totals for sets and parts rose twenty-three percent over the
record sales figures for the previous year. Clichés uttered by
characters in the program soon became national sayings, and
the story line—like the trial of Andy Brown for murder (it all
turned out to be a dream) —was carefully followed by as
many as forty million listeners.

As it affected radio programming in general, *Amos 'n'
Andy* had two important influences. First, the unprecedented
popularity of the show suggested that the radio public was
ready for new types of series. After a decade of music and
speeches, within months a situation comedy had become an
unprecedented national rage. While movie stars like Rudolph
Valentino, Clara Bow, and Charlie Chaplin had affected Americans as a unit, *Amos 'n' Andy* was the first radio
show to produce such a national clamor. And its characters
were soon ranked with Lindbergh, Will Rogers, and Gene
Tunney as "public gods."[25]

It did not require much analysis for sponsors, agencies,

and network officials to understand that there might exist outside radio at that moment other types of programs capable of
matching the success of *Amos 'n' Andy*. NBC was active in this
regard. Before the end of 1929 the network introduced two
new and different programs destined for long careers in broadcasting. In *The Rise of the Goldbergs*—later called *The Goldbergs*—NBC aired the serialized story of the Goldberg family
struggling to adapt and flourish in America. The story was set
in the Jewish ghetto of the Lower East Side in New York City
and, coming as it did almost simultaneously with the Depression, the deprived-but-undaunted Goldbergs presented a relevant picture of the search for meaning in the midst of adversity. Although it was not fully a soap opera, it was a prototype
of the type of daytime programming which would emerge
early in the 1930s and last for almost thirty years.

NBC also introduced the *Rudy Vallee Show* (also called
The Fleischmann Hour) in the fall of 1929, an innovative
variety program which would last throughout the 1930s. Vallee came to radio already famous as a "crooner" with collegiate looks and a pleasant voice that had made him "the
vagabond lover," a heart-throb to young Americans. But on
radio, Vallee added to his own musical offering by introducing
popular and significant personalities as his guests. A typical
Vallee show might feature love and novelty songs by the host,
but also an appearance by the likes of comedians Eddie
Cantor, Fanny Brice, Olsen and Johnson, or Ed Wynn; dramatic actors such as Maurice Evans; or world celebrities like
Helen Keller or Hilaire Belloc. By the early 1930s, according
to Erik Barnouw, the *Rudy Vallee Show* had become so popular it "had replaced the Palace Theater as the prestige booking
of vaudeville."[26] The program was the first variety series to
revolve about a single celebrity and employ famous guests as a
supplement. The program also avoided the serious music that
appeared so heavily in other variety series, aiming its entertainment primarily at middle-class listeners who were numeri-
cally greater and preferred popular music.

If *Amos 'n' Andy* illustrated that listeners were ready for innovative programming, it also distorted perceptions of the popularity of radio. For too long network officials believed that because one program attracted millions of listeners and sold hundreds of thousands of dollars worth of radio equipment, broadcasting was healthy and responsive to listener wants. But in 1931 *Amos 'n' Andy* peaked and began losing listeners. And as they ceased tuning in the program, millions of people stopped listening to all radio programs. This was especially the case among middle and upper-middle class set owners who tired of the program after two years. With the decline of *Amos 'n' Andy*, radio figures collapsed. Whereas in 1930 about 74 percent of all set owners used their sets on an average evening, by August 1933, the total had dropped to 55.5 percent. Within two years the decline of *Amos 'n' Andy* had taken with it almost one-quarter of all radio users.

To offset the loss in audience size, network radio in the early 1930s introduced dramatic series as a new type of programming. In *The Adventures of Sherlock Holmes* and *Rin-Tin-Tin Thrillers,* NBC in 1930 drew upon established characters from literature and from motion pictures to offer thrilling stories to attract listeners. At the same time, NBC experimented with light comedy-romances in the dramatic series *The First Nighter Program.* The next year, NBC added mystery series like *With Canada's Mounted,* and *Danger Fighters*; and CBS entered the field with the short-lived *Count von Luckner's Adventures,* and the eminently popular *The Shadow* and *The Eno Crime Club.* Similar series appearing at this time included *Fu Manchu Mystery, Charlie Chan,* and *Mysteries in Paris.*

Such programming did little to revive the sagging interest in radio. Although *The Eno Crime Club* and *The Adventures of Sherlock Holmes* were among the top-rated shows in 1931, most dramatic series made little lasting impact on listeners and soon faded in popularity. Many reasons could be suggested for such a development: the paucity of good writers, the still-maturing art of sound effects, the preference of Americans for drama in motion pictures rather than radio. But the most pressing reason was the lack of big-name talent. Movie personalities avoided radio, even as two decades earlier theater actors scorned the fledgling "flickers." As a new form of programming, broadcast drama had little experienced talent upon which to draw. Conversely, the success of the *Rudy Vallee Show* was based greatly on the fame Vallee had generated before coming to NBC, and on the celebrity status of the guest stars appearing on his show.

It became clear to network officials that to offset waning public interest, they would have to find well-known personalities to head varied programs—music, variety, drama, comedy—in the future. To obtain such headline talent, network radio would turn in the early 1930s to stage entertainment. And with the development of radio series centered on the biggest names in vaudeville and musical comedy, the revitalization of commercial broadcasting would be accomplished.

Theoretically, the airwaves belonged to the American people. Congress so assured the citizenry in 1924 when it stated that "the ether and use thereof within the territorial jurisdiction of the United States and their Government"[27] was held in the name of the people. By the Radio Law of 1927 those stations obtaining broadcast licenses were obliged to renew them every three years. Now, the government by statute could protect the air in the interest of the people. In practice, however, license renewals were almost never denied, and the government seldom used its leverage to improve program content. Ironically, moreover, because of the intense commercialism that accompanied the establishment of network radio, by the early 1930s the airwaves in practice belonged neither to the people nor to the networks. They were, instead, the realm of the advertising agencies.

The debate over whether or not to sell audio commercials for sponsors' money had been a lengthy one. By the time NBC and CBS began full broadcasting in 1927, it was still a contested issue. To some, commercialism was prostitution of the purpose of radio, for instead of uplifting, educational programming, advertising turned radio into a cheap spectacle hawking stores, medicines, clothes, food, and other materials best left to magazines and newspapers. Few people defended the esthetics of radio advertising, but many argued that without the capital generated from commercial sponsors, radio would never progress—hire significant entertainers, improve facilities, expand the range of offerings—and would eventually fall into disuse. The appearance of the networks assured the future for toll radio, as network officials encouraged commercial sponsorship at the local and network levels. It was no coincidence that the home station of NBC-Red was WEAF, the first toll station in American radio.

Radio commercialism in the beginning was primitive. Ponderous statements about the product or service often sounded more like a speech than a sales pitch. Timid about offending listeners, early sponsors often settled for naming the program after their products, or pinning the sponsor's trade name on the band or singing ensemble. In this manner programs like the *Palmolive Hour,* the *Wrigley Revue,* and the *Stetson Parade* were aired in the late 1920s, and musical ensembles appeared with names like the Sylvania Foresters Quartette, the Champion Sparkers, the Cliquot Club Eskimos, and the Vicks Vaporub Quartette.

As radio entered its second decade, this crude style of commercialism gave way to a more sophisticated art of selling, and the function and significance of advertising agencies burgeoned. At first, ad agencies served sponsors as middle men. They prepared the advertising copy to be broadcast, and they represented sponsors' interests before the networks. As radio became an increasingly lucrative business, ad agencies became more important, and radio program production became the province of the middle men. Soon complete programs and series were developed, written, and packaged by advertising agencies. The potential sponsor then was presented with the final product to decide if he wished to finance it. If agreeable, the network was sold the program "package" and sponsor as a unit. As for the celebrities and regular personnel appearing on the program, they were all hired by the ad agency. In many cases, by the early 1930s even radio announcers were under contract to advertising agencies.

Radio production, in this manner, was taken out of the hands of the networks. Statistics show that the development came fast and decisively. A breakdown of the accounts of one network in 1929 reveals the following:

33 percent of the programs were produced by advertising
   agencies
28 percent were produced by the networks (for its
   sponsors)
20 percent were produced by the sponsors themselves
19 percent were produced by special program builders

By 1937, in the words of a critic for the show business journal, *Variety*,

the 28 percent produced by the networks plus the 20 percent produced by the sponsors was gradually swallowed by the advertising agencies. Currently, network commercial program production stands virtually at zero—attesting to the profit derived from radio by the advertising agencies, and indirectly indicating no compliment to the networks for their style of programming.[28]

While the great movie studios at this time were using contracts and business agreements to create the so-called "star system" of motion picture celebrities, in radio it was the advertising agencies that were developing the audio star system. Rudy Vallee, for example, may have broadcast over NBC-Red, but he was ultimately an employee of the J. Walter Thompson agency—the ad agency which represented Vallee's sponsor, Standard Brands. The famous children's series, *Jack Armstrong*, was originally a product of Blackett-Sample-Hummert, the agency that created, owned, wrote, and cast the show. That agency also produced many of the most successful soap operas, as well as musical programs, comedy serials, and variety programs. Broadcast personalities adapted to the situation. If an umemployed radio actor were seeking a job in radio, for instance, he would not have approached a station or network office, but instead would have applied to the major advertising agencies. That the agencies did a considerable business with the networks is illustrated in the following table of the largest time sales on NBC in 1932.[29]

Name of Agency	Amt. of Time Sales
Lord and Thomas	$5,461,866
J. Walter Thompson	3,080,941
Batten, Barton, Durstine & Osborn	2,005,102
Erwin Wasey	1,345,245
Blackett-Sample-Hummert	1,329,308
McCann-Erickson	1,154,540
N. W. Ayer	1,021,529

This usurpation of production power by the advertising agencies meant a partial loss of control by the networks. By most contracts, sponsors contracted for a period of thirteen weeks, one third of a regular season, and retained an option for the remaining twenty-six weeks. Also, the sponsor usually had the right to approve or disapprove scripts, to withdraw his sponsorship on several weeks notice, or to cancel outright a series he felt was not selling his product. In some cases, a sponsor might cancel an unsuccessful series and replace it with another in the middle of a radio season.

The influence of sponsors and agencies was augmented by the development of audience rating services which emerged in the late 1920s. Before the appearance of companies which scientifically gathered statistical information on American listening patterns, interested parties had to rely upon less accurate methods of measuring popularity. The most common way was to invite listeners to send for a free premium and count the number of responses. Gosden and Correll did this themselves in 1930 when negotiating for a higher-paying contract. When they obtained more than a million responses to their offer of a free map, they received the new contract, as the station, agency, and sponsor had tangible evidence of how popular *Amos 'n' Andy* was with listeners. This same ploy saved the *Tom Mix Ralston Straight Shooters Show* after its first season. Not knowing if its ads for Ralston cereal were being heard by many children, the sponsor offered premiums to those who wrote to the show. The deluge of more than a million letters in a twenty-six-week period convinced Ralston to stay with the program, a decision it maintained throughout the seventeen-year history of the series.

The first significant attempt at audience measurement was the creation of the Cooperative Analysis of Broadcasting (C.A.B.), or as it was often called, the Crossley ratings.[30] The service emerged in 1929, but was not fully operational until the early 1930s. By telephoning listeners in thirty cities and asking them to name the programs they had heard that day, the C.A.B. report gave a statistical picture of the number of people listening to a particular show, and, therefore, hearing a sponsor's message. Until the 1935–1936 radio season the C.A.B. report was the fullest and most accurate measurement service available.

In 1935, however, the coincidental telephone method developed by C. E. Hooper, Inc., replaced the C.A.B. report as the most detailed study of radio listening. The Hooperatings, as they were termed, were based on an energetic system whereby listeners were called during a broadcast and asked questions about the program being heard at that moment. Unlike the C.A.B. method which asked for a recollection of the entire listening day, every day of the week Hooper operators in thirty-two cities were telephoning continuously from 8 A.M. to 10:30 P.M., asking about the programs with which their calls were coinciding.

Until the waning years of radio, the Hooperatings were the unchallenged cutting edge of radio success or failure. By 1949, however, the A. C. Nielsen Company had replaced Hooper—eventually buying out the company—as the standard rating service because it could offer a more accurate picture of the listening audience. The installation of an electronic audimeter in representative radio sets allowed Nielsen to register on a tape inside the apparatus every time the set was turned on, dialed, and turned off. By this method advertisers could learn which commercials were turned off, which guest stars were most popular, and which programs were heard, even in the early morning, since the audimeter was operative twenty-four hours a day.

Audience measurement made commercial control over broadcasting all the more stringent. No longer did a sponsor have to rely upon mail solicitation campaigns to know the extent to which his commercials were being heard. This meant, of course, that if a show did not produce favorable listener statistics, regardless of the star or the esthetic quality of the program, it probably would be dropped by the advertiser and, therefore, the network. Occasionally, networks sustained sponsorless programs. In most cases these were series created by network producers. By airing them, the networks hoped to interest potential sponsors. In some cases, however, sustaining programs were intellectual series that brought prestige, if not revenue, to the networks. In these categories were news commentators like H. V. Kaltenborn and Edward R. Murrow who often broadcast without sponsorship, prestigious dramatic series such as *Columbia Workshop,* and educational discussion programs like the *University of Chicago Roundtable* and *America's Town Meeting of the Air.*

Equipped with accurate audience measurements, and aware that the networks and local stations were dependent upon them for revenue, radio advertisers became a powerful force in the history of broadcasting. By 1948 sponsors were spending in excess of $400 million in advertising. And they exerted a powerful influence on what Americans heard. In fact, program content was often a secondary consideration for sponsors, their commercial messages being more important. According to one critic, the arrangement between radio networks and advertisers was "as if the editor of a newspaper had to farm out the writing of the news, page by page, to the corporations whose advertisements appeared on those pages." Reflective of this commercial control, George Washington Hill, the president of the American Tobacco Company, once commented: "Taking 100 percent as the total radio value, we give 90 percent to commercials to what's said about the product, and we give 10 percent to the show.... I don't have the right to spend the stockholders' money just to entertain the public."[31] The commercial influence in radio was asserted even more blatantly by J. Harold Ryan, president of the National Association of Broadcasters, when he marked the twenty-fifth anniversary of broadcasting by declaring:

> American radio is the product of American business! It is just as much that kind of product as the vacuum cleaner, the washing machine, the automobile, and the airplane. . . . If the legend still persists that a radio station is some kind of art center, a technical museum, or a little piece of Hollywood transplanted strangely to your home town, then the first official act of the second quarter century should be to list it along with the local dairies, laundries, banks, restaurants, and filling stations.[32]

It was attitudes such as these that led the noted radio critic and author, Philip Wylie, to write in 1947: "Radio is as brash as a peanut vendor in a lecture hall; it's as cheap as a popcorn hawker at the opera; it's a beep at vespers and a burp in an anthem."[33] And Norman Corwin, writing two years later, added his own fillip.

> Radio is the only major field of expression today where a high IQ, where boldness, adventure, imagination and audacity in programming are systematically, faithfully and deliberately penalized. Radio has not progressed, but retrogressed. It is not growing up, but down. It once had a toehold on the threshold of the arts, but its great, bulky body slipped on a stuffed banana, the skin of which concealed a hard, compact roll of fast bucks.[34]

Despite the strong control exercised by sponsors over programming, radio would have a major impact upon society. Most listeners did not feel advertiser influence was detrimental to broadcasting. A poll by *Fortune* magazine in 1938 asked Americans which industry best met public demands. The results indicate that even by this early date, a decade after full-time network broadcasting began, the relevance of radio to society was appreciated:[35]

Industry	Percentage
1. Automobile	43.1
2. Radio	29.2
3. Air Transportation	9.8
4. Motion Picture	9.5

Given both the increasing reliance of citizens upon radio and the curtailment of automobile production during World War II, it is safe to assume that by the mid-1940s radio was considered the most responsive industry in the nation.[36]

One of the most comprehensive studies of the effects of radio on society was made by the President's Research Committee on Social Trends which in the period from 1929 to 1932 observed social evolution in the United States. In its final report the committee enumerated 150 specific effects, and suggested that in each instance it was possible to discern secondary effects. Thus, from the conclusion that radio had increased the interest of Americans in sports, the committee derived secondary conclusions that enrollment had increased at colleges whose games were consistently broadcast, that airing baseball games had increased attendance, and that broadcasting had heightened interest in the climate of Florida and California.[37]

Perhaps the most significant influence of radio, even in the early 1930s, was the effect its programming was having upon the homogeneity of the nation. The United States had always been afflicted by sectional, regional, and cultural differences which kept it from becoming a fully united nation. Historical events, linguistic idiosyncracies, and cultural differences all testify to the heterogeneity of the country. Radio increased communication within the United States. Although local stations might have reflected provincialism in their own program originations, network broadcasting transmitted a single standard. The same announcers were heard coast-to-coast; celebrities became nationally known; the values and attitudes projected in radio dramas were heard by millions in every part of the country.

Network radio increased the similarity among Americans because it communicated the same stimuli throughout the nation. It developed a national constituency for its programs and commercials. In doing so it had to avoid offending sectional or regional differences. Forced to find the common denominator among all groups within the United States, radio became the thread that tied together all people. More than print or film, politics or laws, radio united the nation. When, by the late 1940s, more than 90 percent of the homes in America had radio receivers, it seems clear that the homogeneous message of broadcasting was being heard and appreciated. In a single stroke network radio standardized, entertained, informed, and educated its mass audience. In this function, it bound together the American people as had no single communications medium since the printing press.

The impact of radio as recognized by the President's Committee would be even more obvious in the next two decades. Beginning in the early 1930s, radio would evolve into the nation's most popular form of entertainment. So pervasive would be its influence as a leisure activity, by mid-century listening to the radio was second only to sleeping in the amount of time it consumed in the average person's life. Its impact was intelligently summarized by radio scholar Charles A. Siepmann when he wrote:

> Here in America radio is our main pastime. More than 90 percent of American homes have at least one receiving set. Millions have several. The average man or woman spends more leisure hours in listening to the radio than in anything else—except sleeping. The poorer and less educated we are, the more we listen—and naturally so. For radio—cheap, accessible, and generous in its provision for popular tastes—has come to be the poor man's library, his "legitimate" theater, his vaudeville, his newspaper, his club. Never before has he met so many famous and interesting people, and never have these people been at once so friendly and so attentive to his wishes.[38]

The popular acceptance eventually enjoyed by network radio, however, was in jeopardy in the first years of the 1930s. The declining popularity of *Amos 'n' Andy* by 1932 had led to a general diminishing of radio use throughout the nation. The loss of twenty-five percent of all listeners in a two-year period compelled programmers to develop new and enticing shows that would arrest the downward trend. The answer had already been indicated in the success of the *Rudy Vallee Show*. But it would be more strongly presented in the 1931–1932 radio season. The solution, of course, was to develop programs centered on already-established entertainment personalities.

And this was to be most strikingly demonstrated in the appearance of the *Eddie Cantor Show* in the fall of 1931.

Cantor's success was substantial. He brought with him to radio a national reputation as a comedian that had been developed in vaudeville, phonograph recordings, and motion pictures. Now as a broadcaster his humor and infectuous personality captured listeners as fast as *Amos 'n' Andy* had a few seasons earlier. Within a year the *Eddie Cantor Show* was the premier program on the air. More importantly for network radio, the response of listeners to this "personality performer" clearly showed that broadcasting needed headliners—the biggest names in entertainment who would host their own shows. It was with this mentality that radio approached the 1932–1933 season.

The Maturation of Programming, 1932–1939

Radio blossomed in the 1930s. Where earlier programming had relied primarily on musical and discussion shows, in its second decade broadcasting expanded its versatility to offer listeners as wide a range of entertainment and information as could be found in the other popular arts. During this period, radio developed the various genres of expression that were already recognizable in literature and film. Now it produced detective programs, westerns, the serialized melodramas that were the soap operas, comedies, romances, and serious dramas. In quiz shows and broadcast journalism, programming unique to the medium was introduced. With such an array of amusement for audiences trapped by the economic depression and social uncertainty of the 1930s, radio became the great well-spring from which came escape, diversion, knowledge, and inspiration.

National radio needed national reputations—that was the lesson of Vallee and Cantor—recognized personalities who would appeal immediately to audiences throughout the nation. In 1932 the networks turned to such men and women and initiated the most creative new season to date. A fortuitous development for the networks at this time was the virtual collapse of vaudeville. The dog acts, ventriloquism,

slapstick comedy, whistlers, and tap dancers that had been the
content of vaudeville could not withstand the competition of
the electric entertainment media. Radio, movies (especially
the "talkies" that had become standard by 1930), and phonograph recordings made the vaudeville stage shows lackluster
and predictably boring. Radio was new every time a listener
tuned in; films were vivid and engrossing every time a viewer
entered the theater; phonograph records brought the music
and jokes directly into the parlor. These new influences not
only undermined vaudeville as an institution, but created unemployment problems for vaudevillians.

In the fall of 1932 broadcasting presented the most daz-
zling array of new talent it had ever unveiled at one time.
Comedians, the most compelling feature of vaudeville, high-
lighted the new programs. The Marx Brothers, Ed Wynn,
George Burns and Gracie Allen, Jack Benny, George Jessel,
Jack Pearl, and Fred Allen all began their broadcasting careers that fall. Network radio that year also introduced
the vocal talents of singers like Bing Crosby, the Boswell Sisters, Paul Robeson, Ruth Etting, Jane Froman, Gertrude Nies-
sen, and Al Jolson. New that season, too, were news commentators Walter Winchell, Boake Carter, and Edwin C. Hill.

The maturation of radio in 1932 coincided with the election of Franklin D. Roosevelt to the Presidency of the United
States. That FDR understood the persuasive potential of
broadcasting was notable even before his inauguration, for in
December 1932, his popular wife, Eleanor, began appearing
regularly on *Vanity Fair*, an NBC variety program sponsored
by Pond's facial cream, offering her ideas on the state of the
nation, and on women's problems in particular. With President Roosevelt and his New Deal, Americans received a psychological and material antidote to the Depression that had
existed since the last months of 1929. In radio, FDR found
the most effective means of communicating directly with his
constituency, thereby enabling him to explain his activities and
to expand his popular support. Roosevelt's warm, friendly talks
with the American people, the so-called "Fireside Chats," be-

came the hallmark of his administration. During 1933 he broadcast four such personal discussions, always commencing his conversation with the democratic salutation, "My dear friends." Throughout his terms in office, Roosevelt utilized network radio to communicate directly with the people.

Between March 1933, and June 1935, for example, the President broadcast forty formal and informal speeches. And he was heard by the citizenry. C.A.B. ratings show that his post-Inaugural Fireside Chat on March 9, 1937, was heard by 30 percent of the radio audience, and his campaign address on October 10, 1936, was heard by 25 percent of the listeners.

As a corollary to Presidential speeches, the coverage of news events by radio in the 1930s led inevitably to a unique type of reporter: the broadcast journalist. Whether it was reporters like Lowell Thomas or Gabriel Heatter reading the news, or political commentators like Dorothy Thompson or H. V. Kaltenborn making intelligent appraisals of new developments, radio produced new styles of reporting and commentary that matured in this decade. Coincidentally, radio brought speeches and interviews with national and international newsmakers. The controversial actions of the New Deal were praised and blasted in coverage of events as diverse as discourses by members of the FDR cabinet and the 1936 Republican Presidential Convention. Foreign leaders were heard frequently in the United States. Overseas transmissions brought American listeners the diatribes of Fascist leaders Adolf Hitler and Benito Mussolini; but they also brought events as touching as the funeral of Britain's King George V and the abdication of Edward VIII.

When World War II began in Europe in September 1939, it was not surprising to most Americans. Although isolationist and neutral in their foreign policy, via radio Americans had heard the speeches, lived through the crises, understood the concessions, and anticipated the consequences. If it had been an unaware populace that went to battle in 1917, because of radio it was an informed citizenry that by 1939 heard and assessed the unfolding of events in the new war.

The impact of broadcasting through its coverage of news was vital and profound. Yet, as a source of fictional characters and popular culture, radio also placed its imprint upon American society. Out of radio came many of the most popular heroes of the decade. The war against crime, such an important part of actual law enforcement in the 1930s, was aided by culture heroes like Lamont Cranston (The Shadow); Mr. Keen, Tracer of Lost Persons; Britt Reid (The Green Hornet); Steve Wilson, the fighting newspaper editor on *Big Town*; and the comic-strip ace detective, Dick Tracy. Even though the western was not adequately developed on radio until the 1950s, several heroes galloped out of the West (or Northwest in some cases) to defend society against criminality —among them the Lone Ranger and Tonto; Sergeant Preston and his "wonder dog," Yukon King; and the hero of Laurie York Erskine's stories, Renfrew of the Mounted. Radio created heroes of domesticity like the sympathetic Ma Perkins, the paternalistic Henry Barbour of *One Man's Family,* and the self-sacrificing Helen Trent. In the 1930s radio utilized heroes from other areas of entertainment. Babe Ruth, Jimmy Foxx, and Max Baer—all sports heroes—had their own programs. Although Tom Mix had retired from motion pictures in 1933, he became a radio hero (Mix did not play himself) and remained so until 1950. Radio also gave fuller realization to comic strip heroes like Little Orphan Annie, Don Winslow of the Navy, Skippy, Buck Rogers, and Flash Gordon. And besides Renfrew, literature provided radio heroes in the early 1930s like the hard-working Stella Dallas, Tarzan of the Apes, the youthful Frank Merriwell, and the ageless Sherlock Holmes.

Radio heroes, like most champions in American popular culture, were symbols of truth, justice, honor, and other bourgeois virtues. Products of a middle class, commercial, and competitive society, radio heroes embodied the essence of those morals and values upon which the society was founded. Perhaps it would have been expecting too much for a sponsor to finance a program with an antisocial character as its recurring central character. Such would have identified the sponsor's product with an evil personality. Even when the insidious Dr. Fu Manchu was dramatized, the plot stressed the heroic actions of his arch-nemesis, the good Nyland Smith. Such programming, moreover, would have been incompatible with the nature of popular culture in American society as it functions to improve and stabilize society, not to undermine its operative value system. Nowhere was this pattern more closely observed than in the content of those programs designed for children.

Radio aired its programs for children in the hours after school, on Saturday mornings, and in the early weekday evenings. In the early years of radio such programming had been confined primarily to storytelling. Several personalities, among them Ireene Wicker of the *Singing Story Lady* series, and Nila Mack, the writer and director of the long-running *Let's Pretend* program, would perpetuate this style of broadcasting into the 1950s. The air was filled with dozens of network and local "uncles"—like *Uncle Don* on WOR, *Uncle Olie and His Gang* on CBS, and *Uncle Elmer's Children's Hour* on WJAS (Pittsburgh)—who related stories and songs and introduced regular characters like those appearing in 1931 on the NBC series, *Jolly Bill and Jane*: Fritzie the Fiddler, the Bugle Man, and the Three-Legged Piano Man. Parents scrutinized such programs, making certain that their children would not be influenced by adverse ideas, images, or words. When Uncle Wip of WIP inadvertently spoke a profane word into an open mike following a broadcast in April 1930, he was fined by the Federal Radio Commission and soon lost his job.[39] This vigilance was put to an acid test at the end of the decade.

The action and violence of juvenile adventure dramas was roundly criticized by the late 1930s as detrimental to American youngsters. For years network and agency representatives had defended such dramas against scattered attacks by educational groups, women's organizations, and generalized parental criticism. But by 1938, the pressure against mayhem on the air became overwhelming. The adults assailed adventure series aimed directly at youngsters—programs like *Jack*

Armstrong, which featured an athletic teenager fighting pirates, hostile natives, and diabolical gangsters; *Jungle Jim,* an adult character who struggled against enemies similar to Armstrong's rivals; *The Green Hornet,* an urban vigilante whose programs often included beatings, shootings, and murder; and *Howie Wing,* an aviator and do-gooder who usually encountered crime and brutality. These programs often relied on fistfights, loud action, and death to add spice to the plot. They also featured cliffhanger endings guaranteed to draw kids back to the radio the following day. Parent groups, like the Parent-Teachers Association, argued that this programming left children on edge, upset their normal up-bringing by placing destructive ideas in their young heads, and generally made them violence-prone.

But if parents were upset by children's programs, they saved their bitterest criticism for adult-oriented shows that children heard in the evening. They attacked programs like *Gangbusters,* realistic stories of criminals being brought to justice; *The Witch's Tales,* frightening stories of ghosts, murderers, superstitions, and assorted horror characters; and even *The Lone Ranger,* whose hero never killed anyone, but was assailed as a show filled with gunfights and narrow es-capes. Typical of the criticism launched against these dramas was the comment from a Des Moines parent who remarked:

> Our six-year-old has become gangster-minded this past year since he has been allowed to run the radio at his will. He plays G-man constantly and talks at great length about Jack Armstrong and the rest. Most children at this age have adequate imagination without this added stimu-lus which radio brings them. I am very greatly opposed to the various programs for children which employ terror-izing situations.[40]

The criticism of radio and its relationship to children be-came so intense that the networks were compelled to reassess the importance of violence in juvenile programming. In 1939, they either reissued or revised earlier program-policy codes which addressed a wide range of controversial subjects. In meeting the problem of violence in adult shows, the NBC statement—a new revision of its code published originally in 1934 and revised two years later—pledged to listeners that no obscene, profane, sacrilegious, vulgar, or salacious material would ever be aired. As it affected children's programs, the new code spoke in more specific terms.

> All stories must reflect respect for law and order, adult authority, good morals and clean living. The hero and heroine, and other sympathetic characters must be portrayed as intelligent and morally courageous. The theme must stress the importance of mutual respect of one man for another, and should emphasize the desirability of fair play and honorable behavior. Cowardice, malice, deceit, selfishness and disrespect for law must be avoided in the delineation of any character presented in the light of a hero to the child listener.[41]

In a similar vein, the CBS statement of policies—adopted originally in 1935—spoke of social values and the vulnerability of youngsters.

> The exalting, as modern heroes, of gangsters, criminals, and racketeers will not be allowed.
> Disrespect for either parental or other proper authority must not be glorified or encouraged.
> Cruelty, greed, and selfishness must not be presented as worthy motivations.
> Programs that arouse harmful nervous reactions in the child must not be presented.
> Conceit, smugness or unwarranted sense of superiority over others less fortunate may not be presented as laudable.
> Recklessness and abandon must not be closely identified with a healthy spirit of adventure.
> Unfair exploitation of others for personal gain must not be made praiseworthy.
> Dishonesty and deceit are not to be made appealing or attractive to the child.[42]

In these network statements is the essence of all effective juvenile programs. With their emphasis upon recognizable heroes and moral purposes, children's programs were socializing agents bringing to youngsters—in an entertaining context —the values and ideals of American society. One step above fairy tales in their subtlety, these radio shows offered Truth, Justice, Honor, and Decency as lessons. Jack Armstrong never cheated; Don Winslow was not a liar; Joe Palooka never succumbed to evil temptations. Brutality and violence, in this light, not only added verve to the serialized plots, but they substantially augmented the moral lesson. Such mayhem added tension and uncertainty to the stories. They introduced the possibility that the heroes and all they represented might not succeed. This device made the eventual triumph of morality all the more impressive in the minds of young listeners.

The victory of complaining parents in compelling the networks to reconsider their program policies illustrates the functioning of commercial radio in American society. Always fearful of losing their broadcasting licenses, radio stations and networks had to be responsive to the criticisms of listeners. This was especially true when such complaints were organized into a single, sizable movement with political potential. Such a wave of indignation against soap operas in the early 1940s led to a curtailing of such series in that decade. Networks also feared offending sponsors. If commercial programs were intended to raise money from advertising, controversial programming only enraged rather than satisfied consumers. Existing as they did in a competitive industry that sought to please a large audience, the radio networks vigilantly assessed listener reactions to their offerings. This rivalrous situation was even more pressing after 1934 when a fourth major network, the Mutual Broadcasting System, was created. Mutual was created by the pooling of several large, independent stations—WLW (Cincinnati), WXYZ (Detroit), WGN, and the key station, WOR—with the regional Don Lee Network on the West Coast, and several smaller outlets throughout the nation. By 1938, Mutual had grown to 110 stations and by the mid-1940s to more than 300 affiliates.

With such competition, the program producers were quick to spot a trend in listener preferences. The pattern created a history of fads in which an innovative program with great popularity soon became the model after which advertising agencies and networks fabricated similar series. The success of Eddie Cantor led to the inundation of radio by vaudeville comics. Later, broadcasting endured crazes such as those for amateur shows, quiz and giveaway programs, and Hollywood-celebrity shows in the 1930s; situation comedies, detective mysteries, and big-jackpot quiz shows in the 1940s; and westerns in the 1950s. As the airways became saturated with these faddist programs, listeners became satiated and shifted their interests to new types of shows. In this manner, commercial radio developed its range of programming while meeting the popular demands of its mass audience.

In the 1930s radio realized the esthetic extremes of its programming. These poles were manifest in the audience participation shows that emerged in the middle of the decade and the dramatic series which appeared throughout the period. "Audience participation" described those shows that utilized people in the studio or listening audience to provide the substance of the program. This was realized most clearly in the amateur programs, the singing and spelling shows, and the quiz series that occupied the attention of millions of Americans. There was a relationship between these shows, moreover, as they reflected the similar social values. These programs appealed to the sense of individualistic accomplishment that is at the base of American civilization. In a society stressing intelligence, talent, and hard work as the means of self-improvement and economic betterment, the American people eagerly accepted programs that promised a chance to succeed. The coincidence of the worst economic depression in the nation's history only added intensity to those who participated in, and listened to, such broadcasts.

The amateur craze began in 1934 with the appearance of Major Bowes' *Original Amateur Hour*. The show offered talented contestants throughout the country a chance to compete for prizes and possible discovery by talent scouts. Within a year the program was the top show in radio, outdrawing the prestigious *Jack Benny Program*, the *Rudy Vallee Show*, and the popular *George Burns and Gracie Allen Show*. Amateur-

ism swept Depression America. New shows emerged like
National Amateur Night on CBS, *Amateur Revue* on NBC-
Blue, and *N.T.G. and His Girls* on Bowes' own network,
NBC-Red. Amateurs appeared in unexpected places, as in
comedian Fred Allen's *Town Hall Tonight* program where
each week he allotted part of his show to budding performers.

The popularity of amateurism was intense. By 1936,
Bowes was receiving ten thousand applications a week from
singers, tap dancers, one-man bands, saw players, yodelers,
operatic talents, and the like. This popularity was felt also in
local broadcasting. Throughout the United States local stations had their own amateur shows. Here tens of thousands of
hopeful aspirants appeared on such programs as *The Children's Hour* on WNOX (Knoxville), *Opportunity Parade* on
KFRC (San Francisco), *Italian Amateur Hour* and *Spanish
Amateur Hour* on WBNX (New York City), *The Sunsweet
Amateur Hour* on WMCA (New York City), and *The Monte
Carlo Amateur Hour* on KMAC (San Antonio). Critics assailed the amateur craze as banal, exploitative of the talentless,
and offensive to the ears. Radio producer S. L. "Roxy" Rothafel attacked them bitterly, contending that "an amateur hour
is nothing short of a heathen Roman holiday, with the lions of
those past carnivals having a much better chance for survival
than the performers on the modern show."[43] Roxy was at
least statistically correct. Of more than fifteen thousand hope-
fuls who performed for Major Bowes, only a handful of future
talents was discovered, and only one, that being Frank Sinatra
who appeared in 1937 in a quartet called The Hoboken Four,
ever achieved overwhelming success. Yet, amateurism was a
democratic form of radio amusement. It was the average
citizen entertaining his colleagues. It was as close as an audience came to controlling directly the content of its own programming. And it was all done in the name of self-achieve-
ment, the struggle by the individual to "make it" in a competitive society.

By 1937 contests had replaced amateurs as the most popular form of audience participation programming. In a sense,
these shows held more potential for personal success, since

they did not require an obvious talent to win. From such participant shows as Gillette's *Community Sing* where the audience sang along with the show, and *Spelling Bee*, where participants could win up to $5 cash for spelling words, the modern quiz show was created. Even before 1937, however, radio was dispensing prizes to listeners. *Professor Quiz*, which appeared on CBS in mid-1936, offered $10 cash to the contestant best at answering general information questions. And contests were often held in connection with daytime soap operas. Audiences were invited to complete the last line to a jingle, or to write "in twenty-five words or less" a testimonial to the sponsor's product. Prizes in these contests could be as trivial as a supply of the sponsor's product, or as grandiose as a new automobile.

Network radio by 1938 was filled with quiz shows. Bingo, lotto, kino—games that had helped revive sagging movie attendance in the early Depression—were now brought to the millions of listeners drawn to their radio sets. The quiz format was adapted to every type of program. There were sports quizzes, news quizzes, courtroom quizzes, quizzes for children, quizzes that matched men against women, and children against adults. For intellectuals, there were *Information, Please!* with Clifton Fadiman and *The World Game* with Max Eastman. For the jitterbug set, there were *Kay Kyser's Kollege of Musical Knowledge, Beat the Band* with Ted Weems and his Orchestra, *Ben Bernie's Musical Quiz*, and by the early 1940s, *Cab Calloway's Quizzical*. And for the mystery fans, there were quizzes that offered prizes if one could name the criminal in that evening's broadcast. Radio even developed anti-quiz shows in such comedy parodies as *It Pays to Be I norant* and *Can You Top This?*

Perhaps the most controversial quiz program was *Pot (Gold* which debuted on NBC-Red in 1939. Where most q tion-and-answer shows offered only small financial prizes, *O' Gold* gave away $1,000 to anyone who picked up his phone if called during the broadcast by host Ben Grauer. if not listening to the show, the contestant won the prize. A consolation prize of $100 was awarded to those

home when telephoned. Upping the ante in giveaway programs had a dramatic effect on Americans. Movie houses lost
a significant number of patrons during the *Pot O' Gold* broadcast. The program became one of the top-rated shows in radio,
and demands for investigation of all quizzes were instigated.
Critics argued unsuccessfully that all radio quizzes should be
cancelled because they were illegal lotteries and a form of
gambling. Although quiz shows faded in popularity during
the war, they never disappeared completely. In the postwar
era they would reemerge, and reach new heights of popularity.

Like the amateur programs, the quiz and giveaway shows
may not have been esthetically pleasing, but they were fully
compatible with American social values. Instead of talent,
quiz shows called for intelligence as the means of achievement.
Again, the self-reliant individual could succeed if he had the
requisite knowledge. At a time when unemployment, economic sluggishness, and governmental experimentation diminished popular faith in the American system, these radio programs reaffirmed social premises.

In contrast to the simplicity and materialistic quality of
quiz shows, however, radio produced its most artistic achievements in its dramatic programming. Of course, most dramas
were not cultural triumphs. The romantic comedies found on
series like *Curtain Time, Grand Central Station,* and *The
First Nighter Program* followed the hackneyed formula of
boy-meets-girl, boy-loses-girl, boy-gets-girl. And quaint, but
predictable, rural dramas unfolded on *Soconyland Sketches,
Sunday at Seth Parker's,* and *Real Folks.* But in the writing
and production of several important dramatists, radio achieved
its finest artistic hours.

Drama on radio dated back to the WGY Players in the
early 1920s. In the 1930s, however, production improvements
would allow for a more sophisticated broadcast. Network
drama had its origins in the late 1920s when several magazine
publishers sponsored dramatizations of stories found in their
serials. *The Collier Hour* in 1927 began such a practice on
Blue. Soon similar dramas were adapted from *Redbook,
True Story, True Romances,* and *The American Weekly.* At

this time, too, radio actors were utilized in other dramatic genres—the detective story, the western, and the daytime soap opera. Radio, however, had two shortcomings which hindered the offering of refined, above-average drama: it lacked well-known acting talent, and it needed first-rate writers.

Hollywood, the depository of "name" dramatic talent, resisted broadcasting. Although a few movie personalities headed their own programs in the early 1930s—Adolph Zukor, the president of Paramount Pictures, discussed films, and *D.W. Griffith's Hollywood* was a Hollywood gossip show during the 1932–1933 season—the studios barred the stars from "cheapening" their box-office appeal by broadcasting. Advertising agencies, moreover, were reluctant to pay the exorbitant fees demanded by the stars even willing to face the microphones. Nonetheless, radio was drawn to motion pictures. Gossip commentators like Walter Winchell and Jimmie Fidler came to radio in the 1930s. Local stations regularly broadcast movie reviews. One station even aired remote broadcasts from the projection room of a local theater, allowing listeners to hear sections of movie sound tracks. But when NBC-Red introduced *Talkie Picture Time,* a series in the 1933–1934 season which dramatized scenes from motion pictures, it started an irresistible trend. Other shows in 1934 began broadcasting re-enacted scenes from movies, although radio actors, and not Hollywood stars, played the various parts. Here were series like *Forty-Five Minutes in Hollywood,* and *Hollywood Hotel,* the latter hosted, significantly, by the Hearst newspaper gossip columnist Louella Parsons.

Parsons' influential position in the movie industry made it difficult for movie stars to reject her request to appear on *Hollywood Hotel.* She promised publicity for a star's latest film, and a refusal meant the risk of offending the most powerful movie writer in journalism. During her years on the program, Parsons used her leverage to bring the biggest names in Hollywood to her mike. In the process, she broke down much of the resistance of the stars and studios to radio.

With the appearance of the *Lux Radio Theater* the greatest broadcasting vehicle for Hollywood stars was inaugurated.

Originally airing adaptations of Broadway dramas, the *Lux Radio Theater* floundered after its premier in 1934. Within two years, however, the hour program successfully switched its emphasis to Hollywood movies, and changed its broadcasting site from New York City to the film capital. It was a doubly significant stroke. The success of the new format and the transfer of location precipitated a wholesale exodus of radio production to the West Coast. Here the networks were close to the glamor and name-recognition of the film colony. Now that the stars were cooperating with radio, nothing but the brightest future seemed assured. Before the end of the decade, the most important programs in broadcasting were originating from network studios in Hollywood.

The Lux program was an overwhelming radio hit and would remain so until 1955. During its run most of the alluring names in movies acted on it, not just in scenes, but in full adaptations of their greatest film triumphs. William Powell and Myrna Loy appeared in 1936 in *The Thin Man*; Clark Gable and Claudette Colbert in 1939 recreated *It Happened One Night*; James Cagney and Pat O'Brien the same year came before the microphones in *Angels with Dirty Faces*; Cary Grant, Katharine Hepburn, and James Stewart in 1942 played *The Philadelphia Story*; and Humphrey Bogart and Walter Huston in 1949 brought *The Treasure of Sierra Madre*. The series was given even greater stature by the fact that throughout its first decade in Hollywood it was hosted by movie director Cecil B. DeMille. Importantly, the Lux program inspired the appearance of movie stars in other dramatic series. In the late 1930s such programs as *The Screen Guild Players* and *Warner Academy Theater* broadcast adaptations of feature films. *Silver Theater* and Dupont's prestigious *Cavalcade of America* utilized movie stars in original dramas. Underscoring the change of attitude by the studios, in 1938 Metro-Goldwyn-Mayer produced *Good News of 1938* a dramatic-variety series which starred most of the M-G-M celebrities.

It would be incorrect to assume that because radio courted Hollywood personalities, it was unable to develop its own acting talent. By the late 1930s many distinguished actors were emerging in radio, some moving into successful movie careers. Agnes Moorehead, Don Ameche, Art Carney, Arlene Francis, Richard Widmark, Frank Lovejoy, and John Hodiak were among the more well-known graduates of broadcasting. Perhaps the most prestigious alumnus, however, was Orson Welles. Before he left radio for films, Welles emerged as a first-rate actor and director in such series as *The Shadow, Campbell Playhouse,* and *Mercury Theater on the Air.* On this latter program he left his most enduring mark on radio history, a performance which clearly illustrated the potency of this new medium of communication.

The airing on October 30, 1938, of an adaptation of H. G. Wells' novel, *The War of the Worlds,* was meant by Welles and his colleagues to be a Halloween "trick" played on American listeners. By enacting the novel as if Martians were actually invading the United States and radio was covering it, Welles sent a shiver of fear up the spine of the nation. Many of those who missed the opening credits mistook the program for an actual invasion, and when the announcer stated, "Ladies and gentlemen, we interrupt our program of dance music to bring you a special bulletin from the Intercontinental Radio News," for millions of listeners fantasy became reality. Others could not help but relate it to the war scare which Hitler had precipitated a month earlier over the Sudetenland area of Czechoslovakia. The impact of the broadcast was to create a near hysteria in the nation. No one anticipated that radio could have such a devastating control over its listeners. From New York City and Washington, D.C., to St. Louis and Seattle, listeners panicked because of the sounds they heard from a commercial radio drama. If ever radio demonstrated its need to be scrupulously responsible in its programming, it was in that panic broadcast in 1938,[44] for this was a broadcaster's moral equivalent of yelling "Fire!" in a crowded theater.

As well as frothy romances and adaptations of Hollywood films, network radio produced occasional dramatic series that were more artistic than commercial. Such programs were almost always network sustainers—paid for by the networks rather than by a sponsor—that garnered more prestige than Hooperatings. In 1937 interest in such prestige drama became a point of rivalry. CBS drew several of the finest actors in Hollywood to stage radio adaptations of Shakespeare. Among them were Burgess Meredith as Hamlet, Walter Huston as Henry IV, and Edward G. Robinson as Petruchio in *The Taming of the Shrew.* NBC countered by engaging the noted actor, John Barrymore, to enact four Shakespearian plays. His portrayals in *Hamlet, Richard III, Macbeth,* and *Twelfth Night* were solidly praised. CBS also produced other Shakespearian plays in 1937 with noted talents like Leslie Howard, Rosalind Russell, and Tallulah Bankhead. The Mutual network joined the rivalry, producing Victor Hugo's *Les Miserables* as a seven-and-one-half-hour serial starring Orson Welles

The trend toward serious drama did not end with this outburst. In the following year radio broadcast the works of such substantial writers as Ibsen, Marlowe, Gogol, Corneille, Eliot, and Tolstoy. The network contest for cultural leadership even spread to fine music. To counter the success of CBS in airing the Sunday concerts of the New York Philharmonic Orchestra, David Sarnoff in 1937 ordered the formation of an NBC Symphony Orchestra and engaged Arturo Toscanini to be its conductor.

Impressively, during the year beginning May 1938, network radio turned overwhelmingly to fine drama for inspiration. According to *Variety Radio Directory,*[45] radio that year aired 164 adaptations of stage plays, 60 adaptations of prose and poetry, and 208 plays written specifically for radio. Add to this the 138 plays, stories, operettas, symphonic dramas, and dramatizations of books produced by the Federal Theater Radio Division—a New Deal project of the Works Project Administration under the Federal Theater Project—and it is clear that by the end of the decade the networks had made a distinctive commitment to adult drama.

Nowhere was this maturation in radio more apparent than in the celebrated CBS program, *Columbia Workshop.* The series began in July 1936, and was an experimental theater wherein sound effects, production techniques, and innovative writing were often more important than plot. As a sustainer it brought to radio the works of aspiring and acclaimed writers—among them Archibald MacLeish, Pare Lorentz, Dorothy Parker, Irwin Shaw, Stephen Vincent Benét, and James Thurber—whose artistic dramas would have been otherwise incompatible with the generally less mature offerings of network broadcasting. Directed first by Irving Reis and then by William N. Robson and others, and scored by the brilliant musician, Bernard Herrmann, the *Columbia Workshop* was one of radio's most impressive achievements. Many *Workshop* productions became classics of American broadcast drama. MacLeish's *Fall of the City* was a brilliant play in verse form which warned of impending dictatorship and loss of personal liberty. Benét's *John Brown's Body* was a choral and poetic reiteration of the promise of freedom. Among the program's other triumphs were Lorentz's Depression documentary, *Ecce Homo*; Shakespeare's *Hamlet* and *As You Like It*; *The Four Quartets of T. S. Eliot*; and, with its author, Aldous Huxley, as the narrator, *Brave New World*. Many associated with the *Columbia Workshop* entered as unknowns and graduated to successful careers in radio and the other arts. In its several seasons on CBS (1936–1942, 1946–1947, and, as the *CBS Radio Workshop*, 1956–1957) the series created a prestigious legacy for both the network and radio.

Despite the success of network drama, radio seemed always a "poor cousin" to the other popular arts. Trade journals consistently carried stories regarding the lack of name talent being developed in broadcasting, and the failure of radio to produce great writers or directors. Critics also condemned the limitations created by commercialism, considerations of scheduling which always superseded art, and the fact that radio limited an actor to the voice only.

The prominent radio actor Joseph Julian boldly suggested this when he wrote that radio inevitably led to artistic stagnation and to the disintegration of the creative performer. Writing in 1941, Julian alleged that most radio performers lacked "inner satisfaction after doing a radio job," and that, despite a few bright lights, "corn still runs rampant on the airwaves."[46] Although Julian's opinion was blasted by some of the more respected talents in broadcasting—Bing Crosby, Irene Rich, Gene Autry, Les Tremayne, Katherine Seymour, Carleton E. Morse, and Erik Barnouw[47]—his attitude again pointed up the sense of inferiority and anonymity with which many radio professionals worked. Especially hard hit by defeatist criticism was the paucity of fine radio writers.

Most radio writers produced formulaic stories for formulaic series. But even when radio did develop outstanding dramatists, they invariably were lured into writing film scripts or novels. Such was the case with men like Irving Reis, who became a movie director; Ralph Berkey, who graduated from soap operas to Broadway plays; Irwin Shaw, who left *The Gumps* and eventually wrote the best-sellers, *The Young Lions* and *Rich Man, Poor Man*; Herman Wouk, who emerged from the *Fred Allen Show* to write *The Caine Mutiny*; and Arthur Miller, who left composing dramas for *Cavalcade of America* and *The Theater Guild on the Air* to compose award-winning scripts for Hollywood and Broadway.

Although broadcasting served as a training ground for several important writers, it still was not without its own luminaries who developed radio drama into a polished product. Arch Oboler came to radio in the early 1930s when writing and production standards were low, and when an understanding of the medium was generally absent. Oboler described the situation when he remarked:

> Radio in those days was an imitation of motion pictures, and an echo of the stage. No one had really used it as a theater of the mind, had realized that a few words, a sound effect, a bit of music, could transport—in the mind of the listeners—one to any corner of the world, evoke emotions that were deep in the consciousness of the listener.

Oboler scored a quick success in his long-running horror program, *Lights Out*. By 1939, he was the honored "experimental drama" writer for NBC on his own series, *Arch Oboler's Plays*. Although he also wrote for the romantic-comedy series *Grand Hotel*, as well as composing playlets for several NBC variety shows, Oboler's mark was made as an innovative, original playwright.

In Arch Oboler radio found its greatest exponent of using sound effects to maximize drama. One of his more famous plays involved giant earthworms taking over the world, complete with the sound of the creatures devouring everything on earth. In other dramas he turned people inside out, had a chicken heart expand to the point that it destroyed civilization, and caused a man to be trapped half-way while trying, through telepathy, to transport himself through the solid concrete wall of a bank—all possible only in radio where audial suggestion and imagination conspired to create illusion. Oboler also specialized in internal dramas, plays that took the listener into the minds of his protagonists. His drama "Baby" followed the thinking of a pregnant woman awaiting the birth of her child; "The Ugliest Man in the World" traced the pain of a homely man taunted by insensitive people but eventually finding love with a blind woman; "Buried Alive" probed the thinking of a living person mistakenly thought dead and interred; and in 1940, Oboler's dramatization of Dalton Trumbo's anti-war play, "Johnny Got His Gun," took listeners into the mind of a soldier who had returned from World War I as a "human vegetable."

Oboler was a prolific writer. In his first decade in radio he produced almost 800 plays. Although he tried his hand at writing for motion pictures, he seemed wedded to broadcasting. Oboler stood as a spokesman for radio dramatists. In 1938 he chided radio producers for paying so little and expecting so much from playwrights. "To pay $5000 for a guest star and $150 for the words she emotes," he wrote, "is obviously not a method or situation to build a group of eagerly working radio dramatists."[48] In the early 1940s he became the advocate of politicized, propagandistic dramas, a posture which conflicted with network policies adhering to neutrality before war erupted, and only reasonable propaganda after it began.

As late as 1946, Oboler was attacking management, this time for the dishonesty in radio advertising which, he argued, was indecent, untruthful, and depreciatory for broadcasting.

According to him, "Our radio franchise rests on service, not in trumped-up claims and counter-claims of pseudo-virtues, either in ourselves or what we sell."[49] Oboler ended his creative career in radio on a note of bitterness and disillusion. In 1948, after confessing that, "the writing of each play, over these years, has been a nerve-wracking, stomach-turning, head-spinning series of week-after-week crises," he assailed radio as never before. Radio, in his view, had a "rapacious appetite"— expressed in deadlines and cycles of thirteen, twenty-six, and fifty-two successive broadcasts—which allowed the writer no time for reflection or study or replenishment of his depleted inner creative reservoirs. Oboler summed up his medium in a stunning mixed metaphor: "Radio, for the dramatist, is a huge, insatiable sausage grinder into which he feeds his creative life to be converted into neatly packaged detergents." His answer to the dilemma was to pray for the acceleration of the forward movement of television.[50]

If Arch Oboler exploited the audial nuances of radio, Norman Corwin realized the poetic beauty possible within the medium. Corwin's skill lay not in handling radio as a new art but in his ability to write words effectively and to produce a breadth of broadcast drama that ranged from poetic impressions of life and moving patriotic statements to clever satires and sensitive human fantasies. Corwin brought the older art forms—literature and poetry—into the new medium of radio and, more brilliantly than anyone before, demonstrated its esthetic potential.

With a background in journalism and movie public relations, Corwin came to radio in 1937 as a poet. From his local program, *Poetic License,* on WQXR (New York City), he moved the next year to the Columbia network on a personalized series called *Words without Music,* and soon to the prestigious *Columbia Workshop.* At CBS, Corwin's styles began to emerge. His "Plot to Overthrow Christmas" was a delightful holiday fantasy that became a regular Christmas-time feature. His political satire, "They Fly through the Air with the Greatest of Ease," was an attack on fascism which sarcastically was dedicated "to all aviators who have bombed defenseless civilian populations and machine-gunned helpless refugees." In the patriotic series, *The Pursuit of Happiness*, which commenced in late 1939, Corwin further developed as a writer, director, and producer of tasteful, artistic drama.

That radio drama could be an emotive, sophisticated art form was aptly demonstrated by Corwin's work during the war. His impressive contribution to the *Columbia Workshop* in 1941, a six-month series called "Twenty-Six by Corwin," was a singular triumph. Corwin's dramas here extended from the whispy light of dawn which he impressionistically followed around the globe in "Daybreak," to ringing salutes to democracy and Americanism in "The People, Yes!" and in "Between Americans," to a tender escapist fantasy of a determined boy searching the galaxies for his dead dog, "The Odyssey of Runyon Jones." In the series *This Is War* in early 1942, and *An American in England* at the end of that year, Corwin brought to radio the dislocation and hopefulness that were shared by people on both sides of the Atlantic. And when the war ended in Europe and then Japan, Corwin's acclaimed programs, "On a Note of Triumph" and "14 August" happily, yet soberly, proclaimed the coming of peace. In reviewing "On a Note of Triumph," *Variety* epitomized the contribution of Corwin to peace and to radio.

> Here was Corwin the fashioner of beautiful prose, Corwin the exponent of realistic ideals, the Corwin who can make words sing, the poet who glorifies the common man and above all the Corwin who is the master of radio and its assorted techniques. . . . Corwin is the first to prove that radio can inspire great works of art and, by the same token, he disproves the theory that writing for the medium fetters and binds creative talent.[51]

Unlike the disillusioned Oboler, Corwin remained a dedicated practitioner of the craft he had helped create. In the mid-1940s he travelled around the globe using a wire recorder to preserve the voices and sounds he encountered. The result of this four-month excursion to thirty-seven countries was an impressive series, *One World Flight*, broadcast in early 1947. Yet, the future was dim for Corwin. With the coming of television and increased network competition, his narrowly-focused craftsmanship became incongruent with CBS policy. As Erik Barnouw has related it, Corwin left radio in the late 1940s because his work lacked the broad appeal found in many of the top-rated programs. Although he had made epic a-chievements for William Paley and CBS, he was not the dramatist to reach as many people as possible. When Paley offered him unacceptable terms in a new contract, Corwin was essentially out of broadcasting.[52]

For every Oboler and Corwin, radio produced scores of undistinguished writers who quietly plied their trade. Perhaps their accomplishments were little more than repetitions of formulae, turning out predictable plots with uninspiring characterizations. Nonetheless, even with hack writers, through its various dramatic programs, radio emerged by the late 1930s as more than a medium of music and discussion, comedies and quizzes. Even if it was trite art, it was a type of programming that tied broadcasting to the traditions of the theater. Perhaps soap operas were overly melodramatic, the western was still an immature form, and detective shows were ordinary by this time, but radio programming was still theater and it was enjoyed by millions. Many dramatic series became radio favorites. Programs like *Inner Sanctum, Escape,* and *The Mysterious Traveler* entertained listeners for years. And *Suspense,* which began its twenty-year run in 1942, effectively blended Hollywood actors, fine writers, and suspenseful plot development. No dramatist or actor could hope to change broadcasting. It was a reflection of the people and system and culture which produced it. Therefore, in a mass medium, directed by commercial interests and competing for consumer attention, the remarkable achievement is that brilliant dramatists ever succeeded. Their triumphs, moreover, must be shared by the networks which sustained them.

By the end of the 1930s radio was solidly a part of the lives of most Americans. Most homes had at least one receiver; portable sets and car radios made broadcasting a mobile medium; and radio was seriously undermining newspapers as the preferred source of news, and film as the favorite form of diversion. Radio was producing its own cultural personalities —Kate Smith, Arthur Godfrey, Clifton Fadiman—and it was breathing vitality back into the careers of many entertainers from other media—Fannie Brice, Eddie "Rochester" Anderson, Jean Hersholt.

Through its heavy diet of popular music, moreover, radio was playing an instrumental role in rejuvenating national spirits following the Depression. As the austerity of the early 1930s gave way to a broader national confidence by the end of the decade, radio created for its audience—as the title of both the Al Jarvis (KFWB, Los Angeles) and the Martin Block (WNEW, New York City) record programs suggested— a "Make-Believe Ballroom." The dance music called "swing" was largely popularized through radio. Network radio allowed a nation of jitterbugging "hep-cats" to hear remote broadcasts from the more important ballrooms and nightclubs in Los Angeles, Chicago, and New York City. Many big band leaders had their own regular network series, and swing fans could regularly hear the pulsating music of Benny Goodman, Duke Ellington, Glenn Miller, and Tommy Dorsey. With the Lucky Strike cigarettes program, *Your Hit Parade,* radio in the late 1930s made the country familiar with the weekly Top Ten in record sales. As a pervasive supplement to all this live musical performing, radio—on the network, but especially on the local, level—created the disk jockey who played the popular recordings that the dancers and listeners were purchasing.

Yet, radio's greatest challenge lay ahead. During World War II broadcasting would be called upon to play a strategic role in maintaining unity and self-confidence among the American citizenry. Less than twenty years old, radio was compelled to accept the challenge with its incumbent responsibilities.

Wartime Radio, 1939–1945

If there remained doubts by the end of the 1930s that broadcasting was integral to American civilization, the events of September 3, 1939, dispelled those notions. That was the

biggest news day in the history of radio. Within the eighteen
hours between 6 A.M. and midnight, listeners heard live transmissions of several profound events:

1. The declaration of war against Germany issued by the
   British and French governments.
2. An address to the British Empire by King George VI
   of England.
3. A speech by the British Prime Minister, Neville Cham-
   berlain.
4. A speech by President Roosevelt.
5. A speech by the Canadian Prime Minister, Mackenzie
   King.
6. News reports about the torpedoing of a transatlantic
   liner.

Only hours old, the instantaneous communication possible
through commercial radio was bringing the new World War
directly into the living rooms of the American people. Of
course, the events leading to the war had been scrupulously
covered by radio: from the crises to the speeches, from the
threats to the battles. Now that a conflagration had engulfed
Western civilization, radio would continue to function as the
principal source of information for the nation.

In the twenty-seven months between the outbreak of
World War II and the American entry into it, network radio
struggled to remain as neutral as possible. This was especially
difficult for foreign correspondents like Edward R. Murrow
and William L. Shirer. Strongly anti-fascist and, by nature,
Anglophiles, it was no easy task for them to report an un-
biased description of Rotterdam being levelled by Nazi
bombs, or to stand in a London studio of the British Broadcasting Corporation and report on the Blitzkrieg that was being unleashed on the British capital. Eric Sevareid, as a CBS
correspondent who had covered the fall of France, summarized
one of the difficulties of such assignments when he remarked
in 1940:

> After you've gone through this thing called total war
> you're apt to have different standards.... When you've
> seen the homes of civilians destroyed, hospitals bombed
> and helpless women and children killed in the street and

in air raid shelters, you have a new idea of what's important. . . . Everyone over there has narrow escapes from
death every day. It can't help but change your outlook,
give you a new perspective.[53]

Network policies, as well as journalistic professionalism,
tried to keep radio programming as neutral as possible. Even
without governmental suggestion, the networks in September
1939 quickly enunciated editorial postures that included:

1. The avoidance of horror, suspense and undue excitement in reporting the news and the plight of refugees.
2. Scrupulous checking of news sources before broadcasting.
3. Careful labeling of propaganda when used in broadcasting.[54]

One of the first to feel the weight of this neutralist policy was
the noted news commentator, H. V. Kaltenborn. His anti-
fascist commentaries on the news were stifled by CBS. The
network commenced calling him a news analyst, thereby allowing him the right to assess the facts, but offer no opinions.
And when Kaltenborn left CBS and moved to NBC in late
1939, he encountered similar restrictions.

The network policy of neutrality also extended to entertainment programming. Dramatic shows could not involve
sabotage, subversion, or spying within the United States.
Heroes could not be involved for one side or another in the
war. Broadcasters could not openly side with any of the com-
batants. Yet, programs skirted proscriptions by concentrating
upon patriotic topics. By lauding American society and its
institutions, radio effectively proclaimed the principles of democracy, equality, freedom, individualism, and the rule of
law. It was not difficult to link such values with the anti-facist
cause.

There were other signs of distate for the totalitarian
cause. Children listening to *Captain Midnight* in late 1941
heard their hero striking "fear into the hearts of foes of democracy and freedom" in Japanese-occupied China. In February, 1940, the noted film director, Louis de Rochemont, spoke
on *We, the People* of the Maginot Line and the invincibility it

gave to France against a possible German assault. The actors on one broadcast of the *Lux Radio Theater* in 1941 donated their salaries to the China Relief Fund. The newspaper drama, *Big Town*, dealt intermittently with themes of racial and religious tolerance. *The Screen Guild Players* dramatized the politicized films *Meet John Doe* and *Waterloo Bridge*, and indirectly-related films such as *I Met Him in Paris, Shop Around the Corner, Ninotchka*, and *Winter in Paris*. Three weeks after the war began in Europe, the *Columbia Workshop* rebroadcast its acclaimed warning about imminent dictatorship, *The Fall of the City*. And three new programs—*Bulldog Drummond* and revivals of *Fu Manchu* and *The Adventures of Sherlock Holmes*—clearly presented English heroes fighting crime. Probably the most stridently anti-Nazi program in this time was the soap opera *Against the Storm*, Sandra Michael's serial about refugee families seeking new lives in America. Set in a small college town, this soap used refugees and college lectures as contexts in which to make patriotic and anti-totalitarian statements.

Radio certainly sympathized with the Anglo-French position. Thus, when news commentator Drew Pearson predicted in July 1940 that Germany would defeat Great Britain, his comment drew much unfavorable attention.[55] Those few stations that broadcast a pro-German attitude were usually local ethnic stations airing German-language or Italian-language programs for enclaves in Milwaukee, New York City, and Chicago. These were quickly taken off the air. The forces that most effectively kept radio true to a neutralist policy were isolationist groups like the American First Committee.

Although an overwhelming majority of Americans sympathized with the British position, almost as large a majority favored an isolationist foreign policy for the United States. Embittered by sacrifices made during World War I and true to a non-interventionist policy that had been initiated with George Washington, patriotic organizations and citizens carefully audited radio to ensure its impartiality. When they detected political prejudice, these citizen censors loudly complained to the station, network, sponsors, and the FCC. They also utilized radio to spread their own messages. Col. Charles A. Lindbergh was a frequent speaker, arguing that Europe's wars were not America's concerns. Former President Hoover was a strong voice, suggesting in 1940 that if a Nazi peace were established in Europe, the United States should begin developing economic ties with the New Order. Senators like Robert Taft and Burton Wheeler, newscasters like Boake Carter and Fulton Lewis, Jr., and social leaders like Bruce Barton, a Congressman and founder of the advertising agency, Batten, Barton, Durstine & Osborn, also lent their prestige to the neutralist lobby. Theirs was an effective campaign. Governmental and network policy as well as public opinion did not abandon neutrality until the Japanese attack upon Pearl Harbor on December 7, 1941, and the German and Italian declarations of war on the United States four days later.

World War II was a radio war. From the "Day of Infamy" speech delivered by FDR to the Congress on December 8, 1941, to the surrender ceremonies on September 2, 1945, aboard the U.S.S. *Missouri* in Tokyo Harbor, Americans experienced the battle most directly via broadcasting. News correspondents transmitted from the theaters of war, the federal government maintained a liaison with its citizenry through radio, and networks and local stations were eager to interrupt regular programming to bring the latest news flashes. The war affected other areas of broadcasting besides news. Government War Bonds programs such as *Treasury Star Parade, Millions for Defense,* and *Music for Millions* mixed Hollywood celebrities and heavily-propagandized scripts in emotional pitches for bonds. Other official messages—from appeals for scrap metal, used fats and grease, and planting Victory gardens, to conserving the life of rubber tires, squelching rumors, and meeting the strict requirements to earn a Victory-Home sticker—reached listeners.

In the early weeks of the war, all radio rallied to national needs. In the midst of the plots, soap opera characters began discussing Red Cross or U.S.O. volunteerism. Mrs. Edward G. Robinson, representing the women's U.S.O. division for Cali-

fornia, appeared on *Dr. Christian* to appeal for donations to
the organization. *Vox Pop,* the popular interview program,
hosted a survivor of Pearl Harbor, and then used the opportunity to suggest that those who failed to double up in automobiles were guilty of criminal negligence, while those who
took joy rides in automobiles were guilty of sabotage. On the
Kraft Music Hall, host Bing Crosby stressed the importance of
buying war bonds in order to "clip the Nips." The plot of an
Amos 'n' Andy broadcast dealt sympathetically, but nega-
tively, with a wealthy woman who wished to avoid government agencies and start her own private war projects. Shows as
diverse as *Lum and Abner,* the *Quiz Kids,* and the gossip
program, *The Voice of Broadway,* made ringing speeches
about buying bonds to support the American troops fighting
the war. Even local stations entered the crusade. Ethnic stations like WBNX (New York City) and WHOM (Jersey
City) aired anti-Nazi shows in German. Station WGR (Buffalo) created a "Commando Corps" of youngsters to sell War
Bonds and Stamps. Participating children received armbands
for identification, and depending upon the amount of their
sales, they were able to move up in the ranks from "Private" to
"General."

These were impassioned weeks, and the rhetoric of radio
programming testified to the depth of the feelings being
demonstrated. Typical of these intense emotions was the following speech made by the central character in *The Adventures of Ellery Queen,* not usually a program in which the
actors became topical.

> It is true that I spend a great deal of my time editing
> and writing but my major purpose in life is to bring
> criminals to justice—to see that they are put where they
> cannot terrorize decent people again. Today the most vi-
> cious gang of international criminals in all history is
> loose in the world. So we Americans have organized—a
> wrathful army of men, women, and children—to track
> down these criminals together. You're in this army, even
> if you're not shouldering a gun—not everyone can. But
> everyone can take a shot at the Axis just the same—with
> no more effort than it takes to stop at your corner drug

store. Because one 25¢ War Stamp bought from your druggist puts 12 bullets into the magazine of an American's gun—yes, 12 bullets and you may be sure our boys will deliver your 12 messages to the Nazis and Japs without fail. And that 25¢ War Stamp not only means 12 shots at the Axis—it's also an investment because your 25¢ immediately goes back to work earning money for you, money you will get back with interest after it has done its share for Victory. So buy bullets through War Stamps from your druggist tonight. Yes, and tomorrow and the next day and the day after that—buy War Stamps every day until the day of Victory.[56]

As animated as was such rhetoric, there were those who felt that radio needed to paint the enemy in more sinister colors. Arch Oboler enunciated that position when he told a group of radio officials and scholars that radio programs needed an "injection of hatred and passionate feeling."[57] His radio plays that year reflected his position. Oboler created diabolic pictures of what he termed "the Jap-Nazi world" that would materialize if indifferent Americans did not dedicate their energies and money to the war effort. In his fantasy, "Adolf and Miss Runyon," he had Hitler roundly denounced by a typical American woman who then killed him in a car accident. In his drama, "Hate," Oboler heatedly preached that the Nazis were "a filthy, ruthless, bestial crew . . . they hate us and our kind, intend to destroy us and all we stand for. We must kill them with any weapon, by any means, if we are to survive. We must fight; we must hate."[58] In "Chicago, Germany," presented on the *Treasury Star Parade,* he presented a brutal vision of the consequences to average Americans of a Nazi conquest of the United States—an insight which dramatically ended with the comment: "This has been a play about an America that must never happen—that will never happen—NEVER!" Oboler personally explained his commitment to the war on the broadcast of *Lights Out* on December 18, 1942.

A few weeks ago . . . I started a game. Perhaps you heard about it. It's called "They're Here for Me." It's a very simple game. You sit where you are and you think, "The

Japs, the Nazis—they're here for me. Not for someone in
the newspaper, or someone in the town half-way across
the world, someone I don't even know in this neighborhood, or even for my neighbor next door. But for me."
Yeah, a smirky little Jap is standing at the door. He's there
for you—not in the headlines, not just an idea, but actually there for you. It can happen you know. Three million
dead in Europe attest to that fact. . . . Think about that
Jap or that Nazi waiting for you, and then remember
that every War Savings Stamp and every War Bond that
you buy is a bullet, or a bomb, or a tank, or an airplane
between you personally, and the horror of a Jap-Nazi
world. Every Bond that you buy—another bullet, or another bomb, or another tank, or another airplane between you personally and the horror of a Jap-Nazi world.

Although the intensity of wartime patriotism tended to
diminish as the war dragged on, the national military effort
was strongly a part of radio entertainment from 1942 until
mid-1945. As a programming trend it was recognizable in the
number of military men and women who appeared as contestants on quiz shows, and in the appearance of series fully
oriented toward the war effort—series like the award-winning
The Man Behind the Gun, which dramatized the battles of
war; *The Army Hour,* a military variety series; and *Stage
Door Canteen,* an all-star revue for servicemen hosted by
Bette Davis and other personalities. Preoccupation with the
war was noticeable in such disparate expressions as Fibber
McGee and Molly singing "The Star-Spangled Banner" at the
end of one of their shows; Eddie Cantor, Kate Smith, and
Ralph Edwards (host of the popular quiz show, *Truth or
Consequences*) conducting extremely successful War Bond
drives; and the appearance of programs like *Viva America,*
which stressed the warmth of political relations between the
United States and her Latin American allies. Yet, nowhere was
the propagandizing more obvious than in children's programs.
The impressionable minds that had been spared violence by
the network codes in 1939 now became targets of plots that
were as brutalizing as anything intended for adult listeners.

American children fought World War II in front of their
radio sets. To take them into the thick of the battle, there

were the likes of *Don Winslow of the Navy*, the story of a Naval aviator who bombed ships, attacked Nazis, and hated Japanese. *Hop Harrigan* was about "America's ace of the airways." Harrigan was an eighteen-year-old free-lance aviator who presented a "big brother" image to youngsters. But he was an American warrior to the core. Harrigan flew bombing runs, had dog-fights with enemy planes, escaped concentration camps and rescued his wounded pal while dodging German machinegun bullets. The heroes of children's programming fought enemies everywhere. In *Captain Midnight, Terry and the Pirates, The Sea Hound,* and *Jungle Jim* they championed the Allied cause in the air, on the sea, and on land throughout the world. At home, America was protected from spies and saboteurs by the central characters of *Superman, Tom Mix and His Ralston Straight-Shooters, The Green Hornet,* and *Jack Armstrong*.

As if the plots were not involvement enough, throughout the war juvenile listeners were implored on these shows to fight the enemy by collecting scrap metal, used fats, tin, rubber, and newspapers; and by buying War Bonds, writing to servicemen once a month, and planting Victory gardens. Never had a war been so directly taken to American youngsters; never had a war been as total as radio made it. One of the most compelling examples of this attitude is found in the five-point pledge to fight waste that juvenile listeners to *Dick Tracy* swore in 1943:

I pledge
1. to save water, gas, and electricity
2. to save fuel oil and coal
3. to save my clothes
4. to save Mom's furniture
5. to save my playthings

Compliance not only gave a child inner satisfaction, but by notifying the network of his pledge, a child had his or her name placed on a Victory Honor Roll which—the program announcer assured listeners—was sure to be read by General Dwight D. Eisenhower when he received it at Allied Headquarters in North Africa.

The directions taken in children's serials fostered debate among critics. One representative from the Office of Civil Defense assailed their "blood-and-thunder" quality. According to her, such programming "will make American children more of a problem in the post-war world than the worst propaganda-corrupted youngsters in the Axis nations." Others contended that alarm was unnecessary, that this programming had democratic lessons to relate, and that it was principally through war-related action that children would be persuaded to sit and listen. This was underscored by one critic who noted of children's serials: "In a subtle way, they preach love of country in a way that every youngster understands—more effective than anything which could be prepared to teach democratic ideals by a more direct method." In a similar vein, Robert J. Landry of *Variety* alleged that these shows were effective in teaching children the ethical stakes of World War II. He maintained that there was a positive value to be found in those juvenile programs where:

> the modern hero . . . swoops out of the clouds in a stream-lined bomber at 400 miles an hour. . . . He dive-bombs a huge Japanese battleship off the face of the ocean. Where does this leave "The Lone Ranger"?[59]

The domestic stresses of World War II raised in the minds of all people connected with broadcasting the fear of censorship. The fear was chronic in the history of radio, but in the war years it appeared more imminent than ever. In practical terms, there were two types of censorship in broadcasting. First, there was direct interference by the federal government to prevent certain types of programming. Second, there was localized, editorial selection by station managers or network officials. Historically, radio had been much more affected by the latter. By statute and constitution governmental agencies were generally prohibited from interfering in program content. Even the FCC, which controlled the issuance and renewal of licenses, was prohibited from directly telling stations what they should or should not broadcast. Editorial selection, on the other hand, frequently occurred. The motives in such instances were usually clear: the fear of antagonizing listeners by airing controversial opinions, the desire to observe the boundaries of good taste, the fear of offending a commercial sponsor.

In early 1939, *Variety* printed a broad spectrum of opinions from experts in radio programming on the subject of censorship. Most agreed that although there had been little federal interference in the past, there had been many instances of station and network editorial selection. Most confidently hoped, moreover, that should a war crisis arrive, radio would be able to regulate itself without governmental controls. This was ably argued by Edward Klauber, executive vice-president of CBS, who cited three historical reasons for self-censorship: 1) that every mention of censorship is met with increasing opposition; 2) that when the truth is known, broadcasters have been making earnest efforts to handle fairly all points of contention; and 3) that the public knows that broadcasters act swiftly to correct their faults, and the public had come to rely on this type of self-regulation.[60]

When America did enter the war, the hopes of most broadcasters were realized. The federal government decided upon a course of voluntary self-censorship for radio rather than confiscation or stringent regulation of the industry. Nevertheless, the government made its desires for program content known to the stations and networks.

As early as January 1942, the Office of Censorship stated the official position on programs that might provide information helpful to internal spies and saboteurs, or external military and naval commanders. In its Code of Wartime Practices for American Broadcasters, the government asked for voluntary censorship of news, ad-lib talk and game shows, and foreign language programs. Proscribed from such programs were references to the weather, fortifications, war-related experiments, troop or materiel movements, casualty lists, and the like. Stations were urged to watch carefully those quiz and discussion programs where comments from the audience might be heard. Fearing secret coded messages, the government also requested the elimination of programs that accepted telephoned or telegraphed requests for specific songs, "lost and found" announcements, or for announcements of mass meetings. Such materials should only be handled, it was suggested, when requests were received in writing—and then only after station continuity departments had rewritten the requests in their own words. As for foreign language radio stations, the code required all such stations to keep full transcripts, either written or recorded, of their programs. It further requested strict adherence to scripts by announcers and performers. To underline its hands-off policy toward radio, however, the government further declared in the code that

> Free speech will not suffer during this emergency period beyond the absolute precautions which are necessary to the protection of a culture which makes our radio the freest in the world.[61]

While federal officials declined to confiscate equipment or assign military censors to each station and network, they lost little time in informing the broadcasting industry that there were certain materials they wanted aired. Through the Office of Facts and Figures, headed by Archibald MacLeish, and the Office of War Information, under former CBS newsman Elmer Davis, the government issued a slate of propaganda items it hoped would be interjected into regular programs. It set up a Special Features Plan which would utilize network programs and local stations for airing war messages. It also urged programming that touched wartime topics: the issues involved in the war, the nature of the enemy, the nature of the Allied nations, war aims, and the condition of the fighting, working, and home forces.[62]

The coordination of government requirements and radio's responsibilities was enhanced by the fact that many radio personalities and network officials entered governmental service during the war. As well as Davis, CBS Vice-President William B. Lewis joined the staff of the OWI. Jack Benny, Kay Kyser, Jean Hersholt, George Burns and Gracie Allen, Nelson Eddy, and other radio celebrities were recruited in 1942 into a "Committee of 25," a government-sponsored group coordinating fund-raising and morale-building activities. Arrangements such as this benefited both the networks and the government. Network radio now encountered government officials who understood the problems of commercial broadcasting—men and women who would not burden the networks with disorderly programming or ponderous uninteresting propaganda. The federal government in turn received knowledgeable workers skilled in the management of national radio systems, and top-flight entertainers whose reputations lent credibility to an appeal for funds or to a patriotic statement.

There were instances where radio transgressed the federal regulations. Early in the war, Chicago sports announcer Bob Elson had a difficult time breaking his habit of announcing "it's a beautiful day at the ball park," and thus found himself cut off for several seconds during these unintentional "weather reports." Some discussion programs stopped taking live comments from the audience and demanded that all questions be submitted in writing beforehand. Other shows, unable to adjust their formats, simply left the air. When Mutual newsman Arthur Hale inadvertently spoke of atomic research taking place at a site in Pasco, Washington, several military leaders were so enraged they actually demanded an end to voluntary controls and the establishment of military censorship in the United States.[63] Despite such instances, the record of American broadcasters during the war was impressive. Probably the most positive statement that can be made of a nation's communications system was written in the memoirs of the eminent news reporter, Raymond Gram Swing. Concerning his "experience with censorship throughout my career," Swing remarked:

> During World War II, none of my broadcasts was censored, though at the Blue network they were read prior to delivery by someone on the staff. That was, and is, standard procedure in radio and television today; and I find it not only unobjectionable, but proper, since the station is legally responsible for what its broadcasters say.... I am simply reporting that I had remarkably little interference with my freedom to say what I wished throughout my life as a journalist and commercial broadcaster.[64]

It was a significant social achievement for a major combatant to have conducted a war for almost four years without interrupting the flow of entertainment and inquiry that commercial broadcasting had established. It suggested to many that once the battle was ended, radio had a bright and prosperous future before it.

By the end of the war, there were many reasons to expect a thriving future for radio. Because in early 1942 the demands of war production had halted manufacture of radio tubes and receiving sets, manufacturers expected booming postwar sales. Sets could now be repaired, new radios and radio-phonograph combinations could be bought, and, in the spirit of victory and peace, returning Americans could revert to their familiar listening patterns. To entertain this new world, there were more than 900 stations, broadcasting for sixty million radios, owned by thirty-one million "radio families." Further, there were developments within the industry that added sophistication and practicality to broadcasting.

Radio had new prestige. Although the other popular arts had already established awards for distinguished merit, until the 1940s radio had no equivalent of the Academy Award or Pulitzer Prize. Beginning in 1942, however, the renowned School of Journalism at the University of Georgia began granting its annual George Foster Peabody Awards for outstanding achievements in broadcasting. The Peabody Awards rapidly became a most impressive mark of distinction among radio personnel. A perusal of the names of early recipients serves only to confirm this assessment, for among those artists were comedians Fred Allen and Bob Hope; broadcast journalists Cecil Brown, Charles Collingwood, Edward R. Murrow, and Raymond Gram Swing; and director-producer William N. Robson.

As well as recognizing its own talented achievements, radio offered an improved future with the introduction of frequency-modulation (FM) programming. FM promised truer transmission with no interference from static, a situation most appreciated by music lovers. Further, because it was locally-oriented and broadcast with limited coverage patterns, it emerged as sponsorless radio with lengthy periods of uninterrupted transmission. FM had been perfected in the early 1930s by its inventor, Edwin Howard Armstrong. Its marketing had been thwarted, however, by the political and business maneuverings of RCA and its chairman, David Sarnoff. Protecting his own interests, Sarnoff argued that a new alternative like FM would cause consternation within the established world of AM radio, this at precisely the time when television would be emerging. Sarnoff urged concentrating upon developing television and adjusting radio to its impact. Despite the moves by RCA, FM radio became a reality at Armstrong's experimental station in Alpine, New Jersey. By 1945, there were other FM stations scattered throughout the country. And when that year the FCC readjusted to lower frequencies the range in which FM could be broadcast—this over the protests of Armstrong and his followers—RCA dropped its hostility and FM became an unchallenged, operative dimension of broadcasting.

The future also looked promising because during the years of war-programming radio had developed a decidedly egalitarian tone. This was especially true as it related to America's black population. Until World War II, Afro-American characters had been racially stereotyped—whether portrayed by black or white actors—as butlers, maids, and loafers. While black singers and musicians appeared frequently on radio, racial prejudice was clearly evidenced in drama, comedy, and variety programming, as well as in the many types of programs—news, sports, quiz, panel discussion—in which blacks were almost never involved.

The war would begin to change this attitude. Battling a foreign enemy who was steeped in racist ideology, it was difficult for many Americans to decry fascism abroad and tolerate bigotry at home. Beginning in the 1940s, radio and the other popular arts assumed a civil libertarian course. Black talents like Paul Robeson, Juano Hernandez, and Canada Lee appeared in dignified dramatic roles. Radio brought the plight of the black soldier and sailor into American homes in programs as diverse as soap operas and documentaries. Programs explored black culture, probed the meaning of democracy, and envisioned a postwar world of brotherhood. Matters became so affected by wartime cultural liberalism that black actors appeared occasionally in white roles on "color-blind" radio. Importantly, this cultural re-evaluation of the Afro-American, and by association, all ethnic minorities, would spread to social, economic, and political matters once the battle ended.

The hopeful signs of the mid-1940s were enhanced by a new competition in network broadcasting. The creation of the American Broadcasting Company presented listeners with a fourth wholly-independent network. ABC was born after the Federal Communications Commission and the United States Supreme Court ordered NBC to divest itself of its Blue network. According to the court, NBC-Blue had been used to stifle competition with NBC-Red; and since the two chains controlled a substantial number of the high-wattage stations in the country, this constituted a monopolistic practice. In 1943 the Blue Network was sold to Edward Noble, the president of the Lifesaver Candy Company. For $8 million Noble acquired three stations that were owned and operated by the network, and almost two hundred network affiliates. Eventually, the call letters of the network key stations came to reflect the fact that there were now three major corporations in broadcasting. By the 1950s, ABC had changed the name of its key station from WJZ to WABC, as CBS changed its home station from WABC to WCBS. NBC-Red, now simply the National Broadcasting Company, instituted several changes before WEAF finally became WNBC.

The Metamorphosis of Radio, 1945–1960

Ironically, the ending of World War II dealt a serious blow to the radio industry. Since 1939, and more dramatically after American entry into the struggle, commercial radio had been the most vital communications and entertainment medium in the nation. Broadcasters had rallied behind the embattled flag. Government programs and announcements were dutifully aired; regular shows integrated patriotic themes into their scripts; and voluntary self-censorship was carefully and successfully carried out. But the cessation of the war left radio without purpose or direction, and in need of self-appraisal. Waging a crusade so intensely for so many years, by late 1945 radio personnel found it difficult to discover meaning in the new world.

The pages of *Variety* during the 1945–1946 radio season reveal an intense argument over the future of radio. The diversity of opinion was demonstrated in the split between veteran comedians Fred Allen and Eddie Cantor.[65] Allen maintained that radio was still in its infancy, was still a problem child, and needed to develop its showmanship and its writers. Cantor argued that radio had grown up, and that it could now afford adventure, "dare to do different," as he phrased it. At the same time, FCC Commissioner Clifford Durr raised the question of whether or not radio really knew what listeners wanted. He demanded hard-hitting programs that were constructive but not afraid to offend people.[66] The call for more meaningful programming was the essence of the editorials appearing in May 1946, in both *Life* and *The Saturday Review of Literature*.[67] Even more significantly, this was the same point made by William S. Paley, CBS board chairman, in a critical speech in October 1946, before the National Association of Broadcasters, a powerful organization comprised of station and network officials.[68]

Several writers seemed to suggest that radio could rediscover its social importance by developing "socially responsible" programs. According to Carroll Carroll, the writer of Bing Crosby's popular *Kraft Music Hall,* radio needed a cause such as racial and religious tolerance. According to him, the

> fight against intolerance is a long, slow, never spectacular campaign of education in decency and good taste that we, who discovered the propaganda weight of radio during the late war, must carry on for true peace on earth, good will to all.[69]

George Rosen of *Variety* argued that radio's new cause should be to warn civilization of the frightening implications of the

atomic age, an era in which terrible new weaponry made escapist radio irresponsible. Rosen maintained:

> To overcome the awesome realization of the atomic bomb,
> radio must also embrace the one-world philosophy: it
> must enlarge its sphere to global-kilocycle proportions,
> foster an understanding of other nations, a sympathy
> to their way of life, a truthful interpretation of their
> contributions to culture. These must become a pertinent
> part of radio's policy. Radio can in this way make a con-
> tribution to understanding and the outlawing of hate.[70]

In the same progressive direction as Carroll and Rosen,
the producers of the successful series, *Mr. District Attorney,*
Ed Byron and Bob Shaw, argued there was a "noblesse oblige"
inherent in the radio business and that it was the obligation of
broadcasting to battle the evils that menaced Americans. Specifically, they maintained that "the multitude of antidemo-
cratic whispers and rackets perpetrated on the people" must
be exposed in programming. According to Byron and Shaw,
Mr. District Attorney intended "to keep on clamping down
hard on any group or anyone whose purpose is an America
which is not for all Americans."[71]

Radio programming reflected the ambivalence of postwar
criticism. In most instances it returned to escapist shows, yet
social relevance was not totally absent. The top-rated comedy
shows reverted to non-topical gags and clichés, while dramatic
series emphasized escapist romance, mystery, and horror.
Nonetheless, there were popular comedians like Fred Allen
and Henry Morgan who continued, even increased, the tempo
of their social and political satire. The appearance throughout
the late 1940s of realistic series, among them *Dragnet, Treasury Agent,* and *The Big Story*—all dealing with actual criminal events—added a note of authenticity and relevance to
radio drama.

Perhaps the most popular expression of escapism, however, was the resurrection of the quiz show craze. Quizzes had
not disappeared during the war, but their popularity had
waned, and their mass appeal had been curtailed by the code
dictated by the Office of Censorship. But shows like *Truth or
Consequences* and *Quiz Kids* had endured. In the postwar
world the quiz shows would boom. Beginning with *Truth or*

Consequences in 1945, and followed by new shows like *Stop the Music!* in 1948, the giveaway programs abandoned the inexpensive prizes given in the past and began offering jackpots worth as much at $30,000. By 1948 radio was offering annually more than $7 million in cash and merchandise. After years of austerity, this materialism proved irresistible to Americans. In unprecedented numbers they now tuned in the quiz shows, sat waiting for the phone to ring, and fantasized with elated winning contestants.

There was also a markedly relevant nature to postwar programming. This quality was revealed particularly in the radio documentary. Prepared usually by network news staffs, documentaries probed most areas of social concern. From juvenile delinquency to the Cold War, from the consequences of the atomic bomb to alcoholism, American listeners heard radio assume a social responsibility it had avoided in the past. Documentaries were usually broadcast as specials, yet series like NBC's prestigious *Living—1948* presented such probative programs on a regular basis. Add to the documentary the appearance of new panel-discussion programs, among them *Our Foreign Policy, Meet the Press,* and *Capitol Cloakroom,* and it becomes apparent that there was a fuller sense of social responsibility emerging in network radio.

Even in children's programs there was a new urgency. The most explicitly progressive series was *Superman,* which had its hero fighting racial and religious bigotry for several years after the war. The appearance of non-Anglo-Saxon heroes—the Indian brave, Straight Arrow; the Latino avenger, the Cisco Kid—also guided postwar youngsters toward tolerance. Other series spoke to juvenile listeners in terms of contemporary issues. If *Jack Armstrong* dealt with fixing boxing matches, the series was merely reflecting the headlines of the day and offering lessons condemning gambling and organized crime. Cold War themes of sabotage and espionage continued in *Hop Harrigan, Captain Midnight,* and *Sky King.* And later *Tom Corbett, Space Cadet* and *Space Patrol* brought themes of space travel together with more familiar cops-and-robbers plots.

Regardless of the orientation broadcasting took following

the war, it experienced a barrage of destructive criticism from outside the industry. This hostility was compounded, moreover, by business developments which challenged the nature of radio in America. Radio was seriously hurt by a diminishing of listener interest. Soldiers returned to find the same familiar voices, many still broadcasting at the same hour. Radio stars who had been weekly attractions in the early 1930s continued into the early 1950s to dominate the evening hours. Statistics substantiate the inertia in broadcasting. In 1950 there were 108 different network series that had been on the air for at least a decade—twelve of these having been on the air for two decades, making them almost as old as network broadcasting. As the following chart suggests, the same programs also continued to dominate the monthly ratings:

April 1953	April 1948
1. Amos 'n' Andy	1. Fibber McGee
2. Jack Benny	2. Jack Benny
3. Lux Theater	3. Amos 'n' Andy
4. Bergen-McCarthy	4. Lux Theater
5. You Bet Your Life	5. Walter Winchell
6. My Little Margie	6. Fred Allen
7. Bob Hawk	7. Bob Hope
8. Fibber McGee	8. Bandwagon (Harris-Faye)
9. My Friend Irma	9. Bergen-McCarthy
10. Mr. & Mrs. North	10. Arthur Godfrey

April 1943	October 1937-April 1938
1. Fibber McGee	1. Bergen-McCarthy
2. Bob Hope	2. Jack Benny
3. Bergen-McCarthy	3. Bing Crosby
4. Lux Theater	4. Lux Theater
5. Aldrich Family	5. Eddie Cantor
6. Walter Winchell	6. Burns & Allen
7. Fannie Brice	7. Major Bowes
8. Mr. D.A.	8. Rudy Vallee
9. Jack Benny	9. Fred Allen
10. Rudy Vallee	10. Al Jolson

To many who wanted new voices, new programs, and new formats, this time was what one critic called "the era of the doldrums." And as radio continued with its traditional bill of fare, the size of the audience dropped off strikingly. Although this trend would reach its nadir in 1946 and listenership would begin rising, it was a development from which radio broadcasting never fully recovered.

If traditional programming was causing an exodus of listeners, experimentation could be risky. In a period of Cold War with its groundswell of anti-Communist fanaticism, producers could not be too imaginative lest they invite charges of subversion. The radio industry, like the film industry, came under investigation by several governmental agencies. The House Committee on Un-American Activities under Congressman Martin Dies, and later J. Parnell Thomas, sought to expose the writers, producers, and actors who, it purported, were subverting Americanism. Even the FCC was probed by a congressional committee. Out of this paranoia came some of the most divisive years in the history of entertainment. Liberal commentators lost their jobs and the more successful ones, like Drew Pearson, had their reputations sullied. Rumor publications, like *Red Channels,* a book which listed those it claimed to be Communists and "fellow-travellers," destroyed careers and divided the industry into opposing camps. Timorous networks and fearful advertisers dropped controversial actors and writers without investigating the charges against them. In fact, blacklisting—closing the door to employment to anyone considered controversial—became a common practice by the early 1950s. If the unions or craft guilds sought to oppose these unthinking practices, they usually ended up with internal factionalism preventing meaningful action.

Such divisiveness within the industry was only aggravated by the heated rivalry that developed among the networks. With four networks competing for a dwindling number of listeners in an atmosphere inimical to innovative programming, broadcasters reverted to an obvious course of action: pirating stars and hit programs from other networks. In this activity no one outdid William Paley and CBS. In the late 1940s he wooed from NBC some of that network's greatest celebrities. Spending millions of dollars, he brought to Columbia *Amos 'n' Andy*, the *Jack Benny Program*, the *Red Skelton Show*, the *Edgar Bergen-Charlie McCarthy Show*, and the *Burns and Allen Show*. From ABC Paley also obtained the *Bing Crosby Show* and the Groucho Marx program, *You Bet Your Life*. By December 1949, CBS had sixteen of the top twenty shows in the Nielsen ratings. Conversely, in the first four months of 1949, NBC lost almost $7 million in advertising revenue.

Other changes within the industry further revealed the turmoil in which radio found itself as it entered the 1950s. The president of the Mutual network, Edgar Kobak, was fired; the major networks slashed their advertising rates as much as twenty-five percent; and some of the largest accounts —like Kellogg's, Pillsbury, and Standard Brands—dramatically curtailed their spending in radio. On the local level, many stations, seeking new consumers to whom to appeal, began shifting their formats to please black listeners. In matters of programming, transcribed shows, long anathema to NBC and CBS, became increasingly common, and recorded reruns of popular shows became a summer feature by 1949.

These were tumultuous times for radio. Even when the networks pinned their hopes and cash on new series, disappointment was the inevitable result. This was especially the case in the recorded series sold by Frederic Ziv Company (*I Was a Communist for the F.B.I., Boston Blackie, Freedom, U.S.A., Bright Star*) and M-G-M Attractions (*The Hardy Family, Black Museum, Dr. Kildare, Maisie, M-G-M Theater of the Air*, etc.) and in NBC's ninety-minute variety extravaganza, *The Big Show*, which was budgeted at $35,000 per program, but which never delivered the anticipated large audience during its two years on radio, 1951–1953.

These developments suggest that radio was changing. It was a new era, a new social context in which radio had to find a balance or perish. Some like David Sarnoff could contend that radio would not die because too many homes had radio sets. But this was hardly a convincing argument. If radio were to survive, it needed new financial arrangements, programming that suited its changing role in society, and a new awareness of what its function would be in America at mid-century. The prepossessing reason for these considerations was, of course, the fatal threat that the emergent television industry was presenting to radio.

Americans had been living with the promise of television since the 1920s. To a nation enraptured by technology and its electrical gadgets, the ability to see entertainers and orators in the living room seemed the logical extension of radio. Thus it was with the Washington inventor who predicted in September 1925, that within five years every household in America would be equipped with a viewer that would allow people to see what they were hearing.[72]

It was in this spirit of confidence and anticipation that *Variety* headlined its edition of April 16, 1930: "TELEVISION NEAR READY." By the end of the 1930s, moreover, television had become a reality. The marketing of TV sets began in 1938. In May of that year *Variety* printed its first review of a television program, and in the following spring *Billboard* commenced its TV reviews. For the popular fan magazine, *Radio Mirror,* this was indeed an auspicious period. In August 1939, it changed its name to *Radio and Television Mirror,* and the next month announced the first TV giveaway contest in history: six new Philco television receivers for the best answers—in one hundred words or less—to the statement: "The radio or movie star I would most like to see in a television program is: ..." In announcing the contest, the magazine captured the optimistic spirit that television generated:

> Now you won't have to wait until you have the money to be the first on your block—perhaps in your town—to own a Philco television set! The newest miracle, this decade's greatest thrill, may be yours for the price of a postage stamp. ... Only recently put on sale, they're an engineering achievement![73]

Had World War II not interfered with the research, production, and distribution of receivers and transmitters, television would have challenged radio in the early 1940s. With the demands of war, however, the radio and television industries were converted to production for military purposes. But the potential of TV was not forgotten. As the war concluded, manufacturers and network officials were already planning to reintroduce television to American consumers. Perhaps the most accurate observation on the future for video was made early in 1944 by Paul G. Hoffman, president of Studebaker automobiles, when he suggested that within a decade it would be a billion dollar industry employing 4.6 million people. Hoffman argued that the $100 billion Americans had saved during the war would be a strong force in this development.[74]

The emergence of television in the postwar era was a mixed blessing. In some ways it was a complement to radio. Many considered TV an extension of radio broadcasting, some calling it "sight radio," "radio optics," "radio moving pictures," and "radio vision." Many programs in 1945 and 1946 were simply adaptations of radio series, and most TV programs were the same types of shows that radio had utilized. In this regard, television's primitive quiz, dramatic, audience participation, and comedy telecasts were not unfamiliar to radio listeners.

The debt to radio, however, went deeper. It can reasonably be argued that television only began to develop a large following when several of the biggest names in radio began appearing on it, and when some of the largest advertisers in broadcasting transferred their capital to video. In 1948, Milton Berle, Ed Sullivan, Fred Allen, and Edward R. Murrow appeared as featured guests or hosts of their own TV shows. Several radio series—*The Lone Ranger, The Original Amateur Hour,* and *Break the Bank*—became TV features that year. By 1950, some of the best television programs—*The Goldbergs, Suspense, Arthur Godfrey's Talent Scouts, Stop the Music!, The Life of Riley*—came directly from network radio, several with the same sponsors and stars. With such programming, what had begun as "sight radio" began now to destroy its "hearing-only" competition.

The only impediment to the inundation of America by television was the lack of transmitters. But as new stations were erected, the popularity of the new medium exploded. By 1950, in cities like Los Angeles, Philadelphia, New York City, and Baltimore, more people watched TV than listened to radio. Surveys overwhelmingly suggested that once more stations and sets were in use, radio would collapse. Alarmists noted that when cities became saturated with television, radio could hope for no more than fifteen percent of the evening audience. Four years earlier a *Variety* headline had wondered if TV were "RADIO'S FRANKENSTEIN?"[75] The answer seemed to be in the affirmative. In a doomsday vein, a CBS vice-president, Hubbell Robinson, Jr., compared the situation to Custer's Last Stand. "Television is about to do to radio what the Sioux did to Custer," he wrote in 1948. "There is going to be a massacre."[76]

In the 1950s radio producers tried to regather their momentum. In doing so, they would create some of the more impressive series in broadcasting history. Science fiction and westerns had traditionally been children's fare in radio. But in the period of competition with TV, radio produced distinguished adult series in these genres. NBC's *Dimension X* and *X Minus One* presented serious science fiction based on stories by leading writers in the field. CBS concentrated on the adult western. Beginning with *Gunsmoke* in 1952, it introduced *Fort Laramie, Luke Slaughter of Tombstone, Frontier Gentleman,* and as late as November 1958, an adaptation of a television hit, *Have Gun, Will Travel.* NBC also experimented with mature westerns with *Dr. Six-Gun* and Jimmy Stewart's *The Six-Shooter.* A new sophistication also appeared in detective programs. Police dramas like *Dragnet, Broadway Is My Beat,* and *Twenty-First Precinct* were grim, informative dramas that painted an unglamorous picture of law enforcement in an urban context. Private investigator programs like *Yours Truly, Johnny Dollar* and *Night Beat* also had heroes operating within an adult environment. The networks also produced several impressive dramatic series. In these waning days of radio drama they introduced *NBC Star Playhouse, Philco Playhouse,* and *Your Nutrilite Radio Theater.* In late 1955, NBC's last attempt at substantive drama was *Your Radio Theater,* a fifty-five minute showcase whose stars included Fredric March, Herbert Marshall, and Victor McLaglen in

such powerful plays as "Death of a Salesman," "The In-
former," "Lost Weekend," and "There Shall Be No Night."

Despite those creditable achievements, radio as heard
since the early 1930s was dead. In December 1955, the Nielsen
ratings showed that there was not one evening program listed
on the top ten. In fact, the most popular evening show was
Dragnet which was tied for fourteenth place, well behind the
soap operas and variety shows of daytime radio. Startling, too,
was the fact that although that year there were over 46.6 million homes equipped with radios, the average evening broadcast was heard in only 786,000 households.[77] Daytime network
programming could hardly be considered a business with a
future. By the end of 1960 there was not one soap opera remaining on radio. In fact, by that date radio had assumed a
new function and a new appearance in American society.

In the postwar era, television replaced radio broadcasting
as the primary entertainment medium of the mass audience.
In an incredibly short time, it preempted radio as the preferred source for drama, sports, soap opera, variety, comedy,
western, and children's programming. Radio's problems in
readjusting to peacetime conditions were exacerbated by the
threat of the new visual medium. It is in light of this tension
that one must consider the loss of advertisers, the talent raids,
the sinking ratings, and ineffective new programs. The Nielsen ratings in late 1955 only confirmed the obvious point:
radio had lost its audience and now had to adjust to the new
environment. Radio on the network level was now a supple-
mentary, secondary entertainment source. To survive, it had
to do better those things which television could not do. It
also had to find new means of obtaining sponsors. As NBC
President Niles Trammell had predicted a decade earlier,
radio now had to discover "a niche where it can best serve the
public."[78]

The answer to the problem of adjusting to a new environment had already been discovered by most of the independent,
non-network stations. In the late 1940s slightly fewer than
twenty-five percent of the stations in the United States were

not affiliated with one of the four major networks. To meet this rivalry, independent stations tended to specialize in programming not offered by the networks or television. These shows featured music, foreign language programs, sports, and local-interest angles. The independents also concentrated on the portability that TV could not match. They provided programs for the beach, automobile, restaurants, shops, and factories. The independents also appealed to local sponsors, and to groups of sponsors who individually could not subsidize a full program, but who as a cooperative unit shared sponsorship. There were instances where these practices were abused. An FCC document in 1946, the *Report on Chain Broadcasting*, or, as it was popularly called, "the blue book," showed how crassly commercialized some local stations had become. During a sample week in 1945, for instance, KIEV (Glendale, California) devoted eighty-eight percent of its time to phonograph records and other recorded music, interspersed with 1,034 commercials and eight public service announcements. At KMAC the figures were more startling, for it aired 2,215 commercials in a 133-hour period, an average of 16.7 commercials per hour.[79] Although these cases were exceptional, they reveal the dedication to local sponsorship and inexpensive programming that non-network radio had developed.

That the radio networks needed an economic boost was made clear by financial statistics by 1955. During the nine years before that date, gross revenues for the four networks had been declining at a rate of $32 million per year. In this atmosphere, the networks began experimenting with multiple-sponsorship and local programming. Affiliates also were urged to obtain local sponsors instead of expecting a single national company to underwrite a network show. This decentralization of control may have weakened the hold of the networks over their affiliates, but it produced a new affluence for broadcasting. Possessing most of the more powerful stations in the nation, the affiliates found themselves increasingly independent in terms of programming, and increasingly wealthy in terms of time sales. Cut-backs in programs from the networks, and the ability to reach a wider local and regional audience than the weaker-signalled independent stations, soon allowed them to become more profitable than ever.

By the 1960s the networks provided only a remnant of what they once fed to their affiliates. News on the hour, special events coverage, recorded music, and a few features scattered throughout the day—this was the typical offering from NBC, CBS, ABC, and MBS. Radio had to adjust to postwar values, but especially, to the challenge of television. In doing so, it no longer was needed as a comprehensive entertainment forum. Network radio, instead, turned time back to the local stations and concentrated on matters which TV could not do faster, more conveniently, or more inexpensively. This development was well understood by Matthew J. Culligan, NBC's vice president in charge of radio, when in 1958 he told a group of advertising agency officials:

> Radio didn't die. It wasn't even sick. It just had to be psychoanalyzed.... The public didn't stop loving radio despite TV. It just starting liking it in a different way— and radio went to the beach, to the park, the patio and the automobile.... Radio has become a companion to the individual instead of remaining a focal point of all family entertainment. An intimacy has developed between radio and the individual. It has become as personal as a pack of cigarets.[80]

Radio certainly was not dead by 1960. It had simply experienced a metamorphosis. Just as it had always reflected the values and realities of its environment, radio by this date was reflective of a mobile, affluent, and commercialized America, solidly committed to television for its creative amusement, but still requiring radio for music and instantaneous information. Radio in the 1960s would be the realm of the disk jockey and the newscaster. And in the mid-1970s—when there were more than 4,400 AM stations and 3,500 FM stations, and more than 402 million radios in use (compared to 121 million television sets) —this was still the case.

One of the more perceptive personalities in broadcasting was Arch Oboler. Writing in early 1945, he foresaw the demise of radio as he had known it. His article, "Requiem for Radio," stated it bluntly: "Television will supplant 'blind' broadcasting even as sound pictures did way with the silent movies. To deny this is to whistle in the dark of wish-thinking."[81]

What was passing away was an era in American cultural history. What had begun in the 1920s as an experimental toy and a popular fad, had emerged in the next decade as the most compelling medium in communications. Recognized early by American capitalists as a profitable and strategic new industry, radio became an entertainment, informational, and artistic utility. Certainly, it was filled with commercialism. Certainly, too, it was shaped in part by sponsor and agency prejudices. But radio was still functional. To many critics it lacked esthetics. Not enough classical music!, not enough fine drama!, too much soap opera!, they proclaimed. Yet, radio from 1920 to 1960 mirrored the American civilization which it served. If it was commercialized, it was because the entire society was shaped by a capitalist, consumer economy with its penchant for competitive advertising and its advocacy of a business ethic. If it lacked grace and refinement, it was because radio served a democratic audience, a mixture of educational and economic levels which generally appreciated a belly-laugh more than a polite curtsey. Norman Corwin epitomized this situation when he noted that radio

> rises no higher, and sinks no lower than the society which produces it, and if its abuses and shortcomings and perversions seem relatively greater than those of corresponding mass media of information and entertainment, it is only because of radio's relatively greater ubiquity. The local newspaper comes out once or twice daily, the local movie bill changes once a week, but the local loudspeaker, meaning the one in your living room, performs all day long if you will permit it, changing its bill hundreds of times within the range of an average dial in any average broadcasting day.... I believe people get the kind of radio, or pictures, or theater, or press they deserve.... The gist of what I am saying is that the radio of this country cannot be considered from the general culture and modes of the American people. Radio today is neither as good as the program executive will have you believe

in his statement to the interviewer; nor as bad as the intellectual guest at the dinner party makes it out to be.[82]

As a democratic republic, the United States was established, populated, and maintained by relatively simple and
hard-working middle-class people who demanded similar
qualities in their entertainment. By a study of their principal
medium of amusement in the middle of the twentieth century,
it is possible to comprehend and appreciate fuller the nature
of that commercial democracy and the character of the people
who made it work.

2

The Great Escape—
The Story of
Radio Comedy

If one conclusion can be drawn from the history of popular entertainment, it is that Americans like to laugh. It was the work of clowns like Charlie Chaplin and the Keystone Kops who produced mass acceptance of motion pictures. The most compelling dimension of vaudeville was its comedians. When comedy was blended with popular music, it created the immensely popular idiom, musical comedy. Radio, too, owed much of its success to the men and women who made listeners laugh. Although radio had developed impressive musical, dramatic, and news programming by the 1930s, it did not experience its greatest acceptance until comedians—from minstrelsy, vaudeville, burlesque, and musical comedy—flooded broadcasting in the Depression years. Ironically, in the 1950s when television displaced radio as the prime entertainment medium in American homes, it was principally because comedians, many of whom had joined radio in the Great Depression, shifted to video and developed large and loyal followings.

Comedy was the most consistently popular type of programming in radio. While the bulk of broadcasting time was filled with music, those shows highest in the ratings were usually comedies. And while it thrived, radio comedy engrained itself in the lives of Americans as no other aspect of the popular arts. More than the sex symbols and great dramatic talents of the movies, more also than the dynamic musical stars of Broadway and the recording industry, the comedians of the air communicated most effectively with mass society. During the economic dislocation of the early 1930s, the most acclaimed "gloom chasers" were radio personalities such as Ed Wynn, Jack Jearl, and Amos 'n' Andy who regularly brought laughter and light-heartedness to millions. The most well-received entertainers of U. S. troops during World War II were comedians like Bob Hope, Milton Berle, and Jack Benny who travelled throughout the world to visit and amuse the G.I.'s. When it came to raising money for wartime bond drives, the most successful salesmen were entertainers like Eddie Cantor, whose comedic reputation made the seriousness of his sales pitch all the more striking. The persuasiveness of radio comics was also evidenced in the various charitable causes which aligned themselves with comedy spokesmen, such as Jerry Lewis, Bob Hope, and Danny Thomas, for their fund-raising efforts gained lucrative popular support from Americans. Enjoying a following that extended from national fan clubs with hundreds of local branches to the Presidents of the United States, broadcast comedians functioned as national jesters. As such, they occupied a niche within society that was both substantial and crucial.

The Nature of Radio Comedy

The basis for the popularity of comedy on the air was twofold: the result of the exciting and humorous personalities of the comedians, and the therapeutic necessity of laughter. The radio clowns were above all distinctive characters who developed a rapport with their audiences, and each broadcast attempted to renew that relationship. Although they had read and rehearsed their script thoroughly, each week the comedians exhibited spontaneity, wit, warmth, and a sense of commonness with the audience as they sought to make listeners laugh. Many accomplished this with funny sayings or sounds which the audience came to expect within each program. Joe Penner in the mid-1930s became associated with his absurd phrases "Wanna buy a duck?" and "You nasty man!" With Ed Wynn, the high-pitched "So-o-o" that he warbled between jokes may have sounded more like a turkey call than a human expression, but it helped fashion an audial personality that endeared him to Americans for years. And Jack Pearl's mendacious Germanic character, Baron Munchausen, invariably drew much laughter when, after reciting an obvious lie, he asked of his doubting partner, "Vass you dere, Sharlie?" Pearl described the importance of such clichés when he told a fan magazine in 1934,

> I'll stick to that German dialect role. It's my trademark, just like Ed Wynn's "so-o-o," or Joe Penner's duck. We spent years building those things up, just as a manufacturer builds up his business trademark. We'd be crazy to let 'em go.... What does it matter as long as they're laughing? I get letters from people who say that I've made them forget the depression for a while, that I've made them laugh. That's what I've tried to do all my life—what I want to do—just make people laugh.[1]

Comedic clichés frequently were situations or characteristics with which the star of the show found himself involved weekly. Fred Allen's stroll down "Allen's Alley" on *Town Hall Tonight* and later the *Fred Allen Show* allowed him to meet various recurring characters with whom he joked. Jack Benny possessed several familiar clichés—his subterranean vault where he stingily secreted his money, the noisy 1924 Maxwell automobile in which he was still chauffeured, and his grating inability to play the violin—that appeared for more than two decades on his popular program. On the *Fibber McGee and Molly Show*, comedians Jim and Marian Jordan had many zany characters who visited their fictional home at 79 Wistful Vista, as well as an audial cliché, a stuffed closet that loudly unloaded its contents whenever Fibber forgetfully opened it. Throughout the 1940s, moreover, physical attributes, such as the shapes of the noses of Bob Hope and Jimmy Durante, the plumpness and baldness of Bing Crosby, and the skinniness of Frank Sinatra, always prompted approving laughter.

The popular radio comedians did not flourish, however, because of any gimmick or complicated secret. They achieved their preëminence because they had good material, they knew how to tell a joke, and above all, they were funny individuals. As early as 1930 it was clear to a writer in *Variety* that the essence of successful radio comedy was simplicity. According to him, great care had to be taken to avoid patterns of verbal stage comedy like cross-fire, wisecracking, double entendres, complicated gags, pantomime, and mugging. A simple, common audience responded best to simple comedic material. "Radio's axiom for comedians is," he wrote, "be simple and be funny or be fancy and lousy."[2] In this same vein, John V. Reber, a vice-president with the influential J. Walter Thompson advertising agency, remarked in 1933 that radio was a completely ruthless medium which could expose those who were not basically humorous. "Just trying to be funny doesn't go," he stated, for the "comedian has to think and live his humor, or the great listening audience detects the shallowness of his humorous veneer."[3] Jack Benny, the most popular comedian in the history of radio, well understood the necessity of being funny and uncomplicated. He summarized his feelings in 1934 when he told an interviewer:

> No one should ever try to be funny ... because when your audience knows you are trying, and sees you working for a laugh, they're all tired out with your efforts by the time you come to it. For that reason, we try to make our show as off-hand, as natural, as easy as possible. Our motto is: Be nonchalant![4]

As well as personality, radio comedy prospered because Americans needed to laugh. In the world of increasing stress and complexity that has characterized the United States in the twentieth century, humor exercises a cathartic, healthful value as it has allowed harried people for a short while to laugh away personal tensions. In general, radio enjoyed its greatest popularity during a time of unprecedented uncertainty within the nation. Wars, economic collapse, urbanization, increased competitiveness, technological displacement, dramatically-increased population, and religious reevaluation—these were all significant forces at work in America during the Golden Age of radio. Within such an environment, listeners made comedians the most acclaimed entertainers in broadcasting.

Comedy programs were aired usually in the evening hours, thereby appealing to those trying to relax after a day of labor or coping with reality. People tuned in to be amused, to be swept away in laughter, and in the process to find their existences a little more tolerable. And comedy shows were popular. A survey in 1946 revealed that such programs were the most popular form of entertainment programming in radio, as fifty-nine percent of the respondents cited comedy as their preferred evening diversion. Significantly, this type of programming had a statistically lower appeal to farmers and residents of rural communities, suggesting perhaps the salutary importance of such shows in the more aggressive urban context.[5] Milton Berle best stated the necessity of radio comedy for American audiences when in 1940 he wrote:

> There's an ever growing need for radio comedy broadcasts. This world of ours is a sanguinary place. There are always wars between nations and between individuals. People for the most part are serious minded, always worrying about something or other. How to make an adequate living, how to win the girl, how to enjoy life. Therefore, I believe that our minds should be completely at ease when we go out to have a good time, or stay home to listen to a radio program.[6]

Radio produced a style of humor that was designed for an undifferentiated mass audience. For the most part, it avoided topical material—intellectual comedy based upon current events and political personalities—and it especially eschewed that caustic political satire which came to typify much of American humor by the late 1960s. Instead, radio comedy turned inward, poking fun at the comedian and/or his assistants. In this manner, it found laughter in everyone. Such comedy deflated the ego and good-naturedly exposed the futility and the stupidity of taking oneself too seriously. Lest the task of struggling to survive in mass society become too prepossessing, there were clowns like Red Skelton and his characters Clem Kadiddlehopper and Willy Lump-Lump to parody the mannerisms of the "average" man. Lest marriage, home, and family become overly demanding, George Burns and Gracie Allen were there to spoof these important institutions. And lest the work-a-day world become too discouraging, there were the humorous likes of Irma Peterson, the screwball secretary on *My Friend Irma*; Chester A. Riley, the well-intentioned but awkward factory worker on *The Life of Riley*; and Lum Edwards and Abner Peabody, the implacable general store operators on *Lum and Abner*. Through the characterizations and activities of such comedic types, listeners were not only entertained, but they were subtly dissuaded against the pomposity and arrogance that could develop within a society of would-be achievers.

Another characteristic of radio comedy was its penchant for humorously breaking social conventions. To an audience of "average" listeners, earning "average" salaries, and possessing an "average" share of powerlessness within mass society, it was often refreshing to assail in jokes the pretentions, wealth, and influence of social leaders. No comedian better exploited this impulse than Fred Allen.

Allen's humor contained a relatively high degree of sophistication that made him somewhat ahead of his time. For eighteen radio seasons his programs featured various personality types within society. Senator Bloat and Senator Beauregard Claghorn were windy parodies of American governmental leaders. Bloat was always discussing legislation he was introducing in Congress. These "Bloat Bills" promised everything from settlement of the national debt to bifocal lenses for old people with short arms who were unable to put on regular glasses. Claghorn was a loud, loquacious orator who was so Southern in his allegiances that he would never see a baseball game in Yankee Stadium—in fact, never see a game unless a "southpaw" was pitching. Allen enjoyed caricaturing poets. Falstaff Openshaw was an aspiring poet who once explained his talent by saying, "I can't help rhymin'—it comes to me natural, like commutin' to a Babbitt." Humphrey Titter specialized in unusual greeting cards and jingles, and Thorndyke Swinburne was described as "the poet laureate of the Boston Post Road." Allen even dared to satirize the social activity of the "average man" through his character, John Doe.

Doe was an angry, argumentative citizen whom Allen explained as "incensed about forces and people who were hampering his survival."[7]

Few subjects escaped the scrutiny of radio humor. As a democratic form of comedy, it refused to recognize most areas of sacrosanct tradition and levelled its sights on a broad range of topics. In the late 1940s, Henry Morgan was especially incisive in his parodies of great occurrences in history, current events, social conventions, and American perceptions of foreigners. On the *Milton Berle Show* during the 1947–1948 season, Berle dedicated each program to a particular institution, comically "saluting" such topics as health, Christmas, women, literature, public service, and communications. Edgar Bergen used his dummies Charlie McCarthy and Mortimer Snerd to flirt with glamorous female movie stars who were his frequent guests. Such a format not only produced an eminently popular program, but parodied the unrequited flirtations that millions of Americans had with Hollywood personalities. The innocence of children was satirized in Red Skelton's impish character Junior, "the mean widdle kid"; in Sis, the rude little girl who lived next door to Fibber McGee and Molly; in Tommy Riggs' own vocal creation, the mischievous seven-year-old, Betty Lou; and especially in Baby Snooks, the peevish brat introduced by Fannie Brice in 1936 on the *Ziegfeld Follies of the Air,* and a continuous character in various series for fifteen years. Even the image of bandleaders was humorously tarnished by the characterization of Phil Harris on the *Jack Benny Program* as a liquor-loving, woman-chasing hedonist.

The overwhelming popularity of comedy on the air indicates that audiences approved this type of self-defacing humor. According to Constance Rourke in her study of American humor, "American audiences enjoyed their own deflation; they liked the boldness of attack, the undisguised ridicule." As early as 1919, the noted Scottish comedian, Sir Harry Lauder, also understood the comedic psyche of the American democracy when he wrote that, "They've a verra keen sense o' the ridiculous and they're as fond of a joke that's turned against themselves as of one they play upon another pairson."[8]

Radio comedy was a reflection of the democratic society it entertained. Like that society, it was thematically and stylistically concerned with a civilization of common people— drawn from all religious and ethnic backgrounds—struggling to govern themselves while attaining material and emotional satisfaction. As such, this comedy embodied the heritage and reality, the goals and the pretensions, of a pluralistic society living in a relatively classless environment.

One of the most controversial areas in which radio found rich comedic material was in its caricature of ethnic minorities. A staple of stage comedy of the nineteenth and early-twentieth centuries, racial comedy abounded in radio and was warmly received. Some of the most important series in radio history, in fact, exploited ethnic humor. *Amos 'n' Andy* for almost thirty years featured two white men playing the minstrel show stereotypes of black life. Their success, moreover, inspired a rash of blackface imitators in the 1930s with names like George and Rufus, Honeyboy and Sassafrass, Pick and Pat, and Watermelon and Cantaloupe. *The Goldbergs* was a Jewish replica of *Amos 'n' Andy*. Although it was sympathetically written by its star, Gertrude Berg, this serialized story of Molly, Jake, Rosalie, and Sammy Goldberg—and of their star border, Uncle David—filled the air intermittently for twenty years with heavy accents and Yiddish phrases.

Other network series which stressed ethnic stereotypes included *Frank Watanabe and Honorable Archie* which became a coast-to-coast program in 1930 and for three seasons dealt with a white American and his Japanese houseboy, and *Life with Luigi,* which from 1949 until 1953 centered on the tribulations of Luigi Bosco, an Italian immigrant coping with life in the United States. Baron Munchausen first appeared in 1932, and even in 1953 Jack Pearl was using his thick Germanic accent in a summer series, *The Baron and the Bee.* *Duffy's Tavern,* which ran from 1941 until 1951, was not only set in a pub, but many of its characters—the oafish Clifton Finnegan, the thickly-accented policeman, Clancy—also filled out classic Irish stereotypes. In 1941, NBC aired two for the price of one when in *Abie's Irish Rose* it capitalized upon the hit Broadway play about a Jewish young man, his Irish wife, and the comedic conflict that arose from merging these stereotypes.

As well as programs with a fully ethnic setting, racial humor was often found in secondary characters on many of the important comedy series. Eddie Cantor featured Bert Gordon as "The Mad Russian"; Harry Einstein played Parkyakarkas, a Greek comedic figure; and Alan Reed provided the thick Russian voice for Cantor's mike-shy violinist, David Rubinoff. In the 1930s Al Pearce, on *Al Pearce and His Gang,* spotlighted Yogi Yorgesson, a Swedish character; Lily, a black maid; and Mr. Kissel, a Jew. Black characters appeared regularly on the *Jack Benny Program* where Eddie Anderson played Rochester, the valet; on the *Red Skelton Show* where Wonderful Smith portrayed himself; and on the *Eddie Cantor Show, Fibber McGee and Molly Show,* and *The Great Gildersleeve* where the black maids Hattie Noel, Beulah, and Birdie Lee Coggins appeared, respectively. Dialectician Sam Hearn created a Jewish character, Mr. Schlepperman, who in the mid-1930s was a regular on the *Jack Benny Program.* Strong Irish stereotypes were found in Ajax Cassidy on the *Fred Allen Show,* and in the nosy landlady, Mrs. O'Reilly, on *My Friend Irma.* And several programs spotlighted more than one ethnic type. The popular *Judy Canova Show* throughout the 1940s had Geranium, a black maid played by Ruby Dandridge, and Pablo, a Mexican stereotype created by Mel Blanc. And in the mid-1940s Steve Allen starred in *Smile Time,* an afternoon comedy series which presented as regulars a feisty Irish landlady, a dim-witted Mexican handyman, and a lazy black janitor.

Stereotypic ethnic comedy was not without its critics. Since the early 1930s various black organizations lobbied against the minstrel images perpetuated by programs like *Amos 'n' Andy.* The onset of the racist Nazi doctrine and the growing potential for war made radio producers more sensitive to racial and religious jokes by the end of the 1930s. *Variety* reported in 1939 that scripts were being altered and that what was once called "ethnic humor" was now being termed

"intolerance." According to that trade journal, "The growth
of intolerance has forcibly reflected itself in racial or dialectic
humor. Certain races now heatedly resent having themselves
kidded or joked about on the air, even if the kidding or story
telling is done by a member of the race involved."[9] The experience of World War II only increased the pressure against
racial humor. The following Yiddish-accented characterization might have gone unnoticed ten years earlier, but after it
was broadcast on the *Abbott and Costello Show* in April 1945,
it was called disparaging, and a racial stereotype, and was reported to have "created some unfavorable comment in the
trade."

> *Jewish Characterization* (with accent): Good evening,
> gentlemen. I'm from the Friendly Credit
> Company. My name is Auck—Tommy Auck.
> *Costello:* I think before I spoke to your brother—
> Mohawk.
> *J.C.:* But of course, I think so too. Now, Mr.
> Costello. My company makes a practice of
> examining all applicants for loans; a mere
> formality, if I am not too inquisitive. We have
> absolute faith and confidence in your honor.
> *Costello:* See that, Abbott? They trust me.
> *J.C.:* Now, Mr. Costello, please be so kind and
> place your fingerprints on this pad. I'll check
> with Washington later after we take a sample
> of your blood.
> *Costello:* You're gonna take my blood?
> *J.C.:* Oh, just a couple of quarts. We return it after
> the loan is paid up.[10]

Related to ethnic humor was "hillbilly" comedy which
also gained popularity on radio. In vaudeville it had been
termed "Ruben" or "Rube" humor as it ridiculed rural stereotyped characters—typically named Rube—for their awkwardness and generally uncouth manners. Beginning in the mid-
1930s Bob Burns portrayed "the Arkansas Traveler," a rural
and Southern characterization, who perpetuated the clichés of
this comedy. For over a decade Burns would chide his listeners, for instance, for believing that hogs were lazy, reminding
them, "I'd like to see any of you people lay around in the mud

WESLEY, DAVE

Tue Jan 14 2014

Don't touch that dial! : Radio

33029006875108

Hold note:

*
*
*
*
*
*
*
*
*
*
*
*
*

WESLEY, DAVE

Tue Jan 14 2014

Don't touch that dial! : Radio

and come up with forty pounds of bacon." In an authentic Arkansas accent, Burns related anecdotes about his family and friends, such as the time they sprayed the alfalfa with Uncle Slugg's corn liquor and the next day found Slugg grazing with the cattle.

Sometimes radio portrayed these "hicks" within their own environment. The central characters on *Lum and Abner,* for example, ran the Jot 'em Down Store in Pine Ridge, Arkansas. For twenty-four years their serialized program blended folksy wisdom and country-bumpkin comedy as they encountered a range of stereotyped rural characters and ill-fated schemes. Rube comedy was also the essence of the *Judy Canova Show.* Here, however, the heroine was situated in the big city, having migrated to Hollywood from a hillbilly hamlet called Cactus Junction. The quaintness of her country personality was demonstrated weekly in comments such as, "When I found out we are what we eat, I stopped eatin' pig cracklin's and sow belly," or by her admission that she learned to rhumba by driving a tractor with a loose seat. In her new and awkward urban environment, moreover, Canova's observations were always colored by her Rube background. Thus, she might conclude that, when drinking tea, city people extended their little finger as a place to hang the wet teabag.

Despite protests, radio and the listening public never abandoned their taste for ethnic humor. Certainly, the war made writers and sponsors more sensitive to social realities, and the more pejorative dimensions of such comedy disappeared. Nonetheless, American audiences continued to encounter traditional stereotyped personalities. It was not until the late 1940s that programs like *Life with Luigi* and *My Friend Irma* appeared with their respective Italian and Irish characterizations. Although the producers of *Beulah* finally selected a black woman instead of a white man to portray the stereotyped black maid, the appearance in that role of Hattie McDaniel in 1947—and Louise Beavers and Lillian Randolph in the 1950s—did not alter the minstrel model upon which the show was based.

The depiction of America's ethnic minorities as guileful,

awkward, or pretentious was a residual of the humor that blossomed in vaudeville and minstrelsy during the time of massive immigration at the turn of the century. Poking ridicule at accents, mannerisms, personality traits, and physical attributes was ultimately the comedy of a race-conscious society that was anything but a melting pot. It was difficult for radio comedians to abandon successful ethnic material. Most comics and writers had begun their careers in vaudeville. Several, such as Eddie Cantor and singer-comedian Al Jolson, had established national reputations by the second decade of the twentieth century as blackface entertainers.

Not all comedians were oblivious, however, to the negative thrust of their humor. In 1932, the popular bandleader and funnyman, Ben Bernie, noted that he omitted from his gags all references to nationality, politics, religion, and public officials of any nation. According to Bernie, "It's too risky, it isn't kind, not even for a laugh."[11] Yet, through *Amos 'n' Andy* and its imitators, early commercial radio was solidly linked to the derogatory humor of the minstrel shows. Like Rube comedy, "Dutch" humor—the term applied to German-accented caricatures—survived vaudeville and remained in radio as German and Yiddish stereotypes. Despite their general insensitivity, other vaudeville stereotypes—Irish, Italian, Oriental, Scandinavian—also continued to find employment until radio deserted comedy in the late 1950s.

Comedy on radio was necessarily limited in its methods of expression. Because it lacked the visual dimension of theater or motion pictures, humor demanding sight was impossible. Much of the slapstick movie tradition of Charlie Chaplin, the Marx Brothers, or the Three Stooges—pies in the face, pratfalls, and high-speed chases—were understandably incompatible with broadcasting. Although a few comedians in the early 1930s, like Ed Wynn with his funny hats and garish clothing, and Eddie Cantor with his off-mike physical antics, played to the studio audience in visual as well as aural terms, most preferred to rely upon good scripts, vocal inflection, and timing.

Radio comedy also demanded speedy delivery. While the

leisurely pace of W. C. Fields was acceptable in a screen comedy, in broadcasting it was too slow to sustain listeners over a lengthy period. An audience needed time to absorb the images created by the comedian's words, and slack in setting up this imagery and delivering the punchlines undermined the relationship between listener and performer. The following study of the 1946–1947 radio season clearly illustrates that the most popular comedy programs were those with a rapid pace in building up the audience for laughs.[12]

Rank in November, 1946	Name of Program	Buildup Time Between Laughs
2	Bob Hope Show	10 seconds
6	Red Skelton Show	11 seconds
1	Jack Benny Program	13 seconds
3	Edgar Bergen-Charlie McCarthy Show	14 seconds
12	Phil Harris-Alice Faye Show	15 seconds
8	Amos 'n' Andy	16 seconds
—	Burns and Allen Show	16 seconds
—	Joan Davis Show	17 seconds
5	Fibber McGee and Molly Show	19.8 seconds

Radio was, therefore, an unproductive medium for many of the more famous comedians from the movies. Fields never had his own series and had to confine himself to guest appearances in the late 1930s on programs like *Your Hit Parade* and the *Edgar Bergen-Charlie McCarthy Show*. None of the clowns from silent films succeeded in broadcasting, the only notable contribution coming from Harold Lloyd, who in the fall of 1943 hosted and starred in a short-lived series, the Old Gold cigarettes *Comedy Theater*.

The Marx Brothers had an ambivalent career in radio. Their series in 1932 lasted only one season. Individually, moreover, they had only mixed success. Harpo, the silent character, was totally incongruous with a vocal medium and was confined to honking a horn, chasing blondes, or playing the harp. Chico sounded stiff and studied over a microphone. He appeared irregularly on musical programs, usually as a pianist

or guest bandleader, rather than the Italian caricature he perfected in films. As late as 1952, he produced an unsuccessful
pilot program, *The Little Matchmaker*, in which he played
Chico Revelli, a marriage broker. By this time, however, his
ethnic characterization was at best stale, and the show never
became a series. Only Groucho, after years of experimentation,
found popularity in radio. As demonstrated during the 1943–
1944 season in his series, *Blue Ribbon Town*, Groucho's wise-
cracking style often sounded caustic rather than funny. But
when he switched his format and became in 1947 the punning,
ad-libbing host of the quiz program, *You Bet Your Life*,
Groucho hit upon the formula that kept him on radio until
1959, and on television from 1951 to 1961.

Still another force which shaped radio comedy was censorship. Comedians always had to be concerned about censors
with their blue pencils deleting objectionable material.
Whether it emanated from network vice-presidents, advertising agencies, or sponsors, this interference in the content of
programming helped account for the generally noncontro-
versial nature of broadcast humor. The theory behind such
censorship maintained that since a program entered a listener's
home without his foreknowledge of its content, it must contain nothing that might insult his personal attitudes. Unlike a
motion picture or a book where published reviews and public
opinion often informed potential consumers of the content,
radio had no such warning system and therefore had to avoid
matters over which there might arise disagreement. Included
in the list of tabooed items, as summarized in 1939 in the code
of program policies adopted by NBC,[13] were offensive references to physical afflictions and diseases, unpleasant smells or
odors, laxatives or bodily functions, the Deity, profanity, and
race or religion. The censors even looked askance at comedic
reference to various parts of the human body, radio and its
types of programs (especially soap operas), and regional
sensitivities.

Oversights in perusing scripts, or an ad lib by a comedian
during the live broadcast, often caused consternation in a network. No comedian upset his network more than Fred Allen.

Whether it was a controversial spontaneous remark during his show, or a fierce defense of his autonomy in preparing his scripts, Allen tested the tolerance of radio officials. Typical of the heated reaction incurred by Allen was the incident on his broadcast of May 8, 1935, when, to the reply of an amateur performer that her last name was Lee, Allen remarked, "You don't happen to be any relation to the Lee of 'I Surrender, Dear' fame?" *Variety* reported that in anger, "Southern listeners complained that the remark was a grave offense to the name of a great Southern general, statesman, scholar and gentleman, and that if radio comics had to do any insulting, they could pick on folks from up north."[14]

During the 1946–1947 season Allen's censorship argument with NBC reached its peak, as the comedian integrated into his script disparaging quips about network executives. He told his audience during a pre-broadcast warmup in November 1946, that he considered broadcasting vice-presidents to be "fungi growth on the desks of conference rooms." Through the person of Clarence Menser, Vice-President for Programming, the network insisted that it would not allow demeaning wisecracks about NBC management. Matters climaxed during Allen's program of April 20, 1947, when he was cut off the air for thirty seconds because he refused to delete an unflattering joke about the network.[15] Despite their concern over such matters as those raised by Fred Allen, censors were most concerned over two areas of potential humor: sex and politics.

Although no written code spelled out the specifics, there was a general understanding within the broadcast industry that sex appeal would not be used to sell a program. Attractive men and women certainly appeared on radio, and reference was usually made to their beauty; but sexual innuendo was avoided, and explicitness was prohibited. American radio was eminently prudish, and its rigidity was not confined to comedy programming. When General Hugh S. Johnson, retired from the military and from the Roosevelt administration, wanted to devote his weekly commentary to the subject of venereal disease in November 1937, NBC forbad the broadcast. NBC frequently banned from the air popular songs it felt too politically controversial. In 1933 it proscribed "Please, Mr. President," which it thought disrespectful to the Chief Executive; and in 1940 it nixed several war-related recordings, including "Blackout; Hold Me Tight," and bandleader Jimmy Lunceford's "Belgium Stomp." For its part, CBS also censored popular music. With the United States tenuously clinging to its neutrality in 1940, that network banned all war-related songs. When CBS did lift its ban, it first allowed only songs from World War I.

Keeping in mind this tradition of conservatism, it is easy to understand the uproar created by the appearance on December 12, 1937, of actress Mae West on the *Edgar Bergen-Charlie McCarthy Show*. Long a symbol of bawdy sensuality, West brought with her a well-nurtured reputation as a temptress and libertine. Her enactment with actor Don Ameche of a comedy skit about Adam and Eve and their expulsion from the Garden of Eden was suited to her popular image. The nine-minute episode, written by Arch Oboler, not only infringed upon the religious beliefs of many listeners, but West's love-groans and promiscuity in interpreting Eve's seduction of Adam definitely overstepped radio's sexual boundaries. After unsuccessfully cajoling Adam to "take me outta this dismal dump and give me a chance to develop my personality," Eve tricked him into eating the forbidden fruit and being "dispossessed." In this way she declared herself to be "the first woman to have her own way, and a snake'll take the rap for it." The skit ended with one final transgression of the religious and sexual taboos of broadcasting:

> *Adam:* Eve, it's as if I see you for the first time.
>   You're beautiful.
> *Eve:*   Mmm. And you fascinate me.
> *Adam:* Your eyes!
> *Eve:*   Ahhh. Tell me more.
> *Adam:* Your, your lips. Come closer. I wanna hold you
>   closer. I wanna . . .
> *Eve:*   You wanna what?
> (Sound of two loud kisses followed by trumpets and thunder.)
> *Adam:* Eve, wha, what was that?
> *Eve:*   That was the original kiss!

The uproar over the broadcast was startling. Religious organizations, especially the Roman Catholic Church, attacked it as immoral and sacrilegious. They threatened a boycott of the sponsor, Chase and Sanborn coffee, and urged the Catholic League of Decency to expand its Index to include radio as well as film and literature. The Federal Communications Commission investigated the incident, and NBC reacted by banning Mae West's name from any of its future broadcasts. West, herself, was absent from radio for the next thirty-seven years.

Radio avoided political humor as much as it shunned sexual material. The fear here, of course, was of offending the FCC (which issued and renewed broadcasting licenses) as well as insulting listeners' political feelings. Will Rogers was the only humorist to escape such censorship, this because his reputation as a good-natured political critic had been accepted by Americans long before he came to broadcasting. Yet, in a period so heavily involved with fascism, Communism, depression, threats of war, and war, it was difficult for comedians and their writers to avoid exploiting the world predicament.

In March 1937, *Variety* published a list of topical matters that comedy programs were compelled to avoid. These included any type of joke involving President Roosevelt, the Supreme Court, Congress, or specific parties involved in labor strikes. Censorship was also exerted to prevent any interpretative or opinionated gags about Hitler, Mussolini, General Franco and the Spanish Civil War, or the courtship of the American divorcee, Mrs. Wallis Warfield Simpson, by the heir to the British throne, Edward, Prince of Wales.[16]

Despite network policy, political jests were occasionally integrated into comedy shows. They were, however, hardly critical of any government or its activities. The Depression was consistently made the butt of jokes by Burns and Allen, Jack Benny, and Amos 'n' Andy.[17] Fred Allen's broadcast on Christmas night in 1932 ended with the quip that "No matter what other nations reject their war debts, America certainly got even with turkey today." Ed Wynn worked Mussolini into a joke on his broadcast on April 16, 1935. According to Wynn, a woman reading the newspaper remarked to her husband, "It says here Mussolini is going to give a radio to every man the day he gets married." The man replied, "That's silly, why would a man want to get two loudspeakers at once?" Gracie Allen in 1940 took matters one step further when she followed a tradition set earlier by Eddie Cantor and Will Rogers and conducted a gag Presidential campaign. Her pseudo-campaign was complete with a "Gracie Allen for President Convention" held in Omaha, May 15–18.

American isolationist policy in the inter-war period occasionally tempted comedians. When Eddie Cantor guested on the *Rudy Vallee Show on* April 23, 1936, he performed a strongly isolationist song, "If They Feel Like a War, Let Them Keep It Over There," in which, to the applause of the audience, he sang:

> If they feel like a war, on some foreign shore,
> Let them keep it over there.
> If the fools wanna fight, and think might makes right,
> Let them keep it over there.
> From coast to coast you'll hear a million doughboys cheer,
> Our job is to protect our loved ones over here.
> With an ocean between, let us keep our hands clean,
> Let them keep it over there.*

In the immediate aftermath of the Munich Conference in the fall of 1938, Al Jolson and Parkyakarkas insensitively punned about slicing up the Sudetenland area of Czechoslovakia by the Germans. When Parkyakarkas announced that he was going to sue several Ohio cities—Youngstown, Cleveland, and Toledo—for refusing to cash his check, Jolson asked why not Dayton too. Parky replied, "You can't sue Dayton, no checks there." On October 11, 1939, Al Pearce's Milquetoast character, Elmer Blunt, jested about American policy on armaments now that war had broken out in Europe. Attempting to sell corsets door-to-door, Blunt showed one lady "our no embargo model" which, he explained, "allows for free move-

---

*Copyright © 1935. Renewed by Shapiro, Bernstein & Co., Inc. Used by permission.

ment of the arms." Innocently, on October 1, 1940, Fibber McGee "apologized" for saying "china" when referring to the dishes for, as he remarked, "We can't say anything controversial."

During the war years political humor became much more prevalent on radio. Within five weeks of the Pearl Harbor bombing and American entry into the battle, Eddie Cantor set the tone of the new attitude in an open letter to the entertainment world. Cantor suggested that all comedy was now political. "The barrage of laughs that lifts our men, women and children is an important reserve to the barrage of bombs that are hurled forth to meet the enemy," he wrote. "High spirits," Cantor said, "are one of this country's first priorities."[18]

References to the enemy, the draft, the armed services, the President, and to the general commitment now all surfaced in American radio comedy. Comedians like Cantor, Jack Benny, and Bob Hope frequently broadcast directly from military bases, appearing before large and enthusiastic audiences of soldiers and sailors. The radio funnymen also used their programs and their personalities to raise money to sell War Bonds. By early 1942, for example, Fibber McGee had made a national phrase out of his line, "Buy a bond and slap a Jap across the pond"; and on January 29, 1944, Eddie Cantor, just two days short of his fifty-second birthday, broadcast for twenty-four consecutive hours over KPO (San Francisco) and sold $37.6 million worth of war bonds.

The comedy program which most consistently dealt with the political issues of the period was the *Fibber McGee and Molly Show*. Throughout the war years writer Don Quinn integrated into the scripts topical issues, such as women factory workers, war bond rallies, gas rationing, war songs, air raid wardens, and knitting clothes for soldiers. This type of relevant comedy not only aided national morale, but it often explained governmental goals in understandable and succinct terms. In a sense, the McGees reduced American foreign policy to a few lines in 1942 when Molly asked, "What did the President mean by his speech last night, Fibber?," and Fibber replied, "Hands across the sea, Molly ... first arms, then hands across the sea!" Molly concisely explained the governmental decision in early 1942 to stop selling defense stamps and start selling war bonds. To Molly, this simply meant, "We're going to stop defending and start fighting."

The prevalence of political jokes that emerged in radio comedy during World War II insured post-war comedians and writers that the inhibitions about topical humor would never again be as stringent. While many series reverted in the late 1940s to more traditional formats, several significant comedians continued, even into the 1950s, to utilize political humor regularly. This was especially true of comedians such as Bob Hope, Red Skelton, and Henry Morgan. With Morgan, in particular, jokes about political developments and personalities were an indispensable part of his radio style.

While Skelton's character San Fernando Red was a bombastic caricature of unscrupulous politicians, and Hope specialized in good-natured ribbing of politicians and social developments, Henry Morgan demonstrated a blunt style of humor that betrayed a strong element of political liberalism. In his various network programs Morgan was capable of friendly jibes, such as his comment that since Margaret Truman "is now rehearsing and exercising her voice constantly at the White House," he could now predict "that President Truman will be spending more time at his home in Independence, Missouri." He could also make Cold War quips about what American product the Russians would claim next to have invented, or that a good example of a Communist Front was Stalin's stomach. But his acerbic wit was often less generous with other institutions. He assailed banks: "You know, most people think of banks as cold, heartless, large institutions. And they're wrong. There are small ones, too." He derided the post-war housing problem, noting that "America is still true, true to the traditions of its forefathers. When the Puritans landed there were no houses, and we're carrying on that great tradition." Morgan handled congressmen rudely, as he did when he mused over the notion of fining a congressman to insure attendance at meetings: "Do you realize that would keep him on the job all of the time, using every bit of his ability, all his brain power, all his—maybe we'd better leave it the way it is."

Morgan openly displayed his liberal political bias when he poked fun at Eugene Talmadge, the former governor of Georgia, who had been associated with the Ku Klux Klan. In a skit in January 1947, he visited a mythical Southern state, Cornpone, and spoke to a local businessman:

Morgan: Finally, I've investigated business conditions. I interviewed a typical Cornponian manufacturer who said—
Man: Yes, sir, the new governor is great for my business.
Morgan: Splendid! What is your business, Colonel?
Man: I manufacture bed sheets.

Henry Morgan's most biting comedy skit, a lengthy routine in which he combined his attack on housing problems with a pointed critique of American landlords, illustrates the higher level of artistic tolerance that had developed in network radio. Landlords, a fundamental part of the national economic structure, would never have been so openly rebuked by radio—network, advertising agency, sponsor, station—at any period before the post-war era. The following excerpt from a skit broadcast on March 26, 1947, suggests that although networks did not diminish their concern over sexual material, censorship of political humor had abated.

Cornelius: Hello, Pierpont, evict any tenants today?
Pierpont: No, not in this weather. I'm waiting for a rainstorm.
Cornelius: I don't know how you get away with those evictions. Aren't you ever stopped by the OPA?
Pierpont: What's that?
Cornelius: That's the outfit that froze all the rents in my building. I got even, though.
Pierpont: How?
Cornelius: This winter I froze all the tenants.
Pierpont: You know, I had trouble with the heat, too. During the coldest part of the winter I had trouble with the furnace. Couldn't use coal.
Cornelius: What did you use?
Pierpont: Nothing. Anyway, that empty furnace came to good use.

Cornelius: How?
Pierpont: I rented it to a veteran . . .
Cornelius: Tenants! Tenants! There should be a way of
getting rents without having any tenants.
Pierpont: Yes.
Cornelius: What do you do when a tenant complains about
pipes bursting, and dangerous fire hazards?
Pierpont: Well, in that case there's only one thing to do.
Cornelius: What?
Pierpont: I go to Florida.
Cornelius: You know, I have one tenant who keeps
complaining that his roof leaks. What should I do?
Pierpont: Charge him for an extra shower. Say, you
know my eight-story house on Sunset Lane?
Cornelius: I thought it was nine stories.
Pierpont: Eight. The roof caved in.
Cornelius: Any people hurt?
Pierpont: No, just tenants.

The Emergence of Radio Comedy—The Thirties

Comedy had always been a part of commercial radio. In
the 1920s several dramatic programs such as *The Smith Family*
with Jim and Marian Jordan, and *The Rise of the Goldbergs*
(later called *The Goldbergs*) were meant to be humorous.
Musical patter teams like Billy Jones and Ernie Hare, who
changed their name to fit their sponsor (in this regard, they
appeared as The Happiness Boys for a candy manufacturer,
The Interwoven Pair for a sock company, The Best Foods
Boys for the food company, and The Taystee Loafers for a
bread manufacturer—as well as Trade and Mark, stars of *The
Smith Brothers,* sponsored by a cough-drop company) successfully melded jokes and songs into their broadcasts. *The
Eveready Hour,* the popular variety program which debuted
in late 1923 and lasted until 1930, often featured comedians
like Will Rogers, Irvin S. Cobb, Walter C. Kelly, George
Moran and Charlie Mack (the Two Black Crows), and Eddie
Cantor. In its inaugural broadcast in August 1926, moreover,
NBC recognized the importance of radio comedy when, along
with operatic singers and renowned musicians, it spotlighted
the popular comedians Will Rogers and Joe Weber and Lew

Fields. Yet, not until the overwhelming popularity of the blackface humor of Freeman Gosden and Charles Correll did producers fully comprehend the appeal possessed by broadcast humor.

In the tradition of minstrel shows, Gosden and Correll developed two black characters, Sam and Henry, who became favorites of Chicago listeners in the mid-1920s. When in 1928 they changed radio stations and were unable to retain their original name, the pair appeared on WMAQ as Amos Jones and Andy Brown, proprietors of the Fresh Air Taxi Company and the central characters of *Amos 'n' Andy*. In varied formats, the program would remain on the air until 1960. *Amos 'n' Andy* did for radio what Milton Berle and his *Texaco Star Theater* did for television two decades later: it captured the fancy of the nation and turned a popular medium into a mass medium. By 1930, there were Amos 'n' Andy toys, candy bars, comic strips, and phonograph records. The sales of radio sets jumped from $650.5 million in 1928, to $842.5 million in 1929 (the year their WMAQ program was nationally aired by NBC). Six times a week their fifteen-minute serialized program engaged the national consciousness. Switchboards slowed to inactivity as few phone calls were placed; department stores piped in the broadcast so shoppers need not go home; and factories closed early to allow employees to listen. In early 1931 a telephone survey by the Cooperative Analysis of Broadcasting gave *Amos 'n' Andy* an incredible rating of 53.4 percent of those listening.

If the success of *Amos 'n' Andy* illustrated the appeal of comedy programming, other social and economic developments help account for the rise of broadcast comedians in the early 1930s. The onset of the Depression, with its distressing unemployment, long breadlines, and generalized disspiritedness created a social atmosphere in which humor was most appreciated. Throughout the period letters and articles in fan magazines attest to the fact the listeners found comedy of great assistance in fighting personal despair. Although comedians generally avoided dealing directly with economic realities, jokes about the Depression were well-received by studio audiences, and Andy Brown's frequent reference to "de repression" soon became a light-hearted national phrase.

The collapse of vaudeville was also a fortuitous event for radio comedy. An article in *Variety* estimated that about three hundred vaudevillians had quit in 1929, and several hundred left in the first four months of the following year, all convinced "that the future has little in store for them."[19] Where vaudeville entertainers had been reluctant to abandon the stage and enter radio before the 1930s, the collapse of their industry created a pool of underemployed talent from which radio producers could draw in developing new programs. Vaudeville was also an excellent training ground for nationally-oriented radio. Circuit-travelling comics had to develop a style of humor that was acceptable to all types of audiences. Although they made concessions in their acts to local idiosyncrasies, these stage comedians had to please customers from New York City to San Diego with the same type of humor. Drawn as they were from every social class and all backgrounds, vaudeville customers were also less sophisticated than concert or Broadway audiences. The comedians who pleased the diverse patrons of vaudeville, therefore, possessed excellent backgrounds in entertaining exactly what radio was developing—a mass national audience.

Important also to broadcast comedy was that by 1931 all forms of radio programming had reached their peaks and radio began suffering a drastic decline in listeners. In 1930, for example, 74 percent of all set owners utilized their radios on an average weekday. By August 1933, that figure had fallen more than one-quarter to 54.5 percent. This development was, in the words of a contemporary report, "clearly the lowest ebb in listening that radio has ever experienced."[20] It was, therefore, in an atmosphere of collapse within the industry that sponsors and advertising agencies sought innovative and attractive programs. The man who most influenced this search was Eddie Cantor.

Vaudevillian, musical-comedy star, motion-picture personality, and recording artist, Cantor came to radio with his celebrity status already established. His program for Chase & Sanborn coffee premiered in September 1931, and within a few broadcasts was well on its way to national popularity. In less than a year, his was the most popular program on radio, and by January 1933, his C.A.B. rating was 58.4. Cantor revolutionized radio comedy. He abandoned the serialized, homey humor of *Amos 'n' Andy* and utilized the fast-paced gag style made popular in vaudeville. Where earlier comedians had broadcast from quiet studios or were otherwise sealed off from studio audiences, Cantor opened his programs to the public. He thrived on this live audience, convinced that laughter was infectuous and that if he made the studio audience laugh, he was obviously making listeners at home laugh. That Eddie Cantor influenced the future of radio was clearly demonstrated the next year as producers found in similar vaudeville comedians the personalities they needed to revive radio. That year marked the debut for such comedy series as those of Jack Benny, Burns and Allen, Ed Wynn, Jack Pearl, Joe Penner, Fred Allen, and the Marx Brothers. With this inundation of funny men and women, the domination of radio by the comedians had begun.

The gag became the staple of comedy when the former vaudeville entertainers entered broadcasting. On stage, comedians found great acceptance of these short jokes—jokes that ranged from crisp one-liners to curt comedic jabs occurring within a story or skit. Gags could be intricate jokes or simple puns, but invariably they suggested incongruities which took listeners by surprise and prompted laughter. Indicative of gag humor is the following exchange which occurred in the *Joe Penner Show* in late 1937.

Waiter:	(Laughs)
Penner:	Why, Dr. Ludwig. What are you laughing at?
Waiter:	The soup.
Penner:	The soup isn't funny.
Waiter:	Wait 'til you taste it. (Laughs)
Penner:	Say, I thought you were a doctor. Where did you learn to be a waiter?
Waiter:	In my waiting room. Get it? (Laughs)

1st Guest:	Waiter, take this back. I thought I told you to serve alphabet soup.
Waiter:	I didn't want you to read at the table.
Penner:	And another thing, waiter, there's a splinter in my cottage cheese.
Waiter:	What did you want, the whole cottage?
2nd Guest:	What is this terrible stuff on my plate?
3rd Guest:	It's so tough, I can't chew it.
Penner:	Waiter, I must say, this is not very good goulash.
Waiter:	I can't understand it. I used a pair of your best goulashes.

Most celebrated early comedians specialized in this type of unsophisticated humor. Ed Wynn was reputed to have a repertoire of more than twenty thousand such jokes. Jack Benny, later known as a subtle wit, on his earliest programs in 1932 still followed his introduction as "our effervescent comedian" (he was sponsored by Canada Dry ginger ale) with the comment, "Effervescent for me, we would have a nice program tonight." Four years later, Benny was still punfully deferring to his sponsor with his opening greeting, "Jello, everybody!" Utilizing his German dialect, the popular Jack Pearl found an abundance of puns in mispronouncing and misdefining English words. Further, it was with unmistakable pride that David Freedman, the writer of Eddie Cantor's material, told a fan magazine in 1933 that his most successful gag occurred when Cantor, in a deep Russian accent, gave this interview:

Girl:	I'd like to interview you, Mr. Rubinoff. Ah, what a beautiful name. Is Rubinoff your real name?
Cantor:	No, my real name is Quinn.
Girl:	Quinn? Q-U-I-N-N?
Cantor:	No, no, Quinn. C-O-H-E-N. Co-win![21]

Throughout the decade American listeners remained loyal to the pun. Comedy programs continually dominated the top fifteen shows in the ratings, and scholarship at that time revealed that about forty percent of the humor in a typical comedy program consisted of puns.[22] Perhaps the most intense example of this simple style of humor occurred on January 17, 1938, on the *George Burns and Gracie Allen Show* when for almost six consecutive minutes the famous comedy

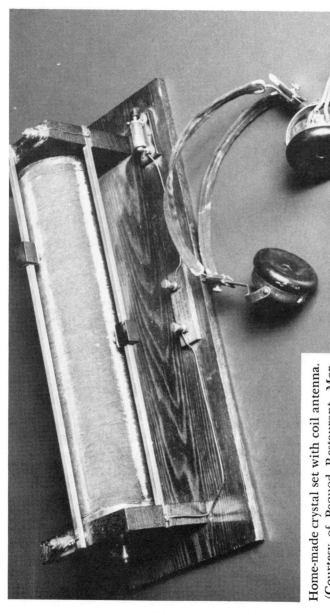

Home-made crystal set with coil antenna. (Courtesy of Pequod Restaurant, Morton Grove, Ill.)

The Atwater-Kent "Breadboard" Model 10 was a popular five-tube receiver in 1924. The speaker was detachable and was purchased separately. (Courtesy of Pequod Restaurant, Morton Grove, Ill.)

The 1926 David Grimes "Baby Grand" radio receiver with detachable speaker. (Courtesy of Pequod Restaurant, Morton Grove, Ill.)

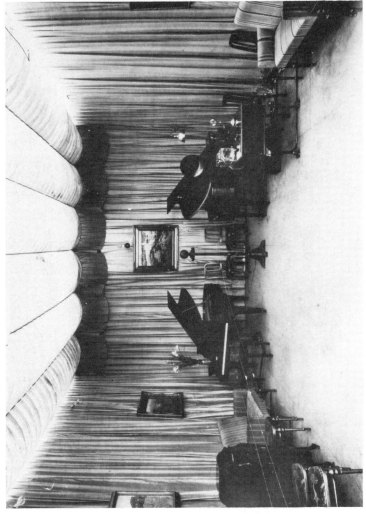

An early radio studio reveals flowing draperies for sound control, and twin pianos for the ever-present sound of music. (Courtesy of WGN Radio, Chicago)

Three generations of microphones (left to right): a carbon
mike from 1922, an improved double-button carbon mike from
1926, and an RCA model 44 mike from the late 1930s. (Courtesy
of Pequod Restaurant, Morton Grove, Ill.)

By the late 1920s radio had become a most popular living room utility. (Courtesy of WGN Radio, Chicago)

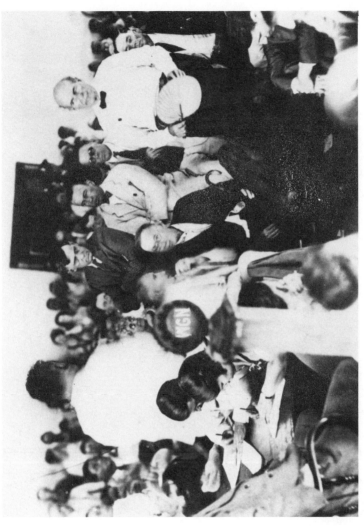

Coverage of current events was an integral part of radio programming since the 1920s. In July, 1925, station WGN (Chicago) made great strides when it broadcast live coverage of the so-called "Scopes Monkey Trial" from Dayton, Tennessee. Here, William Jennings Bryan fans himself near the WGN mike. (Courtesy of WGN Radio, Chicago)

The governmental administrator who had most to do with shaping the structure of commercial radio in the 1920s was Secretary of Commerce Hebert Hoover (left), seen here being interviewed over the air in 1927 by Arthur Sears Henning, chief of the Washington Bureau of the *Chicago Tribune.* (Courtesy of WGN Radio, Chicago)

team, plus their regulars Tony Martin, Ray Noble and John Conte, punned with the names of cities in a skit Gracie called, "The Fantasy of the Cities." The following excerpt presents an extreme expression of this comedic style. Significantly, that month the series was ranked fifth in the nation, with a strong Hooper rating of 27.5; it is safe to conclude that the pun was still a form of humor appreciated by most American listeners.

> *Gracie:* You see, I tell the story by using the names of cities and towns. . . . Now, for instance, Tony Martin is a Richmond who's been Macon a lot of money in Georgia, but he needs a few more Dallas to pay his Texas. Get it?
>
> *George:* Well, that's not Hartford me to understand.
>
> *Gracie:* Oh, you're catching on.
>
> *Tony:* Now, Gracie, if this is a musical number, do I play the part of a singer?
>
> *Gracie:* Well, no, Tony. You've got a little Quincy in Detroit. So you can't Sing-Sing.
>
> *George:* He can't Sing-Sing. Well, Walla Walla, that's very good.
>
> *Gracie:* Very good? As Al Jolson would say, New Haven heard nothin' yet.
>
> *George:* I guess not.
>
> *John:* Am I in this musical number, Gracie, The Fantasy of the Cities?
>
> *Gracie:* Well, I should say you are, Johnny, you're the little Boise that I'm in love with.
>
> *George:* But maybe Johnny doesn't love you.
>
> *John:* Oh, that's alright, George. I'm glad to Yuma her.
>
> *Gracie:* You see, George, Johnny's on my side—you spoke Tucson.
>
> *George:* But Gracie, I'm a very out-Spokane man.
>
> *Gracie:* Well, anyway, the scene Ipswich-es now to a town in Montana. But I can't mention the name of it.
>
> *George:* Why not?
>
> *Gracie:* Well, George, you're not allowed to say Helena radio.
>
> *George:* Well, that was really a Butte.
>
> *Gracie:* It's very funny Anaconda I made it up myself.
>
> *George:* Oh, yes, Anaconda you made it up right out of your own Marblehead.
>
> *Ray:* I say, Gracie, am I in this Fantasy of the Cities?
>
> *Gracie:* Certainly.
>
> *Ray:* Well, do I play another murder victim?

Gracie: Well, yes, Ray. And your name is Valley.
Ray: Rudy Vallee?
Gracie: No, Death Valley. And you're from Texas.
George: Well, maybe Ray can't play a dead body from Texas.
Gracie: Of Corsicana.
George: Well, Ray, you can Troy.

With the ascendency of broadcast humor, gag writers became a critical factor in radio production. Unlike stage performances where a comic could use the same routine throughout his tour, once a program was aired its material could not be broadcast again. With no such institution as the rerun or a rebroadcast at a later date, radio devoured jokes at a tremendous rate. Comedians were, understandably, heavily dependent upon their writers to furnish new and better jokes for each program. The toll could be heavy on the radio comic who lacked able writers. In 1934, *Variety* reported that several name comedians had already exhausted the material it had taken them up to twenty years to accumulate.[23]

Ed Wynn suffered from this problem. During the early 1930s, his *Fire Chief Show* enjoyed outstanding popularity. Wynn, however, relied on his own gags and wrote most of his own scripts. During a thirty-minute broadcast he often delivered as many as fifty-five jokes. His series lasted for three years, until in 1935 he altered his rapid-fire gag style for the more leisurely mode of the *Gulliver the Traveller* program. Without the verve or dynamism of his original program, the new series marked the beginning of Wynn's demise in radio. Despite two other short-lived programs, *The Perfect Fool* in 1937, and the fantasy-comedy, *Happy Island* in 1944, plus an abortive attempt in 1947 to team with his son, Keenan, in *The Wynn Show*, Ed Wynn never regained the popularity his clowning style and material had achieved earlier. In fact, in 1945 Wynn angrily summarized his plight when he announced he was finished with radio since "Radio has changed with these [present-day] gag writers."[24]

The most prolific and controversial writer during the 1930s was David Freedman. He began writing comedy in 1931 when he composed gags for Eddie Cantor, and for three successful years he was the principal source of Cantor's material. Before his untimely death in December 1936—at the age of thirty-nine—Freedman had also written radio scripts for such comedians as Ken Murray, Block and Sully (Jesse Block and Eve Sully), and the Greek-accented George Givot. Freedman was an indefatigable gagster who was highly paid for his services. At a time when an ordinary dramatic script could be purchased for $15 to $75, he was receiving almost $750 for each Cantor program, and $500 for *The Chesterfield Program* for which he wrote the comedic lines for dialectician Lou Holtz. At the time of his death, Freedman was involved in a controversial legal suit against Cantor, wherein he claimed the comedian failed to honor a contract signed in 1929 which guaranteed him ten percent of all Cantor's earnings.

Many of the successful gag writers in this period had come to radio after writing careers in vaudeville. Gagsters like Eugene Conrad, who in 1933 wrote for Burns and Allen, Block and Sully, and Milton Berle; J. P. Medbury, who wrote the early scripts for Burns and Allen; Harry Conn, who produced jokes for Jack Benny, Joe Penner, and Eddie Cantor; and Billy Wells, who developed and wrote for Jack Pearl's character Baron Munchausen; all had experience composing for vaudeville comedians. Nonetheless, the radio medium was different. Freedman admitted that it was more difficult writing for radio than for the stage. "On the stage, if the material is funny," he told an interviewer, "audiences can be made to laugh at any sort of low character, grotesque or buffoon. You can't push such a character on the radio, however," he continued, "because a radio character is a guest in the home. And people don't want to receive 'muggs' into their homes."[25]

Gag writers often utilized elaborate cross-indexed filing systems in which they placed their jokes. Culling material from publications, experiences, other media, and other comedians, the authors arranged the jokes in such a way that if a situation involved an automobile, they could look under "automobile" in their personal files and produce several appropriate gags. The Hal Horn company in New York City was reputed to have about five million jokes arranged in this manner, with three hundred variations filed under "Who was that lady I saw you with?"

This system of arranging jokes was originated by Ralph Spense, a comedy writer for silent movies whose comic titles helped many films to success. As a device in radio production, it allowed a writer to draw from used material, switch details of a basic joke to fit the context for which he was writing, and produce a new variation on a successful gag. This permitted writers to last for years in a business which demanded fresh jokes weekly. It also prompted criticism of comedy authors for lacking imagination and talent. The prolific David Freedman answered such complaints in a letter to the editor of a fan magazine in 1935. Never denying that writers added variations to used jokes, he maintained:

> The futility of trying to create new jokes for radio and stage becomes more apparent with each succeeding broadcast and appearance of the famed comedians. Accusations of plagarism are flung at the latter—and the men who write them—without restraint; often at the hint of an old wheeze, dressed up in modern clothes. I . . . have been criticized with others. That there really is nothing new under the sun, as the Bible states, is further evidenced by the fact that Mark Twain once dedicated a book "to Mr. Smith, wherever he is found," and it develops that an earlier humorist, Artemus Ward, prefaced a book with a similar inscription. Lincoln has been credited with the expressive phrase, "Of the people, by the people, and for the people," yet Theodore Parker, in a recorded address before the Anti-Slavery Society, May 13, 1854, used the same phrase. What's the answer?[26]

As it emerged and flourished in the 1930s, radio comedy established patterns that would endure beyond the decade. The utilization of a comic foil—often called a "stooge"—by the star comedian was a lasting development in this formative period. Comedians discovered early that it was difficult to entertain a mass audience with only a comic monologue. For the sake of variety as well as inventiveness, stooges appeared on almost all comedy programs in the first years of the decade. In some cases they operated as the butt of the jokes told by the star; but in many instances, the stooges actually delivered punchlines or operated as "straight men" setting up the funnier stars. Several comics utilized their wives as stooges. Gracie Allen, Irene Noblette, Portland Hoffa, and Mary Livingston, for example, played the role for their respective husbands, George Burns, Tim Ryan, Fred Allen, and Jack Benny. Stooges occasionally possessed thick foreign accents, such as Cantor's Mad Russian, Cantor's and Al Jolson's Parkyakarkas, and Phil Baker's English butler, Bottle (Harry McNaughton). In several programs even the announcer became integrally involved in the comedians' joking, as did Graham McNamee with Ed Wynn, Jimmy Wallington and Harry von Zell with Eddie Cantor, and Don Wilson with Jack Benny.

The appearance of the stooge allowed for dialogue that was more interesting to an audience. The repartee and unexpected twists in conversation often precipitated the funniest moments of the programs. Further, the stooge allowed the comedian to delineate better his own personality. In reacting to the words or antics of his foil, the principal comedian juxtaposed his own fictional characteristics, thereby making them a familiar part of his program. Without the skeptical Mary Livingston or the openly-doubting Rochester, Benny's stinginess would not have been as humorous. The fictional stupidity of Gracie Allen added charm and understanding to the low-key sobriety of George Burns' character. And the thick dialects of Cantor's stooges made his radio personality seem even more enthusiastic and believable.

Also important to the pacing of most comedy series in the 1930s were the various musical interludes provided by a resident orchestra and vocalist. The music clearly divided each show into segments allowing writers to develop a single, episodic story or a series of unrelated skits. The music also added variety to the broadcast and associated it with the successful variety-show format of programs like Fleischmann's *Rudy Vallee Show,* the Maxwell House *Show Boat,* and *The Collier Hour.* Also, many significant orchestra leaders played behind the radio comedians. In the 1933–1934 season, for example, Ferdé Grofé provided music for Fred Allen's *Sal Hepatica Revue*; Guy Lombardo appeared with Burns and Allen; Ozzie

Nelson and his orchestra backed the *Joe Penner Show*; Paul
Whiteman appeared with Al Jolson on the *Kraft Music Hall*;
and Mildred Bailey and her orchestra provided rhythm for the
George Jessel Show. In several cases these orchestra leaders
also acted as stooges. In all instances, however, a break for a
musical selection from the band, or a solo from singers like
Tony Martin *(Burns and Allen)*, Deanna Durbin *(Eddie
Cantor Show)*, Gene Austin *(Joe Penner Show)* or Frank
Parker and Dennis Day *(Jack Benny Program)* lightened the
comedic format and allowed listeners a pause between the
humorous segments of the broadcast. Typical of this merger of
comedy and music was the pattern on Fred Allen's *Linit Bath
Club Revue* as aired on December 25, 1932:

   I.   Announcer opens program
   II.   Orchestra plays full song
   III. Monologue by Allen—into first scene of skit
   IV.   Vocal solo by Charles Carlisle
   V.   Second scene in skit—Portland Hoffa enters
   VI.   First commercial
   VII. Musical interlude
   VIII. Third scene of skit
   IX.   Orchestra and vocalist—portions of two songs
   X.   Second commercial
   XI   Closing comments from Allen.

   Comedians learned early that their humor was most successful when put into skit form. In 1932, Jack Benny introduced the feature of satirizing current motion pictures, a format he used throughout his radio and television career. By the
middle of the decade, Benny's weekly program—like those of
several other gag comedians—was being written around a
single theme or humorous situation in which he and his supporting characters found themselves. Eddie Cantor, too,
understood the necessity of introducing situational contexts in
which humor could be developed. Although he had begun in
radio as strictly a gag comedian, within a few years he was
openly advising his colleagues to abandon the puns of vaudeville and to develop a more mature form of comedy. "So comedians have either got to stop gagging or get off the air," he
told an interviewer in 1934. "People won't stand for the old

stuff any longer," according to Cantor. Of the older comedic
form, he contended:

> I'd like to get away from gags altogether. What gags I do
> use are only for insurance. Situations are a gamble. You
> can't tell how they are going to hit people. Gags are the
> sure-fire laughs. Then why get away from gags? Because
> the public is sick of them. They know all the answers.
> What's the use of kidding ourselves? We've all got the
> same little books, you know—"Fun in a Smoking Car" or
> "Minstrel Wit and Humor." We rewrite the old jokes,
> dress 'em up, and call 'em new gags. But you can't fool
> the public. They're the same old friends with their
> whiskers trimmed. . . . I've said: Boys, if you'll throw those
> little books away, you'll be better off. Stick to those gags
> long enough and they'll strangle you. Better give 'em
> up.[27]

One of the more successful comedy teams to develop an
innovative style was Stoopnagle and Budd. Called "The
Gloom Chasers" when they emerged on CBS in 1931 as a
comedy-patter act, Colonel Lemuel Q. Stoopnagle (F. Chase
Taylor) and Budd (Wilbur Budd Hulick) developed a zany,
conversational type of humor which was most effective when
presented in short, individual skits. The two comedians provided the voices for most of the odd characters who appeared
on their show, and their skits remained short and simple
pieces which relied upon absurdity, satire, mimickry, and
puns. Typical of their format, in March 1935, they enacted
such humorous vignettes as a sale pitch for a "patented both-
sides-wrong bed" which guaranteed the purchaser that "you
cannot jump out of bed with a smile, but instead you leap
from the couch with a grouch"; an interview with Cornelius
Updrum, a man who always held his hands behind his back
because he carried the front end of a bass drum in a marching
band; and a short skit featuring Stoopnagle as Adelbrit Glad-
pebble, "a dealer in bricks and mortar," who hired Budd as a
replacement for a work horse. When these jokesters dissolved
their act in 1937, their uniquely absurd style of comedy left
radio. Not until the appearance of Bob and Ray (Bob Elliott
and Ray Goulding) in the late 1940s would it re-emerge.

Features such as stooges, musical interludes, and situational skits added variety to comedy programming. They also offset the overexposure that might result from a comedian simply airing joke after joke. All the great radio comics avoided prolonged periods which they operated alone. Even later masters of one-line gags, like Red Skelton and Bob Hope, maintained a monologue for only several minutes before introducing an assistant, guest, or musical diversion. The lengthy comedic monologue, however, was not totally absent from broadcasting. It was a pattern best developed by a group of intellectual humorists who came to radio not from vaudeville, but from successful careers in literature and journalism. At various times throughout the 1930s, radio comedy was enhanced by programs from such individuals as Irvin S. Cobb, Alexander Woollcott, Will Rogers, James Thurber, Arthur "Bugs" Baer, and Heywood Hale Broun. None of the latter three was particularly outstanding. Thurber on CBS in mid-1934, Baer over WOR (New York City) in mid-1936, and Broun in 1931 on WCAU (Philadelphia) and again in 1937 discovered that in radio delivery was as important as composition. Their respective series lasted no more than a few months.

More successful, however, was Irvin S. Cobb. The noted writer appeared as the host of several important network series, including the *Good Gulf Show* during the 1933–1934 season, and *Plantation Party* in the 1936–1937 season. Here, as a "Kentucky Colonel," he was most effective as master of ceremonies and raconteur of stories depicting the character and style of Southerners. Despite Cobb's popularity, the humorous monologue received its most developed and applauded realization in the programs of Alexander Woollcott and Will Rogers.

A renowned critic, author, and wit, Woollcott was the host—and often the only performer—of *The Town Crier,* a literate series in which he presented dramatic and literary reviews, personal reflections, essays, interviews, music, and humor—all interpreted through a personality that was engagingly rich in charm. And Woollcott needed that charm, for, as one admiring critic termed it, he possessed "just about the worst voice that ever poured itself into an offended microphone."[28] Woollcott's program began in 1933, and with sponsors that ranged from Cream of Wheat breakfast cereal to Granger Pipe Tobacco, it remained intermittently on radio until the early 1940s. His was a subtle and intellectual type of humor that, perhaps, escaped listeners more attuned to the broad jokes of the popular comedians. Typical of Woollcott's style was his nostalgic description of the German Kaiser on the eve of the Great War. As broadcast on October 6, 1933, Woollcott mused:

> In Berlin the Kaiser sits on this throne, his gleaming sword in its case, his beard as yet unsprung. It is his proud boast that he has kept the peace of Europe for five and twenty years—he and he alone. And even as he says so—even as he struts his little stage—there sounds from the wings a sardonic laugh. It's the future giving him what will one day be known as "the raspberry."

In the same broadcast, Woollcott humorously summarized his function as a critic, pointing specifically to the danger inherent in the role.

> It has been suggested that at this point each week I should make a recommendation of some book, play or picture. Any such commentator as myself is a little like the tasters employed by the Doges in medieval Venice who all lived in daily, and justifiable, fear of being poisoned. Before the soup was served to the great man, it was sampled by the taster. If the taster survived, the Doge began dunking with a relish. If the taster died in agony, the soup was thrown out, fresh soup was ordered, and—considerably annoyed—the Doge had to send around for a new taster. Well, as taster-at-large to the American public, I hereby report that I have just enjoyed, without deleterious after-effects, a new book from England called *Brazilian Adventure*.

If Woollcott was literate and urbane, Will Rogers was unpretentious and rural in his radio personality. Born in Oklahoma and a successful writer and movie and stage comedian before he came to broadcasting, Rogers was as much a folk philosopher as he was an entertainer. He had appeared on radio throughout the second half of the 1920s, but did not have his own regular program until early 1930. From that date until his death in an airplane accident in 1935, Rogers acted on the air as the court jester and critical wit of the nation. Throughout his career he had joked about politics, and network apprehension about political humor did not thwart him. Rogers gathered his own material for each program and worked without a script. Network censors, therefore, found it impossible to preview his comments, and sponsors refused to censor his material. His barbs could be strong. In his broadcast over CBS on November 11, 1934, Rogers satirized the defeat of the Republican Party in congressional elections several days earlier: "All that was mortal of the Republican Party had left this earth. . . . He passed away just because he wanted to live like a pioneer. He couldn't change with modern civilization." Rogers pounded his point home as he remarked, "and on his tombstone it says: 'Here lies a rugged individual, but he wasn't rugged enough to compete with the Democrats.' "[29]

Rogers had satirized Presidents since the administration of Woodrow Wilson, and on radio he continued that tradition. Although he was especially fond of Franklin D. Roosevelt, he found FDR and his New Deal a vulnerable, but respected, target. Typical of his style was the *Good Gulf Show* broadcast of April 30, 1933. Here, Rogers referred to Roosevelt as a political magician, "a Houdini of Hyde Park," and noted innocently, "They started the inaugural parade down Pennsylvania Avenue, and before it got halfway down there he closed every bank in the United States." But this program also revealed the seriousness of Rogers' humor, for beneath the joking he was a democrat and an optimist about Roosevelt's ability to lead America out of the Depression.

> Now, I understand Mr. Roosevelt—somebody told me— was listenin' in. Now, Mr. Roosevelt, we've turned everything over to you. We've given you more power than we've ever given any man—any man was ever given in the history of the world. We don't know what it's all about. We've tried to run the country individually and collectively and along a democratic line. But, hey, we've gummed it up so. So, you take it and run it if you want to, you know, and deflate, or inflate, or complicate, you

know. Or insulate—do anything just so you git us a dollar or two every now and again, you know. So, you're our lawyer. And we're gonna turn the whole thing over to—things are movin' so fast in this country now that we don't know what it's all about. The whole country's cockeyed anyhow. And we're disappointin' you. And you take it—we don't know what it's all about, but God bless you.

The demands of broadcasting exerted a maturing effect upon American comedy. Faced by competition for listeners, and compelled to create new programs each week, the comedians and their writers created by the 1940s a higher standard of popular humor. No longer could comedians hope to survive on the tricks developed in vaudeville. Burlesque characters, silly sounds, absurd lines, and an abundance of puns had sustained pioneers like Jack Pearl, Joe Penner, Ed Wynn, and Phil Baker. These devices also appeared in series with slapstick comedians like Wheeler and Woolsey (Bert Wheeler and Robert Woolsey) and Olsen and Johnson (Ole Olsen and Chick Johnson). By the 1940s, however, such entertainers had faded in significance and their places were being taken by the more adaptable of the early comedians, and by a "second generation" of comics who brought new ideas and new personalities to American broadcasting.

"Old timers" like Jack Benny, Eddie Cantor, and Fred Allen survived this winnowing-out process, principally because their concept of radio comedy was sound, and their writers were talented. Benny knew, for example, that the excessive utilization of a supporting character or popular cliché would eventually turn audience interest into apathy. Throughout the 1930s, he carefully introduced new regular characters like Eddie "Rochester" Anderson in 1937, and singers Kenny Baker in 1935 and Dennis Day in 1939; and he made intermittent use of subsidiary actors like Andy Devine, Sam Hearn, Mel Blanc, Sheldon Leonard, Frank Nelson, and Ronald and Benita Colman. Similarly, on his program, Eddie Cantor introduced as regulars singers and comedians like Deanna Durbin, Bobby Breen, Harry Einstein, Hattie Noel, and Dinah Shore. Throughout the period Fred Allen also moved characters in and out of "Allen's Alley" and developed such

new features as The Mighty Allen Art Players, Won Long
Pan—his take-off on the Oriental detective, Charlie Chan—
and his weekly joking about the news, the News of the Day
Newsreel.

In this vein, one of the more popular gimmicks to emerge
was the "feud" between Benny and Allen. Supposed disputes
between personalities were not new to radio with these comedians. In the early 1930s a "grudge" had developed between
the popular bandleader and comic, Ben Bernie, and the sharp-
tongued commentator, Walter Winchell. On their respective
programs each belittled the other while listeners laughed
understandingly. The imbroglio between Benny and Allen
began accidentally on *Town Hall Tonight* on December 30,
1936, when Allen ad libbed a quip about Benny's inability to
play the violin. Jack Benny countered on his next broadcast,
and the feud was on. Actually, the battle was made possible in
October 1935, when Allen and his sponsor (Bristol Myers) became clients of Young & Rubicam, the advertising agency
which represented Benny and his sponsor (General Foods).
While each had different sponsors, sharing a common agency
kept the feud fully under control and, therefore, not commercially unprofitable for either side. The battle came to a climax
in March 1937, when the two comedians staged a mock fist-
fight during a broadcast of the *Jack Benny Program*. The two
"fought it out" off-mike in an alley. There was no winner, and
they returned arm-in-arm, "bruised" but reminiscing about
the good old days. Despite the apparent reconciliation, the
feud was a popular comedic device and it continued sporadically until Fred Allen retired from his comedy program in
1949.

Radio comedy matured by the early 1940s because of the
relatively sophisticated and realistic material upon which it
came to rely. Characterization within a program was made
fuller as writers developed personalities with whom audiences
could identify. Instead of the vaudeville style of humor—with
its obvious jokes and unbelievable settings—comedy was more
cleverly integrated into the characters appearing on the program. Jack Benny, whose show eventually ceased being a

comedy-variety series and was written as a situation comedy, well understood this important improvement in broadcast humor. Writing in 1945, he explained how he and his cast fit into this new maturity.

> We feel that, to a certain extent, we represent the audience. In us, they see themselves. It would be foolish for us to knock each other around, because then we would be knocking the audience around ... and when you start doing that—well your sponsor had better be your own brother-in-law. However, one of America's greatest characteristics is our ability to laugh at ourselves. When the audience sees themselves through us, they get a special kick out of the jokes that seem to fit them personally. . . . Throughout, we try to have things happen to us which will be interesting and also, above all, *funny*. That's why so many of our routines and gags come from what we see around us. . . .[30]

"Topping" a joke—creating a string of secondary, but funnier, jokes based upon an original gag, and, thereby, propelling an audience to greater and greater laughter—was not new to the 1940s, but as Benny explained, the process was now more sophisticated and more cleverly related to the well-known traits of the program characters. As an example, he cited the following dialogue between Rochester and Mary Livingston:

> *Mary:* You say you just got into town, Rochester. What took you so long ... was the train late?
> *Rochester:* What train? I was out on Highway 99 free-lancing.
> *Mary:* You mean you hitch-hiked? Why?
> *Rochester:* Well, instead of a train ticket, Mr. Benny gave me a road map.
> *Mary:* Oh.
> *Rochester:* And a short talk on the generosity of the American tourist.
> *Mary:* You mean that's all Mr. Benny gave you?
> *Rochester:* No ... he also gave me a white glove for night operations.[31]

Here the original gag plus three toppers created not only a series of laughs from a continuous image of Rochester hitchhiking, but they skillfully capitalized upon personal qualities known to listeners—Benny's stinginess, Rochester's racial heritage, and Mary's compassion for people exploited by Benny.

It was important to the continued popularity of radio comedy that as the vaudevillians faded in popularity, fresh, young talents emerged to replace them. Bob Hope had developed his comedic skill early on such obscure variety programs as *The Intimate Revue* in 1935, *Atlantic Family* in 1935, and *Rippling Rhythm Revue* in 1936. Specializing in a staccato stream of one-line and two-line barbs (by 1947 his show was delivering eighty-five gag lines per half-hour broadcast), Hope blended this approach with an attitude of apparent nonchalance to create a captivating comedic personality. When he first appeared on his own show for Pepsodent toothpaste in September 1938, the reviewer for *Variety* well understood that Hope's snappy pace was something new and engaging, for he predicted great success for the new personality: "That small speck going over the centre field fence is the four-bagger Bob Hope whammed out on his first time at bat for Pepsodent. . . . He sounded like success all the way. . . . Let him show over a period of time that he can duplicate, and the other comics will be lending a jealous ear."[32]

Rivalling Hope in terms of pace and vitality was Red Skelton. Skelton came to radio in 1939 after a stage career primarily involving pantomime comedy. Yet, patterning his delivery and his penchant for laughing at his own jokes after Ed Wynn, Skelton by the early 1940s became one of the top comedians in radio. Especially effective were the characters he created. The "mean widdle kid" was a rambunctious and scheming brat with whom listeners could not help but be enraptured. In Clem Kadiddlehopper, an addlebrained singing cab driver, listeners encountered a lovable, if doltish, image of ignorant humanity. And in Deadeye, the boisterous and braggart "fastest-gun in the West," Skelton mimicked the streak of self-importance in most people.

In the slapstick comedy team of Bud Abbott and Lou Costello, American listeners found the tradition of vaudeville comedy enlivened by an energetic and disciplined patter style. Emerging from small-time burlesque, Abbott and Costello entered radio through their appearances on the *Kate Smith Show,* an hour-long variety program which, thanks in no small part to the comedy team, by the late 1930s had replaced the *Rudy Vallee Show* as the most popular variety program in radio. In 1942, the comedy team was starred in the popular *Abbott and Costello Show.* Abbott's character was that of the level-headed straight man. Prone to chastising his partner, and always ready to let him suffer the consequences, Abbott's dour personality contrasted effectively with that of Lou Costello. Costello was the comedic force of the act. It was his vulnerable personality—so prone to innocent errors, so gullible around charlatans, and so inhibited in the company of women—that was the most attractive aspect of the team. Audiences accepted the loud screams and inane puns of Abbott and Costello; and they marvelled at their well-timed and thoroughly-rehearsed verbal routines, like the famous "Who's on first?" conversation; but it was the human fallibility of Costello that made the pair one of the leading radio comedy acts throughout the 1940s.

The most consistently successful of the new generation of talents was Edgar Bergen. While Bergen was a ventriloquist with a modest personality, his dummy, Charlie McCarthy, certainly balanced the traits of his operator. Charlie was a blend of rascality, irreverence, and brashness. He flirted with attractive guests and quarrelled pointedly with W. C. Fields. Charlie said the things most people thought, but would dare not utter. Bergen and McCarthy emerged from obscurity in 1936 when, after seeing them at a party, Rudy Vallee suggested they guest on his program. It was Bergen's talent, of course, that produced the banter between himself and the puppet, but it was Charlie's bold personality that made the act a hit. After many guest appearances with Vallee, the *Edgar Bergen-Charlie McCarthy Show* premiered on NBC in 1937. For the next fifteen years the program never fell below number seven in the annual ratings. In fact, in the years 1937–1940 and 1942–1943, Bergen's program was the top-rated program in radio. Although Bergen later developed other puppet characters—the dull-witted Mortimer Snerd, the husband-hunting old maid, Effie Klinker, and the unmemorable Podine Puffington—none ever rivalled Charlie McCarthy for the affection of audiences.

With the appearance of these new comedians, a second generation of radio comics had emerged. By 1940, Al Jolson was fifty-five years of age, Ed Wynn was fifty-four, Eddie Cantor forty-eight, and Jack Benny and Fred Allen were forty-six. In comparison, Bob Hope and Edgar Bergen were thirty-seven years of age, Lou Costello was thirty-two, and Red Skelton twenty-seven. Most of the new comedians had had stage backgrounds, but none was as tied to the traditions of vaudeville as the pioneers of the early 1930s. By the time this second generation entered broadcasting, the capabilities of radio as an entertainment medium were more fully understood. Less attached to the past, the new comics were able to adapt their material to fit these modern dimensions. Therefore, as radio entered the 1940s, broadcast comedy did so with an infusion of young and agile talent. Yet, the most significant comedic development of the 1940s was not its gag comics. Instead, the most important growth in radio humor in that decade was the flowering of situation comedy as the most prevalent type of humor on the air.

The Situation Comedy—The Forties

In contrast to the variety style of comedy, with its big-name hosts, stooges, guest stars, skits, orchestras, and fast-paced atmosphere, the situation comedy of the 1940s relied more strongly on drama—the sense of story with a definite beginning, development, and ending—and hence produced its humor within a strikingly different context. With the gag comedians, listeners could not mistake the spirit of a stage show which they possessed. The prologue by the star, the banter between him and the guest, the skit or skits, and the closing remarks combined to create a spectacle in which listeners were seemingly placed in the audiece of a stage revue.

Situation comedy, however, swept listeners directly into the narrative. These comedies, especially those set within domestic surroundings, opened within a familiar context and stayed there until the program ended. Even those sitcoms that had orchestral interludes and guest stars remained tied to a single story line from beginning to end. In this manner, listeners were taken directly to 79 Wistful Vista each week on the *Fibber McGee and Molly Show*, to 1849 Rogers Lane on *The Adventures of Ozzie and Harriet*, or into Mr. Duffy's bar on *Duffy's Tavern*. In these familiar surroundings—or in new surroundings made familiar because the regular characters were visiting there—the audience was drawn into an episode in which humor and dramatic narrative were blended.

The situation comedy was not new to the 1940s. It had actually been developed in the late 1920s as a result of the success of such early programs as *Amos 'n' Andy* and *The Rise of the Goldbergs*. Both serialized programs presented recurring characters, functioning in familiar surroundings (Amos and Andy ran the Fresh Air Taxi Company, and the Goldbergs lived in the Jewish ghetto of the Lower East Side of New York City), and into whose lives listeners were able to enter. That this type of program hit a responsive note with Americans is noticeable in the fact that by 1930 *Amos 'n' Andy* was the top-ranked program in the nation, and *The Goldbergs* remained intermittently on radio for twenty years.

The development of situation comedy was adversely affected when radio was inundated by vaudevillians in the early 1930s. Used to stage routines and joke-telling, few of these established comedy stars developed successful situation comedies. This is not to say, however, that even at this time sitcoms failed to appear. One of the most appreciated programs in radio, *Easy Aces*, began in 1930. This serial featured the witty conversations and adventures of Goodman and Jane Ace. Housewife Jane was a master of malaprops whose mispronunciations usually contained poignant double entendres. Her misconstructed phrases—"up at the crank of dawn," "working my head to the bone," and "you've got to take the bitter with the badder"—became nationally recognized bon mots. Husband Goodman not only starred in the series, but for the fifteen years it was on the air, he was its sole writer.

Vic and Sade first appeared in mid-1932. Masterfully written by Paul Rhymer, this daytime blend of soap opera and sitcom focused on the antics of the fictional couple, Vic and Sade Gook, who, with their young son, Rush, lived humorously "in the little house half-way up in the next block," in the epitome of small-town America, "Crooper, Illinois—forty miles from Peoria." Throughout the 1930s audiences found in Vic, Sade, Rush, and their silly friends—Dottie and Chuck Brainfeeble, Smelly Clark, Ruthie Stembottom, Uncle Fletcher, and Rishigan Fishigan from Sishigan, Michigan, a distinctive absurdity which set it apart from most of the humor broadcast at this time.

Another important situation comedy to emerge in the 1930s was *Lum and Abner*. This series featured the Rube humor of Lum Edwards (Chester Lauck) and Abner Peabody (Norris Goff), proprietors of the Jot 'Em Down Store in Pine Ridge, Arkansas. The program came to network radio in mid-1931 and for twenty-two years presented a vast range of rural characters and ill-fated schemes. Lauck and Goff provided almost all the voices for the show, from Cedric Weehunt, the local idiot, and Snake Hogan, the village tough-guy, to the money-hungry Squire Skimp, and Grandpappy Spear, the inveterate checkers player. Whether their tribulations concerned such crises as caring for a lost infant, planning a trip to Mars by rocketship, or training the weakling, Mousey Gray, to be a prizefighter, the rustic pair demonstrated the viability of situation comedy.

Despite the chronic popularity of sitcoms, American tastes in humor in the 1930s continued strongly in favor of the comedy-variety mixture associated with the stage comics. A perusal of the C.A.B. ratings for that decade illustrates that while comedy dominated the top-ten rankings each year, until the 1940s the only situation comedy ever so popular was *Amos 'n' Andy*.

With the decline in popularity suffered by *Amos 'n' Andy*, the sitcom format did not re-enter radio in any popular fashion until the end of the decade. Not until the success of the *Fibber McGee and Molly Show* by 1940 did the situation comedy become a strong alternative style. Jim and Marian Jordan, stars of the program, had had ample training in radio humor before attaining acceptance as Fibber McGee and Molly. In the 1920s they had entertained Chicago audiences with *The Smith Family,* and in the period 1931–1935 they had appeared in a sitcom, *The Smackouts,* set in a grocery store that was always "smack out of everything." As the McGees, from 1935 until 1957, they nurtured and refined two characters who comically summarized the conditions of millions of average American families. The series was well-written by Don Quinn, a former cartoonist who had joined the Jordans in 1931 and remained with them throughout his career. The humor, however, was not particularly innovative. Much of it bore the mark of vaudeville in which the Jordans had worked even before entering broadcasting. There were weekly visits to the McGees' home by such distinctive characters as the self-centered and short-tempered Mayor La Trivia, the puny-voiced Wally Wimple, the bratty little girl next door, and the wheezy and incredulous "Old Timer" whose skeptical retort, "That's pretty good, Johnny, but that ain't the way I heared it," became a standard of the program. The weekly adventures encountered by the McGees were also unspectacular. A typical program might center on Fibber finding a wristwatch, wall-papering the house, suffering a toothache, or planning a vacation.

The strength of the program lay in the two central characters. As it was with second generation comedians like Bob Hope and Edgar Bergen, the key to success with audiences in the 1940s was the development of a fallible, recognizable, sympathetic human character with whom listeners could warmly identify. Fibber McGee and Molly were certainly in this mold. They were familiar people, a blend of rural and urban that was awkward and vulnerable enough to affect the serious emotions as well as the funnybones of Americans. Fibber was boastful, but ultimately inadequate, while Molly was nonplussed by her exaggerating husband and always in control of the situation. If Fibber started bragging about his theatrical

Top Programs for Specified Periods[33]
(includes average percentage of audience)

March 1930 to February 1931	March 1931 to February 1932	March 1932 to February 1933
1. Amos 'n' Andy (37%)	1. Amos 'n' Andy (33%)	1. Eddie Cantor (22%)
	3. Eddie Cantor (18%)	2. Amos 'n' Andy (20%)
		4. Ed Wynn (18%)
		5. Jack Pearl (17%)

March 1933 to February 1934	March 1934 to February 1935	October 1935 to April 1936
1. Eddie Cantor (25%)	3. Joe Penner (19%)	2. Jack Benny (26%)
1. Ed Wynn (25%)	4. Eddie Cantor (18%)	5. Fred Allen (19%)
5. Jack Pearl (23%)	4. Ed Wynn (18%)	5. Burns and Allen (19%)
7. Amos 'n' Andy (18%)	6. Jack Benny (17%)	10. Eddie Cantor (15%)
7. Burns and Allen (18%)	8. Amos 'n' Andy (15%)	
	8. Fred Allen (15%)	

October 1936 to April 1937	October 1937 to April 1938	October 1938 to April 1939
1. Jack Benny (33%)	1. Edgar Bergen (40%)	1. Edgar Bergen (42%)
2. Eddie Cantor (25%)	2. Jack Benny (36%)	2. Jack Benney (36%)
5. Fred Allen (22%)	5. Eddie Cantor (25%)	5. Fred Allen (21%)
5. Burns and Allen (22%)	6. Fred Allen (23%)	5. Burns and Allen (21%)
	6. Burns and Allen (23%)	
	10. Al Jolson (21%)	

October 1939 to
April 1940

---

1. Edgar Bergen
   (40%)
2. Jack Benny
   (39%)
4. Fibber McGee
   (29%)
6. Bob Hope
   (24%)

background, Molly was there to deflate his ego by reminding him that the only play he ever wrote had been a disaster. If Fibber whined about the blisters he was getting while digging, Molly was there to mother him condescendingly and then command him back to work. Or if Fibber cracked a corny joke and looked for laughing approval, Molly would remind him sourly, "'Tain't funny, McGee," *Radio Guide* magazine explained the strength of their humor when it cited them in 1936 as two of "those Pagliaccis of the air who were trying their darndest to make America forget its troubles."

> They were Fibber McGee and Molly, whose homely humor might be that of your old Aunt Harriet in Cherokee or mine in Kalamazoo—whose whole philosophy is as sincere as yours or that of your good, kind neighbor next door. In the beginning there was nothing subtle about the McGee brand of humor. It was as honest as the kitchen sink—as unpretentious as your old bone-handled carving knife—and sometimes it was just as suddenly sharp! In fact, theirs was Main Street entertainment, pure and simple.[34]

The *Fibber McGee and Molly Show* was not an overnight success. It took Quinn and the Jordans several years to be accepted by an audience used to the comedy and variety mixture offered by big-name stars. In January 1936, for example, their Hooper rating was 6.6 as compared to 26.8 for the *Jack Benny Program*. Yet, by polishing their style, convincing listeners of the variation possible within sitcoms, and developing recognizable and funny characterizations, within four years their rating had increased to 30.8 compared to Benny's 34.1. By February, 1943, the program set a new C.A.B. rating record of 44.5, the highest rating a half-hour program had ever achieved to that date.

The rise of the *Fibber McGee and Molly Show* led directly to a revival of situation comedy in radio. Eager to duplicate the popularity and profitability of that series, sitcoms proliferated in broadcasting in the 1940s. One of the principal charms of this type of program was its low cost. Relative to the traditional comedy show with a high-priced star, guests, orchestra, and writers, the sitcoms were economically competitive and often more profitable. A comparison of weekly production costs and Hooper ratings for the top comedy-variety and situation comedy programs in January 1944 reveals that the latter were usually less expensive and cost less per rating point than the celebrity shows.

Program Economics
(January 1944) [35]

Comedy-Variety	Production Costs	C.A.B. Rating	Cost per Point
Bob Hope	$14,750	31.6	$467
Red Skelton	$ 8,000	31.4	$255
Bergen & McCarthy	$12,000	29.2	$411
Jack Benny	$22,500	27.2	$806
Abbott & Costello	$11,000	24.0	$458
Fred Allen	$14,000	19.8	$707

Situation Comedy	Production Costs	C.A.B. Rating	Cost per Point
Fibber McGee & Molly	$10,000	31.9	$313
The Aldrich Family	$ 6,500	26.9	$242
Amos 'n' Andy	$ 9,000	17.1	$526
Blondie	$ 5,000	16.3	$307
Great Gildersleeve	$ 5,000	16.0	$307
That Brewster Boy	$ 2,750	13.0	$212

Situation comedies of the 1940s usually related familiar occurrences drawn from the realities of domestic life. A typical show might revolve around something as recognizable as repairing a water pipe, purchasing a new hat, or greeting a visiting relative. But whatever the context, the strength of sitcoms was their blending of this credible, if unspectacular, narrative action with plausible comedic development. In reality no one ever produced as much laughter experimenting with a chemistry set as did Phil Harris on the *Phil Harris-Alice Faye Show* on November 14, 1948. Yet the humorous incidents that happened in that broadcast—innocently spilling hydrochloric acid on the tablecloth, creating an unknown blue and orange mixture, accidentally dropping the mixture and causing an explosion—were all possible developments and, therefore, hilariously comprehensible to the audience. The jokes and skits heard on the comedy-variety shows in the 1930s ranged from unrealistic spoofs and satirical parodies, to fantasies and absurdities, but the sitcoms of the next decade always possessed an aura of suburban middle-class feasibility.

In terms of format, situation comedies fell into three distinctive types. Programs focused on the adventures occurring to a family residing in its own home, or on a group of recurring but unrelated characters operating a business establishment, or—if the central character was mobile and could usually be found in more than one locale—on a distinctive personality.

The most prevalent format was that which concerned the family. Here the family was invariably white, middle-class, and living in a single-family home in the suburbs. For the Andersons of *Father Knows Best,* this meant two proud parents and three energetic children, Betty, Bud, and Kathy, all residing on Maple Street in Springfield, U.S.A. For the Webster family of *Those Websters,* it entailed mom and pop and two children, Billy and Liz, living at 46 River Road in Spring City. And for the Coopers, Liz and George, who had no children in *My Favorite Husband,* it meant living in "a little white two-story house" at 321 Bundy Drive in the "bustling little suburb of Sheridan Falls." A twist to the formula was provided by *The Great Gildersleeve* where "Unk" Throckmorton P. Gildersleeve presided over rearing his niece and nephew, but

still in a friendly and predictable neighborhood in the peaceful town of Summerdale. Whatever the composition of the
domestic unit, all such programs seemed dedicated to the function asserted in the opening to *Those Websters,* that this was
"our weekly reminder that families are fun."

While most family situation comedies centered on the
adult characters, a significant variation on the motif was
found in those series spotlighting juvenile members. The prototype of these shows was *The Aldrich Family,* an eminently
successful program revolving about Henry Aldrich and his
problems with adolescence. Evolving from a Broadway show
and several appearances by the play's cast on the *Rudy Vallee
Show,* Henry and his entourage—his parents, sister, girl
friend, best friend, and other acquaintances—came to network
radio in the summer of 1939. For the next fourteen years their
program was among the highest-rated shows on the air. The
plots were ordinary, but their themes were teenaged. They
dealt with Henry's love problems, his troubles at school, or his
failure to communicate with adults. Although aimed at a typical evening audience, a mixture of adults and youngsters, *The
Aldrich Family* was the first radio series to concentrate its attention on teenagers. Programming for and about children
had always been juvenile in orientation. The Jack Arm-
strongs, Captain Midnights, Uncle Dons, and Little Orphan
Annies of broadcasting made no pretense at trying to appeal
to, or reflect, the sensitive world of the teenager. On the other
hand, adult programming in the evening hours usually
avoided juvenile characterizations unless, like Fanny Brice's
Baby Snooks, they were infantile comics. In Henry Aldrich,
however, network radio presented in prime time a vigorous
and well-intentioned image of the humorously-innocent
American adolescent.

The success of *The Aldrich Family* led to a considerable
number of imitations. *A Date with Judy,* which premiered in
1941, featured a feminine equivalent of Henry Aldrich. Where
Henry had Homer as his best friend, Judy Foster had Mitzi;
where Henry had a younger sister, Judy had a kid brother;
and where Henry's best girl was Kathleen Anderson, Judy's

beau was Oogie Pringle. Also in this format were programs like *Meet Corliss Archer, Junior Miss, Maudie's Diary, That Brewster Boy,* and *The Adventures of Archie Andrews*—all of which debuted in the early 1940s. Certainly such series involved the interactions of family members with mundane problems and comic situations, but the emphasis was clearly on the teenager in the house. The weekly opening lines to *That Brewster Boy* aptly summarized this approach, as they proclaimed:

> This is the story of an average American family, the Brewsters. You'll find people like Mom, Dad, Nancy and Joey Brewster in every town in this country of ours. Yes, that's right, you'll even find boys like Joey in every town, because Joey's problems are universal.

All these series probed the laughable consequences of teenage life. Beneath the humor, however, there was a reality which suggested that along with the comedy, there was pain in being an adolescent. Girl-friend and boy-friend problems could be agonizing for Joey Brewster or Corliss Archer; reconciling parental demands with one's own desires was often difficult for Judy Graves of *Junior Miss* and Maudie Mason of *Maudie's Diary*; and Archie Andrews encountered humiliation as well as humor when he displayed his awkwardness in adult society. In surfacing such tensions, even in a comedic context, radio pioneered in the commercialization and analysis of teenage culture through the mass media. It was a process that television, film, and popular music would develop more fully in the next two decades.

Radio situation comedies were middle-class morality tales. The American family was portrayed as a vital institution in which love, trust, and self-confidence were best developed. Altercations resulted from misunderstanding or a lack of trust; disruptions in social harmony were short-lived and trivial; personal weaknesses were often the signs of tolerant characters; and love and respect permeated the narrative. A disgruntled Henry Aldrich might scream "Jeepers!" "Yikes!" or "Gee Whiz!" when commanded by his father; yet, ultimately, he followed Pop's advice. Dagwood Bumstead in *Blondie* might be indecisive and awkward, but he possessed a compassionate personality. Chester A. Riley, the blue-collar hero of *The Life of Riley*, could exclaim "What a revoltin' development this turned out to be," but listeners knew that the "development" would not destroy Riley's warm family life and sympathetic nature, and that circumstances would not stay "revoltin' " for too long. When Ozzie Nelson was not on speaking terms with his next-door neighbor, it was because of an insignificant misunderstanding that would be happily resolved before the program ended. In this manner, sitcoms provided social lessons. They instructed audiences in the value of friendliness, honesty, respect, tolerance, and other salient attitudes of a middle-class society. These secular parables proffered models which cleverly combined comedy and social message, an act of camouflage that made the sermonizing more palatable. In the process, they became powerful communicators of the values necessary for the well-being of a civilization of competitive, success-oriented citizens seeking still to maximize harmony and eliminate dissension.

The moralistic dimension of domestic situation comedies was appreciated by religious institutions. In 1947 the International Council of Religious Education polled ninety percent of the Protestant churches in the United States to discover which programs most faithfully portrayed American life. Criteria used in the selection was heavily moralistic, for according to a spokesman, the following standards were applied to each series:

> (1) Is the family true to life? (2) Is the family democratic? (3) Does the family recognize God in its everyday living? (4) Is there a high moral tone to the program? (5) Is the sponsoring commercial in keeping with the best in family life? (6) Is there a high type of humor? (7) Does the family show an interest in the community, the nation and the world? (8) Is the home the center of security and strength? (9) Does the program portray the family as improving?[36]

The list of the top ten programs, in alphabetical order, illustrates that American churches well understood the social and moral values underlying radio sitcoms:

Adventures of Ozzie and Harriet (sitcom)
The Aldrich Family (sitcom)
A Date with Judy (sitcom)
Fibber McGee and Molly Show (sitcom)
The Greatest Story Ever Told (religious drama)
Life Can Be Beautiful (soap opera)
Ma Perkins (soap opera)
Mayor of the Town (sitcom/drama)
One Man's Family (soap opera)
Pepper Young's Family (soap opera)

Important, though less numerous, were those situation comedies centering on a business establishment or a distinctive character. *Duffy's Tavern,* set in a pub, and *Meet Me at Parky's,* located in a restaurant, presented humor-laden stories of plans going astray but leading inevitably to happy resolution. *Duffy's Tavern* featured musical interludes and guest stars like Bing Crosby, Rex Harrison, and Ida Lupino, but its sustaining dimension was the weekly predicament encountered by Archie, the manager, and his tavern regulars, Clifton Finnegan, Clancy the cop, and Miss Duffy. One week it might be Archie scheming for a raise or preparing the tavern for the visit of a celebrity, the next it might involve Miss Duffy's constant search for a husband or Archie trying to win money to make the books balance. In *Meet Me at Parky's,* Nick Parkyakarkas, the popular stooge for Eddie Cantor and Al Jolson in the 1930s, emerged as the proprietor of a diner in which problems and beef stew mixed with guest stars, musical interludes, and a cast of comedic regulars that provided a Greek-American equivalent of Duffy's Irish-American realm.

Despite the absence of a home and family, this type of sitcom paralleled the domestic format. Instead of a house in the suburbs, the bar or restaurant functioned as the friendly domicile in which comedy and narrative unfolded. Instead of a family, it offered the host as a surrogate head-of-household, and the recurring characters as the remainder of a pseudo-family. Like the domestic sitcoms, moreover, the problems encountered in these comedy shows were always upliftingly resolved.

Those comedies stressing a distinctive leading character

still adhered to the sitcom mixture of a central personality augmented by surrounding comedic characters. Such principals were neither married nor tied to a business establishment, and therefore possessed physical mobility that rendered location secondary to individuality. By the early 1940s, the *Jack Benny Program,* the leading comedy-variety series of the preceding decade, had evolved into a situation comedy of this type. Benny's escapades took place at home, in his neighbor's house, at his studio, on a train, at the race track, or wherever his writers felt it advantageous to locate their leading character. Without a spouse, family, or home, Benny was free to be situated anywhere consistent with the characterization built into his role.

Both men and women appeared as central characters in this sitcom format. The empty-headed blonde secretary, Irma Peterson, dominated the antics that occurred on *My Friend Irma.* Connie Brooks was the man-chasing center of *Our Miss Brooks.* And the hillbilly actress, Judy Canova, portrayed herself as an unmarried celebrity on the *Judy Canova Show.* Also in this style were programs like *Life with Luigi* which concerned the adventures of Luigi Bosco, a recent immigrant from Italy; and *Amos 'n' Andy* which in 1943 had become a half-hour, non-serialized sitcom vascillating between the schemes of George "Kingfish" Stevens and the dreams of Andrew H. Brown. Although such programs avoided the extreme mobility of the *Jack Benny Program,* their stress on personality and their de-emphasis of family and locale clearly distinguished them in terms of format.

One of the most interesting variations in this type of programming was *Maisie.* The series appeared in 1945 and concerned the assorted adventures of Maisie Revere, a world-wise beauty from Brooklyn who, between show-business flops, drifted from city to city encountering varied occupations, fresh men, and comedic situations. Based on the "Maisie" movies produced by Metro-Goldwyn-Mayer, this radio series presented an image of liberated womanhood that was far ahead of its time. For the sake of respectability, Maisie was engaged to Eddie Jordan, whom she affectionately described as a "good-lookin', sweet-talkin', lovable, lazy, no-good bum." She was only able to commiserate with her fiance, however, during those shows that unfolded in New York City. But Maisie's antics took place throughout the world. She was immediately at home in a London dress shop or a Texas dude ranch. She railroaded, drove, sailed, or hitchhiked her way from one locale to another, demonstrating an earthy understanding of men that was punctuated by a solid slap across the face of the more aggressive wolves. Maisie, however, possessed the proverbial heart of gold. Whether she was working at a blood bank, or spending her last dollar to buy movie tickets for a group of orphans, she was a singular figure whose feminine assertiveness and independence was even more striking when compared to the stereotyped dumb-blonde stupidity of Irma Peterson and the husband-hunting predictability of Connie Brooks.

The Decline and Fall of Radio Comedy—
Into the Fifties

Broadcast comedy did not die in the late 1940s and 1950s. It simply ceased to be relevant to American society. With the advent of television and its success in post-war society, listeners became viewers, audio fell victim to video, and the function of radio humor was preempted by its televised competition. During this period there were many reasons offered in explanation for the decline of comedy on the air. Some said there was a paucity of new talent, others suggested that the jokes were repetitive and boring. It was TV, however, that was the most significant undermining element.

Ironically, the chief catalyst in this development was a comedian whose radio career had been less than spectacular. Milton Berle had never had a successful radio series. In the period from 1936–1948, he had appeared on such forgettable programs as Gillette's *Community Sing, Stop Me If You've Heard This One, Let Yourself Go,* and the quiz show, *Kiss and Make Up.* His biggest break in radio, the *Milton Berle Show,* appeared in the 1947–1948 season, but was hindered by Berle's comedic delivery. His was a screwball comedy style involving physical antics and a group of stooges giving vent to their eccentricities which appealed more to the studio audience than to listeners sitting blindly before a radio. Berle was forever making asides to his live audience and apparently deviating from the script with spontaneous quips and gestures. As a television comic, however, the clowning and mugging that were pointless on radio became important assets. Berle entered television with his *Texaco Star Theater* on September 21, 1948, and within weeks he was the most popular entertainer in the nation. His program of October 19 gained a Hooper rating of 63.2 in metropolitan New York City. This translated to a 92.4 percent share of the televison audience, the highest rating ever achieved by a radio or TV program. What was most important, however, was that Berle's phenomenal popularity stirred other comedians into considering the new medium.

Eddie Cantor had long been sympathetic to television. In the 1930s, he warmly lent his support to the emerging medium, suggesting to readers of radio fan magazines that television would "stage such entertainment as the world has never dreamed of,"[37] and, "Television is a reality. Those who doubt it is here are like the fellows who stood in the streets a few years ago when gasoline engines went by and said—'do you think they're real?' "[38] Yet, like most successful radio comedians, Cantor was leery of TV once its potential had been revealed by Milton Berle. He seemed as much fearful as critical when he told an interviewer in early 1949, "What I have seen on my television set, with the exception of one or two shows, has been the worst kind of junk. It seems that the producers of this trivia have only one thing on their minds—is it cheap!"[39]

Cantor was not alone in his distaste for TV. Jim Jordan was reluctant to join the new medium, telling *Variety,* "We pioneered in radio, but we aren't as ambitious as we were 25 years ago, so we'd rather sit back for a while and let the young blood do the groundwork."[40] Jack Benny seemed more irrational when he wrote in 1946, "Hold off television. Science be damned! Long live radio!"[41] He retained this circumspect attitude for many years for, although he made his television debut in January 1949, **Benny** did not quit his radio career until 1955. Groucho Marx also belittled the new entertainment form, focusing his ridicule on the technological quality of TV in 1949. As he wryly explained it, his was, at best, an ambiguous feeling toward television.

> Despite all this, with bloodshot eyes, I watch this ogre night after night, bored but nevertheless fascinated by its potentialities. How long can I survive on radio against this new monster? When will I become a public charge? Long before midnight this quivering and erratic entertainment signs off, and in a semi-stupor I grope my way to my bedroom where the butler feeds me a double seconol, places ice packs on my eyes, and until I fall asleep chants over and over the immortal words of George M. Cohan, "Don't worry, kid, the only thing that will keep the average American at home is a dame." Thus, reassured I fall into a deep slumber broken by a violent nightmare, excessive sweating and an unconscious desire to jump out of the window.[42]

Similar consternation came from Bob Hope and Al Jolson. Edgar Bergen, however, took a different line of attack. He assailed the degenerating state of comedy writing, claiming that the switch to TV was as much the fault of bad radio comedy as it was fascination with the new medium. He argued that radio wore out talent, sapped the energy, and drained the imagination. "We don't expect our major novelists to turn out a new book every single year," he complained, "but we expect radio comedians and their writers to turn out a frothy half-hour, smart as new paint, every single week."[43] In one of the more public displays of such waning confidence in broadcasting, Fred Allen's poetic stooge, Humphrey Titter, recited the following rhyme on the *Fred Allen Show* on November 28, 1948:

> Farewell to you, old radio jokes,
> I can stand you no longa.
> California weather, and Airwick,
> Azusa and Cucamunga.
> Who's on first?, Jolson's age,
> How big is Durante's nose?
> Cantor with his five daughters,

How sloppy are Crosby's clothes?
Allen's Alley, the "mean widdle kid,"
Sinatra looking so bowly.
Fibber McGee and his closet—tell me,
Which twin has the Toni?
"Coming, Mother," "Listen, Gracie,"
At long last I've made my decision.
So, farewell to you, old radio jokes,
I'm turning to television.

Not all of the leading comedians were apprehensive about
television. George Burns and George Jessel felt that while TV
would create its own artistic dimensions, a good comedy act
from vaudeville or radio could be readily adjusted to its
demands.[44] Ed Wynn, the first big-name star to produce a
kinescoped television series on the West Coast, enthusiastically
supported television. In the summer of 1949, he publicly
chided his colleagues who were afraid to enter it. According to
Wynn, most of the great comedians were hiding their fear of
TV behind criticism of the quality of the kinescope process
and other technical issues. "I have fear, too," he added, "fear
whether the public will accept me on television. But I don't
fear TV itself."[45]

Although network officials clearly recognized that, in the
words of CBS vice president Hubbell Robinson, Jr., "No one
in his right mind can seriously doubt that television is going
to be a dominant factor in American life,"[46] American radio
produced some of its most impressive comedy programs in
these twilight years. In the late 1940s, comediennes emerged
with more importance than ever before. In Eve Arden (Our
Miss Brooks), Lucille Ball (My Favorite Husband), and
Marie Wilson (My Friend Irma), CBS belatedly began to
feature women as the central characters in situation comedy.
Until that time there had been few significant female humorists in radio. Former vaudevillians like Gracie Allen and
Fanny Brice, as well as younger talents like Judy Canova, Cass
Daley, and Joan Davis, enjoyed popularity. Yet, relative to the
number of male comics in broadcasting, the role of the come-
dienne had been limited. In tapping this source of talent, net-

work radio ushered in a new generation of comics who would easily and successfully make the transition to television.

Radio also produced several new male comedians in this disintegrative period. Among the fresh and distinctive talents unveiled by the networks were Morey Amsterdam, Art Carney, Alan Young, Dean Martin and Jerry Lewis, Bob Elliott and Ray Goulding, Danny Kaye, Danny Thomas, and Jackie Gleason. Whether as supporting comics, or as stars of their own programs, except for Bob and Ray, none of these comedians achieved sustained popularity in radio. Instead, their skill would be more fully realized in motion pictures and some of the most successful sitcoms in TV history.

When it appeared as a national program, the *Bob and Ray Show* presented listeners a style of comedy not heard regularly since the demise of Stoopnagle and Budd in the 1930s. They were improvisational comedians whose zany parodies and satires exhibited flawless timing and pace, cleverly hiding the fact that much of their routines was ad-libbed. The two men met at WHDH in Boston in 1946, and emerged on NBC in 1951. Bob and Ray presented a variety of comedy skits on their show, but they were especially effective in lampooning radio programming. They spoofed soap operas with their own series, *Mary Backstage, Noble Wife*; children's programs in *Jack Headstrong, the All-American American*; and detective shows in *Mr. Trace, Keener Than Most Persons*. In the character, Wally Ballou, they presented an image of a bumbling, inept radio newscaster, forever butting into the interview and often cutting short the interviewee. In Steve Bosco they presented an inebriated sportscaster whose "scoops" were usually eight days late—he had all the details except the score. More specifically, their character Arthur Sturdley was a parody of Arthur Godfrey, and was played as a fierce bore, among whose claims to fame was a collection of Hawaiian shirts with a clean change of ukulele to go with each.

In a medium that was losing its battle with television— and this meant the curtailment of elaborate comedy programs and the emergence of a new function for radio—Bob and Ray suited the new role of radio. Unlike comedy-variety or situation comedy, their snappy patter style was concise and easily encapsulated into short time periods. An audience that turned to radio for music and news could appreciate the pace and precision of their humor. At an earlier date, without an orchestra, stooges, or guest stars, their type of comedy would have been incongruous with popular tastes. But in the mechanical and austere style of programming in the late 1950s and 1960s, the *Bob and Ray Show* was perfectly adjusted.

The networks did not surrender easily to TV. In the 1940s they hoped to halt the erosion of programming by bringing celebrities to situation comedy, and by creating new comedy shows. Gertrude Berg was brought back to CBS in *The Goldbergs* in 1949, Ronald and Benita Colman in *The Halls of Ivy* in 1950, and Cary Grant and Betsy Drake in *Mr. and Mrs. Blandings* in 1951 represented an attempt to present man-and-wife teams on radio. Some of the more memorable new programs included *Hogan's Daughter* (in 1949 with Shirley Booth), *December Bride* (in 1952 with Spring Byington), *My Little Margie* (in 1952 with Gale Storm), *I Love Lucy* (in 1952 with Lucille Ball and Desi Arnaz), and the *Steve Allen Show* (in 1950). All enjoyed varying degrees of popularity, but radio's days as a creative aspect of American comedy were drawing to a close.

The collapse of radio humor was most dramatically demonstrated in the fate of Fred Allen. Long the sardonic conscience of his craft, Allen's wit had a touch of intellectuality and critical sarcasm that was unique among broadcasting comics. This probably explains why he enjoyed large audiences in his many years on radio, yet never reached the massive ratings that Benny or Cantor—with their more generalized comedy—were able to garner. Allen disliked the threat that television posed to his profession. He once summarized his animosity by remarking, "Television is a triumph of equipment over people, and the minds that control it are so small that you could put them in the navel of a flea and still have enough room beside them for a network vice-president's heart."[47] He was likewise disgusted with the quality of humor

as it was produced in postwar radio. He attacked the commercialized nature of broadcasting where Hooper ratings were
more important to the networks than the quality of its programming. He wryly joked, "Next time you see a radio comedian with his hair gray before his time, his cheeks sunken, his
step halt, please understand that he isn't dying. . . . He has
been caught with his Hooper down, that's all."[48]

Allen made his feelings abundantly clear when on January 30, 1949, he appeared as the narrator of the NBC public
affairs program, *Living—1949*. The show presented a history
of American humor, and in its final minutes questioned Allen
about the present state of radio comedy.[49] He portrayed radio
as the point "where humor has reached its lowest ebb," and
accused it of having lost all spontaneity since "the king of the
airwaves, the comedian, is rarely more than a mouthpiece for
his writers." Allen cited a recent routine between himself and
Jack Benny as containing more than a grain of truth, for when
Allen began to insult his "rival," Benny replied that Allen
would not dare belittle him if his gag writers were present.
"Radio's so-called wit," according to Allen, "tends to be the
product of tired gag writers and hectic gag sessions."

This bitter assessment was prompted not only by Allen's
analysis of comedy, but also by a combination of ill health,
chronic rancor with the network over censorship, and destructive competition with the phenomenally popular giveaway
program *Stop the Music!* While he could manage high blood-
pressure and wary NBC censors, the prizes and money offered
on the giveaway show ultimately ended his career.

In an energetic, fast-paced hour, *Stop the Music!* called
people at random throughout the United States, offering
prizes and cash worth over $30,000. Within months of its
premier in March 1948, it had captured the imagination of
post-Depression and postwar Americans and had lured millions of listeners away from Allen on NBC and the *Edgar Bergen-Charlie McCarthy Show* on CBS. With television already
siphoning off listeners, the *Fred Allen Show* collapsed in the
Hooper ratings. Where in January 1948, the program was
coasting near the top with a 28.7 rating, by March 1949, it had

plummeted to 7.9. Allen parodied *Stop the Music!*, he ridiculed it, and he even offered to pay $5,000 to anyone missing a call from the giveaway program because he was listening to the *Fred Allen Show*. Allen was beaten by the end of the 1948–1949 radio season.

Feeling that broadcasting had reached the point of buying listeners with expensive premiums and frenetic quiz shows, he left radio in 1949 a disillusioned man. His attempts at television were poorly received, and when Allen appeared in the early 1950s as a panelist on the television show *What's My Line?* his career had sadly degenerated. He was still a panelist on that program when he died of a heart attack in 1956 at the age of sixty.

The experience of Fred Allen in the declining years of radio programming was shared by other comics. In November 1952, Bob Hope was switched to a morning program airing daily from 9:30 to 9:45 A.M. By January 1953, moreover, the ratings on his evening program had dropped to 5.3. Eddie Cantor concluded his career on radio as a disk jockey in the early 1950s. The great topical wit, Henry Morgan, ended up in 1957 as the host of an insignificant quiz show, *Sez Who?* The brilliant newcomer, satirist Stan Freberg, produced in 1957 one of the most original comedy-variety programs in radio. It vanished after fifteen weeks, however, because he could find no sponsor. Among those comedians who remained loyal to radio into the mid-1950s, Jack Benny and Edgar Bergen generated ratings that were at best dismal shadows of the popularity they once commanded.

Radio comedy, which had been integral to mass entertainment for a quarter-century, had ceased to be important to an increasingly television-oriented society. As radio returned inexorably to its original format of music and talk programming, its function as the purveyor of popular humor evaporated. Yet, broadcast comedy left a significant legacy. Comedians had revived radio in the early 1930s, and in the process made it one of the most effective antidotes to mass despair and the Depression. Later, to a nation preoccupied with individual struggle and international combat, radio comedy was a reassuring link with a happier world in which hostility was effectively offset by fantasy—where all gruff bosses were like Dagwood's Mr. Dithers or Rochester's Jack Benny, and where global conflagrations were soothed by the antics of Eddie Cantor's spirited personality, or Fibber McGee and Molly's relaxed self-confidence. While it was reassuring to millions that most of the successful comics of television in the 1950s had their roots deep in the history of broadcasting, it was disappointing to some that the imaginative realm of humor created by radio was gone. Radio comedy had served its audiences faithfully as companion, advisor, model, and entertainer. Its passing into irrelevance in the 1950s signaled the end of a distinct era in the history of American civilization.

3

Detective Programming and the Search for Law and Order

The detective story is one of the most compelling and well-received forms of creative expression in the American popular arts. With its emphasis upon plot, character, and method-of-detection, this genre has enjoyed broad success in literature, film, television, and radio. As a format specifically in radio, the detective story emerged in the late 1920s and within two decades was one of the most prolific types of evening broadcasting. Attesting to its popularity, one critic deduced that by 1945 there was an average of ninety minutes of crime programs broadcast daily, and each show was heard by more than five million listeners.[1]

The strength of the detective drama was twofold: it was relatively inexpensive to produce and it was attractive to listeners. Detective shows were much less costly than the comedy and variety programs which abounded in radio. Furthermore, they returned a significantly higher homes-per-dollar-invested figure than other genres. In 1950, for instance, *Variety* estimated the weekly costs of the *Jack Benny Program* and *Bing Crosby Show* to have been $40,000 each, while the production costs on all but a few detective dramas ranged from $4,000 to $7,000.[2] Although detective shows seldom entered the higher ranks of the Hooper or Nielsen ratings, these less expensive programs delivered more listeners per sponsor's dollar than did prestigious comedy and variety series. The average evening mystery program in 1950 garnered 267 homes per dollar, while variety-musicals gained 215, general drama 187, variety-comedy 163, and concert music 123.[3]

The financially-inexpensive nature of detective series was notable in terms of the acting talent they utilized. Comedians like Eddie Cantor or singers like Al Jolson received lavish contracts before agreeing to perform, but detective dramas did not need expensive "name" actors. What was necessary was a clear and distinctive voice and an ability to read fluidly and to inject emotion into the performance. Producers and advertising agencies had scores of skilled radio actors from which to choose. This situation ensured relatively low wages and obscurity for most chosen performers. Thus, favorite detective series such as *The Shadow, Mr. District Attorney,* and *Nick Carter, Master Detective* might enjoy lengthy popularity, but actors, such as Bret Morrison, Jay Jostyn, and Lon Clark, had to expect lower salaries and much less publicity than other broadcasting personalities.

This is not to say that the creators of radio detective series were so niggardly as to ostracize big-name talent. Edward G. Robinson in *Big Town* and Basil Rathbone in *The Adventures of Sherlock Holmes,* both commencing in the late 1930s, enjoyed great success for several seasons. Yet, not until the threat posed by television was clearly understood by network and agency producers was there an effort to lure Broadway and Hollywood celebrities into detective programs. Then, in the late 1940s and early 1950s, such luminaries as Dick Powell in *Richard Diamond, Private Detective,* Joel McCrae in *Tales of the Texas Rangers,* George Raft in *Rocky Jordon,* and Humphrey Bogart and Lauren Bacall in *Bold Venture* appeared in their own successful series. By this date, however, the future of radio as a significant source for drama was already doomed; and rather than a period of flowering in which stage and motion picture personalities became an integral part of radio production, this was a terminal phase in which radio sought to survive by artificial methods.

In terms of entertainment, detective shows afforded listeners the opportunity to mix the deductive process of intellect with the emotional intensity of fantasy. These programs came in various trappings. But whether it was a traditional private investigator, a detective from a local, state, or federal police agency, an amateur sleuth, or an international crime-solver, the heroes of these series engaged the imagination and transported listeners along a deductive route toward a solution of the crime. On one level, the process was simply resolving puzzles: the writers had hidden clues within the story, and the detective and his audience moved inexorably toward fitting those clues together to name the guilty person or persons. The detectives, however, were more than diverting logicians; and the audience was more than simply listening.

Several scholars have suggested convincingly that detective heroes in the popular arts must be viewed as social and cultural symbols, that more than pure entertainment, such characterizations are important reaffirmations of the moral values at the base of American civilization. Sociologist Orrin E. Klapp contended that heroes were of singular importance because they possessed certain socially-desirable attributes (courage, devotion, prowess, etc.) and they pursued significant goals (overcoming evil, championing justice, etc). Klapp noted that even in this secular era when religious faith was declining, the belief in temporal heroes continued to thrive. In this way, heroes in American culture assumed semi-divine personalities, operating in place of the traditional saints and demi-gods of Western civilization.[4]

Charles J. Rolo took the religious implications of American heroes even further, contending, "The detective story is modern man's Passion Play." The detective, he pointed out, is akin to the average man with his shortcomings: Nero Wolfe overeats, Sherlock Holmes uses cocaine, and Michael Lanyard is a reformed thief. Yet, in Rolo's view, all detectives have "The Call," all are Saviors, possessing the saving Grace that would bring all their observers to the Light. As he argued:

> The hero suspects everyone, for the murderer is Every-man; the murder is the symbol of the guilt, the imperfection, that is in all of us. In his search for the hidden truth the hero is exposed to danger, thrashes about in darkness, sometimes suffers in the flesh, for it is by his

travail that the Savior looses the world of its sins. In the detective's hour of triumph, the world is, for a moment, redeemed. Unconsciously, we die a little when the murderer meets his fate, and thus we are purged of guilt. . . . We exult that Truth has been made known and that Justice has prevailed.[5]

The detective story in general, and its dramatization in radio in particular, functioned as more than a form of fun. Throughout its story and structure, the detective program communicated important moral lessons to American society. The essence of those messages lay in the fact that within each drama the villain never won and the hero never lost. Whether or not a program openly declared that "crime does not pay," this was the message expounded in all broadcasts. In a civilization established upon the principle of private ownership of property—be it land, coin, or life—such a proclamation is a functional necessity. It is an imperative that can never be communicated too often. Those who would achieve private property outside the socially-approved methods must be shown to lose. Such villains must become objects of scorn and contempt, marked as Cain so that owners within society might be on guard when in their presence, and would-be emulators might learn from their example. Radio detective series, in this manner, served as theaters in which to blend this serious lesson within a diverting context, illustrating repeatedly that antisocial villains must be reformed, incarcerated, or executed so that the society of the propertied might be secure and enduring.

The actions of radio's crime-solvers also presented a significant personal message to listeners. This communication was related both to psychological stability and social prosperity within American civilization. When Sam Spade, Johnny Dollar, Sgt. Joe Friday, Lamont Cranston, or any of the numerable detectives encountered crime, it was within a familiar pattern. At the beginning of a broadcast the hero was usually found peacefully and calmly uninvolved. With the introduction of other characters, he inexorably found himself enmeshed in trouble and was physically and intellectually challenged. Accepting this new reality and eventually solving the dilemma, the detective inevitably ended his weekly adventure with a sense of self-confidence and achievement. As these champions of justice acted out their formulaic lives, they actually provided a paradigm for effective social existence. Like the challenges which routinely confronted the fictional detectives, the developments which threaten disorder in the personal life of the listener had to be faced and overcome. The route to stability, emotional and material, was to be found only in such triumph. Detective programs, therefore, supplied millions of Americans with understandable stories of achievement within a competitive, mass society. Whether they are viewed as coping with the potentially-debilitating threat to psychological stability, or through personal labor overcoming the challenge and improving their social condition, the salutary model presented by these sleuths touched the most fundamental aspects of life in the United States.

In this perspective, detective drama attains the status of a secular Passion Play serving to fortify both the civilization and its constituency. In an earlier time and place, such stories would have been embodied in sacred scripture and exegesis. But in the United States in the twentieth century—where the victory of State over Church, and of This-World over Other-World is strongly achieved—citizens must find models in their own popular culture. Because they reached far more citizens than did detective literature or film, radio detective programs performed a strategic role in strengthening the tenor of existence within the American commonwealth.

Despite the omnipresence of social lessons within detective programming, it would be incorrect to consider this radio genre as monolithic. There was, in fact, a great deal of variation in the series as they ranged from the documentary frankness of *True Detective Mysteries,* to the comedic cuteness of *The Thin Man,* and from the intellectual precision of *The Adventures of Sherlock Holmes* to the brutality of *Pat Novak for Hire.* Significantly, there are three strategic criteria which appeared in all detective shows: 1) the attitude of the program toward crime and its solution; 2) the function of the central character's personality; and 3) the view of life and society presented in the story—and depending upon the emphasis within each series, radio detective programs can be divided into three distinctive types: Realistic Detective, Glamorous Detective, and Neo-Realistic Detective. From a study of these typologies, it is possible to gain a clearer comprehension of detective drama on the air and its relationship to American life.

The Realistic Detective

The first crime solvers in radio were Realistic Detectives. Traditional, conservative, and ploddingly rational in their approach to solving crimes, these detectives emerged in local and network broadcasting in the late 1920s. Their popularity was such that they remained an integral part of broadcasting until the end of creative programming.

The stress in the Realistic Detective series was upon the logical process by which the crime was solved. In these programs crime was an undesirable dimension of social reality, and the emphasis upon solving the mystery in an organized, dispassionate manner suggested to listeners that through such a deliberate methodology the forces for Good within society were forever at work eradicating irrational criminality. Everything in such programs, from the personality of the detective to the perspective it presented on life and society, was peripheral and without strategic value to the more realistic goal of finding the villain and thereby carrying out justice.

Typical of the early programs in which the Realistic Detective operated was the local series *Unfinished Play*. This series appeared in late 1929 on WMAQ in Chicago. In this program the emphasis upon the rational process in solving crimes was transformed into a gimmick. Each week the drama would end before the actual solution was revealed; then the sponsor, a local furniture store, would offer $200 as a prize to the listener who could provide the most acceptable ending. Writing a fitting conclusion to dramas with such titles as "The Solemn Murder," "The Mystery of the Vieux Carré," and "Murder in Studio A" certainly demanded literary talent to be judged "the best solution," but inevitably listeners had to demonstrate almost mathematical precision in solving the crime according to the clues cryptically woven into the plot. As awkward as this format might appear, it was a popular style. One of the most successful variants of this approach was the network series, *The Eno Crime Club*. The program was sponsored by the manufacturers of Eno antacid salts, and for five seasons, 1931–1936, was broadcast in two half-hour installments weekly. Described in one show as a "thrill-a-minute radio riddle challenging your detective ability," the scheme of *The Eno Crime Club* was to present in the Tuesday drama all the clues to the solution of a crime. The following day the chief characters, a somber police investigator named Spenser Dan and his assistant Dan Cassidy, relentlessly acted out the solution to the problem. The program was slow and monotonous by later radio standards, and the clichés and atmosphere of the series were reminiscent of gangster movies of the early 1930s such as *Little Caesar* and *Public Enemy*. Nevertheless, *The Eno Crime Club* was an immensely popular series, one fan magazine in 1934 terming it "the oldest, largest and most successful detective show in radio."[6]

The strength of *The Eno Crime Club* lay in its relationship to the criminality which was glaringly a part of American reality in the 1930s. This was the period in which romanticized desperadoes such as "Machine Gun" Kelly, Clyde Barrow, Bonnie Parker, and John Dillinger, as well as the countless hoodlums who made their fortunes from the sale of illegal alcoholic beverages, created in the United States a massive and well-publicized crime wave. Although antagonists on *The Eno Crime Club*, such as Finney the Slug and Pretty-Boy Gregory, were only fictional characters, listeners were certainly aware that their real-life counterparts were operating with impunity throughout the country. And when one character in a broadcast in February 1934, declared, "We need all the help we can get to catch these crooks," many listeners could readily interpolate this appeal from a fictional to a realistic context. In a sense, then, when listeners sought clues in a Tuesday broadcast and tested their results with the program the next evening, they were vicariously participating with investigative forces in the apprehension of America's criminals. In this manner, radio fostered in the impotent, potential victims of gangsterism—the members of the radio audience—a sense of self-confidence and power in the face of crime.

Still another Realistic Detective series which utilized the device of suspending the conclusion was *The Adventures of Ellery Queen*. Drawn from the successful stories written by two cousins, Frederick Dannay and Manfred Lee, the program definitely presented strong personalities. This was especially noticeable in the social and professional interaction between Queen, a writer of detective stories, his father, who was a police inspector, and Queen's female assistant, Nikki Porter. The thrust of the program, however, was upon the deductive procedure utilized in discovering the perpetrator of the crime. To underscore the importance of the intellectual process, during most of the ten years in which *Ellery Queen* was on the air (1939–1948), the broadcasts were stopped before Queen named the actual criminal, and a studio panel of renowned "armchair detectives" was asked for opinions as to the identity of the guilty party. This pattern compelled listeners to rely on their own intelligence, matching answers with such guest celebrities as playwright Lillian Hellman, film writer Harry Kurnitz, and musicologist Deems Taylor. Listeners who successfully solved the mystery, especially when the armchair detectives failed, might take justifiable pride in their intellectual accomplishment.

With their deep commitment to the process of reason, programs in the Realistic Detective format demonstrated and popularized what might be termed the "science" of detective investigation. Such shows transmitted the notion that scientific methodology, as embodied in deductive reasoning, could solve the problems of crime as readily as it was solving the problems of physics. By the 1920s a reverent faith in science had become an integral part of the mentality of most Americans. Surrounded as they were by the technological fruits of scientific processes—commodities ranging from electric refrigerators and transcontinental airplanes to the sophisticated motion picture and automobile industries—Americans developed both reliance on these products and a belief that the quandaries besetting society could be answered through analytical investigation by scientists. Such a mentality was all the more expectable in radio listeners since the invention and mass manufacturing of radio equipment were the results of just such rational research. Thus, as in scientific reality, within the realm of the Realistic Detective there were no unsolvable mysteries. No criminals went undetected, and no puzzles were unresolved. Once the most baffling radio crime was submitted to a rational analysis by human intellect—be it that of the fictional detective or of the listener—its solution was assured.

There was no better hero of crime programming who underscored this faith in scientific investigation than Sherlock Holmes. Based upon stories and incidents in the writings of Sir Arthur Conan Doyle, *The Adventures of Sherlock Holmes* began as a series in 1930 and ran intermittently until the 1950s. There was a definite warmth and human character to Holmes and his assistant, Dr. John H. Watson. This was especially expressed when in the early 1930s the program was sponsored by G. Washington Coffee. As a regular part of each program, the narrator was cordially invited into Dr. Watson's study, there to share a warm cup of the sponsor's product while Watson related another adventure with Sherlock Holmes.

There were also charming personalities in the portrayals of Holmes and Watson when in 1939 Basil Rathbone and Nigel Bruce adapted their successful movie characterizations to a radio series lasting six seasons. Bruce portrayed Dr. Watson as well-meaning, likable, yet awkward—a character who was both assistance and hindrance to Holmes. Rathbone, however, developed his character as a pillar of reason who was not so smart, however, as to be unwise. Writing in 1940 about his role as Sherlock Holmes, Rathbone noted that his Holmes "was a man of the people. He belonged to the man in the street." In further defining this character, Rathbone remarked:

There have been other great detectives in fiction, of course, but somehow they have never been able to get hold of the imagination as has Holmes. There is Philo Vance, for instance, whose exploits have been read by millions in the books of S. S. Van Dine. I played him once on the screen, but somehow, I had the feeling he was a little too smart, that he belonged to Park Avenue and not Main Street. He didn't have the common touch which Sherlock, in spite of his erratic brilliance, manages to convey.[7]

Despite such embellishments of the plot as were found in the personalities of Holmes and Watson, *The Adventures of Sherlock Holmes* must be categorized with the Realistic Detectives. These radio dramas always placed their emphasis upon the mental processes needed to solve the puzzle presented each week. In these radio versions, Holmes retained the skills of reasoning which he possessed in literature. A chemist, physicist, mathematician, and logician, Holmes relied heavily upon the sciences in coping with crime.

His abilities were nowhere better illustrated than in those situations in which he, after a short interview with a total stranger, was able to tell a great deal about that person's background. In such scenes, a spot on the clothing, a personal mannerism, or a subtle accent could be interpreted by Holmes' scientific mind to reveal the truthfulness of the stranger's statements. The world of Sherlock Holmes lacked those cumbersome personal accoutrements which often confused the operations of other radio detectives. There were no women of romantic importance in Holmes' radio adventures, no flirtations, no girl friends, no wife. There were also no fantastic disguises he had to assume in order to utilize his powers, and there was no prepossessing profession from which detective work was only a diversion. Holmes opposed crime because he was a professional consulting detective and because crime was irrational within the social order. In a sense, then, his vocation was the logical outgrowth of his disciplined mentality which, like science, understood everything in order and harmony.

The Realistic Detective series relied upon a style or formula. The clues were integrated into the plot, and the hero and audience were challenged to uncover them and solve the mystery. Some might suggest that repetition of this arithmetical pattern for weeks and years might exhaust or bore radio listeners. Yet, it was the success of these early detective dramas that would lead to a fuller development of investigative heroes. The stylized approach of the Realistic Detectives, moreover, achieved great popularity. According to the ratings from January 1932, *The Eno Crime Club* was heard in more homes than were such giants of broadcasting as Paul Whiteman, Walter Winchell, or Lowell Thomas. And in 1933, the *Sherlock Holmes* programs were more attractive to listeners than the shows of either Al Jolson or the Marx Brothers.[8]

With its emphasis upon investigation and the inevitability of apprehension, the format of the Realistic Detective series lent itself easily to dramatizations of the activities of police departments. In this way radio, as a medium of entertainment, became a salient disseminator of information regarding the achievements of law enforcement agencies. In fact, the first network detective series of importance was *True Detective Mysteries*, a series which began on CBS in late 1929 and continued on radio in various forms until the mid-1950s. Dramas in this series were taken from *True Detective Magazine* and, like this popular and stark publication, related stories which glorified the operations of police departments. These dramas, moreover, followed an effective semi-documentary style which, with its emphasis upon realism in the reenactment of actual crimes, justified its claim to be "a real story of a real crime, solved by real people, with a real criminal brought to justice."

True Detective Mysteries featured another dimension which tied it closely to law enforcement agencies. Beginning in September 1934, the series broadcast as a postscript to each program the description of a wanted criminal, offering a reward of $1,000 for information leading to his arrest and conviction. The first such description was of Charles "Baby Face" Nelson. Although the program was not responsible for apprehending Nelson, this feature strongly linked the radio series to the real world of its listeners. In fact, as *Variety* reported, *True Detective Mysteries* by 1949 was responsible for having captured three criminals through its weekly descriptions of wanted offenders.[9]

The realism that could be achieved within this format was demonstrated strikingly in the fall of 1932 when Lewis E. Lawes, warden of Sing Sing Penitentiary in New York, began broadcasting detective stories under the title *20,000 Years in Sing Sing.* With Lawes acting as the narrator, each week the program dramatized the crimes and punishments of selected inmates of the prison. This was a serious and altruistic undertaking for Lawes. He had written a popular book of the same title that inspired a motion picture in 1933, starring Spencer Tracy and Bette Davis. With the radio series, Lawes commenced an avocation in broadcasting that would last into the next decade. As late as the 1946–1947 radio season, he was dramatizing crime on *Crime Cases of Warden Lawes.* He used his earnings from these activities to fight the evil he exposed on the air. Believing that crime was often the result of poverty, or the deprivation resulting from poverty, Lawes stated that most of his salary from radio went into such projects as the construction of a gymnasium within the walls of Sing Sing, and the financing of the prison welfare fund used to assist needy relatives of the prisoners.[10]

With Warden Lawes' programs and other series in the 1930s, radio detective shows became a popular weapon in the social struggle against crime. This was especially noticeable in the number of non-network programs where, in cooperation with local, state, and federal investigatory agencies, many stations aired series which reiterated the futility of criminal activities. For several years KEX (Portland, Oregon) produced *Homicide Squad*, basing its dramas on the exploits of the local police department. *Calling All Cars,* directed on KFI (Los Angeles) by William N. Robson, as early as 1933 featured not only stories from the Los Angeles Police Department, but utilized Chief of Police James Davis to introduce the weekly stories. *Tales of the Oklahoma Highway Patrol,* broadcast in 1937 on WKY (Oklahoma City), and *State Police*

Dramas on WHAM (Rochester, New York) dealt with state agencies. And *G-Men in Action* on WNAC (Boston) in 1939 became one of the first series to focus upon activities of the Federal Bureau of Investigation.

National broadcasting, however, most effectively entered the war on crime through the creative efforts of Phillips H. Lord. A radio actor and producer in the early 1930s, Lord captured popular imagination in 1933 with his program of folksy wisdom and warmth, *Seth Parker*. Following this triumph, however, he turned his talent to creating series which blended entertainment with a glowing tribute to the law officers protecting America from criminality. For more than twenty years he enjoyed unparalleled success in such programs as *G-Men, Gangbusters, Counterspy, Mr. District Attorney, Policewoman,* and *Treasury Agent.*

All Lord's shows were, as was stated so often in the introduction of *Gangbusters,* presented in conjunction with "America's crusade against crime." In them were to be found simple reaffirmations of trust and confidence in the American system. More than dedicated civil servants, however, his heroes demonstrated a paternalistic attitude toward America and its citizenry. His characterizations of male and female police officers showed them risking life and limb to keep the common people secure. This philosophy was made obvious, for example, in the *Counterspy* broadcast of April 20, 1950, when a patriotic ex-spy told an enemy agent why, since defecting to the United States, he no longer dealt in espionage: "America has been good to me. I've found out what sense really is. . . . See all those people down there—peace of mind and a feeling of trust in belonging to a great and good country like theirs is more than even money can buy."

Phillips H. Lord underscored the realistic nature of his productions by employing police officers to act as commentators during the broadcasts. *Gangbusters,* which premiered in 1936, was narrated for most of its first decade by Col. Norman A. Schwartzkopf, former superintendent of the New Jersey State Police. In 1945 he was replaced by the retired commissioner of police of New York City, Lewis H. Valentine. In addition to impressive narrators, *Gangbusters* also featured interviews with a police official from the locale of the story being broadcast.

The use of actual police officers continued in Lord's *Policewoman* series. This program was broadcast 1946–1947, and concerned events in the career of Sgt. Mary Sullivan of the New York City Police Department. At the conclusion of each show, the real Sgt. Sullivan added personal comments, thereby making the broadcast even more realistic for listeners. Later, perhaps out of budgetary exigencies, professional actors were used in Lord's series, *Treasury Agent,* to portray Elmer Lincoln Irey, retired coordinator of law enforcement for the Treasury Department.

Most of Lord's police series enjoyed popularity with American audiences because they presented a compelling mixture of action, topicality, and morality drawn from actual police cases. This was especially true of *Gangbusters, Counterspy,* and *Treasury Agent.* Yet Lord was most successful in appealing to the basically liberal, law-respecting, and compassionate spirit of the American people in *Mr. District Attorney.* In its premier aired on April 3, 1939, Lord established the spirit of dedication to justice and altruism that marked the history of the series. In that broadcast the District Attorney, who was never given a name except "Mr. District Attorney," was elected to office and then pledged to exterminate all gangster elements within his jurisdiction. The essence of this oath was reiterated in the opening of each broadcast for the next fourteen years:

> And it shall be my duty as District Attorney not only to prosecute to the limit of the law all persons accused of a crime perpetrated within this country, but to defend with equal vigor the rights and privileges of all its citizens.

With a reassuring and paternalistic voice, the District Attorney methodically went about his crime-busting activities. While others in the programs might have demonstrated humorous or fallible personality traits, the central character was always unflappable and rational in his approach to thwarting criminals. Even though the stories and characters were fictional, it could not help but be reassuring to listeners to assume that in reality all district attorneys were the equal of the character introduced as "champion of the people, defender of truth, guardian of our fundamental rights to life, liberty and the pursuit of happiness." As proof of the widespread acceptance of this series, *Mr. District Attorney* in the period 1941–1949 was the top-ranked mystery program on radio.

In broadcasting stories laudatory of American police agencies, radio exercised a powerful influence in the maintenance of law and order in a time of great social tension. In European nations this period of economic depression and international warfare—both cold and hot varieties—precipitated momentous social upheaval as forces from the political right, left, and center struggled to gain and maintain ascendency. Within the United States, however, such patterns failed to develop as the traditional governmental forces were successful in convincing the citizenry that it best could sustain law and order. No law enforcement official better recognized the potential of entertainment radio in communicating this message than did J. Edgar Hoover. While director of the Federal Bureau of Investigation, Hoover cooperated with many producers eager to highlight the activities of the Bureau's agents. As early as 1935 he opened his files to Phillips Lord's short-lived *G-Men* series. He also provided authentic G-men to speak on local radio stations on topics such as "The G-Men and How They Do It," the title of a lecture delivered by agent N. Stapleton in June, 1936, over WNOX (Knoxville).

During World War II, and in the postwar years, Hoover saw the FBI honored in other radio series. *The FBI in Action* debuted in 1943 as only a local series on WGY (Schenectady), but Hoover obviously approved the show for the narrator was an agent from the FBI office in Albany. *The FBI in Peace and War* debuted in 1944 and presented images of his agents dealing with a wide range of criminal activities. In 1952 the transcribed series *I Was a Communist for the FBI* featured Dana Andrews as the actual double-agent Matt Cvetic, whose pose as a member of the Communist Party supplied the bureau with information on potentially subversive elements in the Cold

War era. *Top Secrets of the FBI,* a postwar series which weekly praised the bureau as "the most efficient, the most scientific law enforcement organization in the world," featured opening and closing comments by Melvin Purvis, a former agent who was famous for having shot John Dillinger.

Hoover became so committed to radio programming that during World War II he supervised the creation of an "official broadcast of the Federal Bureau of Investigation." This resulted in April 1945 in the premier of *This Is Your FBI,* a laudatory series which ran for eight seasons on the ABC network. Hoover was so pleased with these programs he delivered a lengthy statement on the opening broadcast, praising the FBI, American troops fighting overseas, and even the sponsor of the series, the Equitable Life Assurance Society. Importantly, in this speech Hoover touched upon the relationship between detective radio drama and the real world:

> It is my sincere hope that the broadcasts will enable you to know more about how to cooperate with your local police officials and every branch of law enforcement in your community. I also hope that you will come to know your FBI as a group of men and women who seek no personal glory, and who are part of a great team serving you, your family, and the Nation.

In the waning years of radio drama, producers and sponsors turned increasingly to the Realistic Detective format, and specifically to stories of police investigation, to fill the void left by departing variety and comedy programs. Thus, the formula developed in the 1930s to promote respect for law and order was being exploited in the late 1940s and 1950s to resuscitate radio. The activities of local police departments received honorific treatment in series such as *Squad Room* and *Under Arrest.* Criminals still at-large were dramatized, and their descriptions broadcast in *Wanted, Somebody Knows,* and *$1000 Reward.* The efficiency of Scotland Yard was praised in *Whitehall 1212;* and the intricacies of courts and the law were the subjects of *Up for Parole, Indictment,* and *A Life in Your Hands.* Patterned after the efficacious hero of *Mr. District Attorney,* several series also were produced in praise of traditionally-overlooked service professions. In this mold were shows like *Special Investigator; Dr. Standish, Medical Examiner*; and *Roger Kilgore, Public Defender*, a series so imitative that the opening oath of *Mr. District Attorney* was refashioned and appeared as Kilgore reciting part of the Declaration of Independence.

The Realistic Detective pattern exercised a powerful influence in maintaining popular faith in vital American institutions. By allowing listeners to investigate vicariously with the series hero—be he a fictional character like Sherlock Holmes, or an anonymous police official on *Gangbusters*—radio made Americans feel a part of the process of law enforcement. From such a feeling grew trust and support for all levels of legal organization. This was a singularly important result, for in the 1920s many police agencies had lost the public's confidence due to the scandals involving inefficiency, bribery, and collusion with criminals. This skepticism was aggravated in the next decade by the pressures of the Great Depression. Yet, beginning in the 1930s, by means of the most popular entertainment medium, the mass of American citizens began hearing of the heroic undertakings of private and public investigative agencies. Strong, positive images emerged of these self-sacrificing detectives who pitted reason, science, and technique against underworld perfidy. Such characters, then, functioned as role models, suggestive to children and reassuring to adults. This facet of the Realistic Detective format was clearly comprehended by a listener writing to a fan magazine in 1939. Developing the idea of how radio helped to combat juvenile delinquency, she commented:

> We are a nation of sometimes lax extremes. For a long while the gangster, racketeer and petty criminal, without interference—swayed the follow-the-leader emotion of our youngsters from movie screen and magazine page. Then came the reckoning. Crime gained an appalling headway. The nicest boys in the neighborhood were forming gangs; turning, despite their parents' efforts, into swaggering little hoodlums. Suddenly America took stock of herself and began tearing down in a frenzy of self-reproach the mockery of manhood she had allowed

thoughtless men to erect. The movies turned an about-face, but though they have done a fine job in rectifying a grave mistake, it is really the radio we must thank for such splendid character formers as—*Wanted by the Law* and *Gangbusters*. Taken from life, these worth-while programs give credit where credit is due. To the man with the badge. The protector of lives, home, and property. More than all the preaching in the world, these programs have taught eager little copy-cats that—Crime Does Not Pay.[11]

The Glamorous Detective

It was inevitable that radio producers and advertising agencies would alter the emphasis in the detective program to develop series in which the personality of the central character dominated the action. Writers of detective fiction like S. S. Van Dine, Dashiell Hammett, Earl Derr Biggers, and Raymond Chandler had been doing this since the 1920s. In motion pictures, the same type of glamorized characterization had enjoyed financial success beginning in the mid-1930s. Even radio had moved in that direction in the early 1930s in *The Townsend Murder Mysteries* program which featured Octavus Roy Cohen's "hayseed" sleuth, Jim Hanvey. Not until the Realistic Detective pattern had achieved solid popularity with American listeners, however, did broadcasters seriously market this new Glamorous Detective.

Where the unhampered flow of plot was primary in the Realistic Detective programs, in this new style the embellishment of characters with irrelevant or peripheral traits was as much a part of the program as the story line. Here, listeners found their traditional "whodunit" augmented with the likes of trivial conversations between the hero and the people he encountered, loquacious descriptions, comedic relationships between the hero and his partner, and even sexual tensions between male and female characters. The process of investigation and apprehension was not insignificant in these programs, and neither was the general image of the society they projected. Often, however, such matters seemed more a concession to logic than a deliberate emphasis of the program.

Instead, the Glamorous Detective series presented listeners with a personalized, attractive, and familiar recurring character that an audience could like for his charm and wit, even more than for his investigatory brilliance.

The heroes of the Glamorous Detective series, more than in any other type of mystery programming, related to listeners on a recognizably human level. The documentary-like rigidity possible in the earliest style now gave way to the hero-as-common-man, a popular theme in democratic culture. Most of the human foibles were present in the make-up of the new crime-solvers. Heroes were fat (*The Fat Man*) and lithe (*The Thin Man*); they were young (*The Adventures of Chick Carter*) and old (*The Adventures of Leonidas Witheral*); some were married (*Mr. and Mrs. North*); some were thinly veiled playboys (*Yours Truly, Johnny Dollar*); and some had questionable sexual relationships (Lamont Cranston and Margo Lane in *The Shadow*).

Many of the characters in this format were private detectives or police investigators, but a sizable number practiced other professions. These ranged from newspaper editor (*The Green Hornet*), lawyer (*Murder and Mr. Malone*), news photographer (*Casey, Crime Photographer*), clergyman (*The Adventures of Father Brown*) to magician (*Blackstone, the Magic Detective*), importer (*The Casebook of Gregory Hood*), circus acrobat (*Mr. Mercury*), and unemployed do-gooder (*The Saint*). In addition to physical and occupational differences, the Glamorous Detectives usually exhibited a wide array of personal eccentricities and personality traits that were inevitably demonstrated in the weekly broadcasts. In this regard, perhaps the most embellished of all these characters was orchid-fancier and gastronome, Nero Wolfe, who in one episode was described by his assistant as, "the smartest, and the stubbornest, the fattest and the laziest, the cleverist and the craziest, the most extravagant detective in the world."

Relative to other types of radio detectives, the Glamorous crime-solvers appear not to have taken themselves too seriously. They lacked the explicit moral tone of the Realistic style; and the self-conscious brutality of the later Neo-Realistic

Detective programs was also absent. Instead, this format was principally an entertainment form with a refreshing stress upon lightness and frivolity. Listeners might encounter the hero of *Richard Diamond, Private Detective,* breaking into song in the middle of his story. The spicy sexual banter between Sam Spade and his secretary, Effie, in *The Adventures of Sam Spade,* or between the characters created by Humphrey Bogart and Lauren Bacall in *Bold Venture,* added a sensual dimension to their broadcasts. Audiences also found as much delight as intrigue in the myriad disguises employed by the hero of *Mr. Chameleon,* or in the "Confucius-Says" type of aphorisms spouted by Charlie Chan.

This new type of detective programming emerged in the 1930s, but did not flourish until the following decade. By the 1950s when detective drama reached its zenith, two-thirds of the series were in the Glamorous style. In fact, even into the 1960s *Yours Truly, Johnny Dollar,* a Glamorous Detective program, remained viable.

The hero and series which spawned the Glamorous Detective in radio was Lamont Cranston, the "wealthy young man-about-town" who masqueraded as the Shadow. It is significant that the program began in 1930 with a Realistic format—the character called "The Shadow" being only the narrator and reader of stories from pulp magazines published by Street & Smith. By the middle of the decade, however, *The Shadow* was amplified by its writers. The character was given an alter ego, magical qualities, a love interest, and a moral purpose. He, thereby, became the investigative hero of the weekly broadcasts.

A striking aspect of Lamont Cranston was that he operated in American society as a vigilante. An independently wealthy man of leisure, he was committed to securing justice, unhampered by the legal restraints that would have thwarted official law enforcement agents. He was, moreover, a man of great prestige and influence, being on such familiar terms with Police Commissioner Weston that he could call upon Weston at any time. Cranston also avoided another social responsibility. Although he was forever accompanied by his "constant friend and companion, the lovely Margo Lane," Cranston and she were never married. In fact, although they were obviously attached to one another, except to call her "darling," Cranston usually abstained from romantic gestures or loving words around his female assistant. Freed, then, of the conditions experienced by most adult males in modern society—regular job, common status, wife and family—Cranston maneuvered on his own to bring criminals to justice. With his greatest weapon being his unique and secret ability to hypnotize men's minds so they were unable to see him, Cranston philanthropically turned his existence into a crusade to better society.

The *savoir-faire* of wealthy Lamont Cranston and the omniscience of The Shadow made for a prepossessing mythical figure who entertained listeners for twenty-four years. Most importantly, however, he symbolized the direct action not affordable to most citizens. To a complex urbanized world, The Shadow offered simple answers that emerged through vigilante processes; in a time of uncertainty, he reasserted the old morality that "crime does not pay"; and when the pressures of existence in the twentieth century produced alienation and boredom, the romantic dynamism of The Shadow provided listeners a model that was exhilarating and desirable.

The success of *The Shadow* influenced creators of radio drama to develop detective series focusing upon personality rather than the science of investigation. Frank and Anne Hummert—who had produced many of the most popular soap operas in daytime radio—developed by the end of the 1930s "the kindly old investigator" in *Mr. Keen, Tracer of Lost Persons*, a series that lasted for seventeen years. Carleton E. Morse adapted the humane characters in his successful *One Man's Family* melodrama and produced Jack Packard, Doc Long, and Reggie York of the A-1 Detective Agency and the *I Love a Mystery* series. And eminent motion picture actors Edward G. Robinson and Claire Trevor lent the prestige of their names and talents to *Big Town*, a series which related the crime-solving activities of newspaper editor Steve Wilson and his able assistant, society editor Lorelei Kilbourne.

The significance of the Glamorous Detective programs, however, lies not with the likability of the principal characters but with the coveted attributes of their fictional existences. If radio in general was an escapist medium which allowed each listener to transport himself by relating to its various entertainment forms, the Glamorous Detective programs afforded an audience the greatest opportunity to transcend reality and enter a fantasy realm of romance, action, invincibility, and rectitude.

As in the case of *The Shadow,* one of the persistent motifs in this style of programming was that of the individual hero assuming responsibility to bring justice to a small corner of the vast civilization. This pattern operated not only as a condition within the plots of the various stories, but also as a lure to the individual listener desirous of escaping his reality for a short while. Listening to the radio was a private activity. It demanded audio attention, especially when involved in a complex story or play. Its nature, thereby, mitigated against conversation and other forms of social interaction. Furthermore, the images produced in a broadcast were also individualistic, each listener experiencing within his own mind's eye the fantasy being aired. In this way the exploits of the hero, acting alone in the name of commonly-held interpretations of justice, affirmed the one-to-one relationship between a listener and the radio set. In doing so, his exploits reinforced the commitment of the listener to sit in mental solitude, to hear, and to transcend.

Reflective of this relationship, many of the Glamorous Detective series featured the exploits of an individualistic hero, operating as a loner or with minimal assistance from others. In this sense, the most appropriately titled series was *The Lone Wolf,* based on the writing of Louis Joseph Vance, and relating the adventures of the character, Michael Lanyard. Other programs, such as *The Falcon, Boston Blackie, The Adventures of Phillip Marlowe,* and *The New Adventures of Michael Shayne,* were also studies of lone wolves. Although they may have flirted or conversed with incidental characters, they wandered through civilization unable to rest because justice was incomplete. Whether they were self-righteous or casual in their approach to responsibility, ultimately they all were compelled to action. Free of restraint, save their inbred codes of justice and honor, these heroes alluringly embodied the desire of many in the audience to wander uninhibitedly.

The romantic appeal became even more compelling when the champion of justice operated within a foreign context. Such programming was alluring to Americans who romanticized foreign travel. Generous doses of intrigue, sensuality, action, and exoticism served to increase listener interest. Before World War II, with the isolationism of American foreign policy carefully reflected in broadcasting, there were few series which glorified the solving of crimes in foreign lands. But during and after the war the pattern was altered, and many crime-solving programs emerged which adapted the Glamorous Detective to a non-American society. Slate Shannon in *Bold Venture* operated a fishing boat in the Caribbean; Jethro Dumont, the hero of *The Green Lama,* fought for justice principally in the Far East; *Rocky Jordan* had its home base in Cairo; *Café Istanbul,* although transferred in its second season to San Francisco, was originally set in the Middle East; and *Dangerous Assignment, The Adventures of Frank Race,* and Orson Welles' roguish hero in *The Lives of Harry Lime* operated in a different foreign metropolis in each episode.

Other Glamorous Detectives were inherently involved in international capers because they were foreign by birth. In such instances, the exotic nature of things foreign was found by definition in *The Adventures of Hercule Poirot,* which featured Agatha Christie's Belgian detective; in *Bulldog Drummond* and *The Adventures of Father Brown,* which both involved British heroes; in *Mr. Moto,* which concerned a Japanese detective; and in the escapades of a Chinese-Hawaiian police inspector in *Charlie Chan.*

Another salient aspect of many Glamorous Detective shows was the existence of an assistant to the principal character. Those assistants who were males often brought a warm and comical personality to counteract the business-like efficiency toward which the series' heroes tended. Thus, Mike

Clancy, with his brogue and his penchant for Irish clichés, such as "Saints preserve us!" was a vulnerable complement to affable but serious-minded Mr. Keen. Archie Goodwin, the assistant to Nero Wolfe, brought his blending of working-class humor and brawn to counterbalance the refined proclivities of his employer. And Tim Maloney provided a likable awkwardness which meshed harmoniously with the intelligent and coy qualities of Inspector Mark Saber in *Mystery Theater.*

Female partners, or at least continuing female characters, played a much different role than did male assistants. In some cases they provided primarily sexual content to the stories. The hero in *Philo Vance,* for example, maintained a flirtatious relationship with his assistant, Ellen Deering; in *The Adventures of Sam Spade,* Sam routinely flirted with his secretary, Effie; and Suzy, the newspaper employee who maintained the mailbox of Alan Ladd's character, Dan Haliday, in *Box 13,* expressed her attraction to him whenever he picked up his mail.

In several other series, however, women played a more integral role in the solution of the crimes under investigation. Brooksie, the secretary and girl friend of George Valentine in *Let George Do It,* travelled with her boss, vacationed with him, and helped him with factual information which, along with his brawn, was needed in solving his cases. Margo Lane often acted as a decoy for Lamont Cranston, offering herself to be kidnapped, attacked, mutilated, or worse, in order to force the hand of the antagonist and to allow The Shadow to apprehend him. The assistant in *Nick Carter, Master Detective,* Patsy Bowen, was not as exploited as Margo Lane, but she often suffered physical and psychic torment in her important role beside her employer. And in at least two series, *Mr. and Mrs. North* and *The Thin Man* (Nick and Nora Charles), the feminine half of the detective team played a role virtually equal to that of her husband in solving cases.

Although the interaction between hero and assistant was a strong ingredient in many Glamorous Detective series, of even greater significance was the relationship of the hero with representatives of the police. Since in radio fiction both private and public investigators labored to rid society of crime, listeners might well have expected to discover an amicable working relationship between the two. This, of course, was the case in many shows. Lamont Cranston, if not The Shadow, usually kept the cooperative Commissioner Weston informed of his plans. Phillip Marlowe often stressed the fact that he worked closely with the police. And Boston Blackie was so intimate with public law enforcement that in one program he even assisted the police department in raising funds for underprivileged children.

Nonetheless, many private detectives and amateur sleuths exhibited a distaste for police officers. This caustic relationship ranged from sarcasm to open contempt. Such tension usually emanated from the rivalry of the two investigatory units seeking a solution to the same crime. Mike Waring, The Falcon, carried on a wise-cracking feud with both a lieutenant and a sergeant on the police force. Philo Vance at least respected rank and was cordial towards the district attorney, but bitter toward Police Sgt. Heath. Richard Diamond, however, possessed a mocking disdain for all police officials. And most of those series dealing with international locales had principal characters who at least distrusted foreign police.

This anti-social rivalry was often a function of the heroes' methods of operation. The Green Hornet, for example, never intended to undermine police authority. In fact, in the early years of the series one broadcast each month would feature as a public service a special Law and Order Roundtable—an educational forum in which racketeering in the United States was discussed by authorities. Reflecting popular sentiment, one fan magazine in 1940 warmly praised *The Green Hornet* for presenting the strong moral lesson that "criminals, in the long run, always must face the bar of justice."[12] Nevertheless, the hero Britt Reid—who was publisher of *The Daily Sentinel* as well as being the vigilante, the Green Hornet—often came into conflict with the local police. In several broadcasts this antagonism resulted in warrants for the arrest of the Hornet, or in the police chasing the hero through the city at high speeds.

The producers of *The Green Hornet,* which premiered in 1936, created in Reid and his oriental valet and confidant, Kato, avenging angels for whom the ends justified the means. On many occasions their activities aroused police anger because they interfered with investigations already underway. The pair also frustrated law officials because they often overlooked legalities in their championing of justice. Even when it ceased to be broadcast in the evening hours and, by the early 1950s, was aired in the late afternoon for juvenile listeners, the series continued to demonstrate patterns that insulted police but were acceptable and natural outgrowths of Britt Reid's personal struggle against criminals.

The theme of tension between the police and the hero of a radio series had a literary origin. In many instances this pattern was a vestige of the hard-boiled detective stories which emerged from pulp literature in the 1920s. The motif gave the hero a more ruggedly individualistic flair and accentuated the personal triumph inherent in his ultimate victory. Although the attitude was more often found in the Neo-Realistic Detective series, many Glamorous Detective programs, adapted from literary roots, retained aspects of their antecedents. Certainly, radio tamed characters such as Raymond Chandler's Phillip Marlowe and Mickey Spillane's Mike Hammer when they appeared in their own series. Yet, Britt Halliday's Michael Shayne—at least as interpreted by actor Jeff Chandler in *The New Adventures of Michael Shayne* in 1949—retained much of his resentful attitude toward police investigators.

In those series where such tensions were noticeable, however, their intention must be understood as a literary residual rather than a subversion of law and order. The antagonism was a function of the detective's personality. And, as if to prove that no anti-social message was implied by this pattern, the private eye and the police usually reconciled their differences when the case was solved and the program concluded.

Regardless of relationships or personality traits, the most obvious ingredient in the Glamorous Detective series was adventure. It was the attractive element that captivated and maintained most listeners, for it was the aspect which most contrasted with the familiar routines of the listener's reality. Dan Haliday in *Box 13* started his weekly adventures by placing a classified ad in the local newspaper—a bold invitation to action reading, "Adventure wanted. Will go any place, do anything." Richard Rogue of *Rogue's Gallery* was apparently more selective in his adventures, boasting in one broadcast that "I collect murders." The hero of *Leonidas Witheral,* a man described as "a New England schoolmaster who looks like Shakespeare and is always getting mixed up in murder," transformed the pedantic world of a school administrator into a life of activity and danger.

Sex was another adventure vicariously experienced by listeners of the Glamorous Detective series. This was especially the case when virile and unattached young heroes of programs such as *The Falcon, Frank Race, Phillip Marlowe,* or *The Lone Wolf* were relating their stories. On the other hand, more esthetic than sexual were the activities of heroes in series, such as *Nero Wolfe, The Saint,* and *Gregory Hood,* as they continually pointed out the relatively more-civilized features of good wine, furniture, orchids, and art. Whatever their behavioral characteristics, however, all Glamorous Detectives were meant to touch the imagination of the audience and to entertain. Perhaps, therefore, the best epithet describing the intent of such programming was frivolously uttered by Simon Templar, The Saint, when a client thanked him for solving a case. To the expression of her gratitude, he replied, "Don't bother. It was fun."

One of the most glaring oversights of the Glamorous Detective format was the absence of a significant number of detective heroines. While women were featured in the broadcasts as stenographers and sex objects, in only a few instances were they the principal characters. In these rare cases, however, the programs were either so cliché-ridden or denigrating that they where short-lived and insignificant. *Meet Miss Sherlock,* which was broadcast in the mid-1940s, concerned the investigative adventures of Jane Sherlock, who was introduced as "as smart a little gal as ever stumbled across a real live clue." Sherlock, however, was not a private detective, but a buyer for an exclusive department store owned by the mother of Peter Blossom, the young lawyer to whom Sherlock was engaged. A more traditional, yet tritely written, undertaking was *The Affairs of Anne Scotland*, written by Barbara Owens, directed by Helen Mack, and starring Arlene Francis. This program premiered in October 1946, and featured Francis as a private eye who worked irritatingly independently of the police and became involved in solving crimes in her own manner. The series was heard on the West Coast and endured only one season.

Candy Matson, however, was the most successful female detective produced in radio. It originated in San Francisco in 1949, and for two seasons was broadcast on NBC stations in the West. Matson was a full-fledged detective who aptly handled guns and recalcitrant antagonists. The writers, however, could not help portraying her both as a pin-up girl and a private eye. Thus, in the opening of one broadcast, the announcer described her:

> Figure? She picks up where Miss America leaves off. Clothes? She makes a peasant dress look like opening night at the opera. Hair? Blonde, of course. And eyes? Just the right shade of blue to match the hair.

As a fitting finale, when the series was canceled in 1951, the writer caused her to become engaged to her male rival on the police force and to announce plans to abandon her career in favor of becoming a housewife.

As mentioned in connection with the Realistic Detective, the only serious image of a female investigator was the *Policewoman* series produced by Phillips H. Lord and spotlighting incidents from the thirty-five year career of Sgt. Mary Sullivan of the New York City Police Department. Those heroines who emerged as Glamorous Detectives, however, all lacked credibility and dignity. Given the serious portrayal of women in other genres of radio broadcasting, the conclusion must be drawn that detective programming, like the radio western, was dominated by masculine values and attitudes. To survive, female characters—whether principals or assistants—had to reflect this condition. To have expected solid, creative characterization of fictionalized female crime-solvers would have been to presume a set of non-sexist preconditions which, of course, were absent from American society as well as from detective broadcasts.

The Neo-Realistic Detective

The appearance of a new style of detective programming in the late 1940s and 1950s represents an important development in the history of broadcasting. While crime had been an anti-social activity in earlier detective formats, the hallmark of the emergent Neo-Realistic format was its emphasis upon crime as a symptom of deeper social sickness. The likable personalities that dominated the Glamorous series now gave way to a group of disillusioned, embittered men who reluctantly went about their professions. These characters usually expressed an abusive tone when dealing with others—be they clients, criminals, police, or bystanders. They also articulated a general disdain for most of the positive symbols of civilization and social order. Instead of stressing the rational process of crime detection found prominently in the Realistic pattern, these programs emphasized ugly crimes investigated by brutalized detectives existing within a depressingly grim environment. There was nothing inspirational in the weekly introduction to *Twenty-First Precinct* which described its environment as

> just lines on a map of the city of New York. Most of the 173,000 people wedged into the nine-tenths of a square mile between Fifth Avenue and the East River wouldn't know if you asked them that they lived and worked in the Twenty-First. Whether they know it or not, the security of their homes, their persons and their property is the job of the men of the Twenty-First Precinct.

There was a desensitized, new realism in these programs, a degrading view of life and society well summarized in a typical opening to a broadcast of *Pat Novak for Hire*.

> That's what the sign out in front of my place says, "Pat Novak for Hire." It's the easy way because down here on the waterfront in San Francisco you can't afford to wait

your turn. If you're gonna make a living down here, you
gotta do everything you can. And you gotta be out of the
henhouse by sunup. Even then it doesn't work out always
because you get trouble tax-free. It's like leukemia: there's
nothing you can do about it. There's no way to duck it.
You might as well try to start a conga line in a cathedral.

Ranging far beyond the scope of the other styles, the Neo-
Realistic Detective programs were reflections in radio of the
sullen realism of hard-boiled detective literature and of *film
noir*. The revolution in detective fiction created by authors
like Dashiell Hammett, Raymond Chandler, and Mickey Spillane represented a re-evaluation by an urban and technological society of a literary art form with its roots in the nineteenth century. By "updating" detective characterization, the
authors of hard-boiled detective stories effectively severed
their linkage with Poe and Doyle, and produced a psycho-
sociological brand of literature which meshed with modernity.
The new authors placed their heroes squarely within what
Chandler called "the bitch city," the squalid ugliness of modern urbanity—a landscape that John Cawelti succinctly described "as a wasteland, as a man-made desert or cavern of
lost humanity."[13] Within that existential locale, the brutal
heroes plied their trade with jaded sensibilities.

In cinema, the atmosphere of the hard-boiled style was
captured in several features of the 1940s, but especially in the
murky pessimism that pervaded *film noir*. These films of the
seamy quality of urban life enjoyed great popularity in the
second half of the 1940s. In their dark, psychoanalytical outlook, films like *Nightmare Alley, Cry of the City,* and *The
Naked City* probed with pessimism the condition of civilization in postwar America. The Neo-Realistic Detective was the
attempt by radio to emulate the success of other popular art
forms in expressing this condition.

Radio, however, suffered from a precondition not nearly
as pervasive in literature or cinema: censorship. The argument
over what could and should be placed over the air was almost
as old as radio itself. Network officials, advertising agencies,
directors, and even writers were well aware that their pro-

grams could easily enter any home, thereby making the right of choice inherent in books and movies less relevant in radio. There was, therefore, a constant concern among the creators of radio shows that they might offend listeners. Compounding the problem, detective series had been a chronic point of contention in broadcasting, as many critics throughout the 1930s and 1940s assailed crime series for being disruptive to adult society and harmful to juvenile minds. Because of such potential and actual criticism, detective shows were fairly tame. Sex was usually innocently present, and words as common as "guts" and "damn" were stricken from scripts. This pervasive self-censorship caused one critic in 1954 to berate their "virginal innocence so far as murder and mayhem are concerned."[14]

Despite the limitations inherent in radio, the Neo-Realistic Detective format was a significant approximation of its literary and film forerunners. While earlier radio detectives seemed to symbolize civility being called to rectify injustice, the Neo-Realistic Detectives lived in a world of injustice and seemed at times to approximate incivility themselves. Within this mood of criminality and social failure, the new detectives were relentlessly drawn into conflict. Such was the masochistic confession of Chicago newspaperman Randy Stone, hero of the *Night Beat* series, when he admitted that "like an iron filing, I was drawn to the magnet of unhappiness." To him, this meant a world of pain and failure—dramatically juxtaposed to the real environment of most radio listeners which he described as a world of "success, promotion, love, and friendship."

Listeners could not help reacting to the fearful picture that these detectives presented. In their purview, the greatest cities of the country—New York, Los Angeles, Chicago, San Francisco—were criminal cesspools with only a cadre of depressed public and private investigators defending them from anarchy. Police Detective Danny Clover, principal character on *Broadway Is My Beat,* spoke of all such cities when he described the downtown of New York as "from Times Square to Columbus Square—the gaudiest, the most violent, the lonesomest mile in the world." If a Sherlock Holmes or a Nick

Carter inspired in the audience a quiet confidence in the pur-
posefulness of detective activity, even in victory the Neo-
Realistic Detectives left listeners with uncertainty.

In theme and content, these series pioneered new dimensions in radio. If murder continued to be the criminal's
favorite act, it was now accomplished with noisy pistol shots
interrupted by morbid groans and punctuated by the explicit
thud of bodies collapsing to the floor. Yet, nontraditional
crimes were investigated. Themes such as juvenile delinquency
and anti-Semitism could be found in *Broadway Is My Beat.*
Dragnet related stories of children running away from home,
adolescent girls posing for lewd pictures, drug addiction, and
the abandonment of children. In programs like *The Line Up*
and *Twenty-First Precinct*, both police dramas in the 1950s,
brutal new dimensions in radio crime were treated as investigators became involved with such matters as the bombing of a
politician's home, the strangling of a sixty-year-old woman,
muggings, contract murder, and attacks on police officers.

To match the new types of crime, Police Lt. Lew Dana in
The Man from Homicide demonstrated similar frankness as,
for instance, when he graphically described the dying reactions
of a beautiful woman who had just been shot: "Her face relaxed, and it was a beautiful face, even in death." Such explicitness was also observable when the hero of *Night Beat*
portrayed the scene in the room of a murdered man: "We
found McMasters lying on his bed, the rumpled silk counter-
pane was slowly changing from chartreuse to crimson. Two
bullets had ripped holes in him through flesh and bone."
And sometimes, as in *Jeff Regan, Investigator*, realistic description could become crude personal observation: he was "a big,
heavy-set man wearing a dirty Panama hat. . . . He had hair
in his ears."

The most colorful writers of such series were David
Friedkin and Morton Fine. Their poetic style in depicting
New York City in *Broadway Is My Beat* is a striking example
of a writing flare which was generally absent from radio. In-
dicative of their naturalism, in one episode they described
Broadway in the summer:

> In the summer heat Broadway is a wasteland—sullen, a
> place of regret. It's a time when the breeze puffs in from
> the river, dies suddenly before it touches your dampened
> cheek. The time when you wake up already exhausted,
> then pause before your office door and consider arson.
> Broadway fans itself with a newspaper, and finds fascina-
> tion watching a fat fly crowd against a sweating window.
> The thing to do is to give up—except you've got a job,
> except you've got to pay the rent, pick up the check, buy
> the beer, leave the tip, meet the installment. July or not,
> you've got to make a living, kid.

The heroes of this format were trapped in an existential
dilemma. Sensing what the French philosopher Jean-Paul
Sartre meant when he said that "hell is other people," these
detectives were condemned by their profession to operate in a
world of ugly people. Out of such a moral, emotional, and
physical contradiction, the Neo-Realistic Detectives emerged
with hatred for their existence. Such was the lesson in an NBC
program in 1949, *Dyke Easter, Detective*:

> Be a detective! Shadow people! Make big money! I'll bet
> I've spent two years of my life waiting on street corners,
> watching for people who never showed up. Do you like
> rain? Tell me about it at 2 o'clock in the morning.

Like all such sleuths, Easter lived with a pain he was unable to
share. This type of hero had no such companion as a girl
friend or a flirtatious secretary—love in the world of these detectives was contemptuous, since revealing an openness to
human warmth was only a sign of exploitable vulnerability.
Should such a character make an attempt at developing a relationship with a woman, he was doomed to failure; and a collapsed love affair meant only more self-castigation, as with
Dyke Easter when he bitterly admonished himself: "The
tougher they are, the harder they fall. Dyke Easter—whip him,
shoot him, tear his heart out. He got paid for it, didn't he?"

The investigators were a hard-boiled, tough breed. Lt.
Dana explained it to a petty criminal he was beating to get
information. "If I'm tough," he sneered, "it's because guys like
you have made me tough." "The bitter Lt. Dana," as one
character called him, reaffirmed his reputation at the opening

of each weekly program when he sneered, "I don't like kill-
ers." This characteristic of the Neo-Realistic Detectives was
accurately diagnosed in Dyke Easter when his love interest re-
jected him saying, "You're not lonely, your anger keeps you
warm." Police Lt. Ben Guthrie, the principal character in
Blake Edwards' gritty series, *The Line Up*, more graphically
punctuated this feeling of anger and frustration. In the broadcast of June 21, 1951, after being rescued by police from a
band of robbers who had kidnapped and terrorized him,
Guthrie turned and drove his fist deep into the face of his
handcuffed chief antagonist.

Still another important theme in many of these series was
a disdain for the wealthy. This was not a rejection of money
since none of the Neo-Realistic Detectives was a do-gooder
who solved crimes without compensation. Instead, their scorn
was focused on the rich leaders of society who, through their
money, had purchased privilege. The hero of *Pat Novak for
Hire,* for example, scorned the power of money—a power that
was amplified because of his relative poverty and impotence
within society. This antagonism also existed in police investigators such as Lt. Dana who sarcastically noted to one wealthy
client that, regarding justice, $9 million spoke much louder
than his police department.

In probing the content and meaning of the various Neo-
Realistic Detectives one cannot help but be impressed with the
array of series heroes created by actor Jack Webb. Working
with gifted writers like Richard L. Breen, Herb Margolis, and
James Moser, with talented young actors such as William Conrad and Raymond Burr, and primarily with director William
Rousseau, Webb in the late 1940s developed a singular detective type whose sarcasm and toughness were the essence of the
Neo-Realistic style. Under various names, and in different
contexts, Webb refined his character in *Johnny Madero, Pier
23, Jeff Regan, Investigator, Pat Novak for Hire* and *Dragnet.*

Even when it premiered in April 1947, *Johnny Madero,
Pier 23* was different from other radio detectives. The reviewer
for *Variety* termed it "a hard-hitting, fast-moving item that
carries a good deal of punch in its dialog."[15] That dialog

would be the undoing of the series, for in early 1949 it was unexpectedly cancelled by Mutual because, according to the president of the network, the writers could not tone down their characterizations. Madero was a caustic, quick-tempered type who owned a boatshop on San Francisco's Embarcadero, but hired out as a detective after hours. As Madero explained his lifestyle in one episode, "I rent boats and do anything else you can blame on your environment." The most striking feature of the series—beyond the incessantly rude banter the hero carried on with everyone he encountered—was the hatred for society which he betrayed in all his undertakings. It was a characteristic Webb further expanded in *Pat Novak for Hire.*

Pat Novak, like his predecessor, was a lessor of boats on the docks of San Francisco. But now on ABC, Webb had an artistic freedom he apparently lacked before. The scripts were riddled with the clichés that had become associated with hardboiled detective stories. A beautiful woman entering his room, for example, was described as "like 118 pounds of warm smoke" and possessing a smile "like a furnace full of marshmallows." Another *femme fatale* in Novak's life had "a voice like a bowl of warm stew" and "she made Cleopatra look like Apple Mary." Novak's weekly nemesis was Police Lieutenant Hellman, described as so mean "he wouldn't give his wife an aspirin if she had concussion of the brain." And the difficulty in solving a case was "like trying to follow a grain of rice in a Shanghai suburb." Nevertheless, through the overextended similes, Webb's character emerged as a powerful but unstable hero with emotional traits bordering on psychosis. In a few exchanges of dialogue, Novak could change from an ambivalent flirtation with an attractive woman, to an unguarded threat against her life, bitterly promising that, "I'll dirty you up like a locker-room towel." There was nothing middle-class about Pat Novak—he was the *lumpen* hero, alienated and mean within a society of normal people. Novak confided that "the only honest guy I know" was a recurring character in the series, Jocko Madigan, whom he described as "an ex-doctor and a boozer."

Webb's fictional character was clearly drawn from literary

inspiration. The hard-boiled formula, as manifest in Webb's interpretation, created a new style in detective programming. In a sense, he admitted this in an episode of *Jeff Regan, Investigator,* a CBS series in 1948, when the following exchange took place:

> *Client:* Regan, you've got a nasty way of talking.
> People don't talk to me like that.
> *Regan:* Yeah. Well this is a brand new crowd of people, frosty top, and we talk like we feel.

The naturalism demonstrated in the "brand new crowd" of antisocial heroes created by Jack Webb had one serious drawback—their personalities were more frightening than reassuring to listeners. Even though victorious in combatting crime, they were never characters from whom audiences could obtain constructive impressions. If the importance of detective programming lay in communicating socially-beneficial paradigms, the negative attributes of Webb's heroes invariably destroyed the salutary lessons created by their weekly triumphs.

With the debut of *Dragnet* in late 1949, Webb compensated for this shortcoming and produced one of the most powerful interpretations of police activity in American popular culture. In the character of Sgt. Joe Friday are to be found many of the attributes of Johnny Madero, Pat Novak, and Jeff Regan. A cold and disciplined personality, Friday mechanically went about his duties for the Los Angeles Police Department. From the opening overview of the city as a reservoir of criminality, to the closing bittersweet announcement of the prison sentences for the guilty, *Dragnet* projected an image of a corrupted civilization defended by dedicated but dis-spirited police, crushed by the enormity of imperfection.

Dragnet utilized a realistic, semi-documentary style that was accentuated by specific references to numbered regulations in the Police Code, by frequent interjections of extraneous material—the request for a glass of water in the midst of a strategic confession, the detailed listing of the contents of a murdered woman's purse, a witness who last saw a runaway child when she came out the side door to empty the garbage, an accurate reproduction of the sound of a photographer in a darkroom printing a picture—and by the monotoned enunciation of the actors which sounded more like a newsreel interview than a radio drama. In this manner, Sgt. Friday became a believable hero, something lacking in Webb's earlier characters, to whom listeners could relate. He became as much a part of the police force as any real-life officer.

The greatest appeal of the program, however, was its underlying moral tone. *Dragnet* utilized irony and understatement to suggest that the capture of a criminal on one broadcast did not mean that others were not committing similar crimes. This can be best illustrated with reference to the broadcast of December 5, 1950. The drama involved the plight of two seventeen-year-old girls who had been lured into the "dirty, rotten business" of pornography. One girl, who had had a "good family, good training" before coming to Hollywood to seek a career in the movies, drowned herself in the ocean, leaving only a repentant note saying, "I'm sorry." Police investigation led to a photographer who printed for Friday a lewd photo of the drowned girl, lustfully assuring him, "Bet you get a kick out of this one—real beautiful girl." The second girl led Friday to two men who had taken and distributed the "filth." They eventually were convicted of rape and lewd conduct. The story was a powerful indictment of pornography and the exploitation of gullible young women. In a moment of morality meant for the audience, Friday preached, "As an organized crime it's one of the most vicious and insidious rackets that exists today." To make its point more poignant, the broadcast ended on a note of irony with the surviving girl accepting a job as a carhop—where she could wear "cute uniforms"—hopefully reassuring the police: "Never can tell, might lead to something."

Because they appeared at the close of the creative era in radio programming, the Neo-Realistic Detective series never attained the popularity enjoyed by the earlier formats. Even though *Dragnet* was the most influential police drama in the

1950s, it is most remembered as a television series which began in 1952. Yet, these series were clear signs of important
developments within American society. They represented a
clear determination in postwar America to come to grips in a
more brutally frank manner with the vices and imperfections
of civilization.

Detective programming in the 1930s and 1940s, even
when dealing with actual police problems, avoided confronting the causes of crime. If *Gangbusters* or *Mr. District Attorney* showed criminals being apprehended, it was always as if
their capture would bring justice and harmony to reality. The
Neo-Realistic Detectives, however, made no pretenses about
their world. They showed environment spawning criminals
and suggested that even though a few villains were now in
prison, the social conditions that created them were still operative. Where the Realistic and Glamorous Detectives usually
possessed a quality of *deus ex machina,* the Neo-Realistic
heroes were earthy people enmeshed in earthy problems.
There was no solid, happy resolution at the end of their exploits, only a hiatus until they could resume their perpetual
struggles—this, they suggested, because the environmental
conditions that bred crime could never be altered by their insignificant weekly achievements.

A cynic might contend that the sex and violence entering
radio by way of the Neo-Realistic style was only an unsophisticated attempt to thwart the rush of listeners to television. This
explanation, however, fails to appreciate the cultural import
of such programming. The Neo-Realistic series were only part
of a great liberal upheaval in American popular culture in the
postwar years. In film, literature, popular music, television,
and radio, interest turned to realistic appraisal of civilization
in the United States. The search to understand the roots of
crime was only part of this reformistic attitude. Bigotry, prejudice, discrimination—their result so horrendously revealed in
Europe at the close of World War II—were powerfully exposed in the cultural media. Through the documentary format, citizens were appraised of problems never popularly dis-

cussed in the past: delinquency, the rearing of children, foreign involvement, divorce, the inadequacy of educational facilities, sexism, and the decay of the cities.

Psychological themes filled novels, movies, and dramas as the process of re-evaluation—a rational investigatory approach not dissimilar to the methodology of the radio detectives— turned to the individual as well as to society. It was, however, a period of debate which inevitably raised questions of how much freedom could be balanced against order. By the early 1950s, about the time radio was undergoing its metamorphosis, the forces of reaction had gained an upper hand, momentarily arresting the process of national introspection.

The Neo-Realistic Detectives attacked crime in a manner compatible with the time that produced them. Products of the late 1940s, they helped to expose imperfections within the American system. In this light, rather than a slick promotional gimmick designed to lure would-be television viewers, these series were positive cultural achievements with intimate ties to progressive realities.

Regardless of the format in which they appeared, detective programs were a significant manifestation of American social principles. More than any other type of adult programming, with the exception of religious broadcasts, detective shows invariably presented listeners with moral models. Certainly, they entertained audiences and sold commercial products, but they also championed the simple pattern of Good over Evil, Truth over Lie, and Civilization over Anarchy. Ultimately, these programs were secular allegories of the middle-class, property-owning society which spawned them; and their heroes were agents of bourgeois America, there to tell criminals and citizens alike that crime did not pay, and that good was always victorious.

As simple as it may appear, this was a vital function. A liberal-democratic nation such as the United States, disdaining totalitarian mechanisms for enforcing governmental will, must persuade its citizenry of the rectitude of its system. Since dissidence is relatively tolerated, and therefore always a viable alternative, methods of suasion must be diverse and potent. In this light, radio detective programming takes on political nuances. These series were not, however, the product of any political conspiracy. Indeed, because they were not, detective series were free of artificiality and pretense. Instead, emanating from the natural proclivity of a social arrangement to maintain its validity, the radio detectives were champions of law and order in the broadest sense of the term.

4

Westerns:
From Shoot-'em-ups to
Realism

The western was the most underdeveloped popular genre in radio. While "cowboy" heroes abounded in novels, magazines, and films, their appearance in radio programming left much to be desired. For the most part, western broadcasts until the early 1950s were designed with children in mind. Although there were several noteworthy series in the 1930s and 1940s that presented mature stories within western contexts, most programs featuring recognizable, recurring western heroes were written to please juvenile audiences. It was not until the premier of *Gunsmoke* in 1952 that a realistic western program was successfully developed for adult listeners. Unfortunately for radio, however, *Gunsmoke* and the other adult series it inspired were unable to blunt the growing ascendency of television over radio broadcasting. Thus, radio realized the potential of the western at precisely the time it was becoming secondary to television as a medium of mass entertainment.

It is ironic that the western failed to flourish in radio, since as a genre it was a purely American product which enjoyed long-standing popular and critical attention. The western was developed in the nineteenth century by such writers as James Fenimore Cooper and Ned Buntline. They related stories of the spread of American civilization through the wilderness, and offered home-grown heroes for an expanding nation. In the present century, the western was refined by a group of writers which included Zane Grey, Max Brand, William Macleod Raine, and Clarence Budington Kelland. These authors, who fully understood the western formula and the variations possible within it, turned out hundreds of titles which spread the genre to a vast audience. In the process, the western became enshrined as a truly American art form possessing a significant relationship to the pioneer ethos of the nation.

Critics have found in the western a fertile field in which to seek the relationship of popular art to social realities. Some have seen the western as a form of folklore, while others relate it to militarism within society. The western has been interpreted in terms of Marx and Freud, as well as Christ and John Calvin. And intellectual pluralists have sought to understand it in terms of psycho-social imperatives, artistic necessities, and structural adaptability. Such overwhelming attention from laymen and critics, however, was not directed toward the western as manifest in broadcasting. Here, it remained immature and stunted until its full realization could have little impact upon the listening public.

The Classical/Juvenile Western

Speaking in 1938 before a group of students at Columbia University, comedian Eddie Cantor remarked that the tastes of children determined much of the business of radio. He contended that in the home, children usually possessed a priority on the family radio. According to Cantor, "If there is one radio in the house the child will probably get the program it wants."[1] The implications of this statement are significant for they suggest that producers, writers, and sponsors were well aware of this pattern among listening families. And given the hours during which children were at home and awake—from the late afternoon following the dismissal of school, until the early evening when they went to bed—Cantor's speech suggested that until approximately 8 P.M. radio sought to entertain mixed audiences of juveniles and adults.

Nowhere was this syndrome more obvious than in the western series. From the earliest productions, such as *Rin-Tin-Tin Thrillers, The Lone Ranger,* and *Tom Mix Ralston*

Straight Shooters, to those programs which emerged in the 1950s, like *Hopalong Cassidy* and *Wild Bill Hickok,* western heroes labored for young listeners. Invariably, the programs were sponsored by producers of bread or breakfast cereals, both traditionally youth-oriented accounts. *The Lone Ranger,* for example, which was heard at 7:30 P.M. for most of its life on radio, in the 1930s was sponsored regionally by several bread companies, and throughout most of the 1940s and into the 1950s, it was paid for by General Mills for its Kix and Cheerios cereals.

Although other types of programs broadcast during the hours children were at home avoided catering to juveniles, the western series were oriented toward youth, due in part to their similarity to the so-called B (budget) westerns of the cinema. From their earliest years—as far back as *The Great Train Robbery* filmed in 1903—movie studios churned out hundreds of such films. They were inexpensive and rapidly-produced movies whose plots were strongly formulaic, but whose principal ingredient was action. In feature after repetitive feature, stars like William S. Hart, Hoot Gibson, Buck Jones, Ken Maynard, and Tim McCoy managed to "head 'em off at the pass," save the town from "low-down sidewinders," capture "bushwackers," and other assorted clichés of the formula. Film historian William Everson has pointed out that although many such films did appeal to adults, B westerns were produced primarily for youngsters.[2]

One of the formats radio westerns borrowed from such motion pictures was the pairing of the star with a comedic partner. The device allowed writers to blend humorous relief with the seriousness of the hero's undertakings. Sometimes the partner was a crusty old-timer who offered not only mirth, but a grandfather-image to youthful listeners. Characters like Gabby Hayes on the *Roy Rogers Show,* California Carlson on *Hopalong Cassidy,* and Packy on *Straight Arrow* brought to their series not only distinctive personalities, but a mature and reliable strength which was a reassuring balance to the bold forcefulness of the central character. A popular variation on this motif was the elderly man telling stories of the West to children. This was most fully developed on the *Tom Mix* programs in the early 1930s when "the old wrangler" would sit before a group of youngsters and relate the adventures of Tom Mix.

The most common pattern in the hero-partner relationship was that in which the "sidekick" produced more laughs than assistance to the central character. Jingles on *Wild Bill Hickok* was a slow-witted type who offered little essential help to the star. In *The Cisco Kid*, Pancho was a Mexican buffoon whose strong dialect and penchant for malaprops seemed more appropriate to vaudeville than evening radio. Language difficulties also provided humorous opportunities for other partners. On *Hawk Larabee* in the mid-1940s, sidekick Somber Jones specialized in puns, and malaprops abounded in the vocabulary of Sleepy Stevens, the partner on the *Hashknife Hartley* series in 1950.

One of the most interesting arrangements was that in which children assumed the role of partner. This certainly allowed youngsters an easier chance to identify with the program. But it also limited the realistic potentialities of the series. There was always something unbelievable about young Bobby Benson being the owner of a ranch and actively solving mysteries with his adult employees in *Bobby Benson and the B-Bar-B Riders*. And somehow Little Beaver, the ward of Red Ryder, seemed incongruous with the action in the *Red Ryder* broadcasts. Even the occasional appearance of Dan Reid, the young nephew of the Lone Ranger, inhibited the maturity of that program. One early western series, *Young Forty-Niners,* over WENR (Chicago) in 1933, maximized the effect of injecting children into the western when it made three youngsters on a wagon train the central characters of the series.

Given the frequency of partnerships in the classical/ juvenile western, it was a rare series in which the hero operated alone. Only in a few instances—for example, Buck Jones, the B western personality, in *Hoofbeats* in 1937; and Jed Sloan, the hero of *Tennessee Jed* in the mid-1940s—did such westerns appear. Ironically, their failure to gain popularity with listeners rested in part with their inability to generate humor in the personality of a serious hero.

This is not to suggest that all partners were *sub rosa* comedians who hindered rather than advanced justice. Tonto, the loyal Indian companion on *The Lone Ranger,* was a dignified and valuable comrade to his *kemo sabe* (a Potawatomi phrase meaning "faithful friend"). Tonto was a strong character whose intelligence and dedication often placed him in strategic operations without which the Lone Ranger could not have brought law and order to the West. The friendship between the two men, moreover, demonstrated a depth and honesty which existed in no other radio western. Tonto expressed the profundity of that comradeship in an anniversary broadcast in 1953, when he solemnly pledged to the Lone Ranger, "Kemo sabe, long as you live, long as me live, me ride with you."

Still another debt owed by the radio westerns to the cinematic B western was the exaggerated and simplistic reality they portrayed. The radio cowboy in the 1930s or 1940s might just as readily break into song as he would fisticuffs. Several stars of "singing cowboy" films, for example, developed radio series in which music was an integral part of the production. Although Johnny Mack Brown failed in his series in this format, both Gene Autry and Roy Rogers appeared in long-running programs. As late as 1950, the former star of the defunct *Tom Mix* series continued the pattern of the crooning western in *Curley Bradley, the Singing Marshal.*

Such programming seemed unable to escape the heritage of the many country-and-western music shows that pervaded early broadcasting. Since the first popularity of country music recordings in the late 1920s, radio had been a favorite medium for singers and musicians of this style. Performers like Bradley Kincaid and Carson Robison and His Buckaroos had well-received programs during the early 1930s. With the increasing popularity of *The Grand Ol' Opry,* which debuted on WSM (Nashville) in November 1925, barn dance broadcasts abounded. Series such as *National Barn Dance* on WLS (Chi-

cago), *Barnyard Jamboree* on WOWO (Fort Wayne), and
Renfro Valley Barn Dance on WLW (Cincinnati) helped
establish in the minds of the listeners the notion of western
stars as singers. Into the 1950s Gene Autry and Roy Rogers
dedicated half of their weekly broadcasts to music. Perhaps the
most striking example of this syndrome was *All Star Western
Theater,* a West Coast series in the late 1940s, which featured
B western personalities such as Tex Ritter, Jimmy Wakely,
Donald "Red" Barry, and Allan "Rocky" Lane. The program,
however, spent most of its time spotlighting the singing of Foy
Willing and the Riders of the Purple Sage.

Despite the contrivance of a singing hero, the central
characters in the radio western had impressive and manly
qualities. They were often introduced as the fastest, smartest,
or best in the history of the West. The hero of *Hopalong Cassidy,* which appeared in 1950 as a transcribed series, was presented each week as "the most famous hero of them all." Roy
Rogers was billed as "the king of the cowboys." Buck Jones'
adventures on *Hoofbeats* promised young listeners to be
"thrillin', red-blooded . . . crammed with action and excitement." And *Red Ryder* always promised "stories of the West
that'll live forever." One of the most extravagant introduc-
tions was that which in 1935 presented *Bob Sterling, American
Ranger.*

> The early West of 1850 was a fabulous country where gold
> could be had for the taking, and men could become mil-
> lionaires overnight. But it was also a lawless country
> where men lived by the rule of the gun. Against the forces
> of evil attracted by the easy wealth to be had, the de-
> fenders of law and order were almost helpless. The one
> bulwark standing between the settlers and the criminal
> element was a body of men who had dedicated their lives
> to the war against crime. These courageous men, who
> daily rode hand in hand with death, were the American
> Rangers. And of all this group whose noble deeds became
> a tradition, the most outstanding was Bob Sterling. He
> could outride, outrope and outshoot any man west of
> the Rockies. But his life hung constantly by a hair for
> there was no western badman who had not vowed to kill
> him at the first opportunity. But Bob Sterling seldom

rode alone—his constant companions were fat, little Mexican, Pablo—as deadly with a knife as most men were with a gun—and weather-beaten old Panhandle, who knew every trick of the gunfighter, including how to beat him to the draw by shooting through his holster.

In the masculine world of the radio western, the role of women was supportive at best. For the most part, females were creatures to be protected honorably, and indulged when it was practical. No hero was married, and none developed serious ties with women. Like medieval knights, these western figures perceived women as images of beauty and domesticity. In this manner, Red Ryder in one episode was anxious to provide emotional and financial support for his Aunt Duchess who was overworked and seriously ill because "she's a woman and keeps thinkin' she's an iron man." The Lone Ranger and Tonto exhibited nothing but honorable intentions in the broadcast of June 30, 1947, when they picked up two young women stranded in the wilds and gentlemanly transported them to town. Even after Dale Evans and Roy Rogers were married in real life, their relationship on radio remained that of buddies who sang duets, rather than man and wife in love with each other. But Hawk Larabee best epitomized this quality of western gentility when he defended a young woman in distress, remarking, in stereotypic dialect, "I'm jest a feller from Texas that don't like seein' a dern saddlebum yellin' at a perty girl."

Only in two important series did the central character approach women in sensual terms. In both cases the relationships were no more than flirtations which never prevented the resolving of injustices. On Gene Autry's *Melody Ranch,* women were often attracted to the singing cowboy. These romances led inevitably to a serenade, but never to more serious involvement. The one series that did produce a philandering hero was *The Cisco Kid.* The program premiered on WOR (New York City) in 1942 and became a Mutual and syndicated feature for many seasons. Although Cisco performed the traditional chores of righting the evils of villains, in the first seasons he essentially was cast as the "Latin lover" who spent as much time kissing señoritas. Insincerity permeated Cisco's relationships with women, however, and the role was basically unbelievable. Interestingly, the series was more successful when, in a later version, it appeared in a traditional vein, with Cisco toning down his functions as a Casanova and paying stricter attention to chasing desperadoes.

Although the Cisco Kid was a Mexican character, the stars of radio westerns were champions of a society that was dominated by Anglo-Saxon standards. For the most part, these were WASP heroes, attuned to the fundamental mentality of the nation. Although in the history of the real West there were Swedish, German, and Afro-American characters, they were not to be found among the principals of the radio western. Traditional Irish names like Mix, Cassidy, Dalton, and Reid linked central characters with one of the more industrious nationalities to settle in the United States. British names also abounded—Rogers, Jones, Hartley, Preston, Sterling, Adams —and established the kinship of such heroes with the Founding Fathers and the Pilgrims.

In many instances, moreover, it was possible to know the villain immediately by the non-English nature or questionable character of his name or nickname. Tennessee Jed in episodes in 1947 struggled against the greatest cattle rustler in America, a character named Sanchez de los Riveros-York. The Cisco Kid bested a fiendish criminal called El Culebra ("the snake"). Hopalong Cassidy captured evil-doers such as a Chinese named Chung who shotgunned his victims, a confidence man named Skaggs, a murderer and bank robber named Bart Cranbaugh, and a "sweet bunch of cutthroats" called the Three Jacks Gang and composed of men with "shady" names such as Link, Slim, Big-Ear, Soapy, and Frenchy. And the Lone Ranger, who fought badmen for twenty-two years, encountered villains with names such as El Diablo, the Crimson Prophet, the Hawk, Jackal, the Cimarron Kid, and the Sandusky Gang.

Despite the fact that most classical/juvenile westerns were formulaic and repetitive, it would be incorrect to consider them inflexible. In several instances these series altered their formats and improved because of it. During World War II, for example, it was possible to reflect concern for the war in western dramas set in either contemporary contexts, or in the days of the Old West. This was most effectively accomplished by *Tom Mix* and *The Lone Ranger*. In September 1939, less than one month after the outbreak of war in Europe, the producers of the *Tom Mix Ralston Straight Shooters* announced their intention to use the series to foster patriotism and "clean thinking" among their youthful listeners. According to their statement, the program would be made more relevant by promoting "wholesome entertainment," "worthwhile educational information," and "inspiration for better living."[3] What it became, however, was one of the strongest propagandizing programs during the war. Throughout the conflagration Mix and his ranch hands battled Axis spies and saboteurs. In 1942 the sponsors of the show even offered, as a premium from Ralston cereal, a *Tom Mix Commandos Comic* which strongly asserted the American cause. Mix struggled until the end of the battle. Lest his audience feel that the victory over Germany meant the end of the war, Mix was there on V-E Day to remind listeners that the war in the Far East was not finished. On the broadcast of May 8, 1945, he lectured, "We've shown Hitler and his gang that we know how to lick bullies and racketeers, but we've still got a big job to do for our brothers, and our cousins, and our uncles, and our dads who are still fighting the Japs."

To reflect national concern with World War II in a western set in the nineteenth century was a more difficult achievement; yet, *The Lone Ranger* accomplished this through the use of allegory. The series had a history of involvement with the war. Even before the United States entered the battle, Kix cereal offered as a premium, in November 1941, a "Lone Ranger Blackout Safety Belt." In the broadcasts of August 10 and 13, 1945—less than a week after the dropping of atomic bombs on Hiroshima and Nagasaki, and one day before the Japanese government surrendered on August 14—the series dealt allegorically with the implications of the impending peace. The first program dealt with a meek sheep rancher, named David Bell, who was actually a physician who had lost his medical self-confidence. Bell's pacificity contrasted dramatically with a belligerent neighbor whose bullying of his son precipitated a nearly-fatal accident. Only when Dr. Bell regained his professional confidence and administered to the wounded child was death averted. The story ended on a compassionate note with the headstrong father, now defeated and pacified, reciting the Lord's Prayer. The second program was even more directly related to the war. It concerned a range war between cattlemen and homesteaders that was thwarted by the Lone Ranger and by the transcending love of a rancher's son and a farmer's daughter. The pacifistic point of the program was underscored when Tonto suggested that the West was a vast territory where with tolerance and understanding people of differing persuasions could live together. The farmer's daughter summarized the spirit of the broadcast, and the feeling of most Americans, when she noted at the conclusion of the fighting, "Farmers can get along with cattlemen. It's a big West....There'll be no more fighting, no more blood on the land." Aired at the end of three and one-half years of international warfare, these broadcasts were striking appeals for humility, gentleness, tolerance, and peace, now that the United States, reluctant at first to go to war, had tamed the bullies and resolved the global dilemma.

While only a few Western series were adapted to treat themes of World War II, more widespread was the revision of these programs with respect to issues of racial tolerance and equality. Throughout the 1930s, Mexicans, Orientals, blacks, and Indians were usually portrayed as inferior to the bold white heroes. In the postwar years, however, themes such as brotherhood and racial justice made notable inroads in westerns. With the major exception of Tonto, early westerns presented few flattering images of non-white characters. Tom Mix's black ranchhand, Wash, was pictured as a slow-witted dolt who added little to the action of the program. Bob Sterling's "fat, little Mexican" assistant, Pablo, sounded like a Latin Stepin Fetchit. Both the Cisco Kid and Pancho were modelled after common stereotypes of the Latin American as a rascalish lover and a lazy clown. And a local series in 1933, *Pat Barnes' Bar-Z Ranch* on WENR, featured Barnes providing all male voices on the show, these being "a Chinese cook, grunting Indian, and a nasal cowboy called Adenoids."[4]

When non-white characters were enemies, their images were harshly portrayed. *Maverick Jim*, which appeared in 1933, pictured Mexican "greasers" as diabolical sorts who used murder and tortue—specifically, the application of a hot iron to the eyes of captured gringos—to effect their villainous ends.[5] Even in the 1950s such stereotypes and prejudices persisted. In one episode Hopalong Cassidy captured a "Chinaboy" who had murdered several men, assuring the Oriental that the courts would now handle him and "he'll soon be taking a long, long journey to join his ancestors." *Western Caravan*, which in the summer of 1950 featured singer Tex Williams in a dramatic role, portrayed Apache Indians as merciless butchers of white men. One white man in this program went so far as to state, without being challenged by the hero, "The only good Indian is a . . ." The anachronistic quality of such characterizations led a reviewer in *Variety* to suggest that in *Curley Bradley, the Singing Marshal*, "the stereotyped colored boy and Chinese house boy were unnecessary."[6]

While racial slurs persisted, the radio western by the late 1940s made a concerted effort to project a more positive image of ethnic groups in America. The revised *Cisco Kid* series was much less stereotypic, and even Wash became more intelligent and less subordinate in *Tom Mix*. But in regard to Indians, the new attitude was especially noticeable. Perhaps the first appearance of the new sensitivity came in the *Red Ryder* series which debuted on the Mutual network on May 4, 1942. The existence of Little Beaver as Red's "adopted son" created one of the first racially mixed families in radio. Although he spoke pidgin English and was often referred to as "Injun" and "the redskin," he was a warm and sincere character who operated equally with children and adults in white society.

One of the more dignified portrayals of the American Indian occurred in a broadcast of *The Cisco Kid* entitled, "The Battle of Wagon Box Corral." The program involved a racially-prejudiced Commission of Indian Affairs and an Army colonel who resolutely defended the honor of the Indians. During the broadcast, the announcer praised the military genius of several Indian leaders, including Cochise, Chief Joseph, and Chief Red Cloud of the Oglala Sioux, and equated their intelligence and strategic skills with those of Alexander the Great, Hannibal, and Napoleon.

The most consistently positive image of Indians, however, appeared on *Straight Arrow*, a popular series which came to Mutual in 1948 and ran until the early 1950s. *Straight Arrow* was a stalwart Comanche brave who "when danger threatened innocent people, and when evil-doers plotted against justice," rode the trail for law and order. In reality, the heroic Indian was a white man, cattle rancher Steve Adams, who had been raised by the Comanches and who was familiar with their language and culture. Whenever he sensed danger, Adams rode to a mysterious cave on his Broken Bow Ranch where he underwent a transformation to become Straight Arrow. The dual character personified assimilation and equality. As a white man, Steve Adams was prestigious and a source of stability and authority within his community. As an Indian, Straight Arrow was pictured as "honest, fearless, and loyal to the land of his fathers."

The nobility with which Indians were portrayed in the series was strikingly demonstrated in the broadcast of January 7, 1950. In that program, Straight Arrow and a Blackfoot guide, Skywalk, risked their lives by moving through a blizzard and high snows to rescue a wagon train full of settlers. The pioneers had been abandoned high in the mountains by evil white men, unscrupulous speculators who intended to purchase the land to which the settlers were headed. If listeners failed to understand the imagery of bad white men and good redmen, the following exchange of views certainly underscored the message:

> *First person:*   How, Skywalk! You sure saved our lives.
> *Second person:* You sure did.
> *Third person:* Hadn't been for you, Straight Arrow
>   would never had come to our rescue.
> *Skywalk:*   You better now?

First person:	Oh, that mountain goat the Comanche brought to stave off starvation. And on top of that, all the grub your tribe toted up.
Third person:	Yeah, and Rufus said Injuns wasn't any good.
Packy:	Heh, I reckon you folks got the proof that they are good, eh?
First person:	We sure have, Packy!

In the strictest sense, the western is set in the past. In literature this historical flavor ties the stories to the pioneer spirit which is essential to the mood of the genre. Certainly, the radio western reflected literary antecedents. But many series were set in the contemporary world, thereby adding modern dimensions to the broadcasts. The hero of *Sky King,* formerly an FBI agent and a military officer during the war, now operated as a rancher and amateur sleuth who flew an airplane to capture criminals. The Cisco Kid, in the version which premiered in 1942, made frequent use of the telephone in tracking down outlaws. The world of the TM-Bar Ranch, the home and headquarters of Tom Mix, was a modern environment complete with automobiles, telephones, and other technological advances.

The series which most stretched the boundaries of the western, however, was the *Roy Rogers Show*. Although it had earlier appeared in a traditional western context, by the 1950s the series was written in an adventure, or even detective, format. Programs centered about such plots as the adversities encountered by Roy and Dale Evans when they visited Washington, D.C.; prospecting for uranium with Geiger counters; investigating a stolen stamp collection; resolving the tensions that arose at a roadside diner during a tornado; and breaking a smuggling ring which used railroad refrigerator cars to transport diamonds from Mexico.

Although the western most properly offers an insight into American values, on radio the genre often was set in Canadian surroundings in stories dealing with the Royal Canadian Mounted Police. That federal police force had been instrumental in the settlement of the Canadian wilderness, and its parallel with American history made it a propitious institution for the radio western. Stories of the Mounties were familiar in the 1920s to readers of pulp magazines such as *Argosy*, *All-Story*, and *Adventure*. One of the first radio series to adopt the context appears to have been *Red Trails* which premiered in January 1935, on WJZ (New York City). More popular, however, was *Renfrew of the Mounted* which appeared in 1936 on CBS, and was heard intermittently until the late 1940s.

The most successful Mountie series was *Challenge of the Yukon* which was produced at WXYZ (Detroit) by the same unit that created *The Lone Ranger*, *The Green Hornet*, and the short-lived *Ned Jordan, Secret Agent*. This series debuted in 1939 as a regional sustaining program, and by the mid-1940s was a regular feature on ABC. The producers did not deny speculation that the stories of Sergeant Preston and "his wonder dog, Yukon King" were little more than plots from *The Lone Ranger* set in the snow and tundra of the Canadian northwest. Nevertheless, the appeal of stories of the Yukon and Northwest Territories was so strong that the series lasted until 1955. It is interesting, moreover, that a Mountie theme was chosen for one of the last western series introduced by ABC, *Silver Eagle*. This program, which concerned the adventures of Sgt. Jim West of the RCMP, debuted in July 1951, and remained on the network for four years.

Despite the fact that the classical/juvenile western was produced for more than twenty years for audiences with large youthful components, it provided poignant reflections of American life. Perhaps because they were broadcast with impressionable youth in mind, they were even more obviously indicators of the dominant values and attitudes of civilization. Furthermore, millions of adults listened regularly to radio westerns. This was especially true of those series aired in the early evening. In such programs as *The Lone Ranger* and *The Cisco Kid*, mature listeners found not only a momentary perpetuation of their own childhoods, but also vital social messages that were applicable to citizens of all ages. Thus, western series were significant communications to all listeners. Specifically, radio westerns transmitted societal standards in three distinct ways.

Champions of the Oppressed and the Weak   In a fully democratic society with respect and equality for all its citizens, there would be no necessity for altruistic champions. Yet, within the historical realities of American society, as well as of Western civilization, injustice, repression, and exploitation have commonly occurred. At least since *Beowulf* in the eleventh century, Western literature has lionized those who have stood against such oppression. It might even be legitimately contended that Christianity and its literature were heroic reactions among the repressed and weak factions of the Hellenistic-Roman world. The radio western was related to these traditions for, of all the genres popularly broadcast, the western most consistently projected its central characters as protagonists of justice and defenders of the mistreated.

Whether it involved defending the legal right of a woman against unprincipled land-grabbers, as did Wild Bill Hickok in one episode in 1952, or answering the desperate plea of an old señora—"If we only had the strong arm of an hombre . . . where does one find such a caballero these days?" —as the Cisco Kid did in a program entitled "Valley of Intrigue," western heroes rode out of the obscurity of the desert or the mountains and into the troubled lives of the downtrodden. It was an egalitarian impulse that seemed to motivate these heroes. Encountering the inequities created by evil men, these champions intervened to rectify the situation. They were social agents whose function was to restructure the democratic harmony disrupted by conscienceless badmen.

It might be Hopalong Cassidy rousting a perfidious sheriff whose power intimidated the townspeople; it could be Straight Arrow inspiring his fellow Comanches to clear their good name by capturing a band of white marauders posing as Indians; or it might be Tex Williams thwarting the evil plans of a ranch foreman scheming to exploit his employer—whatever the good deed accomplished in each regular broadcast, the heroes of the radio western brought momentary resolution to a world of distress. Buck Jones on *Hoofbeats* captured much of this spirit when, in inviting youngsters to join his special Buck Jones Club, he opened the membership to anyone, "if you're a boy or girl who's interested in clean living, outdoor exercise, and seeing that the underdog gets a chance." Such an altruistic message, learned by a generation of radio-listening American children, remained a lingering ideal in many adults. That radio westerns might have been partially responsible for inspiring a heroic mentality in mature Americans was suggested by one publication in the closing months of World War II:

> For millions of American boys—and their fathers—the courageous spirit of the old West has never died. Not as long as The Lone Ranger's famous battle cry of "Hi-Yo Silver" rings out on the airwaves. . . . A whole generation of lads has grown up inspired by his ideas. Many of them are now overseas fighting in a different kind of crusade. But they haven't forgotten the daring hero of their child-hood. From the mud of Italy to the sands of the Pacific, "Hi-Yo Silver" has served them as a rallying call, pass-word, identification. The Lone Ranger is on the job.[7]

The message of self-sacrifice and concern for the abused was an integral part of the western formula. But long before World War II it was linked explicitly to oppressive social and political problems weighing upon the nation. In a guest ap-pearance on June 5, 1933, on the NBC variety program, *Holly-wood on the Air*, Buck Jones spoke to the youth of America and tied together the western ethic and the role of children in combatting the Great Depression. In this remarkable speech, only a partial recording of which exists today, Jones called upon his Rangers—his fans who believed in "Americanism, good fellowship, and helpfulness"—to come to the rescue of the nation.

> Far be it from me to make a patriotic speech. But we've got a man in the White House that's doing a mighty sweet job of organizing America, and headin' her back towards prosperity. With summer vacation time coming around, I want to call your attention to a few little things you can do to help Mr. Roosevelt put this big job over in a big way. Times have been pretty tough, times have come when every youngster—boys and girls, too—must pitch in and do something that will help ma and pa make the home a little happier, and the going a little easier. This

Depression is like a kink in a rope, and you youngsters
can straighten it out by doing a little fancy roping your-
selves, that is if you set your mind to it. You're growing
up, you children, and you've got to look years ahead.

Communicators of Morality Despite its secular structures,
American civilization is based upon the Judeo-Christian ethic
which is most succinctly epitomized in the Ten Commandments. Through whatever cultural medium this fundamental
morality is transmitted, it must be communicated continuously to the citizenry. Children, of course, are heavily exposed
to such messages, and they are usually the most credulous
targets. This exposure is part of the socialization process in
which youngsters are introduced to the values of the culture.
Adults, however, are neither immune to, nor without need of,
moral reaffirmation. The radio western, therefore, served as a
noteworthy means of communication, for it embodied basic
social morality while broadcasting to a mixed audience of
children and adults.

Radio westerns avoided distinctively religious philoso-
phizing. The spectrum of moralizing in them ranged from
simple secular wisdom to paraphrasings of the Scriptures. The
most common types of moral messages were those that implored listeners to work hard, to respect the ways of elders,
and to be honest in all dealings. The writers of *Red Ryder*, for
instance, used the relationship between Red and Little Beaver
as an analogy for all father-son relationships. If Red remonstrated or punished the child, it was for transgressing standards that were familiar to youthful listeners. In one episode
Red was especially strong in fulfilling this role. He scolded
Little Beaver for interrupting his conversation, telling the
youngster, "Children are to speak only when spoken to."
Later, he set up definite boundaries with respect to wagering
money when he noted, "Gambling is one thing we don't do
around here." And Red's aunt continued the lesson in values
with her remark on the importance of love in society, testify-
ing to "the finest medicine any woman ever had—the love
of her friends and family."

Children had their place in the radio western as well as in

society. Even when youth was the center of attention, western dramas reminded listeners of social structure and the responsibilities of the various generations. Bobby Benson was twelve years of age, owned the B-Bar-B Ranch, and was the central character in his series. Nevertheless, he was treated as a child. Although his opinions were solicited and considered by the adults in his world, they were still the ideas of a youngster. His colleagues called him "son" and "kid," and he was sheltered from the occasional brutalities of mature life. In one broadcast, for example, he approached the scene of a gory murder, but his adult employees would not allow him to enter the blood-smeared room.

Another type of guidance children received in radio westerns was encouragement to prepare for the future. By deed and word radio characters suggested the necessity and inevitability of children becoming the social leaders of tomorrow. Whenever Sky King extended himself to capture a villain, he presented a model in responsible adulthood to his audience. But when Little Beaver or another juvenile character entered upon the trail of a criminal, he was unable to carry out fully his pursuit because the apprehending of desperadoes was a function of adult life. One of the most glowing calls for youth to prepare for responsible adulthood appeared in a *Lone Ranger* episode in January 1953. Although the Lone Ranger was pleased to be a model for his nephew, Dan Reid, he warned that the young man should not try to follow in his footsteps. Instead, the Lone Ranger declared:

> Our great country will progress only so long as there are leaders. You and young people like you must educate yourselves to be the leaders. Son, I want you to go to college, to study science and law, history and the problems of government. I want you to learn the many things required so you'll be ready to take your place as a good citizen and carry on where we leave off. Knowing that you're in school preparing for the future, I'll be content to continue helping others bring law and order to the West until you young men can take over.

Religion was rare in the radio western. Although listeners might assume their heroes were all God-fearing, devout believers, writers avoided identifying their characters with a specific faith. A major exception was the *Roy Rogers Show*. In real life, both Rogers and his wife, Dale Evans, openly testified to the intensity of their Christian belief. In occasional episodes from their series in the 1950s this personal sentiment became a part of the radio western. In one program in particular, the couple successfully used religious faith to persuade a young doctor to return to his home and face his fears that a patient had died because of an overdose of drugs he had prescribed. Referring to Biblical passages and Christian adages, they persuaded the doctor that mortals cannot judge when and why death comes; that "It isn't for us to judge, only to have faith and believe"; and that "The Lord works in mysterious ways his wonders to perform."

Despite its avoidance of the "Sunday School" quality that is created when plots become openly religious, the radio western was closely allied to the generalized religious morality which is at the base of American society. Nowhere was this more obvious than in Gene Autry's Cowboy Code, a statement on the intent of the radio western that Autry composed in 1951 as a western Decalogue.

1. A cowboy never takes unfair advantage, even of an enemy.
2. A cowboy never betrays a trust.
3. A cowboy always tells the truth.
4. A cowboy is kind to small children, to old folks, and to animals.
5. A cowboy is free from racial and religious prejudice.
6. A cowboy is always helpful, and when anyone's in trouble, he lends a hand.
7. A cowboy is a good worker.
8. A cowboy is clean about his person, and in thought, word and deed.
9. A cowboy respects womanhood, his parents and the laws of his country.
10. A cowboy is a patriot.[8]

The classical/juvenile western proffered a code of ethics to its listeners. In a world in which values were constantly challenged and questioned, these series stood resolutely for traditional Judeo-Christian concepts of honesty, fairness, goodness, and compassion. It was a moral guidance that adult society could not help but notice. In one of the more elaborate approbations of the morality inherent in the radio western, CBS and General Mills established in April 1949, a National Lone Ranger Council of Honor "to encourage America's youth to adhere to the principles of good citizenship and clean living."[9] To underscore the seriousness of the Council, its charter members were listed as including Bob Hope, Eddie Cantor, Harold Stassen, Father John J. Cavanaugh (president of Notre Dame University), Dr. Norman Vincent Peale, Dr. J. Robert Oppenheimer, Dr. Lewis T. Wright (noted black surgeon), Dr. Abba Hillel Silver (statesman and humanitarian), Jane Froman, Gene Tunney, and Robert Ripley.

Representatives of Civilization   Ultimately, the radio western was the drama of civilized men and women pitted against the forces of anarchy. It was the tale of "the Battle of the West" that was also the story of the effort of society to establish and maintain order. In the opening declaration to the broadcast of *The Lone Ranger* on October 18, 1943, the narrator effectively delineated the issues at stake in all radio westerns.

> The life of a pioneer man was rugged at best. If a man did survive the perils of the long trail—the sickness and disease, the Indians, the chance of losing his team, his wagon, and even his life on the steep, rocky passes—he had by no means won the Battle of the West, for even after he had found his peaceful valley, cleared the land, built his cabin, and finally enlarged all this to a sizable, paying cattle ranch, there were those who sought by fair means and foul to take it all away from him.

With this purview, the plot of the western could extend from the experience of the trek from the overly-civilized East to a new home in the wilderness, to the villainous efforts of a minority to upset the social harmony established by pioneers in the unprotected expanse that was the American frontier. Regardless of setting, however, the heroes of these series regularly acted as catalysts in restoring social stability. Some came as official representatives of law enforcement agencies. Tennessee Jed, for instance, was designated a "secret agent of the President of the United States." Wild Bill Hickok was a United States marshal. And the Lone Ranger—an erstwhile member of the Texas Rangers—was such a believable lawman that on January 18, 1955, Senator Price Daniels of Texas placed in the *Congressional Record* a tribute to the series for serving "as a vital factor in keeping alive in the minds of people . . . the traditions and ideals of the Texas Ranger organization and its work in maintaining law and order."[10]

Most of the champions, however, were drifters who moved from site to site, always finding injustices to overcome. Even if they owned property or had a personal stake in a specific settlement, these heroes wandered the wilderness in pursuit of criminality. They never sought to explain their wanderings since their beneficial achievements seemed always to justify this unconventional lifestyle. Perhaps the closest thing to an explanation of this wanderlust were the words of Hopalong Cassidy in describing his frequent absence from his Bar-20 Ranch: "A man has to move around once in a while; he gets stale if he doesn't."

It was a rough, male world which the heroes encountered. Although female characters were often the victims of crime, they seldom were the perpetrators. Law and order were conditions created and disrupted by men. Fistfights, shootings, robberies, swindles—these were the common crimes, and they were crimes of men. It is interesting that in only one instance did a major network develop a western series with a woman as the central character. In March 1946, CBS introduced *Calamity Jane* and featured Agnes Moorehead in the title role. The scripts may have been poor, but the image itself was an incongruity. The series lasted only three broadcasts.

The heroes of the radio westerns were civilizers. From the outposts of civilization they visited, they pruned those evil influences that would retard development. By their actions they suggested that social perfection was possible if only imperfect elements were removed. These champions were direct descendents of those thinkers of the eighteenth-century Enlightenment who also maintained that utopian society was

possible. Man is basically good, they claimed, and it is the
environment which corrupts man; change that environment
by reforming or removing social corruptors, and heaven will
be made on earth. Certainly, none of the western heroes ever
enunciated such a progressive position. Rather than envision
an idealized future, they acted always as if their tasks would
never be completed for, in the words of the Lone Ranger,
"There will always be badmen." Yet, given enough Cisco Kids
or Gene Autrys, the ideal was theoretically achievable. Perhaps, then, the long-range function of the classical/juvenile
western was to produce within each child and adult an understanding of justice and the perfectability that was only possible when all civilized men and women lived without crime.

The Adult Western

By the time the adult western emerged in radio—in the
late 1940s and early 1950s—it could do little to revive the
fortunes of radio. Clearly, television by this time was becoming the most popular medium of mass entertainment. This
was an ironic development, since in the realistic, adult formu-
lation radio presented the most sophisticated western dramas
in its history. In these new westerns the blending of mature
plot, fuller human characterization, and intelligent theme—
all enacted according to serious dramatic standards—produced
several significant series. Traditionally, the radio western had
been produced for juvenile listeners. In its atmosphere of
secret identities, action-packed chases, and stalwart heroics, the
western suffered for too long from a case of arrested adolescence. The realistic western first emerged in literature, and
as early as 1939 in John Ford's *Stagecoach,* it appeared in film.
In radio, however, it was not until after World War II that
the style was developed, and not until 1952 that its highest
achievement, *Gunsmoke,* was broadcast.

Despite its late entry into adult westerns, radio since the
1930s had been concerned with dramatic programs set in western surroundings and not necessarily intended for juveniles.
Reminiscences of the Old West was a local program on KOA
(Denver) in 1931–1935, which recreated stories from the his-

tory of Colorado and the West. When *Under Western Skies* graduated from a local series on KDKA (Pittsburgh) and became an NBC program in 1938, *Variety* praised the maturity of its stories and suggested that the series was creating a unique audience for adult radio plays of the West.[11] The most successful of these early western dramas, however, was *Death Valley Days*. This series began in 1930 and, under its later titles—*Death Valley Sheriff* and *The Sheriff*—it remained on radio until 1951.

These early series cannot properly be classed with the adult westerns which developed in the postwar era. They lacked continuing, mature characters who gave stability and consistency to the later series. They also lacked believable action and realistic locales that enhanced that activity. Sometimes comedies, sometimes dramas, these series possessed neither the plausibility nor the authenticity which the adult western demanded. The uneven nature of these early programs can be seen in the case of *Death Valley Days*. One episode from the mid-1930s told of Sam Bass, an infamous bank robber and killer. In a style more attuned to *Gangbusters* or other early detective series, it ponderously offered the point that crime does not pay. A second broadcast from the same period was a comedy-drama about two old prospectors and their argument over whether or not to purchase an "unlucky" white burro. After shattering their friendship over the issue, the old men were reconciled when the burro proved instrumental in saving the life of one of them. Such programming caused the prominent radio critic, Robert J. Landry, to refer to the series as "a formula of tall tales of the old frontier."[12] When *Death Valley Days* was restructured and retitled in 1945, it found its niche as a detective series relating stories of the modern sheriff of Death Valley, California.

The authentic adult radio western was a product of the realism in popular culture that developed during and after World War II. Following that conflict, America experienced a sustained period of national and personal introspection. Questions about the causes and brutalities of war led inexorably to inquiries about national shortcomings and personal instabilities. The popular arts reveal it to have been a time of interest in psychology, racial and religious intolerance, economic inequities, and concern about national priorities. In a more mature nation, with increased responsibility in the world and expanded liability at home, Americans expressed a proclivity for more realistic creativity in their literature, cinema, and radio.

One of the first western series to attempt to meet the new requirements was *Zane Grey Theatre,* which was aired 1947–1948 on the Mutual network. Although the stories owed little debt to the author after whom the program was named, the writers introduced occasionally mature themes relevant to an older audience. In one broadcast, for example, the murderer, although apprehended in the end, was spared from hanging when the court found him criminally insane. Nevertheless, the series was unable to break fully with the clichés of the juvenile western format. The central character was Tex Thorne who—astride his trusty steed, Topaz, and accompanied by his side-kick, Sandy Fletcher—uttered such banalities as, "Don't throw lead at me unless you want your lead back with interest," and, "You're a woman—got a right to have a hunch," while describing his bachelor status as "footloose and following the tumbleweed; no woman is dabbin' a rope on my carcass."

Frontier Town, the first adult western, was a transcribed series which appeared in the late 1940s. Because it was recorded and was not affiliated with any specific network, *Frontier Town* never achieved the distribution and popularity it merited. The series concerned the adventures of a western lawyer, Chad Remington. As a hero, Remington was intelligent and serious in his approach to solving the problems he encountered in various frontier settlements. He combined physical strength and legal expertise and thereby presented a formidable opponent to antagonists. Although the series possessed one serious connection with the juvenile format—a comedic partner named Cherokee O'Bannion who spoke like W. C. Fields and was an Irish alcoholic—the themes, dialogue, and characterizations of *Frontier Town* clearly separated it from adolescent westerns.

Typical of the sophisticated dimensions explored in the series was the program entitled "Forest Fire." The story dealt with social apathy and personal greed, as Remington was unable to convince the citizens of a small settlement that there was a danger of forest fires destroying their homes. When a fire did break out, the plot dealt with the vanities of several townspeople. One man stole the critical dynamite belonging to the fire fighters and was blown up when the dynamite caught fire. A second character, the local storekeeper, raised the price of his water buckets to profit from the plight of his neighbors. And in the strikingly mature conclusion, tensions were dissipated and the fire contained as the rains came and the entire town joined in a prayer of thanks.

Although at least forty-seven episodes of *Frontier Town* were recorded, the adult formula it introduced did not succeed in network radio until the appearance of *Gunsmoke* several years later. Network officials in the late 1940s seemed too heavily concerned with detective dramas and quiz shows to develop westerns. The western, moreover, was still strongly identified with children, and there was a sufficiency of series in this style. Even after a pilot program of *Gunsmoke* was aired on July 13, 1949—written by David Friedkin and Morton Fine, later creators of the powerful detective series, *Broadway Is My Beat,* and of the Humphrey Bogart and Lauren Bacall adventure series, *Bold Venture*—neither the program nor the format seemed to impress executives at CBS. Not for three years would that network return to the series.

Gunsmoke premiered on April 26, 1952, as a calculated gamble. For producer-director Norman Macdonnell, and writer John Meston, it was an attempt to create on network radio a new type of show—a western for adults. CBS made a substantial outlay of capital to develop the series and to sustain it for eighteen months until a sponsor could be found. Macdonnell admitted to a fan magazine that he was worried when the series began. He and Meston had produced a unique western hero, Marshal Matt Dillon of Dodge City, Kansas, who was, in Macdonnell's words, "a simple, honest person grubbing out an existence amongst a prairie people and on a

rugged land which unwillingly gives up enough sustenance for
man to keep body and soul together."[13] Listeners and critics,
however, immediately approved the new program. The reviewer for *Variety* wrote of the premier broadcast that the
"series is presented with top thesping and scripting values that
pull it way ahead of the pack of AM [radio] westerns."[14]
During its eight years on radio, moreover, *Gunsmoke* won
many awards which attested professionally to its merit.

It was the success of *Gunsmoke* that led CBS and NBC to
develop more adult westerns. By the end of the decade several
distinctive, if short-lived, series had appeared. NBC produced
The Six-Shooter (1953–1954) and *Dr. Six-Gun* (1954–1955);
while CBS developed the genre more lavishly in *Fort Laramie*
(1956), *Frontier Gentleman* (1958), *Luke Slaughter of
Tombstone* (1958), and *Have Gun, Will Travel* (1958–1960).
Although each of these series had its own idiosyncracies, col-
lectively they presented a picture of life on the frontier that
was fuller, more explicit, and more believable than were earlier
westerns.

The most impressive aspect of the adult programs was the
aura of social doom which pervaded their stories. Mirroring
fears in the minds of listeners living in a nation tense with
internal Cold War conflicts and external military threats,
these series created a social environment in which the line between civilization and barbarity was uncertain, and where
heroes were indispensable. Whether they were bona fide law
men, military officers, mercenaries, or simple do-gooders, it
was apparent that these champions were the principal forces
protecting nascent American civilization from the savagery
which surrounded it in the wilderness.

Antagonists in these shows ranged from brutal bullies and
indifferent lynchers to renegade Indians and men who murdered because they simply disliked their victims. In all of
them, however, the motor force was destructive human passion
unleashed by experience in the West. *Gunsmoke* was especially effective in portraying such an explosive environment.
In one episode, for example, two bullies, for amusement, sliced
off the ear of a weak man's donkey. In another a widow

avenged her murdered husband by killing with a rifle at close range each of the men who had mistakenly lynched him. This program was especially poignant as the woman, a respectable housewife and mother, dispassionately declared when captured, "I don't mind, I really don't mind at all." *Gunsmoke* also made effective use of shoot-outs and ambushes on many of its programs to settle arguments. It was a savagely frank world where rhetoric was minimal and procedures were efficient. Norman Macdonnell aptly delineated that context when he remarked, "Everything was out in the open. There was no subterfuge, no neurosis, no artifices or superficiality. Life was straightforward, bone-simple and honest."[15]

Within towns and other pockets of society, the adult western portrayed a world in which harmony was generally absent. In this regard, Paladin, the mercenary hero of *Have Gun, Will Travel,* in the broadcast of October 11, 1959, described an Arizona settlement in a manner that questioned its right to be called civilized.

> Tombstone was swarming with men, swaggering and bois-terous men in groups, and men alone, lolling in the sun, sleeping off drunks. Along the walks the wagons and the horses were lined up solid. And it was almost impossible to guide my way through the moving crowds in the streets. But eventually I reached the Alhambra Saloon and a glass of cold beer.

This sense of despair and lack of meaning was echoed by one character in a broadcast of *Gunsmoke* when he remarked that the essence of life on the prairie was "we do what we have to do." Such an attitude was also expressed by Captain Lee Quince, the hero of *Fort Laramie,* when he cynically maintained that life in the U. S. Cavalry was little more than "fifty cents a day and all the jerky you can eat."

These depressing moods were made acceptable because of the basic optimism of the heroes of adult westerns. Most would have agreed with the statement of Chad Remington on the premier broadcast of *Frontier Town.* According to him, "This is no backwoods we're living in any longer. It may be the frontier, but it's the frontier of civilization." Even moody

Matt Dillon exuded confidence in the future when he lectured
a group of settlers about to leave Kansas out of fear: "We
have troubles now and then, sure, but it's not as bad as you
think. And in a few years it'll be as safe here as it is in Ohio
right now, or California. And it's gonna be a prosperous
country."

At other times, hope was expressed in terms of the diversity of life possible and flourishing in the patches of civility
in the West. In one broadcast of *Dr. Six-Gun* this was portrayed by a Jewish retired Army officer overcoming adversity
to observe Yom Kippur on the frontier. In an episode of *Luke
Slaughter of Tombstone* it was demonstrated by a refined
young woman from the East arriving in wild Tombstone to
marry a local bachelor. It could even be found in the appearance of "civilized" crimes, such as occurred when Marshal
Dillon's deputy, Chester Proudfoot, encountered a woman
who, through lonely-hearts advertisements, met, married, and
murdered for their money a host of lonely men throughout the
West.

The most consistently optimistic adult western was *Frontier Gentleman*. The series offered "slice of life" glimpses of
frontier society as seen through its central character, J. B.
Kendall, a reporter for the London *Times* touring the West of
the 1870s. While desperadoes and hostile Indians were a part
of Kendall's world, the show painted a picture of the frontier
as a place filled with hard-working pioneers constructing a
civilization in the wilderness. In one program this was seen in
the rivalry of two small towns in the Dakota Territory for the
services of a recently-arrived schoolteacher. In another show it
was a local Texas production of Shakespeare's *Othello*, complete with drawls and improvised passages. There was even
hope suggested when a convicted murderer awaiting execution
spoke to Kendall of his many killings—including seven men—
that began when at age ten he shot his father's horse. In a
mood of self-doubt, the murderer remarked:

> I'd like to ask you a favor, mister. You write what I'm
> telling you in that English paper of yours. You say
> maybe somebody sorrowed when I got my neck broke,

huh. Make it up, maybe, like my wife or kid heard and
they sorrowed. Day comes when a man gets to be alone.
Ain't nothin' more to look at 'cept what's inside. Huh,
I sure hadn't oughta killed that horse.

Another mark of the adult western was the central character whose ambivalence gave him a realistic quality missing
in earlier western series. Unlike the decisive and single-pur-
posed spirit found in *Straight Arrow, The Cisco Kid,* or *Hopalong Cassidy,* characters like Bret Poncett, the hero of *The
Six-Shooter,* stammered in speech as well as decisiveness. As
portrayed by James Stewart, Poncett encountered circumstances which on occasion were unsolvable. In a typical episode he deterred a mob intent on evicting from town the wife
of a mass murderer. Although the killer was executed in
prison, and the mob was dispersed, Poncett was unable to convince the woman to reveal that it was she who had betrayed
her spouse to the sheriff. Even though her father would not
speak to her, and the townspeople despised her, the stubborn
widow exasperated Poncett, and the story concluded on that
note of indecision.

In *Have Gun, Will Travel,* the radio western explored
one of the more interesting personalities to appear as a hero.
Like the television character after whom he was patterned,
Paladin on radio was a man of culture, refinement and impec-
cable taste who resided in elegance in a fine San Francisco
hotel. By profession, however, he was a mercenary, a gun-for-
hire whose decisive nature was offset by the ambivalence felt
by listeners who were uneasy with a hired gunman as the central character. Paladin once explained his function in simple
terms: "I have a certain talent with weapons. When people in
trouble need such a talent, I hire it out to them." Paladin usually contracted with oppressed or exploited people to represent them before hostile elements of society. On those occasions when he was actually hired by an oppressor, he invariably
changed sides in the dispute or was freed of the commitment
when something disastrous happened to his evil employer.
Nonetheless, the crassly commercial nature of Paladin's work
made him generally incongruous with the heroes of radio

westerns. His characterization, however, was possible only in adult western programming.

In another mold was the personality of Marshal Dillon of *Gunsmoke*. Dillon was a strong character whose strength was balanced by his loneliness. As the hired defender of law and order, with a keen understanding of the human condition in the West, Dillon was visible and effective. As a social being, however, he was closed and protective. Even his small coterie of friends—Chester, Kitty the saloonkeeper, and Doc—did not penetrate his personal defenses. The best description of Dillon's character came from William Conrad who enacted the role throughout the life of the series.

> Matt Dillon is neither hero nor villain, but a human being. The best of us are sometimes ashamed of our thoughts, and there are times when the worst of us can be proud of our deeds. Matt Dillon is no different. He is a law-enforcement officer who doesn't like killings. He hates the thought of bloodshed. He's underpaid, never liked the job, but knows it has to be done. At times he's wanted to quit—has quit. But like most people who know the difference between right and wrong—and recognizing that justice could be done by him, probably better than by anyone else available—he has always come back to his responsibility. Matt Dillon isn't perfect but he's willing to try.[16]

Because they were directed toward mature audiences, adult westerns often delved into themes of violence and sex. In none of the juvenile westerns did a hero ever warn a rival, as Chad Remington told one desperado, "If you try to pick up that gun . . . I'm promising you this much, I'll jump you and bang your head until it goes clean through that floor." Nor did a juvenile series ever describe a wounded man as did Bret Poncett when he remarked, "Art didn't get a second chance. The carbine slugs tore into his chest, knocked him off his horse. He just lay there. He was bleeding bad." The West in the adult series was a violent place, and its untamed quality was only aggravated by the presence of human beings. It was an environment in which one of Paladin's enemies was brutally trampled by a stallion, and where Remington philosophized about "sudden death being almost a normal part of life on the frontier." One of the more noteworthy attempts to deal with the violence of the West occurred in a broadcast of *Dr. Six-Gun*. In the story, Dr. Ray Matson, the hero, tried unsuccessfully to enact a local gun-control ordinance. In a mood of frustration mixed with nationalism, he resigned himself to the inevitable:

> Let 'em carry their guns, someday they'll put 'em aside. It may not be as easy as takin' 'em away now, but in the long run, that's a pretty sound document, that Constitution. It's worth sewing up a few bullet holes for.

Sex was another theme absent from the classical series, but intimately a part of the adult western. As early as *Frontier Town*, sex was noticeable. In one show, a bar girl, termed by Remington "a young, so-called lady," was overheard rejecting a proposition for later that evening. She appeased her would-be customer, however, by promising him a date "some other night . . . any other night." One broadcast of *Have Gun, Will Travel* concerned a frustrated married woman who lusted after Paladin. Although her ultimate pleasure was seeing jealous men kill one another because of her, her unsuccessful seduction of Paladin was demonstrative and sensual. And, of course, the character of Kitty Russell in *Gunsmoke* could exist only in the adult western. Ostensibly the manager of the Long Branch Saloon, Kitty was patterned after the prostitutes and madames who worked in saloons in actual frontier settlements. Her close relationship with Matt Dillon—at least that of a friend and confidant—also added a spicy flavor to the series.

Even if not exploiting sex, the adult western presented a franker attitude toward sexuality. In a broadcast of *Frontier Gentlemen*, for instance, J. B. Kendall spoke to a young woman about the death of her illegitimate child and of her liaison with a Civil War hero who fathered the child. One of the most impressive shows in the *Fort Laramie* series concerned the need for women in the fort to carry guns. The broadcast suggested that firearms were needed by adult females to fight off Indians who might attack the fort and its

women when soldiers were away on maneuvers. The show
advocated suicide rather than suffering sexual abuse from the
invaders, for as one female veteran of the fort warned a newcomer, in previous raids some women were killed "and some
[were] carried off by the Sioux—dying's easier."

In addition to violence and sex, adult westerns were impressive for their overt political themes. Certainly, they were
often patriotic. The western by nature is Americana in its
approximation of frontier history. Yet, more explicit pro-
nouncements of support for the United States were not absent.
This was especially true of three series: *The Six-Shooter, Dr.
Six-Gun*, and *Frontier Town*. In the latter series, for example,
patriotic references were noticeable in the remark of Cherokee
O'Bannion, "In any book I've read, it's not supposed to be the
cavalry—it's always the Marines who come to the rescue." It
was also exhibited when Chad Remington remonstrated a
Basque shepherd who despaired at losing her flock to villains. To her comment that "I start to believe the whole thing
is not worth it," Remington quickly retorted, "I've never
heard a Basque talk that way before . . . and certainly never an
American."

More striking, however, was the politically liberal stance
taken by several series on the issue of human rights. Reflecting, perhaps, the national concern with civil rights precipitated when President Dwight D. Eisenhower sent federal
troops into the South to enforce school integration, several
series in the late 1950s took up civil rights themes by focusing
on the oppression and exploitation of American Indians. In
all adult westerns Indians were portrayed more fairly than in
the juvenile series. Most were shown to be peaceful, and those
who killed white settlers were pictured as exceptions rather
than the rule. For example, in a broadcast of *Frontier Gentleman*, a small band of marauding Indians was quickly labelled
"renegade," and its eradication by Kendall and the U. S.
Cavalry was not construed as a loss to peace-loving Indians.

Related to this sentiment was the more general theme of
brotherhood which was also a part of the adult western. Even
a pet raven in *Dr. Six-Gun* shrieked that "all men are broth-

ers." And a sensitive broadcast of *Fort Laramie* dealt with the growing trust between white and red men. In it, while investigating reports of Indian raids, Captain Quince encountered a Jesuit priest who taught reading to a small band of Sioux braves. When Quince met one of those braves, the Indian was impressed that the officer did not shoot him. The priest was thus able to draw a lesson in brotherhood, suggesting to Quince, "Maybe that's the way it begins, with one red man and one white man trusting each other."

In a similar vein of tolerance and understanding, *Luke Slaughter of Tombstone* probed traditional prejudices in the program of April 20, 1958. In a frank political discussion, Slaughter—a former cavalry officer who was now a cattle rancher in the Arizona Territory—defended the Apaches against the barbs of a local bigot.

> *Easterner:* War paint? I understood that the treaties with the Apaches were working out nicely.
> *Slaughter:* They are, when the white men live up to them.
> *Bigot:* Well, that is practically treason against your own race, Slaughter.
> *Slaughter:* If it's treason to compare some members of my own race with Indians like Cochise and Margano, well, I'm guilty. Tell us a little more about what you plan to do, Mr. Fell.
> *Easterner:* Well, I want to paint the strong Indian faces, their customs, the way they live. The people back East have some amazing misconceptions about them.
> *Bigot:* Yes, so has Slaughter. He trusts 'em.
> *Slaughter:* We're trying to understand them.

On occasion, these series were also sensitive to the fate of the Indians since the onslaught of white settlers and exploiters. Marshal Dillon, for example, justified the ignoble actions of Indian warriors when he explained to Chester that the cause of their problems was their great loss to expanding white Americans.

> An Indian's no different from anybody else with too much to drink. No, the problem's deeper than that.... Well, the Indians have lost a lot. They're a conquered

people. That doesn't sit well with many men.... There
are times when it makes him mad.

The adult western also respected Indian traditions and
cultural values. This was demonstrated aptly in the episode of
Have Gun, Will Travel aired on February 22, 1959, as an
Indian rancher, Joe Whitehorse, revealed to Paladin his special love for the land.

> When I walk out of my house, onto my own land, [it]
> gives me a good feeling. I love this place. It has given
> me pain, but there is something ... this is mine, this
> handful of earth here, this is mine.

In this broadcast, Paladin strongly asserted his egalitarian politics by siding with Whitehorse against local white
racists. These neighbors taunted Whitehorse with epithets
such as, "I don't aim to raise my children next to some savage,"
"You Indians have reservations ... that's where you belong,"
and, "I got no respect for a critter knows he ain't wanted, but
hangs on anyway." In the end, Paladin settled the confrontation in favor of the Indian and his pregnant wife. The libertarian implications of the program were made most apparent
when Paladin offered his mercenary fee of $2,000 to the
Whitehorse family with an apology for white racism: "Please
accept it for your child, with my apologies for this imperfect
world we have to offer him, and my hopes for a better one in
his lifetime."

In American popular culture the western has had immense success. It was an irony, however, that radio did not
develop the genre fully until creative broadcasting was in ebb.
Several reasons help account for this condition. Among them
were the reluctance of sponsors to underwrite a western for
primarily adult audiences, network economics which mitigated
against sustaining series, the lack of creativity among script
writers who chose to remain with proven formats rather than
experiment, and the general inertia in radio programming
which over the decades created patterns of imitation and
variation rather than produce the widest possible range of
shows for listeners' tastes.

When the mature western did appear, its full impact could not be calculated. By this time statistical ratings were low relative to the figures earned by programming in the 1940s. Many adult westerns also appeared on Saturdays, a day not intended to attract an optimal audience. And by the 1950s, a growing number of Americans were viewing television and were oblivious to innovations in radio drama. Nonetheless, the adult western enjoyed popularity and respect with those who still cared for innovative radio programming. Interestingly, even into the early 1960s, long after the classical/juvenile series had left the air, several adult westerns were still being broadcast. Thus, one is left with only speculation about the probable impact of the adult western if programs like *Gunsmoke, Frontier Gentleman,* and *Have Gun, Will Travel* had emerged in the late 1930s or early 1940s.

5

Soap Operas
as a
Social Force

As a radio genre, the daytime serial drama was created with
the American housewife in mind. Sponsored by household
products, broadcast in daylight hours most likely to appeal to
homemakers, and heard by an audience that was ninety percent female, these so-called soap operas for three decades engaged, entertained, and educated millions of women Monday
through Friday, from 9 A.M. to 5 P.M. That the soaps were well-
received by their intended audience is seen in the fact that
daytime serials lasted into the early 1960s, far beyond the date
when most dramatic and comedic features disappeared from
radio. In fact, one scholar has made a substantial case for the
notion that traditional radio programming died on November
25, 1960, the day when four long-running serials—*The Second
Mrs. Burton, The Right to Happiness, Young Doctor Malone,*
and *Ma Perkins*—were broadcast on CBS for the last time.[1]

Despite their chronic popularity, like many forms of
popular culture that enjoy mass acceptance, soaps were often
the object of contempt. This was first noticeable in the terms
applied to them. When they emerged in the early 1930s, they
were properly called serials since their stories were never completed in one program and, like the romance fiction and
movie serials from which they gained much of their inspiration, their plots might be expected to continue for many
broadcasts before reaching a full conclusion. Before the end of
the decade, however, trade publications sarcastically labelled

them "washboard weepers," "sudsers," and "soap operas" because they were melodramatic and usually sponsored by manufacturers of facial soap or soap powders.

More debasing attacks, however, came from critics inside
and outside the radio industry. Dr. Lee De Forest, one of the
developers of radio, scorned soaps as "tripe" and contended
that they "could be ordered off the air very easily without
much of a cultural loss to the American people."[2] Marion
Dickerman, the education director of the American Arbitra-
tion Association, assailed them as a "deluge of dirt" in which
the "clear boundary edges of the moral codes are smeared and
obliterated."[3] The editors of *Variety* felt that soap operas
were guilty of providing a "malnutritious diet of pap."[4] And
humorist James Thurber poked derisively at them as a simplistic, formulaic sandwich whose recipe was:

> Between thick slices of advertising, spread twelve min-
> utes of dialogue, add predicament, villainy, and female
> suffering in equal measure, throw in a dash of nobility,
> sprinkle with tears, season with organ music, cover with
> a rich announcer sauce, and serve five times a week.[5]

Perhaps the most vitriolic attack on the serials came from
a psychiatrist, Dr. Louis Berg, who in the early 1940s inspired
a strong movement against soap operas. Berg contended that
they appealed to the basest passions in civilized man, and in
time of war were "little short of treason." Most colorfully,
Berg described the soaps:

> Pandering to perversity and playing out destructive con-
> flicts, these serials furnish the same release for the emo-
> tionally distorted that is supplied to those who desire
> satisfaction from a lynching bee, lick their lips at the
> salacious scandals of the *crime passionnel,* who in the un-
> regretted past cry out in ecstasy at a witch burning.[6]

Soap operas, however, were not without their defenders.
Irna Phillips, one of the most prolific and successful creators
of daytime serials, argued many times that her stories were
simply reflections of reality. According to her, "The serial
drama is not 'such stuff as dreams are made of.' It is as funda-

mental as life itself. Our day-by-day existence is a serial drama."[7] Drs. W. Lloyd Warner and William E. Henry of the University of Chicago concluded in 1943 that, "By dramatizing the hopes and fears of the average American housewife, and her standards of right and wrong, the radio serial tells stories which point out good and evil in a way that ordinary people can understand."[8]

Hobe Morrison, the prestigious critic for *Variety*, felt that many soaps had critical roles in American society. He specifically cited *The Goldbergs*, a serial featuring a Jewish family living in New York City, as promoting religious and ethnic tolerance, for "The message is there and, in the serial's years of daily broadcasting into millions of homes, [it] must have had a definite, if immeasurable, effect."[9] Similarly, a study group in 1947 contended that *Big Sister* had a powerful social effect in that it curbed neuroticism, strengthened marriages, provided techniques for coping with emotional problems, improved women's sense of security and importance, and had a positive effect upon listeners' personalities.[10] Even the critical Thurber concluded that the soaps were a form of daytime "morality play" avidly followed by millions of listeners.

The most telling defense of serials, however, lay in the economics of daytime radio. By the late 1930s the soaps had become a significant source of revenue for the networks. Expenditures for daytime radio advertising rose from $11,331,882 in 1935, to $26,701,845 in 1939. Furthermore, sponsors were able to utilize a greater percentage of the time in a soap broadcast than any other form of radio programming. In 1939 a study made at Kansas State College showed that in the average fifteen-minute serial, 17.8 percent of the time—two minutes and forty seconds—were spent advertising. This was in excess of two and one-half times the amount of time spent advertising on one-hour evening shows. Even thirty-minute evening programs used only 10.4 percent of their time with the message of the sponsor.[11] The soaps also were inexpensive for sponsors to produce. In 1946, for example, the average cost of a typical program—fifteen minutes a day, five days a week— was only $1,400 for actors, writing, and technical assistance.

The World of the Soap Opera

From the 1930s through the 1950s, daytime radio offered millions of listeners the opportunity to escape their ordinary lives and enter the world of romance and action that was the realm of soap operas. In their real existences, housewives went predictably about the business of homemaking. They reared children, prepared meals, cleaned house, shopped, and kept home and family as harmonious as possible. There were, of course, occasional interruptions in this lifestyle as deaths, accidents, illnesses, and financial crises occurred. And during World War II, the exigencies of combat temporarily brought many housewives into essential industries as laborers. Such developments, however, were infrequent; and relative to the decades of normalcy, they were unique experiences. As an antidote to the day-to-day routine of many housewives, it was the soap operas which regularly invited listeners to escape their personal existences and share the intense and varied emotions of the fictional radio characters.

The realm created by the soaps was filled with strong doses of agony, hatred, suspense, love, and tribulation. By following the plots of several serials simultaneously, listeners encountered stimulating fantasies they could incorporate into their own ordinary realities. Thus, the soap operas proffered a world of action where a wide range of human and social developments—murder, marriage, birth, death, love affairs, accidents, divorces, and disease—could be vicariously experienced through regular listening.

Alice Reinheart, who through two decades portrayed several soap opera heroines, has suggested that such emotional extremism resulted from the fact that life was exaggerated in the daytime serials. A soap opera, she remarked, "mirrored the problems in concave mirrors, in mirrors that blew them up out of all proportion. It mirrored the regular, everyday problems that any marriage goes through—but it exaggerated them." The heroes and heroines of the soaps moved emotionally between the poles of joy and despair. No one better captured the essence of these extremes than did Kay Fairchild, the central character of *Stepmother,* when in the episode of July 22, 1940, she remarked:

> All we can be sure of is that nothing is sure. And that tomorrow won't be like today. Our lives move in cycles —sometimes that's a good thing to remember, sometimes bad. We're down in a dark valley that allows us to hope, and to be almost sure that we'll come out after a while on top of a hill. But, we have to remember, too, that beyond every hill, there's another valley.

Uncertainty and anguish were often built directly into the structure of a soap opera. In many instances, it was the result of a marriage of an average woman to a man of wealth and power. Of course, this dramatic device allowed audiences to fantasize about the luxury that came with affluence. But the serials were always careful not to overglamorize the wealthy new surroundings in which such characters operated. While *Lora Lawton* was called "the story of what it means to be the wife of one of the richest, most attractive men in all America," it also warned listeners that the series was the "story of love and riches in a world so many dreamed of, but where so few dreams come true." When the announcer on *Our Gal Sunday* repeated his daily question—"Can this girl from a little mining town in the West find happiness as the wife of a wealthy and titled Englishman?"—most listeners felt that happiness was possible, but that it would be painful to achieve. The same uncertainty surrounded *Rich Man's Darling* which in 1935 related the story of an attractive newspaper reporter who at age twenty had married a millionaire aged forty-five. One soap opera, *Linda's First Love,* went so far with this theme that in 1937 it offered wrist watches as prizes to those letters which best told why Linda, a poor girl, should marry either the rich boy or the poor boy in the story.

Many other serials had suffering integrally built into their foundations. *The Strange Romance of Evelyn Winters* was the story of a successful Broadway playwright, mustered out of the Army with a medical discharge, who found himself the guardian, and eventually the sweetheart, of the attractive twenty-year-old daughter of his former colonel who had been killed in action. *John's Other Wife*, which premiered in 1936 and lasted for six years, was based on the motion picture *Wife vs. Secretary*, and related the jealousy of John's spouse toward his secretary. Later, however, it evolved into "the story of the happiness and the heartaches of a second marriage." And the harrowing struggle to find success in show business was the theme of several soaps including *Myrt and Marge, Broadway Cinderella*, and *Mary of the Movies*.

Despite the pain and turmoil, the potential for finding happiness was always present. Even the titles of several soaps suggested that "life can be beautiful," that one had "the right to happiness," and that there was always a "bright horizon" on "the road of life." In one of the more striking testimonies to the power of positive thinking, the opening lines to *Woman of Courage* proclaimed it to be "the moving story of a wife and mother who is unafraid because she knows if you believe, you can win—nothing in life can defeat you—and that what is right will be." Altruistically, *Dr. Paul* was always introduced warmly as "radio's wonderful story of love and service to humanity."

Related to the theme of happiness in daytime serials was the confession of one writer that at the basis of his successful soaps was the so-called "Cinderella story." According to Robert Hardy Andrews, the author of such series as *Betty and Bob, Just Plain Bill*, and *Judy and Jane*, "Cinderella is the spirit of make-believe. She is the princess of dreams-come-true." In an interview published in 1935, Andrews explained further the integration of wished-for happiness into his stories.

> She represents what every man, woman, and child, deep down in their hearts, really want. . . . Cinderella represents life as people would like to see it lived. In her never-ending story, justice overcomes cruelty and injustice, riches supplant poverty, virtue is rewarded, and romance comes to complete the dream.[12]

Nowhere was this happiness more apparent than in the plots of the soaps. Regardless of the pain, there were wholesome love affairs, marriages, births, business successes, recoveries from illnesses, worthwhile children, and personal triumphs. As morose as they might be at times, soap operas could also generate moments of joy, as when Sylvia Field brought home her baby in 1943 on *When a Girl Marries* and boastfully declared, "It feels simply super colossal! As if you'd accomplished the most important thing in the world!" Although Chichi Conrad cried throughout the sad times on *Life Can Be Beautiful,* she also shed many tears of happiness over the loving warmth of Papa David Solomon who ran the Slightly Read Book Shop, her husband, Stephen Hamilton, and their infant child. And in 1941, when wealthy Carter Trent proclaimed his love for "commoner" Peggy Young of *Pepper Young's Family,* it was in the most affirmative terms: "I love you more, darling, and I expect to go on loving you more every time I see you. Every time I'm near you, it's, well, it's just going to mount and mount until I don't know where it'll end. I guess nobody will ever have loved anybody as much as I love you." In thousands of such moments during the history of the soaps, listeners found that after all the anxiety, love and tenderness made life worth enduring.

If tender moments justified existence in the soaps, it was the institution of the family in which such loving experiences were most successfully achieved. Many serials revolved totally around the activities of members of a family. Irish-American families were spotlighted in series such as *Today's Children, Mrs. Wiggs of the Cabbage Patch,* and *The O'Neills.* Jewish-American families were the focus of *The Goldbergs* and *The Foxes of Flatbush.* Strong, but fatherless families appeared in *Ma Perkins, Manhattan Mother,* and *Young Widder Brown.* And a motherless family flourished in *Bachelor's Children.*

There were large and small families, wealthy and poor ones, some that lived with knowing anguish, while others existed calm and confident. Some families, such as Pepper Young's household, grew up, married, and had children during the life of the serial; others encountered death in the soaps, such as when Chichi's husband and baby died in the mid-1940s.

But, whatever the condition or the evolution of the serial family, it always remained what one character in *The Carters*

of Elm Street termed "the magic ring of happiness and home."
Soap opera characters struggled through their fictional lives to
realize this social balance. The heroine of *Stella Dallas* spent
her radio life acting out of "mother-love and sacrifice" to see
that her married daughter had happiness. And Linda Young
on *Pepper Young's Family* lived in shame and depression
throughout the 1950s because she could not bear another child
to replace the one lost in an earlier hospital fire. Yet, no one
better summarized the idealized significance of the family as a
social unit than did Carleton Morse whose *One Man's Family*
was a domestic serial broadcast in the evening for more than
twenty years, and as a daytime soap opera for five years. His
was one of the programs which most glorified the American
family. Although the following excerpt was broadcast on April
27, 1947, when *One Man's Family* was still an evening program, Morse's pristine evaluation of the family remained consistent throughout the life of the serial. Conversing with his
son, Morse's leading character, Henry Barbour, said of the
family:

> *Father:* The American home is the backbone of this
>   nation. The American family is the life blood of the
>   American democracy, the seed of our way of life.
>   If we let that seed die, if we kill the divine spark,
>   then we've killed America.
> *Son:*   Well, when you come to think of it, that's one of
>   the first things Hitler did in Germany: broke up
>   families, made a mockery of marriage and home ties,
>   put a prize on license and illegitimacy....
> *Father:* Is it any wonder that we've made the home and
>   the family our theme for fifteen years?...We are
>   dedicated to it and rededicated to it, world
>   without end. Amen.

   Soap operas were a seductive and significant dimension of
American life for two generations. Listeners strongly identified with the characters. When *Ma Perkins* or *Lora Lawton* offered premiums for a boxtop or two of the sponsors' product,
tens of thousands of replies followed. When a character was
married or gave birth in the story, listeners sent cards and
gifts. Helen Mencken, who played the operator of a sewing

shop in *Second Husband,* even received a sewing machine when in the story the woman she portrayed moved from Montana to New York to set up a new store. The latest developments in story lines became points of conversation between neighbors, and occasionally thousands of fans even sent letters of protest to actors, networks, and advertising agencies when they disapproved of the direction in which serial characters were headed.

Ultimately, soaps were successful because the world they created was relevant and important to their audiences. Although many advertising agencies might have argued differently, the serials were not simply forms of advertising, as important to selling the sponsors' wares as were the commercials. Instead, they represented stylized glimpses into the dramatic potentials of living. They were insights into middle-class lifestyles in which the humdrum and the extraneous were removed, and the essential retained. Traditional, critical, and defensive in their moral view of life and society, soap operas were educative models which, in the American commercial democracy, disseminated the conservative message necessary for a society to stay together. The serials, therefore, were products of a bourgeois culture wherein citizens learned of critical values, of themselves, and of their fellow citizens. The premise of all soaps was the commonness of the American experience—what was described in one episode of *Betty and Bob* as "the same emotions, the same passions, the same hatreds, the same love, the same prejudices [that] stir men and women everywhere." The daytime serials were ritualistic dramas wherein fictional characters met and overcame adversity, while identifying listeners learned better to comprehend themselves, their cultural standards, and the community of the nation.

Soaps in the Depression Era

In treating the soap opera as a scholarly subject, most writers have spent time and energy trying to name the first such program. While some trace it back to the 1920s in programs such as *The Smith Family, Amos 'n' Andy* and *The*

Goldbergs, others place its premier about 1930–1931 in series like *Moonshine and Honeysuckle* and *The Stolen Husband.* While this historical pursuit has a certain academic value, it directs attention away from more important questions about daytime serials. More significant queries are: when they did emerge in the early 1930s, why did they become popular with American listeners, and what was there about this period that made it possible for such programming to become the favorite of millions? In answering these questions one learns more about the relationship of radio to life in America.

The soaps were a product of the Great Depression. Certainly, the development of network radio in the mid-1920s was important to them. So, too, was the success in the late 1920s of night-time domestic comedies, such as *Amos 'n' Andy* and *The Goldbergs,* which demonstrated the viability of serialized stories. It was the great economic collapse of the 1930s, however, that created the social environment in which soap operas could first survive. The Depression put men and women out of work, it broke apart families, and it threatened the confidence which held together the entire society. While governmental ineffectiveness served primarily to aggravate the national predicament, generalized pessimism and perplexity were to be found in popular attitudes throughout the nation.

The popular arts reflected this national mood. In literature, theater, music, and film the sense of helplessness was notable. Radio also mirrored the realities of the Depression. Radio comedy, for instance, achieved its primacy at this time as it served to make listeners laugh away unpleasantness—at least for a thirty-minute broadcast. In a similar vein, soap operas emerged in the midst of the turmoil and grew in popularity throughout the 1930s. Harrison B. Summers, in his survey of network programming, has shown this, for in 1931 the number of "women's serial drama" programs was three; while in 1934 it was ten; in 1936 it was thirty-one; and in 1939 it was sixty-one.[13]

Thematically, many of the early daytime serials appealed directly to listeners feeling the bite of the Depression. *Betty and Bob,* which premiered in 1932, was the story of a young

married couple who had been disowned by the husband's millionaire father and was forced to work and save, as did most
listeners. *Marie, the Little French Princess* in 1933 told of a
wealthy young woman of nobility who found a happier and
more romantic life living as a commoner in the United States.

In *Mrs. Wiggs of the Cabbage Patch* listeners encountered
in 1936 a character whose fictional suffering and discomfort
was always worse than the reality of the audience. Both
Painted Dreams (1931) with widowed Mrs. Moynihan, and
Today's Children (1933) with Mrs. Moran presented large
Irish-American families headed by philosophical, elderly
widows coping with the problems of Depression life. And in
Ma Perkins in 1933 the public found a model of strength and
determination which was meant to offer courage to listeners.
This point was well understood by a reviewer when he de-
scribed Ma as:

> a resourceful, courageous widow fighting the problems of
> hard times with the same indomitable spirit that you and
> you and you are showing in like circumstances. Thus, be-
> sides laundry soap, Oxydol [the sponsoring soap powder]
> urges upon the country a philosophy of patience and reso-
> lution. Not money and high position, but kindly hearts
> is the big thing in life. . . .[14]

Although they were created to capitalize upon both the
frustrations and the hopes of female listeners, soaps possessed
a fundamental formula which allowed for their development,
even when the economic crisis passed. It was a structure which
Hubbell Robinson, Jr., then of Young and Rubicam advertising agency, described as being "based on four cornerstones"—
1) simple characterization; 2) understandable predicament; 3)
centrality of female characters; and 4) philosophical relevance.[15] First, the successful soaps established simple, recognizable figures. The attempt was to create ordinary characters
to whom ordinary listeners could relate. Typical of this format
was Bill Davidson, the central personality in the popular *Just
Plain Bill*. A homespun philosopher and helpful neighbor,
Bill was a barber in the small town of Hartville. Even the
theme song of the program, "Polly Wolly Doodle," suggested

good-naturedness, traditionalism, and familiarity. Bill's personal characteristics were aptly summarized by one critic who described him as, "calm and quiet and gentle and sympathetic and tolerant and understanding and kind, but still firm and strong and wise."[16] With such an arsenal of positive traits, recognizable to the average listener, Bill Davidson for more than two decades encountered and resolved problems that varied from domestic misunderstandings to murder.

Similarly recognizable were the human characterizations on programs like *The Goldbergs* and *Clara, Lu and Em.* In Molly Goldberg, the center of a Jewish family coping with urban life, author and actress Gertrude Berg established a warm-hearted, believable, motherly character who moved generously in and out of the lives of the family members. *Clara, Lu and Em,* on the other hand, presented three realistic small-town women—slightly gossipy, a little naïve, and terribly involved with the problems of being housewives and mothers—who demonstrated bonds of friendship that were familiar to most of their audience.

Establishing understandable situations was fundamental to the formula of a successful daytime serial. Although detractors might argue that this guaranteed the programs would be produced with the intelligence of a twelve-year-old in mind, the writers actually created predicaments and concerns that never overshadowed the personalities of the fictional characters. On occasion, soap heroes became involved in complicated court battles, difficult assignments, and trips abroad; but for the most part, their lives centered on commonplace developments. Romantic concerns dominated the soaps, from courtships and births, to jealousies and divorces. Domesticity was also a favorite topic as scripts were often concerned with such homey themes as preparing a meal, rearing children, cleaning house, and arranging a party.

Due to the slow-moving pace of the typical soap opera, a week or more might be taken up with such predictable situations as packing for a trip, coming home from the hospital, or gossiping about other characters. It once took "Just Plain Bill" Davidson more than a week to give a customer a haircut. The heroine of *Pretty Kitty Kelly* spent three weeks going up a few floors in an elevator, and once when Alice Reinheart's two-week vacation occurred, the character she was playing, Chichi Conrad, left the room to take a bath and did not return from the bathroom until the vacation was completed.

As a third cornerstone, soap operas usually featured women as principal characters. The titles of many serials from the 1930s suggest this preoccupation with feminine interests: *Aunt Jenny's True Life Stories, The Romance of Helen Trent, Manhattan Mother, When a Girl Marries, Girl Alone, Arnold Grimm's Daughter, Stella Dallas,* and *Valiant Lady.* Others implied at least equality between women and men: *The Carters of Elm Street, Betty and Bob, Billy and Betty,* and *Vic and Sade.* Although series in the 1940s presented male doctors and lawyers in strong central roles, men usually played weak roles relative to the strong heroines. Unbalanced, emotionally vulnerable, lacking strength, and generally persuaded or pushed by the serial heroines, the leading men in soap operas were definitely the weaker sex. In fact, except for their professionality—they were usually the doctors while the women were the nurses—there was little in the soap opera world that men could lord over women.

According to Alice Reinheart, radio actors often complained about being "so sick of playing this wishy-washy husband who comes home and is told how to live and what to do and how to do it. . . . It was always the woman who was the strong character." No one was stronger or more determined than the widowed Ma Perkins, who maintained a lumber yard and a household and was described in the opening episode on December 13, 1933, as

> a woman whose life is the same, whose surroundings are the same, whose problems are the same as those of thousands of other women in the world today. A woman who spent all her life taking care of her home, washing and cooking and cleaning and raising her family. And now, her husband's death pitched her head foremost into being the head of the family as well as the mother.

The final dimension of the soap opera formula involved a philosophy that was integral to the personality of the leading characters. Here such homilies as "the meek shall inherit the earth," and "virtue is its own reward" were personified in people like Bill Davidson and Stella Dallas. Such bits of religious philosophy or folk wisdom had been accepted as truths for generations. In this way soap characters and stories became reaffirmations of commonly-held beliefs. And listeners could recognize not only the plight of the heroine, but also the repudiation of truth which her predicament represented. According to Hubbell Robinson,

> it is easy to be emotional about a character whose activities you have followed through a series of mishaps or defeats and triumphs and for whom you are rooting. It is doubly easy if that person seems to you to represent a force for good, and who represents a point of view you share.[17]

This inner goodness in soap characters was not always subtly blended into their personalities. On many occasions listeners found their enduring, honest, saintly principals blatantly moralizing to them. In an episode of *Lora Lawton* in May 1948, for example, Lora pontificated, "I think that life in general is bad enough without unhappiness stemming from temperament being allowed to make it worse." Ma Perkins, who was extremely fond of enunciating moral conclusions, typically expressed herself to her audience in mid-1938, noting that

> anyone of this earth who's done wrong, and then goes so far as to try and right that wrong, I can tell you that they're well on their way to erasing the harm they did in the eyes of anyone decent.

This type of sermonizing from a respected soap opera personality also dramatically occurred in *Pepper Young's Family* in 1941 when Sam and Mary Young were discussing their daughter's decision to dress according to her own fashion rather than pretentiously try to impress her wealthy future in-laws.

> *Sam:*   Honey, imagine her saying a thing like that—
> about it being more important what kind of person
> you are than the kind of clothes you put on.

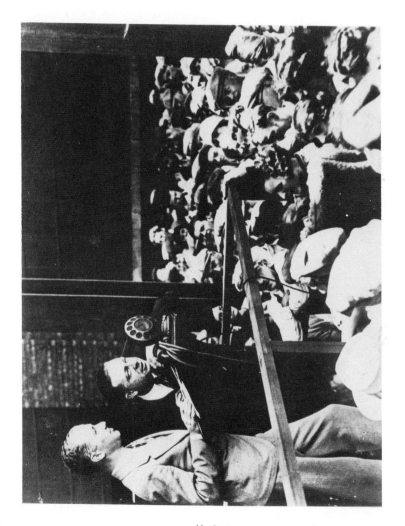

Two of the most popular radio performers of all time were Freeman Gosden (left) and Charles Carrell who emerged in Chicago radio as "Sam and Henry," and later as the nationally-known team of "Amos 'n' Andy." (Courtesy of WGN Radio, Chicago)

Left: One of the most important personalities of radio in its first decades was crooner Rudy Vallee, whose musical variety programs helped spread the popularity of broadcasting. (Courtesy of Kraftco) *Right:* George Jessel (left) and Eddie Cantor brought vaudeville and stage comedy styles to radio in the early 1930s. (Source: Wide World Photo)

The "fireside chats" begun by President Franklin D. Roosevelt were effective devices through which the Chief Executive kept the American people informed of his efforts to control the Depression and carry forth his New Deal program. (Source: Wide World Photo)

The Mills Brothers gained national recognition over the air in the early 1930s. Four decades lates they are still popular favorites. (Courtesy of Kraftco)

Above: Bing Crosby was already a recognized star of screen and recordings before coming to radio in the early 1930s. (Courtesy of Kraftco)
Right: "The King of Swing," Paul Whiteman, led his famed orchestra on radio for two decades. (Courtesy of Kraftco)

Kraft Music Hall was a long-lasting musical variety program hosted by several important celebrities. Here, an ad for the program during the 1934-1935 season when Al Jolson and Paul Whiteman were the featured regulars. (Courtesy of Kraftco)

Left: The most popular of the second generation of comedians who entered radio in the mid- and late 1930s was ventriloquist Edgar Bergen, seen here in 1937 with his monocled dummy, Charlie McCarthy. (Source: Wide World Photo)

Right: The infamous "feud" between Jack Benny (left) and Fred Allen in the mid-1930s was only a publicity gimmick designed to attract listeners to both programs. (Source: Wide World Photo)

Left: Jerry Colonna played the comedic foil, or "stooge," for personalities such as Bob Hope and Bing Crosby. (Courtesy of Kraftco) *Right:* Bob Hope emerged in radio in the late 1930s and quickly became one of the nation's most popular and respected comedians. (Source: Wide World Photo)

Left: One of the more popular "swing" band leaders was Jimmy Dorsey. Remote hookups brought home listeners the pulsating music of the jitterbug live from dance halls, night clubs, and hotels throughout the country. (Courtesy of Kraftco) *Right:* Louis Armstrong appeared on many musical programs, but his own show in 1937 was short-lived. (Courtesy of Kraftco)

Left: The creative talent whose dramatization of *War of the Worlds* plunged the nation into an evening of panic in October, 1938, belonged to Orson Welles. Even before that broadcast Welles had been a successful radio personality, appearing in dramatic roles including that of Lamont Cranston, hero of *The Shadow.* (Source: Wide World Photo) *Right:* A successful writer of radio soap operas for three decades, Irna Phillips had little difficulty making the transition to television serials in the 1950s. (Source: Wide World Photo)

During World War II commercial radio became the primary source of news for the American people. Two distinguished broadcast journalists to emerge at this time were Edward R. Murrow (left) and William L. Shirer of CBS News. (Source: Wide World Photo)

Above: The sensitivity and poignancy of his dramatic productions made Norman Corwin one of radio's most celebrated writers. *Right:* Bob Burns, whose "Arkansas Traveler" characterization helped keep "rube" comedy popular in the United States. (Courtesy of Kraftco)

With the popularity of domestic situation comedy in the 1940s, the family of bandleader Ozzie Nelson—(left to right) Ozzie, David, Harriet, and Ricky—became a national favorite on *The Adventures of Ozzie and Harriet.* (Source: Wide World Photo)

> *Mary:* Ah, it was a nice speech, wasn't it?
> *Sam:* Oh, you bet it was. And it shows the stuff she's made
> of, too. You know, Mary, I'm proud of my daughter.
> *Mary:* You ought to be, Sam.

The soaps reflected more than the economic and social dislocation of the Depression. They and their producers changed with the times by introducing fresh and relevant themes, and by creating new series which focused upon more contemporary values. By the end of the 1930s the flourishing and flexible daytime serials were probing areas of interest not found in earlier programs. Few of the early soaps dealt with career women, but by 1940 many featured women as professional achievers. The heroine of *Hilltop House* managed an orphanage, while the principal character in *The Story of Mary Marlin* became a United States Senator.

Female lawyers were the focus of *Her Honor, Nancy James* and the highly successful *Portia Faces Life.* A nurse was the heroine of *The Woman in White,* and nurses appeared regularly as supporting roles in several serials dealing with doctors and hospitals. *The Life and Loves of Dr. Susan* was a short-lived program which premiered and concluded in 1939, but *Joyce Jordan, Girl Intern* began in 1938 and, under its subsequent title, *Joyce Jordan, M.D.,* survived for a decade and was revived for the 1951–1952 radio season. By the end of the Depression, other career women were noticeable in prominent roles in soaps. Several heroines owned or managed small businesses. Ellen Brown ran a tea parlor on *Young Widder Brown,* Brenda Cummings owned a sewing shop on *Second Husband,* Connie Tremayne opened a lingerie store and later managed a factory on *Arnold Grimm's Daughter,* and the heroine of *Jenny Peabody* was the proprietor of a small hotel. Other leads were actively involved in careers outside their homes. The principal character of *Kitty Keene, Inc.* ran her own detective agency, Patricia Locke of *Manhattan Mother* was a businesswoman, and the heroines of *Rich Man's Darling* and *Jane Arden* were newspaper reporters.

Until the late 1930s, the only network soap opera devoted to a career woman had been *The Romance of Helen Trent* which, in the cliché that opened the show daily, told the story of a thirty-five year old fashion designer who,

> when life mocks her, breaks her hopes, dashes her against the rocks of despair, fights back bravely, successfully, to prove what so many women long to prove in their own lives: that because a woman is thirty-five or more, romance in life need not be over, that the romance of life can extend into middle life, and even beyond.

Certainly, the appearance of professional women in soap operas helped to create new predicaments which differed from the domestic operations of most serials. But this new emphasis also reflected the fact that between 1930 and 1940, as the economic crisis gradually eased, the number of working women rose by almost 16 percent. Daytime serials, therefore, mirrored a growing sophistication within American society—a maturity which accepted women as careerists, no longer totally relegated to home and family.

By the end of the decade, daytime serials also shed some of their sexual exclusivity and featured more males as heroes of their own series. Yet, these newer soaps, plus the few early programs centering on men, were still intended primarily for female listeners. When men did serve as central characters, they fit usually into one of three distinct stereotypes, none of which was incongruous with those soaps with feminine leads. In such programs as *Young Doctor Malone* (1939) and *Terry Regan, Attorney at Law* (1937) the principals were professional men. Youthful, handsome, and unmarried at first, these men were shown as dedicated to their careers. Other such dedicated heroes appeared in *The Road of Life* (1937) where Dr. Jim Brent practiced his medical profession, and in *Bachelor's Children* (1935) where Dr. Robert Graham nobly practiced medicine while raising the eighteen-year-old twin girls entrusted to him by a dying war buddy.

A second style of masculinity was featured in those serials dealing with older men who acted as social philosophers. Here were grandfatherly characters whose strength lay in intelligence, experience and inner confidence. Cracker-barrel wisdom came from the heroes of *David Harum* (1936) and *Scatter-*

good Baines (1938), both small-town luminaries whose ideals and accomplishments were reassuring to their neighbors. In this category also was Reverend John Ruthledge who, on *The Guiding Light* (1938), offered patience and understanding as the formula for living a good life.

The final stereotyped male lead was an easy-going, sometimes humorous characterization which stood in opposition to the melodramatic types normally found in soap operas. Honest, slightly naïve, even eccentric, this type of man usually mixed seriousness and comedy in his adventures. Larry "Pepper" Young of *Pepper Young's Family* (1936) emerged as a wholesome, gregarious teenager whose family was "your friends, the Youngs," and whose daily routines took listeners into his dates, disappointments, parties, and loves. Even as an adult by the late 1950s, Pepper remained a relaxed and gullible personality. More humorous, but equally well-intentioned, was the central character of *Lorenzo Jones* (1937). Lorenzo was portrayed as an impractical but lovable inventor whose main concern—when he was not inventing oddities like a three-spouted teapot with separate spouts for weak, medium, and strong brews—was his devoted wife and partner in mirth and light-heartedness, Belle.

Despite modifications in traditional patterns, soap operas continued for the most part to focus on familiar heroines operating within routine situations. New serials like *The Carters of Elm Street, When a Girl Marries, Those Happy Gilmans,* and *The Couple Next Door* featured the dramatics of family life, while *Our Gal Sunday, Kitty Foyle,* and *Backstage Wife* continued the theme of women of a lower social standing marrying wealth or fame and moving into higher society. The traditional image of the strong woman facing, either alone, or without understanding, the rigors of contemporary life was found in new serials such as *Valiant Lady, Girl Alone, Stepmother,* and *Stella Dallas.* And matriarchy continued in those households headed by the widowed heroines of *My Son and I, Margo of Castlewood,* and *Young Widder Brown.*

By the late 1930s, the soap opera had been formed as an

American popular art form. Although new serials would appear, and older ones would alter their emphases to relate to changing realities, the genre was fully defined. Furthermore, the most prolific and successful creators of daytime serials—Frank and Anne Hummert, Elaine Carrington and Irna Phillips—had made their impact felt in radio. The Hummerts did for the radio serial what Henry Ford did for the automobile industry: they created a "factory" in which they sketched out story lines and acted as general supervisors for a group of anonymous writers who labored to flesh out the suggested plots and create the final products. During the 1930s this scripting system allowed the Hummerts to create dozens of soap operas. By 1936 they were broadcasting more than one hundred scripts each week for more than thirty different sponsors.

Frank Hummert was one of the pioneers of soaps. He told one scholar that his idea for such programming was predicated on the success of serial fiction in newspapers and magazines. According to Hummert, "It occurred to me that what people were reading might appeal to them in the form of radio dramas."[18] From this insight came some of the most popular serials in the history of radio. Included in this listing were *The Romance of Helen Trent* (1933–1960), *Just Plain Bill* (1933–1955), *Backstage Wife* (1935–1959), *Our Gal Sunday* (1937–1959), *Lorenzo Jones* (1937–1955), *Stella Dallas* (1937–1955), *Young Widder Brown* (1938–1956), and *Front Page Farrell* (1941–1954).

The Hummerts were business-like about their soap opera empire. In the early 1930s they created Air Features, Inc., and a subsidiary, Featured Artists Service, Inc. These organizations handled production and casting details for the Hummert productions, but neither Hummert received compensation from them. Instead, they were employed by the advertising agency of Blackett-Sample-Hummert, an organization so powerfully influenced by Frank Hummert that, even though he was not a partner in the organization, for prestige value his name was listed equally with the owners, Hill Blackett and J. G. Sample.

And when Hummert left that agency in 1944, he established Hummert Radio Productions, Inc., and operated as an independent producer.

Despite an efficient approach to the manufacture of soap operas, the Hummerts were protective of their creative function. The many writers who wrote dialog and otherwise filled out ideas were forbidden by contract to credit themselves as originators of the programs. Although they did not disallow a writer being cited as the realizer of an idea by Frank and Anne Hummert, they took precautions against anyone other than themselves becoming too identified with a series. Thus, writers were frequently replaced or reassigned to other serials. During the period 1937–1938, for example, Lawrence Hammond wrote for three different programs, *John's Other Wife, Backstage Wife,* and *Young Widder Brown,* while Marie Baumer was routinely shifted from *Young Widder Brown,* to *Our Gal Sunday,* to *Backstage Wife,* to *Second Husband,* and to *Stella Dallas.*[19]

Frank Hummert strongly defended the system which was devoted to mass production, low costs, standardization, and specialization. According to him, while it was not humanly possible for him and his wife to produce every line of the scripts broadcast in their name, the "initiative, the conception, the detailed synopses and essentially direction, tone, casting, and nature of the series" were theirs. He denied, however, that his system did not recognize a collaboration in the usual literary or dramatic sense; but Hummert argued that the salary the writers received made them employees, not designers.[20]

The empire built upon soap operas by Frank and Anne Hummert was an impressive organization. From their estate in Connecticut, they relayed their plot sketches and summaries to a corps of writers, script readers, and typists. Here the summaries were expanded, refined, and turned out as final scripts. The Hummerts were demanding. Scripts had to be prepared up to six weeks in advance of broadcast. Even if completed, a new idea or a whim to be incorporated into the plot could necessitate completely rewriting weeks of scripts. Salaries paid to writers were low—in 1938, only $25 for each eleven-minute script—and work was heavy, as the flow of words from the "factory" reached six and one-half million annually.

   In contrast to the strenuous business environment in which they operated, Frank Hummert described the world he and his wife created for radio listeners as concerned with "the everyday doings of plain, everyday people—stories that can be understood and appreciated on Park Avenue and on the prairie."[21] Into these serials about ordinary people was added a mixture of uncertainty, suffering, and turmoil that created the dramatic element so effective in the soaps.

   One of the more compelling patterns in the Hummert productions involved the frail but determined heroine of humble birth who had married into money and prestige and spent every episode struggling to ward off jealous female competitors for her husband's affection. The heroine of *Our Gal Sunday* was an abandoned orphan, who had been raised by Colorado miners, now married to "England's richest, most handsome lord, Lord Henry Brinthrope." Mary Noble, the central character in *Backstage Wife*, was "a little Iowa girl" and the jealous, defensive spouse of Larry Noble, a handsome Broadway star who was the "dream sweetheart of a million other women." But Amanda Dyke, the principal of *Amanda of Honeymoon Hill*, was the most disadvantaged of all. She was described each week as "a girl who has nothing in life except her own beauty—neither education, nor background, nor any real contact with the world." Her wealthy young husband, Edward Latham, had to take her away from her strict father and endure the condemnation of his own family. It was in this context of alienation and hatred that the couple sought "happiness on Honeymoon Hill in Virginia."

   While the Hummerts were primarily producers, not writers, of daytime serials, Irna Phillips began as an independent writer. Her first program, *Painted Dreams*, premiered on WGN (Chicago) in 1930. This drama of the hopes and realities of the Moynihan family was the first fully-developed daytime serial broadcast specifically for a female audience. Phillips became so committed to the series that she also appeared as one of the characters. Nevertheless, after two years and 520 scripts, she moved to NBC and created the highly successful *Today's Children*, which for six years was one of the most popular soap operas in radio. Because of her success and the demand from advertising agencies for more serials from her, Irna Phillips by 1940 had established her own smaller version of the Hummert system of mass production. In this modified arrangement Phillips helped to plot the shows, and she approved all final scripts. To do the actual writing, she employed a group of anonymous writers who received up to $500 per week for producing such series as the *Road of Life, The Woman in White, The Guiding Light,* and, until 1943 when she sold the serial, *The Right to Happiness.*

By the end of her first decade in radio Phillips had written or supervised 6,000 scripts and was earning about $200,000 annually. Unlike the massive operation of the Hummerts, which could have as many as a dozen different series broadcast weekly, Phillips confined her efforts to four or five quality serials per season. She also avoided the fantasy that sometimes entered the Hummert product, and preferred dramas about people caught up in more realistic predicaments. *The Road of Life,* a story about doctors, endured on CBS for twenty-two years; *The Guiding Light* concerned a minister whose private and professional life for the twenty years of the serial was dedicated to helping others; *The Woman in White,* involving the professional and romantic experiences of a young nurse, lasted for eleven years on NBC; and *The Right to Happiness* (a spin-off from *The Road of Life*) for twenty-one years related its story of people in search of the happiness described as "the sum total of many things—of health, security, friends, and loved ones."

The success of Irna Phillips' serials came from her devotion to reality and from her careful understanding of the women who comprised her audience. She frequently consulted community and social organizations to obtain current thinking on urgent problems. For example, at the end of World War II, she enlisted the aid of several veterans', parents' and teachers' organizations to gain their views on postwar issues.

She was especially concerned with problems such as the adaptation of families to returning disabled veterans, the paradox of women in the home and on the war job, juvenile delinquency, and marriage problems created by the war. She integrated such issues into her daytime dramas, convinced that women in the audience were interested primarily in the home and all that it represented.

Phillips contended that the principal urge of women was to create a warm and protected family. According to her, the American woman sought "to build securely for herself a haven, which means a husband, a family, friends, and a mode of living—all wrapped up neatly and compactly into a tight little ball with the woman as the busy center of the complete, secure little world."[22] To develop tension, Phillips introduced into this ideal, threats and disruptions perhaps familiar to her listeners. Thus, the challenge of the "other woman" or the "other man" might be a force that propelled a plot for many episodes. So, too, did matters such as illness, thievery, children, or childlessness function in her stories. Hers was a tight, secure universe assaulted by realistically evil, unsteadying forces with which listeners could identify.

Elaine Sterne Carrington came to soap operas after several successful years as a free-lance writer for such magazines as *Saturday Evening Post, Good Housekeeping,* and *The Pictorial Review.* Throughout her radio career she maintained the writer's conservative desire to do it all herself. Instead of the elaborate system of the Hummerts, or the modified style of Irna Phillips, Carrington produced her materials alone. Lying in bed, smoking a cigarette and relaxing, she dictated scripts to her secretary. After careful editing and some rewriting, the scripts were completed. In this manner she produced such long-running serials as *Pepper Young's Family,* which was a mainstay at NBC from 1936 until 1959, *When a Girl Marries,* which ran from 1939 to 1957, and *Rosemary,* which appeared on NBC from 1944 to 1955.

Carrington was a woman of impulse and verve whose lack of pretension did not betray the fact that she was the highest paid writer of soap operas. Mary Jane Higby, the leading actress throughout most of the life of *When a Girl Marries,* recalled Carrington as impish, loving risque stories, and comfortably poised as she entered the elegant offices of NBC, dressed in lace and furs and wearing a pair of gum-soled shoes.[23] Carrington admitted that although she had to provide a yearly story outline to her advertising agency, she never managed to stick to it. Instead, she preferred to let her characters grow naturally out of the situations in which they found themselves. And she often defended soap operas from critics, asserting, "If they aren't a hifalutin' form of art, they frequently contain profound wisdom expressed in universal terms."[24]

One of the most striking aspects of Carrington's programs was the effusively romantic quality they often demonstrated. Reflecting her own happily married life with a successful lawyer and two children, her stories dealt usually with love and family. In her typically gushing style, in one episode of *Rosemary,* she had the heroine and her girl friend, Joyce, discussing love.

Joyce:	Oh, Rosemary, I'm so happy.
Rosemary:	Are you, dear? I'm glad.
Joyce:	I never knew what it was to be happy before— not really happy . . . not deeply, warmly happy. Happiness is a funny thing, isn't it, Rosemary?
Rosemary:	Yes, . . . I guess it is.
Joyce:	Suddenly it comes—just like a ray of sunshine— one minute you've been living in a gray world and then you are living in a world of blazing sunlight. I guess I sound goofy, don't I?
Rosemary:	No, you just sound happy.
Joyce:	Happy! Rosemary, it's when you wake up in the morning with this—this choking feeling of utter joy . . . sometimes it seems as if your body is too small to hold so much happiness crammed into it.
Rosemary:	Darling, you haven't known anything like this before, have you?
Joyce:	Nobody has. Oh, I don't mean that I'm the only person in the world who was every happy this way—that would be foolish—but I mean nobody unless she's in love with the man who's

in love with her can feel it. It's as if—as if—
well, as if you belonged to a small society and
you can only get in when love has unlocked
the door.[25]

With the emergence of Carrington, Phillips, and the
Hummerts, as well as scores of writers of other major and
minor soap operas, the daytime serial as it would flourish for
more than a quarter-century was fully established.

One of the most interesting dimensions of this entertaining popular art form was its use for political purposes. Private
interest groups were the first to exploit the daytime serial for
partisan ends. As early as 1934, a strongly anti-New Deal
organization, the National Industrial Council, created *American Family Robinson* as a means of attacking Franklin D.
Roosevelt and his remedial policies. In this transcribed serial
that ran for two years, the hero, Luke Robinson, was the editor of a small-town newspaper, the *Centerville Herald,* and
was stridently anti-socialist, pro-business, and Republican. In
frequent discussions within the story line, Robinson and
others attacked Roosevelt's social policies as utopian and disruptive. Robinson's political bias was even evidenced in the
name which he suggested for his wife's radio club for women.

> *Mrs. Robinson:*   I was telling you about the radio club for
>   women. Oh, I've had such wonderful
>   responses to the idea. There are hundreds
>   of answers from Centerville alone. And
>   so many good names suggested, well, I
>   hardly know which to choose. There's the
>   Save America Club, and the Sound
>   Recovery Club, and the Economic Freedom
>   Club. Which of those do you like best? . . .
> *Mr. Robinson:*   Well, why don't you call it the Woman's
>   Forum for the Promotion of Constructive
>   Thinking as Contrasted with Radical
>   Theories in Government and Business. . . .
>   Well, how about the Ladies' Aid for
>   America?
> *Mrs. Robinson:*   Oh, now, don't be funny.
> *Mr. Robinson:*   No, no, I'm not being funny. It would
>   mean just what it says: Ladies who are
>   aiding in the preservation of American
>   principles.

Most explicitly, in a later episode Robinson's son-in-law, Dick Collins, engaged a western rancher in a conversation that summarized the thrust of the entire soap opera.

Rancher: That's just what it [the ranching business] is—terrible! Now you take you fellas back East. I understand business has all been took over practically by professors. And all you fellas have to do is set around and let somebody else do the worrying. Wonder when they'll take over the ranching business. Isn't anything I'd like better than to have some government agency come out here and run my business for me while I sit back and listen to the radio and read Shakespeare like I always wanted to. . . .

Collins: I gather that you want the government to do all the work and the worrying and make up all the deficits on the rent side of your ledger, while you act as a sort of retired vice-president, eh?

Rancher: Sure. Ain't that the general idea?

Collins: Not by a long shot. If your ranch were taken over, you'd find yourself looking for a job. If you were lucky enough, you might be able to get a government job managing your own ranch on a salary. Then, you'd have all the worry of making the thing go, and none of the profits. No, the time hasn't come yet when you can get much for nothing, even from Uncle Sam. Our wisest economic leaders are trying to help business stand on its own feet. That's the only way we can preserve that independence which is supposed to be our national characteristic.

Rancher: Well, maybe so. But I set as great a store by my independence as the next one. But what I say is, wouldn't do my independence no harm to get some of those benefits they're passing around so free like. And while they're doin' all this national plannin', I don't see why they can't work up a plan that'll make the ranchin' business pay.

Collins: Oh, you fellas are all alike. You seem to think that the United States Treasury has got a big window in it, with a "Paying-Teller" sign on it, and all you have to do is step up and hold out your hand. National planning would mean more than just keeping your pockets filled. If the

> government forced people to pay you a high price
> for your cattle, it would force you to pay a
> high price for the things you buy. Individual
> rights and government planning just don't go
> together. If carried out, national economic
> control would destroy individual freedom, and
> regiment America into a collective society. . . .
> People have got to decide whether they're going
> to favor plunging into a lot of radical experiments
> that endanger the jobs of everyone, or return
> to time-tested principles.

While *American Family Robinson* failed to undermine Roosevelt's popular support by the time of the Presidential election in 1936, it set a precedent for conveying political messages through the medium of the radio soap opera. In late 1938, the Republican Party of Iowa used this tactic. In the eight weeks before the congressional elections of that year, it ran *The Park Family* on three stations in Iowa. The serial stressed the value of Republican positions, while relating the story of the Parks. That same year the United Auto Workers sponsored a thirteen-part daytime serial on WJBK (Detroit). This series, *Flivver King*, was a dramatization of Upton Sinclair's controversial book based on the life of Henry Ford, a book that was difficult to find in Detroit since police had barred street vendors from selling it.

Network soap operas, as opposed to these special-interest, non-network serials, avoided taking openly political positions. Their primary concerns were entertaining listeners and selling commercial products. Nevertheless, it was not out of the question for a character to become involved in topical matters. This was especially the case in the first half of the 1930s when plots occasionally referred to the Depression or to conditions prompted by it. Probably the most explicit involvement of a soap character with topical affairs, however, occurred in *Ma Perkins* in mid-1938. During the time of the Great Purge Trials in the Soviet Union, the plot of this soap opera concerned Ma and two anti-Stalinists, Gregor Ivanoff and his wife, Sonya. Ivanoff was being hunted by Russian secret agents who found him in Ma's quiet home town, Rushville Center.

To insure his capture, the agents had kidnapped his son and threatened to kill him unless Gregor surrendered. Matters reached a climactic point in the broadcast of May 31, when the Stalinist secret police shot at Ivanoff through the window of Ma's home. Although they missed Gregor, the Communist agents accidentally shot Sonya. She died in Gregor's arms as the closing theme music swelled in the background and Ma Perkins stood by in amazement.

Soap Operas Go to War

As a fully-formulated radio genre with a certain precedent for involvement with topical matters, the soap opera played a significant role in the American war effort during the 1940s. By integrating into their plots war messages, themes, instructions, and propaganda, the soaps helped rally American women to understand and fulfill their critical role in the confrontation. It might have been a government announcement to save used cooking fats needed in the manufacturing of ammunition, or to turn in scrap cans and other used metals needed to build tanks. Sometimes, it was a soap heroine admonishing a friend to give blood for the war effort. Or it was a development within the plot such as the return of a wounded or amnesiac soldier, or even the death in battle of a heroine's son. However it was done, the daytime serial was effective in conveying to millions of listeners political and personal messages necessary for survival.

Almost contemporaneous with the outbreak of hostilities in Europe in September 1939, the implications of the Second World War were made known to American housewives in *Against the Storm*. Written by Sandra Michael, this serial debuted six weeks after the war began and told the story of two young refugees from Central Europe trying to adjust to life in America. Set against the backdrop of the battle, the program probed issues such as democracy and its ideals, and the meaning of fascist brutality. By setting the series in a small college town, Michael was able to inject lengthy statements of principle—spoken as lectures by the professors—which otherwise might have sounded plodding and out of place in a soap opera. Further, using the guise of a lecture by a distinguished visiting professor, Michael arranged for famous personalities to appear on her program. On April 24, 1941, poet Edgar Lee Masters read selections from his *Spoon River Anthology*. On November 3, 1941, the poet laureate of Great Britain, John Maesfield, read from his work via shortwave from London. Twice in 1941 folk-singer John Jacob Niles lectured and sang on the program. Michael had even scheduled President Roosevelt to broadcast on her soap opera, but the entry of the United States into World War II in December 1941 compelled the Chief Executive to cancel his appearance.

Against the Storm was a powerful and acclaimed soap opera. Critics at the time praised its maturity, and in 1942 it was presented a Peabody Award as "a case of merit in a field of mediocrity." Though it left the air in December 1942, when Sandra Michael withdrew from writing it, the serial created a warm, poetic world in the midst of international turmoil. Even in its opening statement, the program appeared philosophical as the announcer softly asserted,

> Against the storm keep thy head bowed,
> For the greatest storm the world has ever known,
> Came to an end one sunny morning.

Against the Storm was undoubtedly one of the best propaganda programs on the air, capable of great idealism as well as powerful invective. At a time of world conflagration, this soap stressed the rational and humanistic values of democratic America, and spoke of the simplicity and gentleness of an ideal life. This was the essence of the program of October 15, 1941, when a newspaper reporter related to a refugee the meaning of America as they sailed through the morning mist and into New York harbor. Reading a portion of the inscription on the Statue of Liberty, he softly spoke of the peace that America provided.

> Give me your tired, your poor,
> Your huddled masses yearning to breathe free, . . .
> Send these, the homeless, tempest-tossed to me:
> I lift my lamp beside the golden door.

The peaceful life was also the theme of a conversation between a mother and her daughter on the broadcast of June 20, 1940. Here in pastoral terms a placid, American Eden was described.

> *Daughter:* ... when I came in the gate here, I saw you bending over that flower-bed, the butterflies skimming around over your head. I thought, that's the way summer ought to be for everyone. It looked so good, mother. The house and the garden—and you, looking so pleased with your flowers. And I wondered if it makes any sense to believe in things like that anymore.
>
> *Mother:* Do you know of anything that makes any better sense, Siri?
>
> *Daughter:* No.
>
> *Mother:* Well, then, I think we ought to believe in the good things—with all our might and with all our hearts.

Like all good propaganda, *Against the Storm* mixed its softness with polemic statements. This was aptly demonstrated when someone remarked to a refugee from the Nazis that "Hitler has done a lot for Germany." Her response represented one of the strongest political statements by any character in soap operas.

> I can tell you what he did for the German people! He held them up at the point of a gun, took their children from them, poured poison into the minds of the new generation, harnessed them all, the young and the old, to his insane machine of war. He put Germany into slavery, and he sent the slaves out to enslave others, and to war against everything decent and free in the whole wide world. That's what he did for his people and never, never let anyone tell you anything else! Is the persecution of one human being not sufficient to condemn a man as a criminal? His Nazis have persecuted and murdered thousands, in cold blood. Suppose he had built the most wonderful national order ever conceived, would you say it was justified if the ground of his nation were soaked with the blood of innocent people? And that maniac did not try to build a great nation. He built a slave state, whose purpose is the destruction of all free states everywhere.[26]

In its own way, *The Light of the World* was as much a wartime soap opera as *Against the Storm*. Debuting in March 1940, *The Light of the World* dramatized the *Bible* in contemporary language and sought to meet a spiritual need at a time of worldwide disillusion. The soap opera created a controversy when it first appeared on NBC. Radio and the other popular arts had evolved rigid rules concerning religious dramatizations. Although there had been several financially successful motion pictures—*King of Kings* and *The Ten Commandments*—as well as theatrical productions in this vein, radio had failed to achieve an acceptable format in which to produce Biblical stories. In fact, the infamous "Adam and Eve" skit performed by Mae West and Don Ameche on the *Edgar Bergen-Charlie McCarthy Show* almost three years before had served only to make radio critics more skeptical. In 1935, the Montgomery Ward department stores had sponsored a thirty-minute Biblical program, *Immortal Dramas*. But the company felt so uncertain about mixing its advertisements with the solemnity of the stories, the department store was mentioned briefly only at the beginning and the end of the broadcast. The program was cancelled after only thirteen broadcasts.

The popularity of *The Light of the World* attested to the skill and foresight of Frank and Anne Hummert who produced it. Beginning with the story of Adam and Eve, the serial traced the *Bible* chapter by chapter until the program left the air in 1950. General Mills, the sponsor, cautiously worked in commercials for Cheerios, Bisquick, and other products at the beginning and end of each broadcast, but these announcements were not specially edited and were similar to advertisements on its other serials. The writers, however, were careful to assure listeners that the program was "presented as a living, human monument to man's faith in God," and that it was "reverently told." Furthermore, at the close of each show the announcer noted that all dramatic materials had been prepared with the assistance of "nationally-known Biblical authorities of various faiths."

More than a technical triumph, however, the success of

this soap opera suggests the mood of American society in 1940. Diplomatically if not emotionally aloof, Americans viewed the Nazi onslaught through Western Europe in the spring of 1940 from their posture of isolationism. Certainly Americans were pleased that such brutality was not happening in their country. But many must have felt betrayed by science, nationalism, and governmental leaders who had promised peace and prosperity in their time. In somber, understandable terms, *The Light of the World* offered listeners a reaffirmation of the religious source from which American civilization had emerged. Moreover, the serial projected itself beyond the listeners' world and declared for itself a universal orientation, as it was daily introduced as "the story of the *Bible,* an eternal beacon lighting man's way through the darkness of time." In an era of international crisis the program proffered reassurance to those who feared, and faith to those who doubted. In January 1941, it was rated fifteenth among the sixty serials broadcast daily. Although its popularity waned toward the end of the war, *The Light of the World* retained a respectable rating throughout its tenure and was a prestigious series for network, sponsor, and producer, as well as for radio.

Wih the exception of *Against the Storm* and a short-lived, insignificant Mutual soap, *Helen Holden, Government Girl,* daytime serial dramas were not quick to adapt their plots or formats following the entry of the United States into World War II. Radio scholar, George A. Willey, has suggested that a full commitment to the war effort did not enter daytime serials until the middle of 1942.[27] Perhaps the time lag was the result of using scripts and stories that had been prepared months before the war began; perhaps, also, the advertising agencies and sponsors were ambivalent as to the advisability of blending war themes into the serials. Yet, once the decision to introduce war-related material was made, the soaps became a consistent medium through which the sacrifices and goals of wartime were communicated.

Early in the war several programs touched upon home-front realities by having younger males face the issue of enlistment or conscription into the armed services. As early as

March 1942, this dilemma was confronted by characters on
David Harum, Amanda of Honeymoon Hill, Jones and I, and
Ma Perkins. In the first two serials, the young men were re-
jected for reasons of health. But in the latter two soaps—
despite enlistment being complicated by having to decide
whether or not to marry their respective girl friends—the
characters entered the Army.

The only popular serial to focus directly upon the war in
the first months of hostilities was *Against the Storm.* It had
had an anti-Nazi direction since its inception, and by early
1942 it was stressing Gestapo brutality and persecution in
Germany. Nevertheless, by the fall of 1942, soap operas were
strongly committed in plot and emphasis to the American
military cause. A survey revealed that in August and September military-related deaths occurred in five CBS soap operas,
while a nonservice death happened only once. A fuller treatment of the war, however, was best realized in new soaps developed with the war in mind, in special broadcasts and obvious plots produced in cooperation with the United States
government, and in strong depictions of familiar serial personalities having to cope with the realities of the homefront.

New programs dealing specifically with the problems of
wartime America were not usually successful. In May 1941,
NBC had attempted to reflect pre-war conscription and military training in an ill-fated series, *Buck Private and His Girl.*
During the war, new serials tried again to exploit domestic
conditions. *Lonely Women,* which premiered in June 1942,
focused on "the universal cry of womanhood—loneliness," as
it was aggravated by the conditions of war. Written by Irna
Phillips, the serial emphasized several characters who lived
lonely existences at a hotel for women. It followed their efforts
to find companionship in a society being depleted by war of its
young men. The theme of a group of differing personalities
contending with the exigencies of war became a familiar format in other new series. The problems of women left at home
was the subject of *Brave Tomorrow* beginning in October
1943, and *This Changing World* in July 1944. *Lighted
Windows* dealt with the problems of an idealistic American

family as it faced the social and physical demands of war. *Sweet River* in January 1944, was concerned with a small town and how it dealt with the war. And *The Soldier Who Came Home* (renamed *Barry Cameron* in 1945) premiered in 1942 and treated the readjustment of a wounded veteran and his family.

Two of the more noteworthy new serials avoided such limits of characterization and reflected the war in more imaginative ways. *The Open Door,* which was written by Sandra Michael, the erstwhile author of *Against the Storm,* debuted on NBC in June 1943, but lasted only a year. Much like her earlier program, this serial treated the war philosophically and intelligently. It focused on a college dean encountering various characters touched by the war. In unfolding the individual stories of these people, the program reiterated its anti-authoritarian convictions. In fact, the egalitarian political persuasion of the program was noticeable from the beginning, as each broadcast opened with the announcer proclaiming:

> There is an open door to a good way of life,
> To all men, for all men.
> This open door is called Brotherhood,
> And over its portals are these simple words:
> "I am my brother's keeper."

Woman of America began on NBC in January 1943, and approached the demands of war in an allegorical manner. Set in the Old West following the Civil War, its story of the strength and determination of a pioneer woman, Prudence Dane, held obvious implications for wartime female listeners who, themselves, were being called upon to be courageous and persevering. Tracing the exploits of the heroine as she moved westward in a covered wagon, the serial stressed the equality of men and women fighting to establish and maintain civilization. It was a struggle which the narrator, the great-granddaughter of the fictional Prudence Dane, suggested was analogous to the world of 1943 where "the women of America are once again fighting side by side with their men in the factories, farms, and homes."

Throughout the war the sponsors, writers, and broad-casters of soap operas cooperated with the American government. The central characters in many series made supportive references to federal programs such as rent control, conservation programs, crusades against absenteeism, and the sale of war bonds. On occasion they mentioned recent important political developments, integrating into their stories references to speeches and trips by national leaders, discussions of recent military battles, and considerations of pressing social issues. To keep radio writers abreast of the latest policy decisions, the Office of War Information (OWI) three times each month provided pamphlets explaining governmental programs. While there was no compulsion to use these pamphlets, if a writer wished to introduce into his serial such matters as man-power shortages or economic fluctuations, he was equipped with the latest official information which would insure exact-ness and compatibility with the war effort.

As part of their commitment to the war, radio stations and networks also carried special programs and series pro-duced in association with federal agencies. In October 1942, for example, CBS and NBC, as well as the producers of *Our Gal Sunday* and *Stella Dallas,* cooperated with the OWI in a week-long adaptation of those two soaps into vehicles explaining the war to American listeners.[28] By utilizing the regular characters of these soap operas to dramatize special stories treating wartime problems, the OWI spread govern-mental war themes in an entertaining, but propagandistic, manner. The cast of *Our Gal Sunday* treated the efforts and suffering of the Allies in prosecuting the war, while the actors and writers of *Stella Dallas* considered the Merchant Marine and the importance of cargo ships to the war. Such use of the popular serial was part of the government's "Victory Front" (on CBS), and "Victory Volunteers" (on NBC) informational projects.

Although both projects were discontinued after seven weeks, they utilized several other serials before then. Week-long adaptations in the "Victory Front" effort occurred on *We Love and Learn, Big Sister, Life Can Be Beautiful,* and *Aunt*

Jenny. And the "Victory Volunteers" programs appeared on *Portia Faces Life, Ma Perkins,* and *Young Widder Brown.* Typical of these polemic projects was the treatment of *Life Can Be Beautiful.* The fourth episode of its Victory Front week dealt with the imagined results of a Nazi occupation of New York City, and the brutal handling by the invaders of Chichi, Steven Hamilton, and Papa David Solomon. Hamilton, a lawyer and a paraplegic, was sent to a concentration camp because he would not practice law according to *Mein Kampf.* Chichi was sexually attacked by German soldiers, but managed to stab one of them to death in the struggle. And Papa David Solomon was savagely beaten because he would not renounce God and pledge allegiance to Hitler. Despite the violence, Papa David managed to utter a ringing statement of American idealism and hope.

> We believe in God and humanity. Without either one men become beasts like you. With them, no matter what happens—whipping with the strap, torturing, killing, or even worse—even life can be beautiful, and someday it will be again.

During the war spokesmen for the national military effort utilized soap operas to appeal directly to American women. As special guests they were usually introduced at the beginning of the program and made their statements before the story actually commenced. In this manner, Eleanor Roosevelt appeared on *The Story of Bess Johnson* and spoke with the heroine about the role of women in the war. Susan B. Anthony II discussed women in wartime industry on a broadcast of *Bright Horizons;* and Mrs. Theodore Roosevelt, Jr., and WAVES commander Mildred H. McAyer spoke on *Aunt Jenny's True Life Stories.*

Occasionally, speakers were integrated into the plot of the story. Thomas M. Reardon, the first Marine to land on Guadalcanal, appeared on *Bright Horizons* as part of a war-bond tour visiting Riverfield. Adet Ling, the daughter of Lin Yutang, the noted Chinese writer and scholar, spoke as a guest on *Young Doctor Malone* in 1943, appealing for blood plasma for Chinese Relief at precisely the time when the story was set in China and was strongly advocating postwar cooperation between China and the United States. The most frequently visited serial, however, was *Woman of America,* which on twenty-one occasions replaced the opening commercial for Procter and Gamble's Ivory Snow with a war message from a guest speaker. These speakers were usually war heroes or women involved with the national effort, and they all brought definitions of the responsibilities of women at home and on the job during the hostilities.

The federal government also worked directly with the producers of soap operas to spread the propagandistic word. The Department of War cooperated with Frank and Anne Hummert in producing in 1942 their short-lived series, *Chaplain Jim, U.S.A.* This serial focused on an American clergyman serving on various battlefronts, and as such, was the only soap opera to deal specifically with military action overseas. Late in the war the OWI experimented with radio characters passing from one program to another. In May 1945, that agency assisted Irna Phillips in merging her two consecutive fifteen-minute serials, *Today's Children* and *Woman in White,* into a half-hour broadcast. In this special program the characters from both soaps visited one another and in the process discussed the problems of rehabilitating wounded veterans.

Despite the new pressures and demands of life on the homefront, soaps remained the most popular programs in daytime broadcasting. Listeners stayed loyal to their "stories," and even newer, flashier types of programming—quiz shows, conversation programs, and musical variety shows—failed to break that allegiance. Government agencies were aware of this sustained popularity and, as a supplement to their cooperation with commercial serials, actually developed their own soap operas.

The Department of Agriculture produced a limited serial, *Give Us This Day,* which in five broadcasts treated issues involving food production and distribution. More elaborate, however, was *Hasten the Day.* A weekly broadcast of fifteen minutes, this OWI program related the story of the

Tucker family which had moved from the country to the big city so that Mr. Tucker, the head of the household, could work in a war factory. The serial began in mid-1943 and lasted until the end of the war, and each program dramatized a different theme of homefront life. The entire Tucker family was a testimonial to citizen cooperation with the government. Mother canned food, the children saved scrap metal and were hospitable to soldiers on leave, and when not laboring at the factory, father was looking for ways to stop waste and promote economy. Even the Tucker house, an abandoned gas station which the family had converted into a comfortable home, provided a model for listeners adversely affected by the national housing shortage. As if these characteristics were not enough, each broadcast of *Hasten the Day* explored pressing problems such as rent control, the nature of rationing, national patterns of food distribution, and the efforts of American farmers to produce crops for the war effort.

Despite the development of new programs or governmental intervention, daytime serials dealt with the war most frequently and most effectively by integrating relevant themes into their regular plots. In this way, the strongest patriotic messages were communicated and made a working part of the serial world. The most common device to lend relevance to such stories was to place soap opera figures in wartime surroundings. This allowed a soap to continue with familiar stories of accidents, tragic diseases, romances, jealousies, and childbirths, but it added an important dimension to topicality and patriotism. The popularity of this pattern was such that by the fall of 1943, seventy-five percent of the twenty NBC soap operas with contemporary settings were involved with the war.

Much as they had done in the early months of the conflagration, conscriptions and enlistments occurred throughout the war. By finding an eligible male character 4-F, a soap opera could continue its normal story line and avoid charges of draft dodging. But, many serials patriotically surrendered characters to the cause. Husbands entered the military on *The Right to Happiness, Helpmate, Backstage Wife, Rosemary, This Changing World,* and *The Story of Mary Marlin.* Sweethearts were given up by heroines on serials such as *Portia Faces Life*, *Young Widder Brown*, and *Pepper Young's Family*. And sons went forth on *Vic and Sade* and *The Goldbergs*. These were noble sacrifices which only mirrored the actual experiences of millions in the audience. In the cases of actors Alfred Ryder of *The Goldbergs* and Billy Idelson of *Vic and Sade*, their fictional inductions occurred because in reality they did enter the military.

Just as millions of Americans were flooding into war-related employment, so too did the principals of many soaps. Factories producing war materials became soap opera locales. Pepper Young, who had been classified 4-F by his draft board, did his part by working in a war plant. By the fall of 1942, Danny O'Neill of *The O'Neills* was the manager of a plant constructing secret weapons for the government. And the hero of *David Harum* was also a plant manager. Several female characters entered war industries. Peggy Farrell of *Front Page Farrell*, and the heroines of *Stella Dallas* and *Kitty Foyle*, all labored in factories to help win the war. War-related work was featured on *Lora Lawton* as the heroine, a young Midwestern woman, moved to Washington, D.C., to become the housekeeper, then sweetheart, then wife, of a shipyard owner. And the rewards of voluntary labor were featured on *The Strange Romance of Evelyn Winters* as Evelyn spent much of her time as a volunteer worker for the Red Cross Blood Bank.

Most dramatic were those soaps that developed elaborate stories which involved the war and its consequences. Injuries and amnesia occurred to many characters who served overseas. For months Mary Marlin's husband was lost in the war zone, only to be discovered in a hospital in Tunisia with his eyes bandaged. Bill Roberts, the husband of the heroine of *Rosemary*, returned from the war with a severe case of amnesia. As he gradually regained his memory, he recalled having married another woman and fathering a child with her. One of the more convoluted cases of war injury happened to Walter Manning, the fiancé of Portia Blake in *Portia Faces Life*. While in the Army he worked for Intelligence, but after being wrongly accused of spying for the Germans, he resigned his commission and became a foreign correspondent. The Nazis, however, captured and tortured him for his military secrets. Eventually rescued and exonerated, Manning faced an uncertain future for he now required intense psychiatric rehabilitation.

Throughout the hostilities, military and homefront themes drifted in and out of the serials. One of the characters of *Lonely Women* mixed romance and intrigue as she was secretly married to, and then made pregnant by, a man accused of being a Nazi spy. Portia Manning became involved with espionage in 1944, and when *Portia Faces Life* moved from NBC to CBS, she continued to pursue enemy agents, despite the rule at CBS forbidding spy stories in network broadcasts. Strained relations developed in several soaps when sweethearts and husbands went off to war, and lonely women were compromised when returning mates discovered their women had found new romantic interests during the separation.

Although almost 300,000 American men died in battle during World War II, only one important soap opera character died in action. In early 1944, Ma Perkins' son, John, was killed in Europe, and the report of his death caused a furor among listeners, program officials, and radio executives. Critics complained that in wartime the millions of listening wives and mothers should not be reminded of the grim potential of war. Yet, in answering such anger, Roy Windsor, supervisor of the program for the Dancer, Fitzgerald & Sample advertising agency, touched upon a significant aspect of the soaps. Windsor claimed that such events could not be avoided if radio were going to be honest and try to portray life as it really was. "If it can happen to Mrs. Slotnik and Mrs. Smith," he argued, "why can't it happen to Ma Perkins?" His final point suggested that this death was written into the story to make it relevant and, hopefully, instructive to all listeners.

> We did not use the death of John, Ma Perkins' son, as a story device, and we do not intend to bring him back in later episodes. He's dead, and the point is that we gave Ma Perkins the same problem as other mothers face. We also believe that, in the face of the type of character Ma Perkins portrays, the episode will give strength to her

listeners who have already faced the same kind of tragedy
or may in the future. We are willing to face adverse
criticism on the terms that we have done something
honest in radio.[29]

The verities of life on the homefront were also reflected
in soap operas in terms of what was no longer present. Lavish
meals and other aspects of luxury were replaced by meal planning to stretch food and a general attitude of austerity. The
secularity of prewar serials evaporated during the war years,
and characters increasingly used phrases such as "God bless
you," and, "I'll pray for you," a development which Anne
Hummert called "religious consolation," a direct result of the
fact that "people need it now."[30] The most striking disap-
pearance, however, was the almost-absolute elimination of the
automobile. In reality, the number of cars on the highways
had diminished because of rubber and gasoline rationing as
well as the retooling of the auto industry for the production of
tanks, trucks, and other vehicles of war. In a soap opera, therefore, it would have been anachronistic as well as unpatriotic
to have a character courting his girl friend in a car, or even
taking a leisurely weekend drive. With this wartime mood,
serial writers even avoided placing characters in accidents involving automobiles.

During the war years soap operas were under constant
attack from reformers, educators, and network and advertising
officials who felt they lacked taste and relevance in the 1940s.
The Federation of Women's Clubs, championed by its organizations in New York City and in several cities upstate, assailed
the serials as unfit for broadcasting. Their chief intellectual
spokesman was Dr. Louis Berg who alleged that listening to
soaps could cause serious medical repercussions, including
tachycardia, arrythmias, increased blood pressure, profuse per-
spiration, acute anxiety, tremors, vasomotor instability,
nocturnal frights, vertigo, and gastro-intestinal disturbances.
Such criticism, plus the search for new listeners and new
revenue, led network and advertising executives to seek alternatives to the daytime serials. Such experimentation was evident in 1943, for instance, as the weekly number of hours in

which non-serial shows were broadcast jumped from six and one-half in January to more than eighteen by December.

Criticism and innovation, however, never broke the loyalty which many American women felt toward soap operas. These serials were aimed specifically at the typical housewife who maintained a home, raised children, and did her own shopping. Advertisements were meant to inform her of consumer products and why she should purchase them, and the stories were intended to attract her fantasy and sense of romance. Like much of popular culture in the United States, the esthetic quality of the soaps was incidental. They were primarily commercial entertainment forms. To sell the cereals, flours, floor waxes, detergents, and other sponsoring products, they sought to be important to their listeners. Only by such pertinence could they expect to attract and hold a large enough audience to remain on the air.

Like all forms of American popular art, they avoided universals and esthetic concerns and focused, instead, upon those themes and attitudes that would appeal to a mass audience. If romance was a constant theme, and if wartime developments abounded in the first half of the 1940s, it was because these were pertinent to the interests and concerns of most listeners. And if wealthy clubwomen, intellectuals, and network leaders were critical of such programming, it was because they shared neither the tastes nor the attitudes of the millions of "average" housewives for whom soap operas were intended. The failure of the critics to understand mass society was only underscored by the fact that it was during World War II—a period when loyalty and industriousness were vigorously solicited through the soaps by the federal government—that they chose to attack this popular type of entertainment.

Soap Operas in the Postwar World

Following the war, daytime dramatic serials adjusted their orientations to reflect new features of American life. Some made a break with wartime themes by introducing important new characters or changing locales in their stories. Others developed new careers for their heroes. As it was with the American public, the serials put away military concerns and resumed familiar patterns of behavior. Above all, they returned to tales of romance. Traditional stories of love—love that was unrequited, suffering, jealous, insecure, or tested—flourished in the serial world as normal times returned to America.

The soap operas took advantage of the postwar interest in psychology to introduce mental problems as a source of plot development. The emphasis was noticeable at this time in literature and motion pictures, as well as in various types of radio dramatic programming. In the soaps, however, the portrayal of psychological problems was more prevalent than in the other forms of the popular arts.

Illustrative of this development was the case of Dr. Jim Brent on *The Road of Life*. After eight successful years as a surgeon in Chicago, he moved to New York City in 1945 and devoted himself to neuropsychiatric work. His chief assistant was Dr. Carson McVicker, a beautiful heiress who had turned to psychiatry as the result of a nervous breakdown several years earlier. Within this relatively sophisticated context, however, recognizable human predicaments soon emerged. Within a few years Dr. Brent had drifted, from an unhappy marriage ending in divorce, through four love affairs, each with its own unhappy dimensions. His affair with Dr. McVicker led eventually to her resignation from the hospital following another nervous breakdown. His liaison with Maggie Lowell was ultimately the result of Dr. McVicker's naïveté in hiring her as a lab assistant. Beth Lambert came to spy upon Dr. Brent and his top-secret governmental experiments, but she ended up as his third lover in the postwar era. And before the 1940s had ended, he was involved with Jocelyn McLeod (whom he eventually married), one of his patients, who was many years his junior.

Psychological materials filtered into the soaps in varying manners. The introduction of a doctor or nurse specializing in psychiatry was a favorite device. *King's Row*, appearing in 1951, concerned a psychiatric hospital. The heroine of *This Is Nora Drake*, a series which lasted from 1947 until 1959, was a nurse in the Mental Hygiene Clinic. And in various episodes of *Big Sister,* doctors often were heard discussing Freudian theories and the latest developments in Russian medicine.

Nevertheless, the most common means of introducing psychology into a serial was to have one of the main characters develop amnesia. A holdover from wartime soaps when shell-shocked veterans often developed loss of memory, amnesia became common in peacetime serials. In series like *The Second Mrs. Burton, Young Widder Brown,* and *Wendy Warren and the News,* amnesia allowed characters to develop entirely new lives and plots. In many such cases, love blossomed only to be thwarted at the point of marriage by the return of memory to the injured personality. Even Lorenzo Jones, the harmless inventor who lived an innocuous life with his beloved wife, Belle, suffered amnesia in late 1952 and before NBC cancelled the series in 1955, he had met, wooed, and almost married another woman.

The nervous breakdown and related emotional complications flourished in the soaps after 1945. Men were frequently the victims of such illnesses. The hero of *Young Doctor Malone* suffered his breakdown in 1948, and Ruth Wayne's husband, Dr. John Wayne, experienced his collapse in *Big Sister* in 1952. In 1954 the heroine's husband on *Wendy Warren and the News* suffered from general mental confusion for several months. And neurotic and psychotic males appeared in many soaps throughout this period. Women, of course, suffered their fair share of emotional problems. In 1951 two characters—Chichi Conrad on *Life Can Be Beautiful* and Peg Martinson on *This Is Nora Drake*—endured psychosomatic paralysis as a result of accidents. Meta Bauer on *The Guiding Light,* after bearing a child conceived out of wedlock and enduring a loveless but necessary marriage, was acquitted in 1951 of the murder of her husband on the grounds of temporary insanity. Yet Ma Perkins' daughter, Fay, was the most emotionally abused heroine of this period for she once suffered simultaneously from amnesia and psychosomatic paralysis.

During the late 1940s much popular analysis was directed toward the subject of juvenile delinquency. In radio this was

notable in terms of news specials and documentaries on lawlessness among American youth. Soap operas also reflected the
national concern as several serials integrated into their stories
youthful gangs intent upon crime. In the process, they were
able to make important statements about the nature and
causes of delinquency. When in 1948 *Hilltop House* returned
to the air after a lengthy hiatus, it began with the story of a
nine-year-old incorrigible child, who with his slingshot had
blinded a playmate in one eye. The judge in the case spent
much of one episode berating the boy's mother for failing to
rear him properly.

In 1949 Papa David and Chichi became involved with
Chuck Lewis, the leader of a dangerous gang of thugs. Although adults were unable to reason with Lewis, it was the
compassionate and understanding Chichi who finally was able
to relate to him. When she had first found refuge at the
Slightly Read Book Shop in the late 1930s, she had been a
member of a street gang. Drawing upon her experience and
understanding of gang life, Chichi illustrated that with the
correct attitude delinquents could be approached and reformed. Wherever there were adolescent children in the soaps,
they were vulnerable to juvenile delinquency. Even well-
adjusted Brad Burton, the son in *The Second Mrs. Burton,*
was tempted in 1950 toward a life of petty crime. Only at the
last minute, when he realized the criminal intentions of his
young friends, was he able to abandon them and turn back to
the respectability and honesty that his soap opera parents had
inculcated in him.

Other glaring realities the soaps had to face in the postwar period were the threat within the radio industry from new
forms of daytime broadcasting, and the challenge outside the
industry from the growing popularity of television. Although
the soaps had been able to withstand the challenge of programming innovations during the war, they never regained
the domination of daytime broadcasting they possessed in the
prewar years. Using figures compiled by Harrison B. Summers,[31] the number of soap operas broadcast each January in
the period 1941–1956 was as follows:

1941 — 60	1947 — 33	1953 — 28
1942 — 55	1948 — 36	1954 — 27
1943 — 40	1949 — 33	1955 — 26
1944 — 44	1950 — 32	1956 — 19
1945 — 47	1951 — 27	
1946 — 40	1952 — 35	

The growing number of variety and giveaway programs occupying time slots formerly held by daytime serials was partially responsible for the decline in soap operas. By the middle of World War II, when, because of rationing, advertisers no longer needed to worry about selling effectiveness in selecting their programs, many agencies began gambling on new types of daytime programming. Although agency executives were not agreed on what type of show would come to dominate daytime radio, they were convinced that all but the best of the soaps would fade away once the war ended. Typical of this new sentiment was R. J. Scott of the Schwimmer and Scott agency who told an interviewer in late 1943, "I think that big daytime variety shows will take a commanding position in radio as soon as talent is available, but that will not be until the war is over. In the meantime, new comedy-dramas and the smaller variety shows will undoubtedly take over many of the daytime spots."[32]

Although soaps were not eclipsed as readily as some authorities anticipated, many popular new programs emerged in daytime radio. Tom Brenneman's audience participation program began in 1943 as *Breakfast at Sardi's* and gained fame under its subsequent name, *Breakfast in Hollywood*. Until his untimely death in 1948, Brenneman made this hour show one of the top ten in daytime broadcasting. Quiz and giveaway series like *Grand Slam* with Irene Beasley, which premiered in 1943, and *Queen for a Day* with Jack Bailey, which began in 1945, also drew listeners away from the soaps and into new listening patterns. And successful daytime variety programs like Don McNeill's *Breakfast Club* and the *Arthur Godfrey Program*—series which had been on radio since 1933 and 1945, respectively—helped to introduce other non-serial programs to network radio.

By 1950 a significant pattern emerged from the competition of the serial and non-serial radio programs. Except in those cases where a new show was hosted by an attractive and dynamic personality, soap operas remained more popular with the daytime audience. Only a few hosts, like Arthur Godfrey, Jack Bailey, Art Linkletter of *Art Linkletter's House Party,* and Tommy Bartlett of *Welcome Travelers,* successfully competed against the soaps. Despite the generally mediocre popularity of non-serial programming, however, the newer type of shows continued to enter daytime radio.

The reason for this development lay in the dynamics of commercial sponsorship. The daytime serials were sponsored traditionally by large manufacturing companies. When many of the significant advertisers, like General Mills and Pillsbury, began leaving radio for television by the late 1940s, they abandoned soap operas. Most of the newer shows, however, had either several small sponsors who shared the broadcasting expense, or local advertisers whose messages were carried only on individual stations airing the network show. The former, multi-sponsored, and the latter, cooperatively sponsored, programs helped keep networks economically healthy even though traditional radio was succumbing to television. What had begun during the war as an interest in non-serial entertainment had become within a decade an economic necessity for the radio networks.

The challenge of television became even more overpowering in the early 1950s when viable daytime programming entered TV. In many cases, former radio soaps moved into the rival medium—*The Guiding Light* in 1952, *Valiant Lady* in 1953, and *Portia Faces Life* in 1954. Even programs new to television, like *Search for Tomorrow, Love of Life,* and *Hawkins Falls,* sounded as if they had been nurtured in radio. Television attracted the actors, writers, and the advertisers whose existence had made radio so rich. Television also offered the soaps as plays, with viewers able to see as well as hear the melodramatic stories. It was an attractive combination which radio producers labored valiantly to offset.

One of the more interesting shifts in plot structure that

radio developed to meet the threat of television was the addition of fast-paced excitement. The traditional pace had been slow in radio, the argument being that a listener should be able to miss two or three consecutive programs and not lose the story line. Now, compelled to become more exciting and more attractive, the radio soaps stressed action. Murder became a favorite event in daytime serials. *Perry Mason,* the soap opera based on the stories of Erle Stanley Gardner, and *Front Page Farrell,* which featured a newspaper reporter who specialized in murder mysteries, related stories of homicide with regularity. But murder appeared often in the traditionally romantic serials, from *Our Gal Sunday* and *The Right to Happiness,* to *Just Plain Bill* and *Rosemary.* Indicative of the new spirit in soaps was the frankly brutal language Meta Bauer used on *The Guiding Light* when threatening her husband: "You're talking to a woman who'd rather see you dead before she can trust a small boy into your care. I'd kill you first, Ted. I'd kill you! I'd kill you!" Anthony Loring on *Young Widder Brown* became intimately involved in murder and it took courtroom trials in 1951 and 1956 to clear him of two different deaths.

Taking 1951 as a year of alarm in the production of daytime serials, a few statistics suggest the intensity of that feeling. During that year there were approximately thirty murders committed on fifteen different serials. Twelve occurred on *Front Page Farrell,* three on *Perry Mason,* and two each on *Our Gal Sunday* and *Wendy Warren and the News.* Add to that at least eight attempted murders, three fatal accidents, and a typhoid epidemic on *Rosemary,* and the violence that had been seeping into the postwar serials had become a flood.

Another reaction to television was the creation of new serials which, it was felt, added relevance or unique dimensions to daytime broadcasting. *Wendy Warren and the News* was introduced in 1947, and thoughout its eleven years on radio it began with the fictional character, Wendy Warren, reading the news from a radio station along with the actual newscaster, Douglas Edwards. Following the capsulized news, Wendy left the studio and entered her serial world. ABC in

1951 tried to revive *Lone Journey*, a serial which had expired eight years earlier, by shifting its locale to the Judith mountains of Montana. Here it became the story of a New York City businessman who abandoned urban life and sought meaning in the country.

No successful soap opera had been devoted entirely to life in the motion picture industry (although *Backstage Wife* and *The Romance of Helen Trent* eventually settled their characters in Hollywood), and the rise and fall in 1950 of *Nona from Nowhere* kept that record intact. The most common format in the new serials was medicine. Just as psychiatry and sickness had become familiar themes in the older, established soaps, they were the subjects of such new programs as *King's Row* and *The Affairs of Dr. Gentry* in 1951, and *The Doctor's Wife* in 1952.

The networks also sought to add prestige to their daytime programs by adding impressive titles and names to their offerings. In this line, both Mutual in 1949, and ABC in 1951, tried to revive *Against the Storm*. A sensitive, moving serial when it premiered in 1939, it had won in 1942 the highest award in radio, but left the air at the end of that year. Even though it featured the original writer, Sandra Michael, the series was not popular in its revived format. A more successful attempt at prestige was made by bringing Carleton E. Morse to daytime radio. The most celebrated production by Morse had been *One Man's Family*, an evening serial which began on the West coast in 1932, and became a highly popular network feature the following year. Morse also had created such other series as *I Love a Mystery* and *I Love Adventure*. In 1951 he also introduced *The Woman in My House*, a traditional soap opera with Morse's familiar strong sense of paternalism and family. In 1955, Morse developed a daytime version of *One Man's Family*, his epic of the Barbours which, like *The Woman in My House*, presented a conservative image of family living. Both serials lasted until 1959.

When the last surviving soap operas were cancelled by CBS radio in November 1960, the *New York Times* misinterpreted the significance of the event when it wryly noted that they "along with their long-suffering relatives and friends were sent to the Valhalla of soap operas with the blessings of the network."[33] It was the radio serial that was unceremoniously shuffled off to an insubstantial paradise. The genre itself survived and found success in the triumphant medium, television. While they were flooding the daytime airwaves for three decades, the soaps clearly established for themselves a niche that even the demise of creative radio programming could not destroy. Expropriating many of the important developers of the radio serials, including the renowned Irna Phillips, television networks merely transplanted the audio soap opera to the exciting new visual medium. It was misleading of the *New York Times,* therefore, to suggest that like so many aged and irrelevant heroes of the past, daytime serial dramas were no longer vital to America in the 1960s.

What ended in late 1960 was only a chapter in the history of broadcasting, not a type of programming. Radio had too deeply integrated the soap opera into the lifestyle of millions of Americans. Here the soaps functioned as advisors, socializers, companions, and friends. They provided everything from philosophy and inspiration, to household hints and gossip. And above all, they had been entertainment. With such a function for daytime, housebound audiences, soap operas clearly would remain a vital and undiminished part of American popular culture.

6

The Development of Broadcast Journalism

Dependent as radio was upon newspapers jealous of their own prerogatives, upon sponsors reluctant to offend potential customers, and upon network executives sensitive to private and public criticism, it was a singular accomplishment that American broadcasting ever developed a significant news format. Yet, it not only produced influential news reportage, but, with the creation of programming peripheral to current events, radio also established the most important development in twentieth-century reporting—broadcast journalism. During the years in which radio was the ascendant popular medium, this novel dimension in journalism affected not only the opinions of listeners, and the public's general level of knowledge, but also the direction of governmental policy and the evolution of the nation. Furthermore, by the mid-1950s the achievements in radio news had established the groundwork for even greater achievements in television.

As it matured in radio, broadcast journalism developed several distinct aspects. Reporting the news was, of course, the primary responsibility. Whether this entailed reading dispatches into a microphone, or venturing into the streets of a foreign country to uncover news, radio eventually displaced newspapers as the principal source for Americans of information about current events. The panel discussion and news interview programs were outgrowths of broadcast journalism. As such, they were stylized news conferences in which questioning and discussion created a more informed audience and led many times to newsworthy revelations. The radio documentary was also a product of broadcast journalism. When it flourished in the postwar years, it proved a persuasive format through which to present extended analysis and interpretation of the news. The most significant aspect of radio journalism, however, was the news commentator. At once a reporter and an editorialist, by the mid-1930s the commentator represented the highest form of opinionated broadcasting in a commercial medium where freedom of speech and program content were often secondary to economic profitability.

Considering the commercial interests that opposed news programming, the development of broadcast journalism was all the more striking. Newspapers and wire services generally opposed radio news as an encroachment upon their domains, and a threat to their financial well-being. Many newspapers countered by operating radio stations, thereby making radio news an extension of their own publications. As early as 1922, sixty-nine stations were owned by newspapers. Furthermore, believing radio could bolster public interest, in many instances newspapers sponsored local newscasters as, for example, the *Brooklyn Daily Eagle,* which financed the first radio efforts of H. V. Kaltenborn in the early 1920s on WEAF and WOR in New York City.

By the time of the Great Depression, however, radio had begun to make serious inroads into newspaper circulation. Americans turned increasingly to broadcasting for their entertainment and information. This was especially vexing to most publishers since newspapers printed daily radio logs without charging stations or networks an advertisement rate. By 1933 exasperation led to action as the Newspaper Publishers' Association, the principal organization of newspaper owners, determined to blunt forever the effectiveness of radio newscasts. The allies of the publishers in this "press war" were the major news wire services in the United States: United Press, Associated Press, and the International News Service.

The wire services had an ambivalent history in their relationship with radio. In 1922, the Associated Press had cautioned its subscribers against providing its stories for broadcast. As the number of stations owned by newspapers increased, however, the policy of the AP became increasingly untenable. In 1925 the news agency relaxed its position, agreeing that radio stations had the right to broadcast those wire service stories that were of paramount national and international concern. Three years later, moreover, all wire services agreed to permit their material to be aired twice daily on radio newscasts; and in 1929 they began to sell their news directly to radio. Depression economics, however, brought a sudden change of policy to the wire services. By 1933, they protectively conspired with newspaper publishers to thwart radio news programming.

To destroy fledgling broadcast journalism, many major newspapers agreed to demand a fee for publishing radio logs. Recognizing that the struggle against radio was a fight for advertising revenue and for customers, newspapers also intimidated the sponsors of radio newscasts by suggesting that they choose which of the two media they preferred to use for their advertising. The wire services, for their part, united to prevent network stations from receiving their product. And all non-network local stations were compelled to pay for the right to broadcast wire service bulletins. This two-pronged attack upon broadcasting was the most serious assault upon freedom of the press and the right of Americans to be informed in the short history of radio.

The radio networks responded with their most powerful weapon when they formed their own news bureaus. Through the efforts of men like A. A. Schecter, Jr., of NBC, and Paul White of CBS, radio set up rudimentary news-gathering staffs that used telephones and telegrams to obtain the news. Oddly enough, in several instances these network bureaus actually "scooped" their established rivals. And when in September 1933 CBS formed its own Columbia News Service and established news bureaus in New York, Los Angeles, Chicago and Washington, D.C.—as well as placing correspondents in every American city with a population in excess of 20,000, and in many foreign capitals—it became clear that rather than arresting the development of radio journalism, the challenge from newspapers and wire services was being successfully met by the networks.

By the end of the year the press war ended with a compromise. Meeting in what one writer called the "smoke and hate-filled rooms" in the Hotel Biltmore in New York City,[1] the two sides agreed to terms that called for the abandonment of news gathering by the radio networks, and the creation of a Press-Radio Bureau to provide the networks without charge enough bulletins to produce two five-minute newscasts daily. Furthermore, radio commentators were restricted to generalizations and news more than twelve hours old. And all broadcasts of Press-Radio Bureau materials were to be without sponsorship. There is no doubt that the losers in the agreements would have been the radio networks had not other developments materialized. Network officials in December 1933 still did not envision the potential, or the necessity, for radio to gather and produce its own news. The expense and the gamble involved in such an undertaking were great risks to take in the midst of the Depression. The terms of the Biltmore Agreement, then, guaranteed radio executives that broadcasting would have a news function, albeit one that was subservient to newspapers.

The future of broadcast journalism was rescued by the reactions of non-network broadcasters. Many independent-minded affiliate stations, as well as small regional networks (such as the Yankee Network servicing the northeastern part of the country) and a number of independent news services refused to accept the compromise made by NBC and CBS. These organizations were able to gather and broadcast their own news so successfully that they effectively undermined the controversial agreement. Because they were decentralized and scattered throughout the nation, they were less vulnerable to pressures from the large networks based in the East. These maverick organizations eventually forced the wire services to retreat from their hostile position and begin selling their news to all radio stations that cared to subscribe. For their part, many newspapers met the change of events by purchasing broadcasting stations and recognizing that radio was to be a medium of news as well as entertainment.

Although networks did not produce effective news-gathering organizations until the mid-1930s, it is ironic that modern radio was born broadcasting news. The airing over KDKA (Pittsburgh) of the results of the Harding-Cox election on November 2, 1920, wedded radio and news from the beginning. In September 1921, KDKA began regular news broadcasts directly from the newsroom of the Pittsburgh *Post*. In July 1922, WJAC (Norfolk, Nebraska) began a daily news broadcast. Three months earlier H. V. Kaltenborn had begun his career as a news commentator on WEAF. Other stations introduced even fuller treatments of the news. WJZ (Newark) in February 1923 began a daily fifteen-minute summary of the news. By 1925 station KOIN (Portland, Oregon) was billing its newscast as the "Newspaper of the Air." And in the late 1920s, WOMT (Manitowoc, Wisconsin) was broadcasting news "every hour on the hour."

Despite the swelling of the number of news programs, other aspects of the evolving broadcast journalism appeared in the 1920s. The use of radio in Presidential politics began as early as November 11, 1921. On that date an Armistice Day address by Warren G. Harding was carried by radio. Throughout his short tenure in office Harding was an avid supporter of broadcasting. Many of his speeches were aired, and his ownership of a 25,000-meter receiver brought much favorable publicity to the new medium.

Radio was an influential addition in 1924 to the national conventions of the Democratic and Republican parties. Nineteen stations covered the Presidential nominating conferences held that summer in New York City and Cleveland, respectively. An estimated fifteen million citizens heard the proceedings. According to the noted radio impresario, Samuel L. ("Roxy") Rothafel, these broadcasts played an important role with the electorate as the uncomplicated selection of Calvin Coolidge contrasted dramatically with the turmoil surrounding the choice of a Democratic nominee, John W. Davis, on the one-hundred-and-third ballot. Radio, in this manner, exposed questionable political processes. It also brought to many listeners a sense of political weakness, listening as they were to supposedly democratic organizations nominating candidates in less than equitable manners. Roxy suggested in 1925 that by exposing political maneuverings, radio was exerting a reformist force. Before preferential primary elections had been instituted in most states, Roxy noted that

> broadcasting of the event planted a germ that may sometime burst out into a political epidemic of a new sort, in the form of a more equitable system of choosing candidates. It will be the natural demand of a people who have come to realize their political insignificance through constant exposure to events completely beyond their choice or authority.[2]

It was appropriate in this first "radio" Presidential campaign that Coolidge was inaugurated before twenty-three million listeners as the oath of office and his inaugural address were broadcast from Washington over two networks linking twenty-four stations throughout the nation. Furthermore, Coolidge possessed the perfect image for the first President to be helped to election by radio. Famous for his conservatism and his silence, the Chief Executive fit perfectly the mold of the new politician which, according to Frederick C. Hicks, eastern director of the Republican National Committee, radio was creating as "thousands of invisible auditors are conscious of the importance of delivering messages free from boastful predictions and demagogic utterances."[3]

In its first half-decade, radio journalism developed the important function of live coverage of special events. Sporting contests were the first broadcasts of this type. As early as July 1921, station WJY (Hoboken) transmitted from ringside the heavyweight championship boxing match between Jack Dempsey and Georges Carpentier. Radio coverage of the baseball World Series began in the fall of 1921. Soon collegiate and professional football games were being regularly broadcast, and announcers like Graham McNamee, Phillips Carlin, Major J. Andrew White, and Ted Husing emerged as the first "sportscaster" celebrities in the nation.

Another type of coverage of special events in these years was the airing of speeches by famous statesmen. In the early 1920s political leaders, such as Woodrow Wilson, and visiting foreign dignitaries, like Georges Clemenceau and David Lloyd George, addressed millions through American radio. In July 1925, station WGN pioneered the broadcasting of legal proceedings. Sustaining a cost of $1,000 per day for the rental of telephone lines, this Chicago station aired the final sessions of the Scopes trial in Dayton, Tennessee. Through its remote transmission from the courtroom, listeners were able to hear the legal and Biblical argumentation of Clarence Darrow and William Jennings Bryan as they debated the merits of Darwin's theory of evolution as taught in the schools of Tennessee.

It had always been a dream of the developers of radio programming that the principal goal of broadcasting should be moral uplift. Pioneers like Dr. Lee De Forest envisioned radio disseminating classical music, university lectures, and wholesome drama. Once it became a medium for advertisers after 1922, however, more democratic impulses entered radio, and it became primarily a medium for popular, mass culture, rather than for the more elite cultural forms its originators had desired. Nevertheless, one of the goals of those pioneers that did survive the advertisers was the use of radio to inform the mass of Americans about governmental policy, to debate the merits of such directions, and to create, thereby, an informed citizenry.

By the late 1920s radio had clearly established a role for such programming. Political commentators, such as Frederick William Wile on CBS and David Lawrence on NBC, offered interpretive analyses of news events. Speeches on political topics were often presented by experts, and politicians made frequent use of the air to make known their opinions. Indicative of this development, in the Presidential campaign of 1928, the Republican party spent more than $435,000 on radio advertising (21.6 percent of its campaign budget), while the Democrats spent $650,000.[4] Thus, as well as its emerging function of reporting the news, broadcast journalism in the 1920s established a definite importance for radio in the exchange of ideas. The implications of such precedents would be more fully realized in the following decade.

Although the official foreign policy of the United States in the inter-war period was one of isolationism, it was not an ignorant American population that adhered to such non-involvement in European and Asian affairs. Especially in the 1930s, when the challenge to American isolationism and world peace was greatest, radio kept listeners informed of the latest political developments. Whether it was broadcasting a panel discussion or a significant event, the speech of a European demogogue, or a remote pickup from the battlefront of a small war, radio was used by the new electronic journalists to bring current events to listeners in a manner that was more vivid and immediate than print journalism.

By 1939 a poll conducted by the Elmo Roper agency showed that more than twenty-five percent of the population relied upon radio to obtain most of its news. More impressive, an overwhelming majority felt that radio news was more objective than newspapers and that radio commentators were preferable to newspaper columnists and editorialists.[5] Furthermore, during World War II, when speed and accuracy were demanded by citizens in the reporting of battlefront news, broadcast journalism became even more popular with Americans. By November 1942 a survey of ninety-five localities showed that seventy-three percent of the respondents received most of their news about the war from radio, while only forty-nine percent listed newspapers as a major source for such information. And in the spring of 1946, a national survey demonstrated that radio had nearly replaced newspapers, as sixty-one percent of those polled listed radio as their major source of daily news, while only thirty-five percent cited newspapers.[6]

Throughout the 1930s radio journalism continued to expand its coverage and improve its techniques. One of the most impressive developments was the appearance of several important panel discussion programs which brought to American listeners all sides of current debates. The longest-running series was *The University of Chicago Roundtable,* which premiered in February 1931, and left the air in June 1955. Although it occasionally featured celebrities, such as Prime Minister Jawaharlal Nehru of India who appeared in 1949, and T. S. Eliot who appeared in 1950, the weekly program usually presented university professors and researchers discussing topics that ranged from science to poetry, and from Presidential policies of Jeffersonianism. *The Roundtable* enjoyed an immense following and provocative broadcasts could generate as many as 16,000 letters to the offices of NBC. At one point during its existence, more than 21,000 listeners subscribed to the transcripts of the program.

More visceral than *The Roundtable* in its exchange of ideas was *America's Town Meeting of the Air*. This public affairs program began in May 1935 on a controversial note. The program considered the topic, "Which Way for America?" and presented as panelists Raymond Moley (member of President Roosevelt's Brain Trust) supporting democracy, Norman Thomas as the spokesman for socialism, A. J. Muste favoring communism, and Lawrence Dennis (editor of *The Awakener*) supporting fascism. Throughout its span of broadcasting that lasted into the late 1950s, *America's Town Meeting of the Air* was not squeamish about confronting its listeners with strongly opposing opinions. New Deal advocates, such as Harold Ickes and Robert H. Jackson, frequently pitted their pro-government interpretations against the pro-business ideals of critics of President Roosevelt, such as Wendell Willkie and General Hugh S. Johnson. The verbal battles of inter ventionists and isolationists were broadcast on the program, and foreign personalities occasionally appeared. Internal social issues were frequently discussed on the show. The program presented a wide range of attitudes, such as those of Walter White of the NAACP, Father Flanagan of Boys' Town, Al Capp, creator of the *Li'l Abner* comic strip, and Arnold Toynbee, the noted world historian. The theory behind the series was to revive the town meetings of earlier centuries by inviting guest authorities to air opposing opinions and then allowing a lively radio audience to question those speakers. It was a format that was both popular and educational.

Panel discussion programming blossomed in the 1930s. Listeners could hear topical problems discussed in depth on such series as *American Forum of the Air*, which remained on NBC for more than twenty years, *People's Platform* on CBS for fourteen years, and *Northwestern Reviewing Stand*, produced by Northwestern University for Mutual for twenty years. One prominent series went so far as to develop a juvenile version of itself, *High School Town Meeting of the Air*, which was broadcast in the mid-1930s. These series presented a wide range of opinion, and since they were usually sustaining programs, there was no interference prompted by the commercial interests of a sponsor. Interestingly, when *Reader's Digest* assumed the sponsorship of *America's Town Meeting of the Air* in the 1940s, there was open fear that an advertiser would inhibit the objectivity of the series. By that time, however, the tradition of free speech in panel discussions was so entrenched that even if the new sponsor had wished to interject its opinion, it probably would have met resistance.

As well as the panel discussion, broadcast journalism in the 1930s saw the emergence of the news commentator as a distinctive entity in radio. More than a reader of news, these commentators were editorial writers who added their informed interpretations to much of what they reported. At a time when audiences listened and did not demand slides and film to enliven news reports, commentators came to dominate newscasting. They offered listeners a wide range of personalities and opinions as they spoke on topics as diverse as European political developments and domestic charities.

It is interesting that although such newscasters offered substantial points of view, they often represented commercial entities. Many were backed by sponsors, and their survival on radio depended upon their ability to reach and maintain sizable audiences. This often caused misgivings among the commentators. To a man like H. V. Kaltenborn it was prostituting his journalistic ethics to read commercials, yet Walter Winchell not only dramatized the products of his sponsor, but with phrases like "lotions of love," with which he signed off his *Jergen's Journal*, he integrated the sponsor's product directly into his delivery.[7] Most commentators, however, were careful not to let their personal philosophies bend before the pressures of advertisers. In this manner Kaltenborn lost his sponsor, General Mills, in 1939 when his outspoken position in favor of the Loyalists in the Spanish Civil War prompted a group of American Catholics to threaten a boycott of General Mills products unless he abandoned his criticism.[8]

Radio commentators in the 1930s were often print journalists who had abandoned newspapers for broadcasting, or who maintained careers in both media. Among the former, Floyd Gibbons and William L. Shirer came from the *Chicago Tribune,* Edwin C. Hill from the New York *Sun,* Raymond Gram Swing from the Philadelphia *Public Ledger,* H. R. Baukage from the Associated Press, and Boake Carter from the Philadelphia *Evening Bulletin.* Among those who maintained viable newspaper columns were Walter Winchell, Dorothy Thompson, and Drew Pearson. It is interesting, however, that several of the more impressive commentators emerged with no newspaper experience. In this category were personalities such as Lowell Thomas, John Daly, Edward R. Murrow, and Gabriel Heatter.

Like their diverse backgrounds, the radio commentators who emerged in the 1930s possessed a wide range of political persuasions. *Variety* in July 1945 presented a study of the principal commentators of the day.[9] From a consideration of that survey, it is possible to substantiate the breadth of interpretation that these newsmen represented. A significant number of the commentators possessed biases that were labeled "reactionary." These included men such as Bill Cunningham, Arthur Hale, Rupert Hughes, John B. Kennedy, Fulton Lewis, Jr., and the highly controversial Upton Close. Associated with such positions as hostility to the New Deal, labor, and interventionism, Close blamed Roosevelt for driving the United States into war and often lashed out at "the smirch of communistic propaganda" that, he felt, permeated much of American broadcasting.[10]

Among the group of "liberal" commentators were the more distinguished broadcast journalists. Cecil Brown, for

instance, was given a Peabody Award in 1942, and Edward R.
Murrow received the same award in 1943. Others included
William L. Shirer, Raymond Gram Swing, and Walter Win-
chell. Between these two poles, *Variety* cited "conservatives"
such as Lowell Thomas, Bill Henry, John Daly, and H. R.
Baukage. It also named as "middle-of-the-road" such com-
mentators as Charles Collingwood, Ned Calmer, Quincy
Howe, and George Fielding Eliot.

Whatever their persuasions, the importance of this type of
radio journalist was twofold. First, in broadcasting news these
commentators brought to radio recognizable political postures
which, ultimately, were advocacies of policy. In an era of
controversy and confrontation in world and domestic affairs,
these news analysts offered their own reasoned, but subjective,
interpretations for listeners to consider. As early as 1936, for
instance, Floyd Gibbons on NBC opposed any type of American involvement in the Spanish Civil War; Winchell warmly
applauded everything President Roosevelt did; Dorothy
Thompson in 1940 called for American entry into the European War; and Boake Carter and Fulton Lewis, Jr., strongly
supported the isolationists in the America First movement.

A second importance of news commentators was the educative effect they had on their audiences. These broadcasters
allowed listeners to test the validity of their own conclusions,
to confirm or refute those interpretations, and to learn in the
process. Rather than condemn American radio for presenting
a cacophony of opinions, each cancelling the others, broadcasting, then, should be commended for tolerating the varieties of Truth. In a liberal-democratic country such as the
United States, a relatively-free citizenry is condemned to its
own level of intelligence. Unlike monolithic regimes where
only one answer is permitted to broadcasters since it is considered *the* Truth, American radio—even in time of great
crises such as the Depression and World War II—tolerated
diversity of opinion. Listeners were compelled to learn for
themselves the correct position from which to understand the
news of the world. This is not to suggest that the range of
political commentary was without limitation. There were, for

instance, no Marxist or fascist news analysts on network radio. Yet, relative to other political regimes, the commentators who emerged in the 1930s represented the broadest spectrum of ideas in radio of any nation.

Radio produced scores of analysts whose broadcasts were an important part of the years of Depression and World War. Nevertheless, it is possible to distinguish several exceptional commentators whose style and message made them especially influential with the American public. H. V. (Hans von) Kaltenborn was the doyen of news broadcasters, even in the 1930s. He began his career in 1922, and was a constant radio personality until he retired in 1955. Kaltenborn brought to his programs an alert, serious style which he maintained by always standing before the microphone, as he felt sitting while broadcasting made one relaxed and off-guard. Born in Milwaukee in 1878, Kaltenborn was the offspring of a Hessian noble family, and throughout his life he maintained a sense of dignity and pride in his Germanic background. He abhorred Nazism as repugnant to German values. When on October 3, 1939, he broadcast news of the death of the American religious leader George Cardinal Mundelein, he could have been speaking of himself when he said of the Chicago prelate, "As a man of German ancestry, he was naturally profoundly disturbed about the pagan aspects of the Nazi creed."

Kaltenborn's liberal politics involved him in occasional controversy. In the 1920s he spoke frequently in favor of the League of Nations. In January 1934, he aroused the wrath of the attorney general of Alabama when he stated that the young black men involved in the Scottsboro Trial should be tried elsewhere because they could not receive a fair trial in Alabama. His hostility toward General Francisco Franco, the Roman Catholic Church, and German intervention in the Spanish Civil War angered many American Catholics and German-Americans living in the Midwest. And his certainty of an election victory for Thomas E. Dewey in November 1948 led to a light-hearted mimicking of Kaltenborn by newly elected President Harry S Truman.

Kaltenborn blended an efficient style of broadcasting

with an ability to elucidate without a prepared script. Being a well-travelled man, he frequently offered side comments on the cities or areas from which his stories originated. He was also not adverse to explaining to his listeners legalistic terms, such as "cloture," that might arise in his newscasts. Despite his erudite approach to radio, Kaltenborn occasionally demonstrated a wry sense of humor. Thus, in a broadcast in September 1939, when he switched from 10:30 P.M. to an early evening time slot, he told his listeners that they could no longer blame him for keeping them from bed, although now he might be accused of interfering with their dinner.

Kaltenborn was especially effective when broadcasting from foreign locations. In 1936, during the early days of the Spanish Civil War, he once transmitted directly from a battle in progress. In 1938 he produced 102 broadcasts from Germany in eighteen days during the Munich Crisis. And, in World War II, he broadcast from the headquarters of General Omar Bradley in France, and General Douglas MacArthur in Australia. The success of this style was evidenced during the war years. In the years 1942–1945, Kaltenborn maintained the highest Hooper rating average (15.9) of any radio commentator with the exception of Walter Winchell.

If Kaltenborn epitomized the dedicated professionalism possible in broadcast journalism, Floyd Gibbons represented the fact that in the 1930s the dimensions of news commentary were still broadly defined. He blended the skills of a journalist with the flair and verve of a showman. It was an attitude toward news and broadcasting which was shared by as prestigious a newsman as Lowell Thomas who told an interviewer in 1934, "There aren't any news broadcasters. . . . On the networks we're really entertainers. . . . My talks are planned as entertainment, not education."[11] Gibbons' journalistic style was a virile one. Although he had been a foreign correspondent for the *Chicago Tribune* for fourteen years, and a popular commentator throughout the early 1930s, Gibbons saw himself as an explorer. A five-part biographical series printed in the fan magazine, *Radio Mirror,* in 1937, appropriately was titled, "The Personal History of Floyd Gibbons, Adventurer."

Except for a few weeks on WGN in 1925, Gibbons began his broadcasting career in 1929 in an NBC series, *The Headline Hunter.* The program featured Gibbons relating newspaper "shop-talk," much as he told stories of adventure in 1930 in his popular series, *World Adventure.* His first news program was sponsored in 1929 by *Literary Digest* magazine. Here, because he wrote his own material and desired to speak more than most fifteen-minute programs would allow, Gibbons developed his famous rapid-fire style of delivery. He was once clocked at 217 words per minute. In this manner, he was able to speak between four and five thousand words in a quarter-hour broadcast. His delivery became so popular that by 1933 he had helped establish a correspondence course for would-be radio announcers, the Floyd Gibbons School of Broadcasting, that advertised on the back covers of fan magazines:

> Have *you* an idea for a radio program? Can *you* describe things? Have *you* a Radio voice? Are *you* musically inclined? Have *you* the ability to write humor, dramatic sketches, playlets, advertising? Can *you* sell? If you can do any of these things—*Broadcasting needs you!*[12]

Throughout the first half of the decade, Gibbons refined his style into an effective crusading pitch. On the Nash *Speedshow* he cautioned against the involvement of the United States government in the Spanish Civil War. On the General Electric *House of Magic* series, his commentaries urged a widespread understanding of science in American life. And on a series sponsored by the Libby, Owens glass company, his constant championing of safety glass helped launch a successful national campaign to require such glass in new automobiles.

Despite the popularity of his political commentaries, Gibbons was never a fully committed newscaster. He was, however, always an adventurer. In 1931 he flew to the Far East with Will Rogers, and entered Manchuria, marching part of the way with the invading Japanese army. His broadcast from Mukden on the morning of January 20, 1932, was the first war broadcast ever sent to the United States from a foreign country. His cordial interview with Benito Mussolini in

1935 may have been responsible for his receiving special treatment by invading Italian armed forces when he covered the
Ethiopian War. In fact, much of the early American understanding of that war resulted from the fact that Gibbons was
the most active foreign correspondent there.

An athletic man with a patch covering his left eye, his
physical appearance enhanced the adventurer image his newspaper and radio career developed. Gibbons must have been
unimpressed with such series as *Your True Adventures,* a giveaway program on CBS in 1937 in which he related stories sent
in by listeners eager to win a prize of $25 for the best story of
the evening. When the popularity of his style waned, Gibbons
left radio. He died in obscurity in September 1939.

The journalistic exhibitionism that surrounded Gibbons
left him vulnerable to criticism. With a new breed of professional radio journalist being developed by the end of the
decade, he was an anachronism. Charitably, *Variety* noted in
his obituary that his "rapid-fire style of announcing" had become "passé after a time."[13] In love with the new medium of
communication, but more in love with being "on the spot"
when world events were taking place, Gibbons was caught between the glamor of the world of the foreign correspondent of
the past, and the disciplined reality of the professional commentator of the electronic age. Perhaps the best epitaph for
his career was written as part of the flattering series in *Radio
Mirror*:

> His has been the story of a man who represents, as nearly
> as any man can, the modern counterpart of the wander-
> ing troubadours of old. They went around their little
> world on foot, gathering news and retelling it in the
> form of songs. Floyd goes around his big world . . . by air-
> plane, train, and fast motor car, gathering his news and
> retelling it in the form of type and brisk, clipped prose
> over the air. The difference is only on the surface. Down
> underneath, Floyd and the troubadours are the same—ro-
> mantics, wanderers, restless pryers into whatever excite-
> ment is going on.[14]

The range of coverage exhibited in emerging news commentary was most expansive in the programs of Walter

Winchell. Although generally considered a broadcaster of Broadway gossip, Winchell probed all aspects of human experience to draw material for his shows. A typical Winchell broadcast might include comments on an illicit love affair, a European dictator, automobile safety, a scandalous crime, and patriotism. A man who was at once a great influence upon public opinion and a scandalmonger, Winchell's journalistic style fell somewhere between the disciplined professionalism of Kaltenborn and the impulsive flare of Gibbons. He was, in the words of an admirer in 1939, both "the historian of trivialities and the serious crusader."[15]

Born of an immigrant Jewish family which struggled to survive in the ethnic melange that was Harlem at the turn of the century, Winchell was reared on the tough, realistic streets of urban America. This gave him a grim but aggressive style which he demonstrated throughout his career. As a teenager he had tried his hand at vaudeville. Working with such neighborhood boys as Eddie Cantor, Georgie Price, and George Jessel, Winchell realized by 1920 that the vaudeville stage was unsuitable to his personality.[16] He turned to journalism, and by the time he entered radio in 1932, he had become the most powerful columnist in the Hearst newspaper chain. Winchell's Broadway information and scandal column was the most widely read of its type in the country. His arrival in radio served only to broaden the scope of his interests, and the expanse of his professional reputation.

Winchell personally knew the saints and sinners of his environment. In the 1930s he became a close friend of President Roosevelt and J. Edgar Hoover; at the same time, he was an intimate of many New York City mobsters. In 1933, Winchell was one of the first radio commentators to attack Adolf Hitler; he also assailed the German-American Bund as subversive, not only to the United States, but to all civilization. And he was a powerful fighter when he took up a cause. With his staccato delivery, accentuated by the sound of a telegrapher's key, his broadcasts left the image of strength, exactitude, and honesty. During his career he became the most influential antagonist against such issues as the House Com-

mittee on Un-American Activities headed in 1944 by Martin
Dies, Communist subversion at home and abroad, the arrest
and trial of Tokyo Rose, and racial and religious bigotry.
Equally, as a proponent of causes, Winchell lent the consider-
able influence of his broadcasts to support the New Deal, the
American commitment during World War II, and Senator
Joseph McCarthy.

Winchell was the most popular commentator in the history of radio. Throughout his more than twenty years on the
air he was the top-ranked commentator in the popularity
polls. At one point in March 1948, his fifteen-minute weekly
program was the number one program in the Hooper ratings.
Broadcasting officials recognized the importance of Winchell.
When in 1948 he signed a two-year contract for ninety broadcasts for the Kaiser-Frazier automobile company, he received
$1,352,000 and thereby became the highest paid personality in
radio. In 1950, he received from ABC a lifetime contract
which guaranteed him a minimum of $10,000 per week as long
as he was physically and mentally capable of broadcasting. If
he became unable to perform, he was guaranteed $1,000 per
month.

The emergence of renowned news commentators like
Winchell, Gibbons, and Kaltenborn by the 1930s helped radio
exert its unifying influence upon American citizens. Certainly,
there was unity in the United States by reason of federal institutions and processes. But radio as a medium of communication reaching millions of listeners simultaneously, represented
as powerful an assault upon sectional and parochial mentali-
ties as any single force in American history. Broadcast journalism, thus, promoted the unity of the nation. Through radio
the entire country experienced the agony of Col. and Mrs.
Charles A. Lindbergh in 1932 as they lived through the kid-
napping and murder of their infant son. When the alleged
perpetrator of the crime, Bruno Richard Hauptmann, was
tried in 1935, radio was in the courtroom to keep the nation
informed. The next year Gabriel Heatter launched his national career by the impressive performance of extemporizing

for fifty-seven minutes from outside the state prison in Trenton, New Jersey, on the evening Hauptmann was sent to the electric chair.

By way of radio, local disasters became national calamities. Thus, in 1933, after an earthquake destroyed much of Long Beach, California, radio made the after-effects a cause for national concern. In 1937 listeners everywhere shared the anguish of announcer Herb Morrison as he wept into his microphone when the German dirigible, *Hindenburg*, exploded while mooring in Lakehurst, New Jersey. And the mounting tension in Europe was carefully monitored by American listeners. Nowhere was this better illustrated than during the Munich Crisis in September 1938, a period which H. V. Kaltenborn termed the "top listening period in American radio" during the 1930s. As more than 200 journalists from NBC and CBS gathered material for one thousand transmissions from Europe, in the living rooms of America listeners learned how the Anglo-French appeasers made their latest concessions to Nazi aggression.

Radio afforded its listeners the opportunity to evaluate political personalities on a scale never before possible. Every President since Harding understood the necessity of utilizing radio as a means to approach Americans as a single, mass audience. Franklin D. Roosevelt best realized the potential and the method of successful broadcasting. Rather than confine his use of radio to campaign and holiday speeches, Roosevelt employed it to speak directly to a national audience "as often as circumstances warrant." Beginning on March 12, 1933, when an estimated fifty million listeners heard his first so-called "Fireside Chat" seeking help to thwart the run on American banks, Roosevelt clearly demonstrated the persuasive intimacy that radio permitted. According to the noted newscaster Edwin C. Hill:

> It was as if a wise and kindly father had sat down to talk sympathetically and patiently and affectionately with his worried and anxious children, and had given them straightforward things that they had to do to help him

along as the father of the family. That speech of the
President's over the air humanized radio in a great governmental, national sense as it had never before been
humanized.[17]

Roosevelt had broadcast speeches earlier when he was
governor of New York. In the same manner, as President he
often used radio to approach the nation as a single state.
Roosevelt, thus, became what one magazine termed "a radio
president . . . the first chief executive of our land to realize the
enormous part that radio plays in our national life, the first
statesman to utilize radio to mould and weld public opinion."[18]

Other American and foreign political personalities made
use of radio. Eleanor Roosevelt was heard frequently in the
early years of her husband's Presidency. She appeared as a
regular feature on programs sponsored by such commercial
entities as Pond's facial cream, Simmons bedding, Johns-
Manville, Remington typewriters, and Selby shoes. Her impact
upon listeners was summarized in a fan publication in 1936:

> Her discussions of pertinent problems facing the women
> of today are helpful, broadminded, courageous and un-
> derstanding. She contributes to charity all her earnings
> from radio work. The first lady of the land has become
> the first lady of the American airwaves.[19]

By the late 1930s, Americans often heard on network
radio shortwave transmissions of the important public speeches
made by the European dictators. Assisted by translators who
interrupted at intervals to explain what Mussolini, Hitler, or
their subalterns had been saying, the decadence of Europe
entered the homes of concerned Americans. Radio also brought
listeners the pomp and circumstance of the Old World as, for
instance, it did on May 12, 1937, when NBC broadcast seven
consecutive hours of live coverage of the coronation ceremonies for King George VI of Great Britain.

Next to President Roosevelt, however, the most compelling political personality to use radio to speak to a single
nation was the Roman Catholic priest, Father Charles E.
Coughlin. A flamboyant crusader who broadcast regularly
from his church in Royal Oak, Michigan, Father Coughlin

became in the 1930s the most vocal and popular proponent of Italian-style fascism for America. Although he began broadcasting in 1926, not until the Depression did Coughlin consistently range beyond purely religious matters and turn his attention to politics. His radio sermons attacked Communism and socialism, capitalists and international bankers, Jews, and the American system of democracy. Coughlin also directed his bitter analyses against Presidents Hoover and Roosevelt.

In 1936 his popularity was so great that he helped form a third political party, the Union Party, which ran Congressman William Lemke for President. Although Coughlin declined in importance after the election, he continued sporadically on radio until by 1940 he had so alienated Americans and their social, economic, and religious leaders that he was unable to return to radio.

At the height of his popularity, Father Coughlin was heard nationally over a special network which reached millions of listeners and brought him considerable sums in donations to continue his crusade. Although he was not a news commentator or newscaster, Father Coughlin was definitely a force in the development of broadcast journalism. Radio was integral to his appeal. He once told an interviewer that "the free radio has taken the place of the free press as the bulwark of liberty."[20] And as ill-conceived as his opinions might have been, his existence on radio was a testimony to the wide perimeters of free speech in American broadcasting. The achievements in radio of Father Coughlin, therefore, were as vital as those of any newscaster. He strained the limits of tolerance, but he continued broadcasting. He vilified Franklin Roosevelt at the time of FDR's greatest popularity, and still found access to radio. Father Coughlin, thus, was one of the developers of the ethic of broadcast journalism which sought Truth, but allowed the American listeners in search of it to choose from a wide range of interpretations.

The most impressive result of two decades of news and commentary broadcasting was, by the time of World War II, the development of an informed and better-educated citizenry. This was demonstrated immediately after the beginning of the war when a poll conducted by Time-Life Publications showed that while only one percent of those questioned favored American involvement, an overwhelming eighty-three percent desired an Anglo-French victory over Germany; only sixteen percent were undecided, and one percent favored the Nazis. Of course, radio was not the only popular medium informing Americans of European developments and of the significance of fascism. But, a large percentage of Americans received their news through radio. And in times of crises, when information was desired quickly, most Americans turned to radio. Unlike the confusion that typified public opinion in 1914 at the outbreak of World War I, radio played an important function in unifying public sentiment by 1939. It was an educational achievement that would only be enhanced by the performance of radio newsmen during the war.

Perhaps the most dramatic display of the potential of radio news occurred in 1939–1940 as American correspondents broadcast the Nazi onslaught as it raged across Europe. From broadcasters such as Eric Sevareid in Paris, William L. Shirer in Berlin, and Edward R. Murrow, Robert Trout, and Charles Collingwood in London, listeners in the United States heard bombs and bullets tear apart European civilization. With a style that was objective and informed, these reporters sent their descriptions to the networks for airing on scheduled and special newscasts. In one moment Shirer might be analyzing the movement of German troops on the Eastern Front, and in the next he might talk about the dejection of the German people now that war had arrived, or about the beauty of visiting Amsterdam with the lights on after eight months of blackouts. Murrow might describe Trafalgar Square as German bombs fell from the London sky, or he might be describing, as he termed it in a broadcast in January 1940, "what this war is doing to men's minds, for this is a war for the conquest of men's minds."

Sensitive to strong isolationist sentiments in America, radio newscasters were hard pressed to remain objective as they reported the spread of Nazi militarism. Although journalistic ethics placed a premium on reporting news in a vocabulary free from prejudice, it must have been a strain for network correspondents to remain implacable in the face of unchecked fascist aggression. Nonetheless, one listener writing to a fan magazine in 1939 suggested that for the most part, American broadcast journalists were meeting their responsibilities. According to her:

> Reports of bombings and such have been given in a cool, calm, objective manner with no attempt to draw conclusions or place the finger of blame, only to giving reports from the various sources as reported. Of course, there have been several commentators who let their prejudice and emotions run away, but on the whole, the war news has been delivered to us in a highly satisfactory manner. If our radio can continue in this vein, we Americans will be better prepared to throw off propaganda. America *must* stay out of this war! This is one of radio's prime responsibilities.[21]

Once most of Europe and East Asia were under the control of the Germans and the Japanese, and once the United States had entered the battle, the role of the broadcast journalist became more difficult. Transmission facilities were frequently unavailable overseas, and jamming and other types of interference often prevented broadcasting. So-called "mobile" transmitters were usually heavy and cumbersome, and broadcasters complained regularly of equipment failure. Nevertheless, newscasters went to the fighting fronts and transmitted their observations to a public grown accustomed to being well informed. In covering American military action in Southeast Asia in 1943, for example, Eric Sevareid of CBS parachuted with troops into the jungles of Burma. Commentators from the United States, like Cecil Brown of Mutual, often travelled abroad to interview soldiers and dignitaries for their broadcasts. And the actions of George Hicks of ABC epitomized the activities of frontline broadcasters. On the evening of June 6, 1944, while aboard an American warship off the coast of Normandy, Hicks recorded the reactions of crewmen as they came under enemy air attack, the din of anti-aircraft guns and airplane engines punctuating his commentary. For his coverage, Hicks received a Peabody Award in 1944.

At home, commentators backed the American war effort, some because they felt it was the duty of American strength to right the international balance of power, others because they felt that since the United States was attacked by the Japanese and had war declared on it by Germany, it was necessary for the nation to protect itself. All domestic commentators, however, would have agreed with a broadcast in mid-1945, by Gabriel Heatter of Mutual, when he offered a prayer for the American troops:

> Merciful God, watch over these men. They march in a crusade for humanity and freedom. These are not men of hate or vengeance. These are humble men. Men whose hearts will never forget pity and mercy. They fight to give all the children of men peace on earth. They fight to banish tyranny and fear. Merciful God, our homes are empty—our hearts are torn with this desperate vigil. Into your care we give our prayers—our lives—our sons—all that we are and can ever hope to be on this earth. Send these men back to us, home to us, for they are part of man's spirit, of man's dream of a world which is free and where kindness lives. Watch over these men—who are meek and humble—we whose faith is strong ask this. Send these men back to our hearts and our homes—this is our prayer.[22]

Despite the heroics and resourcefulness demonstrated by broadcasters in obtaining war news, one of the chief concerns for newscasters and commentators was the threat of governmental censorship. Even before the war had begun, many in radio felt that once the United States entered the battle, commercial radio would be appropriated by the government and converted into an arm of the national war effort. Such considerations were not new, for as early as 1933 the question of radio and the next war was discussed in a radio fan publication.[23] Although a federal take-over never occurred after American entry into the war in 1941, two governmental organizations were quickly created to supervise broadcasting on the homefront: the Office of Censorship and the Office of War Information. They were kept busy overseeing commercial radio for, as *Variety* reported, by mid-1942 there were 202 weekly broadcasts of war news (CBS, 72; NBC, 40; Blue, 52; Mutual, 38), and 173 war-related commentaries per week (CBS, 49; NBC, 26; Blue, 41; Mutual, 57).[24]

Although censorship was distasteful to newscasters and commentators, it had been a fact of radio life for the years since the Federal Communications Commission had banned blasphemy, profanity, obscene allusions, and the like from the air. During the war, moreover, the Office of Censorship (OC) specifically proscribed strategic information from radio. Information about weather conditions, ship and troop movements, war production and other related developments were not allowed. Occasionally, the OC moved against specific speakers, as in November 1943, when it refused to allow King Carol of Rumania to deliver an address on CBS.[25] For the most part, however, American censorship was voluntary. The OC reviewed scripts, but only from those commentators who desired it. According to Erik Barnouw, only Drew Pearson and Walter Winchell—both of whom broadcast sensational news and comments—regularly offered their scripts for perusal.[26] Broadcast journalists, for their part, loyally adhered to the voluntary standards. According to statistics from the OC, moreover, of the seven thousand network news broadcasts in 1942, slightly more than two percent violated the voluntary code, most of these mistakes being inadvertent mentionings of weather conditions. In the first quarter of 1943, furthermore, only seventeen of the two thousand network news programs had had such infractions.[27]

Rather than overseeing actual radio operations, the Office of War Information (OWI) was created to coordinate all government-sponsored broadcasts, and to provide radio and newspapers with information regarding the course of the war. The agency was headed by the respected former CBS news broadcaster, Elmer Davis, who had left commercial radio to assume this post in 1942. As a former broadcast journalist, Davis was aware of the dangers of censorship. Yet, he probably would have agreed with the group of newspaper editors who admitted on *American Forum of the Air* in February 1943 that because of wartime conditions occasional censorship was necessary.[28] If the OWI desired to censor information, it accomplished it by delaying dissemination of its news to the media. In most cases, however, what appeared to be censorial conduct by the OWI actually emanated from military officers who refused to keep Davis' organization fully and rapidly appraised of the latest military developments. More than once, Davis clashed with military officers in defense of the right of the public to be informed.[29]

The voluntary position on censorship taken by the government was a reflection of both the consensus within the country regarding the war, and the confidence of the New Deal administration that it could withstand a critical appraisal of its war efforts. Thus, in 1943 when officials at CBS, on their own prerogative, exerted restrictive controls on their newscasters, criticism was forthcoming from all corners. In late September 1943, apparently fearing the influence over public opinion of its broadcasters, officials at CBS ordered its commentators—among them, Edward R. Murrow, William L. Shirer, Quincy Howe, Ned Calmer, and George Fielding Eliot —to desist from injecting personal opinion and editorialized news into their broadcasts. Such an edict, of course, violated the essence of broadcast journalism as well as the faith of the federal government in commercial radio. Within days it had become a *cause célèbre*. One of the most stinging rebukes of CBS policy came from Dorothy Thompson in her commentary on the Blue network on October 3, 1943. She appealed for public support against the CBS policy:

> This question doesn't affect me, because it's not the way the Blue Network works. We on this network are subject to the censorship of the Federal Communications Commission, barring obscene or blasphemous statements or allusions. We are also subject to the Office of Censorship, code of wartime practices, in protection of American security. And the network imposes on us only these additional regulations: that we must be accurate in news state-

ments, observe good taste, and use common sense. The public is the real censor. If it doesn't like the news commentators, those that employ them soon hear about it, and there is no more contract. The question affects you as listeners. Do you want to hear fearless viewpoints or don't you? Are all broadcasters to become mushmouths? Are you afraid of being unduly influenced or aren't you? And if men whose background and insight is recognized can't express opinions, who should express them?[30]

Criticism of the CBS decision came also from the chairman of the Federal Communications Commission, James L. Fly. He told a meeting of the Radio Executives Club on October 7, that this policy would accord tremendous power and discretion over news to a single person, and that it would establish an editorial policy at the network. In an effective understatement, Fly concluded that any policy that would require commentators like Murrow and Shirer to "mouth secondhand opinions would serve no good purpose."[31] Even before Fly spoke, however, the most effective attack on the CBS decision came from the censored commentators who refused to abide by it. *Variety* reported that within a week of the edict, commentators like Murrow, Howe, and Everett Holles were continuing to inject opinion into their broadcasts.[32] The futile and embarrassing effort by a network to censor its own newsmen was effectively finished by the end of the year for, in one of the more ironic statements of the war, the director of news broadcasts at CBS, Paul W. White, spoke out against the governmental bureaucrats for "stupid censorship" in delaying the broadcast of Eric Sevareid's accounts of his recent treks through the war zones in Burma, China, and India.[33]

Given the doubts and anxieties existing on the homefront, however, wartime radio news proved invaluable in keeping citizens abreast of the latest military developments. Nowhere was radio more responsive to this responsibility than in its coverage of the Allied invasion of France on D-Day, June 6, 1944. Even before the OWI acknowledged the landings on the coast of Normandy, network newscasters were reporting

German communiques which announced Allied parachute landings and bombardment of the French coast from sea and air.

An example of the sophistication of American broadcast journalism by this date was the coverage offered by CBS. With Robert Trout indefatigably anchoring the special coverage, CBS began full-time broadcasting of the event at 12:40 A.M. Eastern War Time. The network utilized several of its commentators stationed in New York City to add depth to the terse reports from Washington and overseas. George Fielding Eliot explained military aspects of the invasion. Ned Calmer, who had been a correspondent in France for several years, assured anxious listeners that the beaches along the Normandy coast were smooth and easily approachable. Historical perspective was provided by Quincy Howe, and John Daly read dispatches from eyewitnesses to the invasion of "the Allied troops storm-[ing] the fortress of Hitler." John W. Vandercook placed the strategy in chess terms when he called it "a Queen's move." And Quentin Reynolds, a veteran of earlier invasions in Italy, summarized the significance of the day when he noted, "If they live to be a hundred, June 6th will always be D-Day to them."

The most impressive dimension of the CBS coverage that day was the many live transmissions from Europe. American listeners were able to hear shortwave broadcasts from Allied leaders to the people of Western Europe. Such personalities as King Haakon of Norway, and the prime ministers of Belgium and the Netherlands were heard speaking to their respective countrymen. General Charles de Gaulle was heard broadcasting to Nazi-occupied France. Interpreters provided complete translations of these foreign language speeches, and instantaneous summaries of the speech of Prime Minister Winston Churchill to the House of Commons were also beamed to the United States.

Further coverage was provided by CBS correspondents in London who continuously fed the network the latest news and features. Edward R. Murrow, chief of the CBS bureau in the British capital, read and embellished upon official Allied statements. In a recorded feature, Charles Collingwood interviewed soldiers as they entered landing craft and prepared to move toward enemy territory. Richard C. Hottelet recalled his view from a warplane as Allied troops flooded the French shore. Amidst the tension and feverish activity, however, Murrow still found appropriate time for a look at the human side of the scene in Britain as he described the cramped but active quarters from which he was broadcasting, augmented by an elderly English charwoman who obliviously went about scrubbing the floor.

With the end of the war, American broadcast journalists seemed pleased with their performance. Although only a year earlier he had written of the "inadequate" performance in reporting the war,[34] Edward R. Murrow on his broadcast of September 16, 1945, summarized the satisfaction of newscasters when he declared,

> I have been listening to the radio. Some of what I hear I don't like. Maybe you feel the same way. But there is something altogether unique about this American system of broadcasting. . . . During the last nine years I saw something of what radio can do when it is used to tell the people what to think, when it is used to dull the critical facilities, when the right to listen is denied. If you doubt that radio is a powerful medium, you should see how it can warp men's minds when it becomes an instrument of national policy. I do not believe that American radio is perfect. But I am persuaded that the listener in this country is better served than is the listener in any other country with which I am familiar.[35]

Wartime experience left a significant heritage to American broadcast journalism. The courage and tenacity with which many radio reporters had fulfilled their responsibilities created a sense of importance for audio news within society. With its speed and range of coverage, radio thus became the most reliable medium of communication through which to obtain news. Newspapers and magazines could offer only depth of coverage to rival the instantaneousness of broadcasting. Moreover, with the maturation of news analysis, radio commentaries compared favorably to those in the print media.

Murrow, again on his broadcast of September 16, 1945, epitomized the spirit and confidence of broadcast journalism as it
faced America at peace:

> Radio, if it is to serve and survive, must hold a mirror
> behind the nation and the world. If the reflection shows
> radical intolerance, economic inequality, bigotry, unem-
> ployment or anything else—let the people see it, or rather
> hear it. The mirror must have no curves and must be held
> with a steady hand.[36]

Throughout the remainder of the 1940s, the liberal crusading spirit that emerged from the war was notable in radio
journalism. Drew Pearson was especially vital in this sense in
July 1946 with his attacks upon the Ku Klux Klan and upon
the white supremist former governor of Georgia, Eugene Talmadge. To make his criticism even more dramatic, Pearson
travelled to the steps of the Georgia statehouse in Atlanta and
in a rainstorm broadcast his quarter-hour program on ABC.
Pearson also created a furor a year later when he charged that
Representative Robert F. Jones, nominated to the FCC by
President Truman, was a former member of the notorious
Black Legion, a racist and revolutionary secret society of the
mid-1930s.

In a less flamboyant manner, Raymond Gram Swing of
ABC urged radio to take a more active role in educating listeners and spreading what he termed a "greater social intelligence." He was especially aroused on his final ABC newscast
on January 25, 1948, when he chided broadcasters for being
too "lax in projecting social problems with stimulation and
excitement, and as a means of uniting the people."[37] At
CBS, Murrow became a vice president in 1946 and for the ten
months he served in that post, he brought his liberal views to
bear on news programming. He introduced programs such as
As Others See Us, a series delving into the image of America
abroad, *CBS Is There* (later called *You Are There*) which
used regular news reporters to recreate historical events, and
CBS Views the Press, a controversial series which critically
assessed radio and print journalism.

The press conference became an integral part of radio in

1945 with the debut of two significant series, *Our Foreign Policy* and *Meet the Press*. Both series presented American and world leaders being questioned by renowned journalists. Although the former series lapsed after several years, *Meet the Press* ultimately branched into television and until the present day has provided a rich source on both media for better understanding contemporary history.

The most active area of broadcast journalism explored in the postwar period was the presentation of radio documentaries. The documentary was an attempt to present deep analysis of critical issues and relevant historical materials by presenting dramatic re-creation and actual voices in a written script. Such packaging added theatricality and educative value to the reporting of news, and it helped emphasize the import of matters needed to be considered by an informed citizenry. With one notable exception, until this period the documentary was practically absent from broadcasting. *The March of Time*, which appeared on CBS from 1931 until 1945, was the first serious attempt in radio to present news in a documentary format. By reproducing with professional actors the voices and actions of current newsmakers, this weekly series recapitulated news events and presented them in a style which blended traditional reportage with melodrama.

During the war, of course, the necessity of informing Americans about battles, political developments, and domestic conditions compelled networks to produce more in-depth studies of significant occurrences. With this impetus, by the late 1940s radio had evolved toward a full realization of the potential of the documentary. The most aggressive network in this field was CBS. In 1946, it established a special documentary unit. Under the direction of Robert Heller, this organization followed a policy of "creating an explosion" with its documentary programs treating subjects ranging from pressing, contemporary social problems, to the life and letters of Abraham Lincoln and the state of American education. Its format was quickly adopted by the ABC and Mutual networks, and by mid-1947 both of these organizations were steadily producing documentaries that often gained critical praise. As for NBC, it occasionally produced documentaries. But instead of the one-time or short-series patterns in which documentaries usually fell, NBC executives preferred regularly scheduled public-service programs that were less complicated to produce and presumably less expensive to the network.

In seeking to understand the tenor of life in the postwar period, a perusal of the topics of documentary broadcasts reveals a broad, generalized evaluation of American society and its values. The implications of the atomic age were often considered. In 1946 and 1947, ABC produced special broadcasts on the anniversary of the bombing of Hiroshima. Atomic energy was the focus of *The Sunny Side of the Atom* on CBS in July 1947, and on a four-part series, *Atom and You,* on Mutual in September 1948. One of the more ambitious documentaries produced at NBC was a four-part series, *The Fifth Horseman,* which in the summer of 1946, probed various aspects of the atom and its relationship to postwar society.

Documentaries also presented glaringly shameful pictures of inequities within American life. ABC revealed the ugliness of inadequate housing in May 1947, in a special broadcast, *Slums.* Mixing recordings of slum dwellers with a frank discussion between representatives of private institutional investment organizations and public housing advocates, the program clearly left its listeners with the conclusion that the menace of slums could only be solved by American citizens and government realizing that they must take care of public health and security.

Juvenile delinquency was a frequent theme in documentary programming. One of the more impressive achievements in this regard was *The Eagle's Brood,* produced by CBS in March 1947. The broadcast featured Joseph Cotten and Luther Adler and probed with brutal frankness the deleterious effect delinquency was having upon American democracy. It suggested, moreover, that it could only be cured by the people most responsible for it: members of the adult generation. There were other social maladies that received probative treatment by the radio documentary. A Mutual program in December 1947, *Wanted: A Baby*, discussed the black market in buying and selling babies; *A Short Life and a Merry One* was a CBS study in 1947 of the state of public health; *Malice Toward None*, an NBC broadcast in February 1948, was indicative of many public affairs programs promoting brotherhood among all citizens; *Marriage in Distress* on NBC in September 1948 dealt with the alarming rise in the American divorce rate and the collapse of marriages in general; and *1960?? Jiminy Cricket!!* utilized characters from Walt Disney motion pictures—Donald Duck, Jiminy Cricket, and the Seven Dwarfs—to dramatize on ABC in September 1947 a timely scientific treatise on the future needs and resources of America.

While newscasters and commentators spent much time keeping listeners abreast of world political developments, the radio documentary investigated social problems around the world. In such a manner, many Americans could not escape the conclusion that domestic inequities were matched by problems abroad. In a five-part series, *The Third Horseman*, NBC in the fall of 1947 introduced audiences to the famine and death being created by food production problems around the world. In *Crusade for Children* in August, 1948, CBS blended guest stars (including General Dwight D. Eisenhower) and the documentary to proclaim the plight of children orphaned and maimed by war, disease, and famine. The most stunning moment in this program occurred when Edward R. Murrow introduced a tape recording of a blind and armless Italian boy, a victim of bombings during the war, who was trying to learn Braille by using the tip of his nose.

Mother Earth, an NBC documentary in late 1948, focused upon man's plundering of the earth's natural resources. And a striking achievement in this vein was *One World Flight*, a special series of broadcasts on CBS in December 1947. Utilizing wire recordings made during his four-month tour of the world, Norman Corwin presented aural images of a single world that was ideologically divided into two Cold War camps. Instead of showing the traditional view of world leaders and common people determined to develop a single world, Corwin's frank series suggested tension, hatred, and self-interest ruled most people.

Most documentaries were special broadcasts heard only once. But in *Living—1948,* introduced in February 1948, NBC commenced a long-running, continuing series of documentaries. Aired on Sunday afternoons, this half-hour series changed its title each year and lasted until *Living—1951.* Subject matter on the program ranged from the most current political developments—speeches by many of the presidential candidates in 1948, a post-election explanation of his inaccurate polling by George Gallup, an analysis of the Marshall Plan—to considerations of social problems confronting postwar American civilization—air pollution, cancer, housing, population growth, mental health, highway safety—and to subjects that were not usually the focus of documentary programs—the circus, the state of American humor, the status of women, the Olympic games, baseball, and prayer in American culture.

One of the more compelling programs was "Ride the Tiger." Broadcast on February 2, 1949, the show was structured as a birthday message to George Washington, but it amounted to a consideration of the legacy of the American Revolution, and its rivalry with the Communist Revolution for ascendancy in the contemporary world. Eschewing shallow rhetoric and patriotic clichés, the program called for the rededication of the United States as a world force for revolutionary change. It warned that Lenin had realized the importance of ideology and technology as revolutionizing exports, and that it was time for America and its citizens to assist the have-not nations of the world. The essence of the program was crystallized in a dramatized conversation wherein a French woman warned an American friend.

> *Woman:*   Through the things you make, through your
>   movies, your magazines, you Americans have
>   become the terrible instigators of social change
>   and hope.

American:	Whoa! Yes, I suppose we do think of ourselves as peddlers of light and progress, but as the agents of revolution ...
Woman:	Oh, don't be naive. Being an agent of revolution is the great role of our times. If you don't play it, others will.

Broadcast at a time when American foreign policy was only beginning its deep involvement in the rehabilitation of war-torn Europe, and its commitment to assisting economically- and technologically-underdeveloped nations, this program in the *Living—1949* series illustrated the timeliness and perceptiveness that the radio documentary could achieve.

Certainly, the Cold War affected broadcast journalism. Even in as moderate a series as *Living,* the implications of the great ideological struggle between Communism and Americanism was obvious. In the postwar years, that protracted international rivalry would have decisive effects upon American news analysts. As part of its pattern of free speech, American radio had always employed conservative and ultra-conservative commentators. Since the late 1930s, broadcasters like Fulton Lewis, Jr., and Upton Close were heard regularly on national radio. Moreover, others like Walter Winchell found themselves more and more allied with conservative commentators as their patriotism, a liberal virtue when the international threat was right-wing fascism, became increasingly reactionary as the fear of leftist Communism mounted. Assisting this evolution in popular thought were the many congressional investigations which insinuated that Communist Party members and their fellow-travellers were actively subverting American film, radio, and television, as well as government, trade unions, and other socio-political institutions.

By 1949, sponsors had sensed the new mood of conservatism and had begun to withdraw support for radio newsmen they felt might alienate listeners with their moderate or liberal slant to the news. When William L. Shirer lost his sponsor and his prime-time broadcast at CBS that year, he resigned and blamed his fall on the incompatibility of his liberal views with network policy. As early as January 1947, the liberal political

journal, *New Republic,* reported that since the end of the war
the four networks had already dropped two dozen left-of-
center commentators.[38] One year later, *Variety* reported that
not only had more liberal journalists dropped away, but that
those who remained were "not only conservative, but what's
worse, not intelligent."[39]

Among those conservative commentators who were definitely not unintelligent were Fulton Lewis, Jr., and Walter
Winchell. Lewis had been an isolationist broadcaster on
Mutual in the early 1940s, and his criticism of the policy of
the New Deal did not end with the war or the death of President Roosevelt. By 1948, Lewis was the chief radio spokesman
for the anti-Communist side in the Alger Hiss case. Lewis
prominently featured the statements of politicians like Richard M. Nixon who accused Hiss of being but one link in the
chain of Soviet spies and traitors in the United States. Lewis
also painted with the same anti-Communist brush many whose
reputations might have been expected to be above reproach.

In his broadcast of December 6, 1948, for instance, he
noted that

> behind the scenes, for your information, this Alger Hiss
> was one of the fair-haired pets of Mrs. Eleanor Roosevelt,
> and those who want to see this case followed out to its
> full conclusion are fearful that that fact will influence
> the Department of Justice, cause it to turn the facts
> against Whittaker Chambers in favor of Alger Hiss.

And Lewis would use the Hiss case to question rhetorically the
purpose and loyalty of the Truman administration, when he
remarked:

> The frightening part of the whole thing is this: this inci-
> dent we stumbled into quite by accident . . . how many
> more like it are in existence unknown to us? Does this
> begin to answer the question of why our State Depart-
> ment behaves so peculiarly whenever Soviet Russia is in-
> volved in anything? Does this begin to answer the silly
> procedure about giving the racehorses back to Soviet-
> dominated nations after the war? And the reluctance to
> do anything about the Chinese aid program? And the
> other dozens of unanswerable mysteries that come along

day by day to contradict the purported policy of firmness toward a nation that is causing us tremendous trouble? It's worth thinking about, and this case particularly is worth watching, too, lest by some remote chance those fears about the Department of Justice might be true.

Primarily because of his hostility to totalitarian government, Walter Winchell on ABC by the late 1940s had evolved from an outspoken liberal to an inveterate anti-Communist. And what made Winchell most effective was that he was the most popular commentator in radio. In September 1947, he unleashed a vitriolic attack upon the Soviet Union. His attacks prompted the Russian ambassador in Washington to denounce him as a warmonger. But Winchell's blasts were eagerly accepted by many Americans seeking to comprehend the new posture of America in world affairs, and trying to understand the aims of Soviet policy. According to Winchell:

> The Third World War is already being fought.... We are losing it.... When the Communists are ready, there will be fifty Pearl Harbors, atomic explosions erasing our cities.... The Communists have germ warfare already.... The cholera plague in Egypt is suspected abroad of being a Soviet experiment.... The next countries the Russians intend to grab are Italy and France as a base to attack Great Britain.... Trained Communist spies are among us locating targets for the sneak attack.... We must start rearming now.[40]

Clearly, at this time there was being established in American society a hostile political environment in which loyalty was questioned as readily as policy was criticized. The tensions, in fact, began almost as soon as the war had ended. On September 4, 1945, for example, Edwin C. Hill of CBS suggested in his broadcast that Roosevelt and Henry Wallace were responsible for the Pearl Harbor disaster four years earlier.[41] Earl Godwin of ABC on November 1, 1945 staunchly defended the controversial House Committee on Un-American Activities as it engaged in "the age-old fight of God and the Devil, Light versus Darkness, Christianity versus Heathenism."[42] And Upton Close of Mutual that same month lashed out at "Communistic propaganda" in the American media, and warned that "the nation is getting sick and tired of voices spouting the Moscow line."[43]

The fever of anti-Communism spread to other journalistic endeavors. Communism was frequently exposed in documentaries. One of the most celebrated broadcasts on ABC was *Communism—U.S. Brand,* a network special in August 1948, which relentlessly exposed American Communism as an allegiance to a radical foreign power and, therefore, treasonable. A timely and well-produced program, it won a Peabody Award for its skill in revealing the purported subversion being carried on by native American Communists.

The spectre of anti-Communism even reached the gossip columnists. On November 9, 1947, Louella Parsons publicly warned Humphrey Bogart not to let his liberal politics involve him with Communists, for although "Humphrey Bogart is a loyal American," and "actors, of course, should have their civil rights protected," he should "stop, look, and listen before you get yourself involved in causes that can be grossly misunderstood."

Throughout the 1950s broadcast journalism expanded technique and coverage. The perfection of tape recording by the late 1940s made it practical to include the voices of newsmakers in news and documentary programs. And although documentaries faded in popularity in 1949, within two years they were on an upswing again, due primarily to the interest in factual programs generated by the broadcast of the investigation of organized crime conducted by Senator Estes Kefauver. As might be anticipated, crime became a favorite topic in these documentaries. Programs ranged in focus from studies of gambling and illegal immigration from Mexico, to narcotics and the threat of organized crime. By the end of 1951, moreover, utilization of actual voices of newsmakers, a documentary technique, was being successfully employed by local reporters in regular newscasts in Chicago. Here, primarily at WMAQ (NBC) and WBBM (CBS), roving reporters were recording newsmakers, and even broadcasting directly from the scene of local events.[44] It was a technique that would be widely duplicated later.

The most ambitious innovation in this regard was the introduction on December 15, 1950, of *Hear It Now*. Produced and written at CBS by the team of Edward R. Murrow and Fred W. Friendly, this program was patterned after a series of successful record albums produced by the same team. Narrated by Murrow, the "I Can Hear It Now" albums brought voices of newsmakers of the past thirty years into the homes of millions. The radio venture attempted to do the same for contemporary newsmakers, to develop, as Friendly termed it, "pictures for the ear." On the premier program, for instance, listeners heard a variegated broadcast which included actual interviews from Korea, Montana, New York, and Lake Success. Heard on that opening program were, among others, George C. Marshall, Bernard Baruch, Walter Reuther, Judy Holliday, and Carl Sandburg. The series enjoyed immediate popularity. Broadcast during prime time at 9:00 P.M. on Fridays, it received a Peabody Award after its first few months on the air. It also inspired imitative programming by other networks as both *Voices and Events* at NBC, and *Week Around the World* at ABC adopted the format. *Hear It Now* eventually gave way to television. After leaving the air in June 1951, it reappeared five months later as a CBS television series, *See It Now*.

While innovative strides were being achieved in broadcast journalism, the political climate within the United States in the early 1950s was disintegrative. Pressures of the Cold War, coupled with the fears and ignorance of many Americans regarding Communism and domestic and international political forces, created a climate in which many mistook the self-assuredness of anti-Communism as a sign of Truth. When publications like *Red Channels* listed 150 celebrities and accused them of being Communists, fellow-travellers, or former members of subversive organizations, a sizable portion of the population accepted the publication's assertions unquestioningly and condemned those on the list as treasonable and dangerous.

When in December 1950 NBC broadcast a public service program sponsored by the American Civil Liberties Union honoring the Bill of Rights on the 159th anniversary of its adoption, hundreds of letters and telegrams protested the airing of such "pro-Communist" material.[45] One radio newsman, Don Hollenbeck of CBS, in 1954 was driven to suicide, in part because of chronic newspaper attacks upon his loyalty and patriotism.[46] Two strategic developments help account for this intense national distrust.

With the outbreak of war in Korea in June 1950, American troops were once again involved in open hostilities. Less than five years after World War II, soldiers were being drafted, uniformed, trained, and shipped overseas to wage a war that was never satisfactorily explained. Although it was alleged to be a war to stop Communist aggression by North Korea, it often assumed the guise of a battle to unite the Korean peninsula under either South or North Korean hegemony. And after nearly three years of war, the conflagration ended in a stalemate—neither side defeated, neither side willing to use atomic weaponry, and neither side making any headway in conquering the other.

Radio coverage of the war was adequate, but the public taste for the battle was not there. Communications with the Far East were never as sophisticated as the shortwave facilities in Europe during World War II. There were no Murrows standing glamorously in Trafalgar Square, although Murrow did make two journeys to Korea and reported from foxholes and military installations. There was no George Hicks to report on enemy aerial bombardment of American shipping, nor an H. V. Kaltenborn to travel abroad to interview universally-respected American generals. In fact, in this war the President of the United States actually discharged his commanding general on grounds of insubordination. Yet, the most pressing reason for the climate of internal distrust rested with the domestic politics of anti-Communism.

If the rise of anti-Communism as a popular crusade had been disruptive of national consensus in the late 1940s, in the next decade it came to challenge the fundamental principles of the American republic. This was the result of the coalescing of the crusade around the aggressive, brutal personality of

Senator Joseph R. McCarthy of Wisconsin. Not since Father Coughlin during the Depression was a champion of the political Right so able to exploit the communications media and build himself a national reputation as chief inquisitor in the purge of the disloyal.

McCarthy stood before microphones and announced that he had the names of hundreds of Communists who had infiltrated the government. Utilizing his chairmanship of a special Senate investigatory committee, he cajoled and threatened subpoenaed witnesses, intimidated elected officials, and ultimately questioned the loyalty of the leadership of the U.S. Army. A skillful propagandist, McCarthy was able to exploit the confusion prevalent in a nation thrust suddenly into the leadership of the non-Communist world. For four years his ruthless behavior kept political leaders from both the Democratic and Republican parties silent in the face of his strength, and public opinion surveys showed he enjoyed massive national support. By the spring of 1954, for instance, a Gallup poll revealed that less than thirty percent of the public disapproved of his tactics.

McCarthy was not without powerful supporters and detractors among broadcast journalists. Especially strong in their backing of him were Fulton Lewis, Jr., and Walter Winchell. Raymond Gram Swing, on the other hand, resigned a position with the Voice of America because he felt the State Department would not support employees maligned by McCarthy.[47] When McCarthy in 1954 charged that the legacy of the Democratic administrations since 1933 was "twenty years of treason," Elmer Davis eloquently answered the allegation by challenging the Republican party to chastise McCarthy.[48] Yet, the most significant journalistic enemy that McCarthy created proved to be Edward R. Murrow.

Although by early 1954 Murrow was anchoring the *See It Now* and *Person to Person* series on CBS-TV and broadcasting a daily radio news program, *Edward R. Murrow and the News,* he became the first powerful media figure to risk his career by attacking McCarthy and his crusade. As his biographer has pointed out, Murrow's argument with the

Wisconsin senator was not with anti-Communism or the exposure of traitors. Instead, he opposed the unconstitutional
method by which, without seeing any evidence, without being
permitted to face their accusers, and without due process of
law, Americans were being accused of crimes against society.
On March 9, 1954, on the regular telecast of *See It Now*, Murrow openly criticized McCarthy. He televised edited film in
which the Wisconsin senator was seen brutally questioning or
uttering innuendoes about innocent citizens. Murrow accused
McCarthy of lies, half-truths, and exploitation of his sena-
torial immunity. Drawing upon personal democratic principles that had been forged and confirmed in his years as a
radio foreign correspondent, Murrow ended his program not
with a castigation of the senator, but with a charge to the
American citizenry:

> We will not walk in fear, one of another. We will not be
> driven by fear into an age of unreason if we dig deep in
> our history and our doctrine, and remember that we are
> not descended from fearful men, not from men who
> feared to write, to speak, to associate, and to defend
> causes that were for the moment unpopular. This is no
> time for men who oppose Senator McCarthy's methods to
> keep silent, or for those who approve. We can deny our
> heritage and our history, but we cannot escape respon-
> sibility for the result. There is no way for a citizen of a
> republic to abdicate his responsibilities. As a nation we
> have come into our full inheritance at a tender age. We
> proclaim ourselves—as indeed we are—the defenders of
> freedom, wherever it continues to exist in the world. But
> we cannot defend freedom abroad by deserting it at
> home. The actions of the junior senator from Wisconsin
> have caused alarm and dismay amongst our allies abroad
> and given considerable comfort to our enemies. And
> whose fault is that? Not really his. He didn't create this
> situation of fear, he merely exploited it—and rather suc-
> cessfully. Cassius was right: "The fault, dear Brutus, is
> not in our stars but in ourselves."[49]

Although the senator was given time a month later to
reply to Murrow's critique, McCarthy's popularity and invincibility began to wane. By the end of the year members of

the Senate had found the courage to castigate and eventually to censure him. By the next year, the entire movement was in disarray and public support for McCarthy's methods had collapsed. Murrow never believed that he had been responsible for such a transformation. Yet, he never doubted that broadcast journalism had a duty to offer informed and reasoned analysis, especially at times when a conspiracy of silence existed among other social institutions. In that *See It Now* telecast, Murrow was the first voice; others followed his lead. It was the highest achievement of broadcast journalism to that date.

It is significant that Murrow, one of the most important commentators in the history of radio, earned his greatest broadcasting achievement after he entered television. There can be no doubt that television by this date had replaced radio as the principal medium for information in mass America. McCarthy had been successful with radio and print media. But on television, his flamboyance and aggressiveness became liabilities. His rhetoric of crusade and purge became on television a revelation of his self-serving, shallow mentality. The age of television news was born on the evening Senator McCarthy was exposed.

Ominous for the new age, moreover, was the radio broadcast on May 19, 1954, in which CBS correspondents joined other experts to discuss the future of Indo-China now that the French colonial power had collapsed at Dienbienphu. As narrated by Lowell Thomas, this hour-long conversation was especially interested in the nature of American involvement in the fighting there, the stake of the United States in the war, and "what the U.S. could do about straightening out the situation." Perhaps anticipating what would eventually become in Southeast Asia, America's first "television war," a reviewer wrote of the broadcast:

> There were no pat answers, but for the listener it meant a new slant on that vast, far-off area. Threaded into a good part of the survey was one statement which everyone seemed to echo—that French colonialism is about ready to write its own obit and that Indo-China must be guar-

anteed freedom or the nation would be throttled by the Commies.[50]

Radio had been born in news, and by the mid-1950s, as its executives searched for new formulas by which to keep network broadcasting viable, radio returned to news. With the premier of *Monitor* at NBC in June 1955, the magazine format was applied to a full weekend of broadcasting. The pattern of *Monitor* was impressive. Mixing news, features, music, comedy, interviews, and the like, the format attempted to cover forty hours of programming from Saturday morning to Sunday evening. Although several traditional programs like *Fibber McGee and Molly* and *Meet the Press* were integrated into the program structure, most of the programming was new. *Monitor,* thus, produced a radio "magazine" that was deeply indebted to the news and documentary styles developed since the 1940s.

This omnibus type of programming was emulated by other networks. Mutual in July 1955, introduced its "Companionate Radio" pattern, and in November 1955, ABC premiered its radio magazine format, "New Sounds," which simulated the *Monitor* style in the weekly evening hours. The success of *Monitor,* however, was not matched by another NBC production, *Weekday,* which for five hours daily organized daytime programming in the same magazine format. It premiered in November 1955. Although *Monitor* would last until the late 1960s, the other formats were ineffective against the challenge of television and local programming. By the 1960s, the prime function of network radio had dwindled to providing hourly news and special features to various local affiliates and subscribers.

In the three and one-half decades in which broadcast journalism was born and matured on radio, Americans experienced a growing sophistication and reliability within this new profession. The notion of the free press was expanded to include free broadcasting and telecasting. The localized audiences of the newspaper world became audiences of millions through broadcasting. The flow of information to the citizenry took a quantum leap through the electronic media. And

The King Cole Trio, led by singer-pianist Nat "King" Cole, came to network radio in the mid-1940s. (Courtesy of Kraftco)

Above: Al Jolson (left) harmonizes with Ed Gardner ("Archie the manager" of *Duffy's Tavern*) during rehearsal. (Courtesy of Kraftco) *Left:* Al Jolson as he appeared with Jimmy Durante on *Kraft Music Hall* in 1948. (Courtesy of Kraftco)

The relationship between children's breakfast foods and radio adventure serials for kids is apparent in this ad in 1943. (Courtesy of Quaker Oats)

As this 1950 advertisement reveals, radio's Western heroes were usually drawn with juvenile listeners in mind. (Courtesy of Quaker Oats)

Above: Harold Peary created the character Throckmorton P. Gildersleeve on *The Fibber McGee and Molly Show* and in the early 1940s made him the central figure of the popular situation comedy *The Great Gildersleeve.* (Courtesy of Kraftco)

Above: The radio dramas of Richard Durham in the 1940s represent the most consistent outcry against anti-black bigotry and racism in American broadcasting history. His series, *Destination Freedom,* elevated Afro-American history and radio characterization to new levels of dignity.

Left: Jack Webb brought to radio in the late 1940s the toughest breed of private detectives ever heard on the air. His pioneering characterizations climaxed in the award-winning *Dragnet* series which enjoyed success on both radio and television. Webb is seen here accepting an award in 1953 for *Dragnet.* (Source: Wide World Photo)

the speed and efficiency of broadcasting came to mean faster and more in-depth news for a population with an ever-increasing level of intelligence. Broadcast journalism was not without its faults. But the most constructive criticism came not from effete politicians fearful of its probing style and search for truth, but internally, from those who sought an even more effective professionalism. A product of radio, broadcast journalism had become one of the crucial dimensions of American freedom in the contemporary world.

7

Stride Toward Freedom— Blacks in Radio Programming

The world of fantasy created by commercial radio programming was the most popular medium of entertainment in the United States from the 1920s until the 1950s. Tens of millions of citizens tuned in thousands of stations to hear news, sports, drama, comedy, and the various other formats by which broadcasters had adapted radio to aural entertainment. To staff such operations, moreover, the stations and networks employed countless numbers of writers, directors, actors, and technicians, Thus, aside from its popularity, the radio industry was a massive commercial operation.

Despite its tremendous need for personnel, however, the industry in its so-called Golden Age offered only limited opportunities for black men and women to develop. In fact, of all the popular arts, commercial radio possessed one of the more effective policies of discrimination along racial lines. It was manifested in the failure to employ black technical operators or actors, and it was evident in the strident stereotyping of black characters in actual broadcasts. That radio was a medium unfriendly to black talent was obvious to Carleton Moss, a black writer, who told an interviewer in 1950 that prejudice in broadcasting was only a reflection of its existence in the general society, that "all American radio takes its cue from the official government. We are automatically under a Jim Crow setup."[1]

It was also apparent to Professor L. S. Cottrell when he

327

wrote in 1939 that the "totally unrealistic" image of blacks in
radio was epitomized in "the stereotyped conception of the
Negro as a simpleton, or a 'bad actor,' or a doglike creature
with unbounded devotion to his master or mistress."[2] It was
also the meaning of the bitter letter written in 1946 by William H. Tymous, secretary of the Washington Veterans' Congress, wherein he criticized radio for depicting

> the American Negro as a buffoon, lazy, shiftless, super-
> stitious, ignorant, loose and servile. If the Negro menial
> is a good workman, he is again caricatured as ignorant,
> cunning and servile. If he has had any schooling, he be-
> comes in many instances even more the target for the vici-
> ous, evil stupidity of our hatemongers. It goes without
> saying that this "typing" of the entire race is false and
> distorted. This is not the democratic way of life for which
> so many of our fallen comrades paid so dearly with their
> lives. This is the Hitler pattern. This is American fas-
> cism.[3]

Nonetheless, the Afro-American was always a part of
popular radio. He was there as a singer, instrumentalist, or
bandleader. His music was there, played by the many small
dancebands that flourished in the 1930s, and by the great
white radio orchestras—like those of Paul Whiteman or B. A.
Rolfe—throughout the Golden Age. Whether portrayed by
black or white actors, the Afro-American was also there in the
many comedies which caricatured members of the race as a
butler, a maid, or a loafer. The point is that blacks were never
completely excluded from radio as their talent and culture
were too rich and compelling for advertising agencies to avoid
totally. But what always did exist within the industry was a
racist impulse which perpetuated familiar, pejorative stereotypes in which blacks were cast. It was a condition with which
few black entertainers were satisfied. It was also unsettling
for many white radio personalities who felt that such a policy
was not only unjust, but a distortion of impressive talent.

Little scholarship exists on the subject of blacks in radio.
That which does exist has been neither exhaustive in its re-
search, nor comprehensive in its consideration of the issue.
The common interpretation is that until the late 1930s, radio

was not fully closed to black personalities. But, as Erik Barnouw contended, once the "lily white" dramas became popular, blacks faded in importance as actors and characterizations.[4] This is also the interpretation of Estelle Edmerson whose master's thesis, completed in 1954, is still the most significant study of the subject. Yet, taking into account the full history of radio broadcasting, as well as the development of blacks in radio and other popular arts, it appears that a reevaluation is needed.

The study of blacks in radio is bifurcated. On one hand, it is the analysis of black professionals appearing in their own programs or as guests on white shows. It is also the study of white actors playing the roles of black characters. Because listeners could not see the racial identity of the actor speaking into a live microphone, and because most white Americans had preconceived notions of how a black voice sounded, it was possible to employ white actors to portray blacks. Thus, by studying these two categories—blacks as blacks, and whites as blacks—a fuller picture and interpretation of the Afro-American and his struggle against prejudice emerges.

Blacks as Blacks

Although audiences at home had no way of discerning from a voice the skin color of a broadcaster, black professional entertainers were invariably cast in Afro-American roles. Such a pattern caused one critic to label radio as "the worst offender of the Negro entertainer."[5] Yet, within the curtailed scope of activity permitted their talent, blacks were a part of radio from its earliest days. As musicians, for instance, they had been contributing to broadcasting since the early 1920s. Whether in obscure jazz ensembles, large dance orchestras, religious choirs, or as performers on recorded music, Afro-American talent was integral to the development of popular music on radio. As early as 1924 the Hampton Institute Choir was appearing on stations in New York City. The vaudeville and film personality, Flournoy Miller, told Edmerson that he and his famous partner, Aubrey Lyles, were broadcasting in 1922. And by the late 1920s black musical performers like

Noble Sissle, Fess Williams, and the Pace Jubilee Negro Singers were heard on the air.

In the early 1930s, with the new networks developing a more professional and mature attitude toward radio, Afro-American singers and musicians were appearing regularly. In 1932 and 1933 Paul Robeson was the featured singer on programs sponsored by General Electric and Eastman Kodak. At the same time Ethel Waters had her own program sponsored by the American Oil Company. Fats Waller, Duke Ellington, and Art Tatum had sustaining series. Among the talents appearing on other network series were the Mills Brothers, Nina Mae McKinney, the Four Southern Singers, the Four Sheiks of Harmony, The Babolene Boys, and Jules Bledsoe.

Important, too, were the many dance orchestras that were broadcasting. From radio studios, night clubs, and dance halls, black bands played the pulsating, rhythmic music which, by the second half of the decade, would be picked up by white bands and captivate the nation as "swing" music. Typical of the popularity of "Harlem dance rhythms" in the early 1930s, the radio log of the *New York Times* for the week beginning November 27, 1932, reveals broadcasts by such Afro-American musicians as Chick Webb, Don Redman (four nights per week over two different stations), and Cab Calloway (seven nights per week over three different stations).

As well as popular music, black gospel music was also an important part of radio programming by the 1930s. Choral groups, like the Southernaires, appeared regularly in their own shows, or as background singers on the many minstrel programs, such as on *Plantation Nights* on KFI (Los Angeles) in 1932, where the "imaginary locale is an old Southern plantation where darkies come to serenade the owner."[6] In October 1933, station WBZ (Boston) reported that more than one percent of its air time was devoted to Afro-American spirituals. This figure is more impressive, however, when it is noted that this was a larger figure than that for detective dramas, political speeches, or quiz shows at that station.[7] The interest in gospel music probably was responsible for the CBS decision to broadcast from the Church of God in Washington,

D.C., the religious services of the Elder Solomon Lightfoot Michaux, a feature which irregularly appeared on radio until the 1950s.

Although they did not flourish on radio, black comedians were also an ingredient of early broadcasting. The greatest demand for these entertainers was to fill the stereotyped roles of stage comedy. This form of humor drew its impetus from minstrel shows and their eventual offshoot, vaudeville. Here the comedy dealt in broad ethnic and racial characterization which was rigorously offensive and of questionable entertainment value by the 1930s. Nevertheless, black actors accepted such roles because they needed employment. Thus, Ernest Whitman and Eddie Green appeared as a "coon act" on the Maxwell House *Show Boat* program in its first season on NBC. Hattie McDaniel brought her "mammy" personality from the *Optimistic Doughnut Hour* over KNX (Los Angeles) in 1932, to the *Show Boat* series in the early 1930s. In the period 1930–1933, Lillian Randolph played with Billy Mitchell in a comedy feature, *Lulu and Leander,* on WXYZ (Detroit). Johnny Lee appeared in *Slick and Slim,* an all-black series on WHN (New York City) in 1932. And the stereotyped humorous black maid and butler appeared in network radio as early as 1932 when Georgia Burke portrayed Gardenia on the soap opera, *Betty and Bob,* and Ernest Whitman portrayed Awful on *The Gibson Family.*

These were not necessarily facile assignments for the black actors. Several complained of the difficulty they encountered trying to effect the accents of minstrel show end men. Lillian Randolph studied for three months with a white vocal coach before developing her dialect. Johnny Lee admitted that he, too, "had to learn to talk as white people believed Negroes talked." Failure to develop the proper minstrel accent might have been professionally disastrous. Wonderful Smith, a popular comedian on the *Red Skelton Show* in the 1940s, confessed that he was dropped from the series in 1948 because, "I had difficulty sounding as Negroid as they expected."[8]

If black entertainers contributed to radio in its early years, this achievement was practically limited to music and

comedy performances. As dramatic actors, there was little
opportunity for blacks. One of the few exceptions was the
popular CBS series, *John Henry, Black River Giant.* The
series was broadcast in 1933 and featured Juano Hernandez,
Rose McClendon, Dorothy Caul, and Jack McDowell. According to an early fan magazine, it was "a fresh and startling program" which stood out, "for John Henry was a *man.*" Speaking of his role, Hernandez noted that John Henry was a
legendary figure emanating from southern labor gangs, and
that there were three qualities that made a hero in such conditions: "First, he must be powerful in his strength; second, he
must be bad; and third, he must be a success with the ladies.
John Henry, the legend says, was a powerful, bad ladies'
man."[9]

Black dramatic actors found employment scarce. They
were only cast as blacks, and since many white actors had
mastered the minstrel accent, there was competition for the
few roles that did exist. A few feeble attempts were made,
nonetheless, by black actors who sought to create enduring
radio series and to develop their own theatrical organizations
to employ their services. In 1935, WMCA introduced *A Harlem Family,* a serial drama produced for the Adult Education
Project of the New York City Board of Education. Although
the local series did not remain long on the air, it featured an
all-black cast, and was written and directed by blacks. The
same station also probed an uncharted dimension of black
entertainment when, in 1935, it broadcast Mercedes Gilbert as
"the colored poetess." In 1933 the noted black opera star, Ken-
neth Spenser, appeared in San Francisco as the lead in an all-
black series, *Deacon Brown and His Peacemakers,* which
featured a blending of gospel songs, stereotyped humor, and
dramatic story line. Also in the early 1930s, Carleton Moss
organized a group of legitimate actors into the Lafayette
Players. This ensemble, which broadcast weekly radio dramas
of black life on WJZ (New York City), included Ernest Whitman, Rose McClendon, Richard Huey, Leigh Whipper, Frank
Wilson, and Edna Thompson.

All of the black dramatic series were short-lived. This is ironic, however, because research in 1935 showed that tastes among black audiences tended strongly toward drama. A poll of movie exhibitors revealed that black theater patrons preferred: (1) "Drama, the heavier the better, and if sentimental, heavily so"; (2) "Mystery, with especial emphasis upon the more horrific films"; and (3) "Gangster."[10] Interestingly, musicals were ranked fourth, and comedies were sixth. The answer to this incongruity, however, lies in the economics of radio and its reflection of American popular tastes.

Although there were more than thirteen million Afro-Americans in the mid-1930s, the vast majority lived in poor conditions. Only in the large Eastern and Midwestern cities did they create a sizable consumer force. Figures from the federal census of 1930 reveal, moreover, that blacks owned significantly fewer radio sets than did the rest of the population. As the following chart suggests, compared to other demographic entities, blacks were not listening to radio as much as whites because receivers were not as available.

Color and Nativity of Families With Radios[11]

Group	Urban	Rural-Farm	Rural-Non-Farm
Whites	56.3%	24.0%	37.4%
Foreign-Born Whites	46.2	32.0	35.1
Blacks	14.4	0.3	3.0
National Average	50.0	20.8	33.7

Given these figures, radio advertisers were unwilling to sponsor programs that appealed specifically to black audiences. Even black businessmen failed to invest regularly in such programming. This situation was compounded by the fact that white audiences, basically ignorant of black realities and prejudiced toward them, accepted blacks in entertainment only in traditional terms of comedy and music. Such bigotry lay deep in the social, political, and cultural past of the United States. And by this date little had been done to correct such attitudes. Therefore, white advertisers, who aimed their commercials at the broadest consumer group possible,

were often unwilling to sponsor black talent. They feared becoming too closely associated with Afro-Americans, thereby
alienating white consumers.

Speaking in 1950, black actor Frank Silvera suggested that
if Pillsbury were to sponsor a show with a black actor outside
the acceptable stereotype, and "if it gets out that [they] were
pushing Negro talent on a Pillsbury program, the next thing
you know it would be branded as 'nigger flour' and it would
never move."[12] This was also the opinion of Chet Huntley
who suggested that such sensitivity on the part of sponsors
also resulted in less news coverage of the black community: "I
presume that the reason for less Negro news was due to sales
resistance. Sponsors would probably fear boycott of their
products."[13]

Afro-American business and civic leaders did not fail to
react to these prejudiced conditions. In 1930 the Harlem
Broadcasting Corporation attempted to purchase a radio station in New York City. Although its negotiations failed, this
black organization also supported local black talent by buying
time on local and network broadcasts. Still another black
company, the Gold Star Radio and Television Corporation,
tried without success in 1937 to purchase the rights to erect all-
black stations in New York City, Philadelphia, Chicago, New
Orleans, and Los Angeles.

Private citizens and civic institutions occasionally attacked stereotyped programs inimical to Afro-American interests. In this regard, newspapers were active. In 1931 the
Pittsburgh Courier, a black weekly journal, sought to petition
the Federal Radio Commission to cancel *Amos 'n' Andy.* Although it was unsuccessful in its drive, the newspaper made
three strong points about the program: 1) that it represented
the exploitation of blacks for the commercial benefit of
whites; 2) that the characters in the series were detrimental
to the self-respect and general advancement of black society;
and 3) that the series placed business activities between blacks
in a negative light.[14]

Four years later the Baltimore *Afro-American,* then the
largest black newspaper in the nation, conducted a similar

campaign. This undertaking, however, was aimed at all stations and programs which insulted blacks. This weekly newspaper asked readers throughout the United States to inform it of epithets, belittling remarks, and racial disparagements heard on the air. The journal, in turn, promised to publish the names of the offenders, and to seek retribution through complaints to the sponsors of such broadcasts.

Although "lily-white" dramas gained greater popularity in radio by the end of the 1930s, black musicians and comedians continued to broadcast. Many such entertainers had their own programs. In 1935, for example, several musical personalities had local and network radio series. These included Nobel Sissle, the Mills Brothers, the Ink Spots, Bob Howard, and Adelaide Hall. In 1936 Duke Ellington appeared on NBC in his own show. The following year Louis Armstrong had a network series sponsored by Fleischmann's Yeast, but it ran for only thirteen weeks. And in 1938 *Recitals in Rhythm* featured Maxine Sullivan.

Blacks were also affected by the amateur craze which swept radio in the late 1930s. *Vine Street Varieties,* hosted by blues singer Jimmy Ruffin, was aired in 1938 over WHB (Kansas City, Missouri). The same year KEHE (Los Angeles) produced a talent revue directed at the 65,000 Afro-Americans residing in that city. Two programs called *Amateur Night in Harlem* began in New York City in the spring of 1935. The one on WNEW soon left the air, but the WMCA production eventually gained sponsors and remained on that station for fifteen years. In 1952 the program was shifted to the ABC network and ran for two more years as *The Original Harlem Amateur Hour,* hosted now by celebrities such as Lucky Millinder, Ethel Waters, and Dizzy Gillespie.

Black entertainers also appeared as regular, featured characters on several musical and comedy programs in the second half of the 1930s. The Fisk Jubilee Singers were heard on *Magnolia Blossoms* over WSM (Nashville). Clarence Muse lent his rich baritone voice to Irvin S. Cobb's popular *Plantation Party* series in 1936. As well as having her own show, singer Maxine Sullivan in 1938 was a regular on the CBS

musical, *Saturday Night Sewing Club*. Comedienne Hattie
Noel in 1938 was a hit on the *Eddie Cantor Show*. But the
most successful black actor in a radio series was also one of the
most controversial, for in mid-1937 Eddie Anderson began his
long association with the character "Rochester" on the top-
ranked *Jack Benny Program*.

In his role as Benny's valet and chauffeur, Anderson
played Rochester as a strong, yet stereotyped personality.
Woman-chasing, dice-throwing, and shiftlessness were all part
of his radio character. Critics would suggest later that because
Rochester often stood up to his employer and showed up
Benny's comedic traits—cheapness, impracticality, pretentious-
ness, boorishness—he was actually a positive black character.
Despite Rochester's assertiveness around Jack Benny (done,
obviously, for comedic effect only), he was a stereotyped character and created no significant breakthroughs toward a mature portrayal of blacks. In his early years with the program,
Rochester was especially identified with the conventions white
society derogatorily associated with Afro-Americans. This condition was strongly illustrated in the *Jack Benny Program*
broadcast on April 3, 1938. With Benny and Rochester on a
train returning to Los Angeles from New York City, the following dialogue touches upon several familiar clichés.

> *Benny:*   Well, we would have been home yesterday if
>   you hadn't gotten off at Albuquerque to look
>   at those Indians.
> *Rochester:* I thought I'se back in Harlem.
> *Benny:*   Harlem? I told you before, all those people at
>   the station were Indians.
> *Rochester:* Indians?
> *Benny:*   Yes.
> *Rochester:* Well, just the same, I saw a papoose eatin'
>   a pork chop.
> *Benny:*   Well, what of it? He can be an Indian and
>   still eat a pork chop.
> *Rochester:* I know, but he had it between two slices
>   of watermelon.
> *Benny:*   Alright, you win. But I want to tell you
>   something, Rochester. This is the last time I'm
>   going to take you to New York. You're supposed

to help me. The only time I saw you was when
you needed money. Why you spent more
than I did.

Rochester: That ain't no record.

Benny: Never mind that. And another thing, you lied
to me. You told me you needed the money
for a new suit. Now, where is it?

Rochester: The suit?

Benny: Yes, the suit!

Rochester: You mean the one I had my heart set on?

Benny: Yeah, where is that new suit I gave you the
money for?

Rochester: Well, I'll tell ya, boss. I was on my way to
the store and got mixed up in a game of African
badminton.

Benny: Oh, so you lost your suit in a crap game, huh?

Rochester: Yes, sir. I rolled myself right out of the
Easter parade.

Although such racist imagery was not always written into
Rochester's lines, as late as 1950 black organizations protested
specific broadcasts which, they felt, went beyond the boundaries of good taste.

When in the mid-1930s the large variety programs turned
increasingly to the use of celebrity guest stars to attract listeners, many black personalities appeared on the most popular
shows in radio. During the period 1935–1937, for example,
Shell Chateau, hosted by Al Jolson and later Wallace Beery
and Joe Cook, welcomed entertainers such as Cab Calloway,
Paul Robeson, Bill Robinson, the Juanita Hall Choir, Stepin
Fetchit, Thomas "Fats" Waller, and Juano Hernandez. The
Rudy Vallee Show in this period hosted such black actors and
musicians as Bill Robinson, Rex Ingram, Eddie Green, Fats
Waller, Mantan Moreland, Cab Calloway, Mrs. Jesse Owens,
Amanda Randolph, the Charioteers, and Flournoy Miller. Importantly, these appearances did not relegate the guests to
playing stereotyped characterizations. When Bill Robinson
guested, the production staff of the *Rudy Vallee Show* built
an elaborate stage where his famous tap and soft-shoe dances
could be picked up by the microphones. Such treatment was
uncommon for a guest star making only a single broadcast.

More impressive, however, was Paul Robeson's role on *Shell Chateau* in the fall of 1935. As well as sing a rendition of his popular song, "Water Boy," Robeson enacted a scene about a stalwart African chief, Neabongo of the Balu tribe, who pitted his authority against the fervor of his people for war. Speaking forcefully at a meeting of the tribe, Robeson asserted:

> Silence! The drums lie! There will be no war for the Balus! For fifty moons have we had peace, and peace we will keep. We want no war. And on this side of the river there will be no war. We have all we need. We have homes; our crops are good; we have water from the great river. We do not need war. And war we will not have! Do you want your fathers and brothers killed? Do you want your wives and daughters carried away into slavery by men of the North Country? Lobengula, have you forgotten the last time we beat the war drums? Have you forgotten your son—shot through the heart by the poisoned arrows of the Acholie? If the warriors of the North Country cross our borders, then we will fight. But while I am chief, we will attack no one. Your wives and daughters will not be carried into slavery. Your sons will not be killed. Remember the law. We have had happiness with the law. We must all be friends. We must all work together. The Balus will have peace. (Murmurs of approval from the tribe.) Let us remember Chonga, our great ancestor. Let us be strong. Let us be wise. Come, into our canoes. Away we go!

It was a bold performance, intended to exploit Robeson's well-known leftist and pacifist politics, as well as to tie in with his recent portrayal of an African chief in the British motion picture, *Sanders of the River*. In this broadcast, Robeson's characterization of a proud, rational, and strong leader of men was possibly the most sophisticated role given a black actor in the history of American radio before World War II.

By the beginning of the Second World War, participation by Afro-Americans in radio was expanding its boundaries. This is not to suggest that prejudice had been surmounted within the industry. But advancements were achieved especially among local stations, where advertisers and station management recognized the growing importance of appealing to black listeners. On November 30, 1935, station WJTL (Atlanta) pioneered black news programming when it initiated a fifteen-minute daily news broadcast devoted entirely to Afro-Americans and read by Afro-Americans. In mid-1937, *Afro-America Speaks* was introduced as a weekly feature on WKY (Oklahoma City). This series featured man-in-the-street interviews with residents of the black community. On WSBC Jack L. Cooper pioneered black broadcasting in Chicago. By 1939, Cooper weekly was airing five and one-half hours of programs meant specifically for black listeners. His shows contained live performances by local choirs, recorded swing music, and a public service feature, *Search for Missing Persons,* which that year helped families and the Chicago Police Department locate seven hundred missing people throughout the country.[15]

There are even indications that by the late 1930s live blues performances were being broadcast in Jackson, Mississippi.[16] With the opening in 1941 of station KFFA in Helena, Arkansas, and the debut that same year of Sonny Boy Williamson on *King Biscuit Time,* this form of Afro-American folk music came to radio on a regular basis. The Williamson series was so successful that within a few years KFFA had commenced two other live blues programs sponsored by Bright Star Flour and by Mother's Best Flour, and featuring, among others, the bands of Robert Nighthawk and Robert Jr. Lockwood.

Still another format in which Afro-American talent was innovatively utilized was the quiz program. In July 1941, *Cab Calloway's Quizzical* brought to WOR (New York City) a blend of music, humor, and audience participation in an all-black quiz show. In February 1942, when Mutual, of which WOR was the key station, was unable or unwilling to make this local hit program a network feature, it was acquired by the Blue Network. On this network, the show emanated weekly from different black communities on the East Coast and in the Northeast. Although it was cancelled after six months on the Blue Network, the program represented another expansion of black talent into an area of broadcasting traditionally reserved for whites. Despite such innovations,

however, it would not be until World War II that conditions
for blacks in radio would be altered, substantially and irre-
versibly.

Whites as Blacks

American radio was not particularly accommodating to
black actors. Although Afro-American comedians found occasional employment in broadcasting, most of the preferred
black roles were filled by white actors. This was possible, of
course, because audiences did not see the person to whom they
were listening. Stations and networks found it preferable to
hire whites to play such characters as Amos 'n' Andy, Beulah,
and dozens of other comedy types. Furthermore, such representation had been standard for a century before radio. Since
the 1830s, minstrels had utilized blackface comedians who
used burnt cork, coarse wigs, and stereotyped dialect to entertain generations of white patrons. Radio, therefore, simply in-
herited and perpetuated a tradition deep in American popular culture.

Radio also imitated the other popular arts in the manner
in which it characterized blacks. Except for band leaders and
singers, those roles depicting blacks were almost always insensitive distortions of Afro-Americans for, as "lovable" and
humorous as were comics like Amos 'n' Andy, they were most
objectionable because they represented the *only* depiction of
black life consistently broadcast.

Specifically, the stereotypes generally conformed to one of
three familiar types: Coons, Toms, and Mammies. The Coon
was derived directly from minstrel shows. He was above all
the clown of radio—murdering the English language with
malaprops, conniving to fleece a comrade out of money,
bumblingly avoiding gainful employment, and wheezing out
his words in ignorant accents unfamiliar to actual blacks.
Above all, the Coon confirmed the racist slur that black society was populated with stupid and scheming indolents.

To counter this portrayal, however, radio presented the
Tom whose goodness and gentleness could never be disturbed. The Tom might be religious, relatively sober-minded,

or even grandfatherly, but he was primarily the submissive, "good nigger" whose existence gave reassurance to white audiences that there were forces of reason at work within the black community. Thus, the Tom was an antidote to the unpredictable rascality of the Coon.

The Mammy, however, existed for the sake of humor. She was the image of black womanhood, which was a blend of quick temper, earthy wisdom, and love for her wards. No one could bake like a Mammy, and no one could shriek like one, either. She was, ultimately, a comic type who would take backtalk from no person, but who added feminine warmth and intuition to the stereotype of Afro-American life.

These minstrel-based caricatures were found not only in radio, but in the various media of popular culture—film, theater, print, and music. Such unflattering typologies, moreover, were not reserved for blacks. At the turn of the century, when the wave of struggling immigrants was so high, America made its humor at the expense of groups such as Italians, Jews, Germans, and Greeks. Decades before, the Chinese had been famliar targets of disrespectful representations. Yet, the black was the oldest ethnic minority to be pejoratively stereotyped. In a society where his assimilation was hampered by skin color as well as legal and extra-legal servitude, the Afro-American was practically a resident alien. As such, blacks were uprooted from their historical past, denied economic independence, and thwarted in attempts at social self-fulfillment. As a general group they lacked power and wealth, vital factors within an achievement-oriented society. Blacks remained chronically at the bottom of the social scale, therefore, and were continually vulnerable to the ridicule of those above them.

Ironically, the chief complaint against stereotyping in radio was that such distortion was the only image of Afro-Americans being broadcast. Still, a program like *Amos 'n' Andy*, for instance, enjoyed apparent popularity among black listeners. For several years after it disappeared from the top Hooper ratings, in the South, heavily populated with blacks, it remained a solid favorite. A fan magazine in 1933 illustrated the ambivalence that surrounded such programming. It noted that while black lawyers were seeking a court injunction against *Amos 'n' Andy*, a charity group in Harlem had telegraphed its thanks to the stars of the show "for being friends of the Negro race."[17] Years later Dr. E. I. Robinson, president of the Los Angeles branch of the National Association for the Advancement of Colored People, a strong foe of the program, suggested that he was not opposed to the program as much as he was to the one-dimensional view radio gave to blacks. Speaking in 1950, Robinson remarked, "The sooner they're off the air, the better it will be for the Negro. Radio points to one side of the Negro, the worst side, most frequently."[18]

Although the Georgia Minstrels and other minstrel programs had broadcast in the early 1920s, it was not until the success of *Amos 'n' Andy* in 1929 that the tradition of minstrel comedy was accepted nationally as an institution in radio. Portrayed by two white comedians, Freeman Gosden and Charles Correll, the blackface characters within two years became the favorite radio personalities of millions of Americans. Erik Barnouw has related how factories altered their working shifts to allow employees to listen to *Amos 'n' Andy*, Monday through Saturday from 7 to 7:15 P.M. Their popularity was legitimized, moreover, when President Herbert Hoover invited them to perform at the White House. And they were largely responsible for the rapid rise in the sale of radio sets and parts which rose from $650,550,000 in 1928, to $842,548,000 in 1929.[19]

As the blackface characters, Gosden and Correll made records for the Victor Company, launched a comic strip that was syndicated by the Chicago *Daily News*, appeared in 1930 in a feature motion picture, and in 1933 even provided their minstrel voices for an animated cartoon. In this manner *Amos 'n' Andy* became part of the American lifestyle. In March 1930, the New York Telephone Company confirmed this fact when it reported that during their broadcasts rows of operators now sat idly where they had always been active with families using telephones to plan evening activities.

Amos 'n' Andy remained an enduring radio feature. Despite several changes in format and networks, the program continued until the late 1950s. The characters lived in Harlem and conducted much of their humorous business from the Mystic Knights of the Sea Lodge Hall. Here were found all of the stereotypes which radio borrowed from minstrelsy. Amos, described by Gosden and Correll as "trusting, simple, unsophisticated," was the Tom who brought sobriety into each program. Andy Brown, "domineering, a bit lazy,"[20] was the oafish Coon who perpetually was chasing women and being swindled by his friends. One of the auxiliary characters created by Freeman Gosden eventually came to dominate the program. In George "Kingfish" Stevens, the series presented the Coon stereotype of the wheeler-dealer whose plans for quick money frequently involved cheating his friends, but never involved getting a job. The Kingfish, thus, was the classic "shiftless loafer" whose indolence forced him to become a schemer, and whose scheming alienated him from "respectable" people. This dilemma was explained in a conversation between the Kingfish and his shrewish, Mammy wife, Sapphire, in the broadcast of April 22, 1947:

Sapphire:	George Stevens, I done made up my mind that I'm gonna have a husband that dresses good, knows nice people, and is got a steady job.
Kingfish:	Sapphire, you mean to say that you is gonna leave me?
Sapphire:	George, I know why you're a no-good bum. It's on account of your association with Andy Brown. Why don't you try to meet a nicer class of men?
Kingfish:	Well, I ain't got da opportunity to meet 'em, they's all workin'.
Sapphire:	Well, that Andy Brown is the cause of it all. What has he ever accomplished?
Kingfish:	Well, yesterday he had a run of thirteen balls in da side pocket without leanin' on da table.
Sapphire:	Now, that's exactly what I mean: Andy hangin' around a pool table all day. Why don't he go to a cultured place like a public library?
Kingfish:	They ain't got no pool table there.

The success of *Amos 'n' Andy* inspired many blackface

imitators. As early as 1929, *George and Rufus* appeared on WOV (Brooklyn). Other groups in the 1930s included such teams as Honey and Alexander on WBT (Charlotte), Moonshine and Sawdust on *The Gulf Show,* Buck and Wheat on *Aunt Jemima,* and Rastus and Jasper on the *Modern Minstrels* program. Some of these groups possessed outlandish names, such as Sugarfoot and Sassafrass, Anaesthetic and Cerebelum on KGW (Portland, Oregon), and Watermelon and Cantaloupe on the *Corn Cob Pipe Club* program over WEAF (New York City). Two white men who enjoyed popularity as minstrel comics were Pat Padgett and Pick Malone. At one point in the mid-1930s they broadcast on Monday nights as Pick and Pat on the *Dill's Best Show,* and on Thursday evenings as Molasses 'n' January on the *Show Boat* program. Such blackface duets also appeared as male-and-female groups. Here, radio produced such teams as Conjur and Caroline on WOR, Magnolia and Sunflower over WGY (Schenectady), Lulu and Leander on WXYZ, and Emmaline and Easy, also on WGY. In most instances, the female character was actually portrayed by a white man speaking an octave above his normal voice. In the case of Lizzie Titus and Mrs. Emma Potts, a female minstrel duet on WLW (Cincinnati), however, both women were played by men.

One of the most popular and long-running network series featuring a white actress as an Afro-American character was *Aunt Jemima.* Even before she became a radio personality, Aunt Jemima was a commercial figure created by Quaker Oats for its pancake flour. As portrayed by Tess Gardella, a white woman, the jovial Mammy figure made Victor recordings in the 1920s and achieved success on Broadway in 1928 in the Jerome Kern musical, *Showboat.* Her role in the musical probably was responsible for creating her radio series the same year. As played by Gardella and her successors—Harriet Widmer in 1935, and Vera Lane in 1943—Aunt Jemima was a fat and happy Mammy figure whose songs, conversation, and pancake commercials kept the morning program on radio until the 1950s.

If Aunt Jemima captured many of the attributes of the Mammy, and the minstrel duets capitalized upon the Toms and Coons, Jimmy Scribner in *The Johnson Family* possessed the widest possible range of black caricature. In this serial which began in 1936, Scribner, a white man, demonstrated the twenty-two separate Afro-American voices he had developed. Even a stereotyped program like *Folks from Dixie,* which in 1933 broadcast on NBC its weekly "humorous sketch of Negro life," was enacted by several men and women. But Scribner, operating originally at WLW, and later on the Mutual network, played every role for over a decade. In 1948 Scribner developed a similar program solely for children. In *Sleepy Joe* he played the story-telling Tom role, as well as the voices of all the animals in his tales—voices that were also stereotyped black characterizations. Scribner's success, no doubt, encouraged the Liberty Network to syndicate from Dallas, in 1951, a white man, Brooks Read, in a similar *Uncle Remus* series.

The resentment that many blacks felt toward such consistent stereotyping of both blacks as blacks, and whites as blacks, was profound and telling. One critic aptly summarized this hostility when in 1931 she challenged the racist impulse in radio:

> The radio should not be prostituted to the teaching of race inferiority or spreading mischievous propaganda that will generate contempt or antagonism between the races. The Negro is permitted to sing spirituals or do burlesque stuff over the radio, but not to speak over a nation-wide network. He is never given a nation-wide chance to talk to people of this country. What is the fear? Why the boycott?[21]

For the most part, such condemnation was not seriously heard by those involved with radio programming. Not until the threat of war emanated from Nazism—the most perfected form of racism in the Western world—did a sizable number of radio officials move to offset bigotry in American broadcasting.

Wartime Radio and Stereotyping

As ironic as it may sound, World War II had a salutary effect upon the image and position of blacks in American broadcasting. With its strong rhetoric regarding fighting for Truth and defending social convictions, the war galvanized in many black actors and white sympathizers the decision to speak forthrightly against racism and its restrictive grip on the American popular arts. The Nazi enemy, moreover, presented Americans with an insidious picture of the implications of bigotry. Thus, there arose in many people an awareness of the paradox of fighting against a racist enemy abroad, while practicing segregation and exclusion at home. Out of such conditions developed the most important re-evaluation of the role of Afro-Americans in American society since the Civil War.

More than any other person, Paul Robeson was the catalyst who sparked this black artistic re-evaluation. Two months after the outbreak in Europe of World War II, Robeson's dramatic singing of the "Ballad for Americans" on the CBS series, *Pursuit of Happiness,* raised the entire issue of the position of blacks in American society. Written in 1935 by a young poet, John Latouche, as a hymn against intolerance and persecution, the poetic lyrics were set to stirring music in 1939 by Earl Robinson. This lengthy song traced the history of the United States as it evolved toward the realization of the freedom and democracy inherent in the Revolutionary War. Reasserting ideals like the brotherhood and equality of all citizens, the song found pride in the fact that America was a nation of nations filled with "everybody who's nobody" and "nobody who's everybody." And when Robeson's powerful bass voice proclaimed the inexorable march toward freedom and human rights—"Out of the cheating, out of the shouting/ Out of the murders and lynchings./ Out of the windbags, the patriotic spouting/ Out of uncertainty and doubting"*—he spoke for millions who felt that the time had arrived to rebuke prejudice.

---

*Copyright © 1939, 1940, renewed 1967, 1968, Robbins Music Corporation.

Coming as it did at a time of acute national self-appraisal, "Ballad for Americans" was enthusiastically received by the nation. In the broadcasting studio Robeson received an ovation that lasted fifteen minutes after the program left the air. He was called upon to perform it again on CBS radio in August 1940, in a special broadcast called *All God's Children,* and in September 1943, on *Stage Door Canteen.* In 1940 the song was orchestrated by the Philadelphia Orchestra and performed at the Republican National Convention. That same year Robeson recorded it for Victor records in a special two-record album. Clearly, "Ballad for Americans" captured the ethos of pride and reaffirmation that gripped America in those early months of the Second World War.

Robeson, however, did not remain idle after his initial success. Long a champion of racial equality, and an admirer of the Soviet Union as the fullest realization of equality yet established, Robeson became a stronger proponent for change than ever before. In public he assailed films and songs that he felt slurred black citizens. In 1942 he announced that he would no longer sing songs like "Glory Road," or other "popular folk songs or ballads that picture the Negro as ignorant or crude, or even savage." And his animosity toward films which discredited blacks caused him to announce of his own movie, *Tales of Manhattan,* "If they picket the film when it opens in New York, I'll join the picket line myself."[22]

On radio, Robeson promoted respect and self-respect for black Americans. On programs such as *Freedom's People* in September 1941, and a special salute to black actor Canada Lee on WOR in June 1941, he helped trace the development of Afro-American culture. When he praised the Loyalist side of the Spanish Civil War on a local special entitled *Five Songs for Democracy* in September 1940, he made it clear that Afro-Americans had a duty to stand for freedom. And when in June 1943 he appeared on an NBC special program, *Labor for Victory,* several weeks after the Detroit race riots, he represented the fact that although the riots were a setback, the cause of freedom was still viable. Robeson was also used by the American government, and several times during the war he lent his talents to propaganda broadcasts. Thus, for example, to assist the Office of War Information in February 1944, he narrated a shortwave transmission to Europe, North Africa, the Near East, and South Africa commemorating the 135th birthday of Abraham Lincoln.

Robeson's model was not lost on other black performers. Several important entertainers joined his protest over the condition of blacks. The cast of the successful musical, *Carmen Jones*, in mid-1944 refused to play in Louisville or Washington, D.C., because of discrimination against blacks. In October 1944, Katherine Dunham spoke to an audience in Louisville and announced that her modern dance troupe would never perform there as long as blacks were forbidden to sit on the main floor among whites. "Maybe after the war," she told the audience, "we will have democracy and I can return."[23] Less than three months later, Lena Horne cancelled a USO performance in Little Rock because Afro-American soldiers were not allowed to see her evening show, while even the kitchen crew—composed of Nazi prisoners of war—was in attendance. In a similar vein, by the end of the war black newspapers were expressing a general displeasure with the forthcoming Broadway theatrical season because it did not display the serious, positive side of black society.

Throughout the war special broadcasts paid tribute to black accomplishments. This was especially true of black soldiers who constituted a sizable portion of the American armed forces. In 1943, *Fighting Men* was a Mutual broadcast which had black servicemen relating their wartime experiences. That same year in a commemoration of the 116th anniversary of the black press, black war correspondents were heard for the first time broadcasting via shortwave from war zones in Europe and North Africa.

Men O' War was an all-black musical program produced by the United States Navy and emanating from Great Lakes Naval Training Center in Illinois. It began as a state-wide broadcast in 1943, but by the end of the war it was a weekly feature on CBS. The importance of black servicemen was dramatized in an episode of the CBS series, *They Call Me Joe*, a special twelve-week series in the summer of 1944, which focused upon the ethnic diversity within the American armed forces. And Chet Huntley's award-winning series, *These Are Americans,* produced in 1944 on KNX (Los Angeles), also dealt with blacks. In 1945, moreover, stories about black soldiers, factory workers, and journalists appeared in a CBS special, *The Negro in the War.* The seriousness of this program was underscored when the announcer read a cabled message from General Douglas MacArthur which stated, "There is no differentiation because of color among the soldiers of my command."[24]

In one sense, the irregular appearance of special broadcasts might make them seem insincere tokens meant to exploit the fact that black soldiers were needed to win the war. Yet, relative to the portrait of Afro-Americans in radio before the 1940s, these special programs were significantly progressive. They pictured blacks as substantial, heroic, even red-blooded and All-American citizens. Here, minstrel images were consistently shunned for the first time in American radio as blacks were presented in equality.

Afro-Americans even appeared as continuing characters in such traditionally white programming as soap operas. In mid-1942 a black soldier appeared in *Our Gal Sunday.* He returned several times during furloughs, and was used to spark conversation between Sunday and her husband about the loyalty of black servicemen to the United States. The same theme occurred on *The Romance of Helen Trent* where a new character, an Afro-American doctor, saved the heroine's life and eventually became a staff physician in a war factory.[25]

The persistent appearance on radio of black cultural leaders like Robeson, Langston Hughes, Richard Wright, and Marian Anderson also signified that wartime respect for blacks would not be mere tokenism. Because of their personal reputations as fighters against discrimination, by their broadcasts these personalities were proclaiming the necessity and inevitability of freedom. One of the more dramatic statements on this issue came as part of a dramatization on WABC (New York City) of the maiden voyage of the all-black naval destroyer, U.S.S. *Booker T. Washington*. In the broadcast, one crewman triumphantly proclaimed, "The *Washington* has got to be better than any ship that sailed the sea, 'cause our skipper is colored and the Hitler forces at home have said that it won't work."[26] The implications of such a statement—the labelling of anti-black forces as Hitlerian, the expression of black pride, and the militancy of the crew—could not have been mistaken by listeners.

Despite such progressive developments, the traditional comic roles to which black characterization had been relegated continued to flourish in radio. This was especially true of network entertainment broadcasting. Certainly *Amos 'n' Andy* continued to enjoy great popularity, becoming in October 1943 a half-hour situation comedy instead of a fifteen-minute serial or a variety show as it had been in the past. Eddie Anderson's character, Rochester van Jones, the valet on the *Jack Benny Program,* was not only popular, but by the 1940s, strategic to the success of the series. And in 1943 one writer could attack big-time broadcasting for maintaining such racist practices as never introducing black guest stars "with the appellation of Mr., Mrs., or Miss."[27]

New stereotyped characters were developed in this period. The maid, Beulah Brown, was introduced in 1940 on NBC's revived *Show Boat* series, but that Mammy figure gained greater popularity in late 1944 when she appeared on the *Fibber McGee and Molly Show.* Played by a white man, Marlin Hurt, Beulah eventually evolved into her own series, *The Marlin Hurt and Beulah Show* (later *Beulah*) in 1945. In the new series Hurt portrayed himself, Beulah, and her dim-witted boyfriend, Bill Jackson. When he died suddenly the next year, Hurt was replaced by another white man. Not until 1947 when Hattie McDaniel assumed the role was Beulah played by a black woman. Yet, even with Afro-American actors in the roles, these characterizations were less than innovative and flattering.

Black maids flourished in the early 1940s. In 1941, Lillian Randolph began portraying Birdie Lee Coggins on

The Great Gildersleeve; in 1943, Ruby Dandridge appeared as Geranium on *The Judy Canova Show*; and Lillian Randolph the following year enacted the role of Daisy on *The Billie Burke Show*. Stereotyped maids also emerged in several soap operas: Georgia Burke played Lily on *When a Girl Marries*; Gee Gee James was Tulip on *Hilltop House*; a maid named Clohe was introduced on *The Right to Happiness*; and another one appeared on *Life Can Be Beautiful*.

As well as the preponderance of roles depicting blacks as housekeepers and cooks, other caricatures of black life came frequently to wartime radio. When *Amos 'n' Andy* became a situation comedy, black actors were hired to fill subsidiary roles formerly handled by Gosden and Correll. Ernestine Wade became the haranguing Sapphire; Eddie Green played the lawyer Stonewall; and Amanda Randolph became Sapphire's shrewish mother, Mama. Mantan Moreland and Ben Carter were regular Coon comedians on the *Bob Burns Show* in the 1944–1945 season, as was Nicodemus Stewart on Rudy Vallee's program for Sealtest foods in 1941. Dewey Markham appeared in early 1945 as a black ranch hand, Alamo, and joked with white actor, George "Gabby" Hayes, on *The Andrews Sisters Eight-to-the-Bar Ranch* program. Butterfly McQueen's portrayal of a stupid secretary on *The Danny Kaye Show* in 1945 was not identified as a black characterization. But the role, itself, was scarcely a positive image. One of the few non-comedic black actors who appeared regularly in radio at this time was Juano Hernandez. He played exotic types on several children's programs, including the African Kolu on *Jungle Jim*; the black assistant, Lothar, on *Mandrake the Magician*; and various Indian characters on *Tennessee Jed*.

Nonetheless, the liberal lesson of World War II was not lost on network radio. In increasing numbers, national series and special broadcasts challenged the prejudices of the past. Beginning in 1942, *Casey, Crime Photographer*, a popular crime drama on CBS, featured a non-stereotyped black photographer, Ernie, who was played by Juano Hernandez, and later by Herman Chittison and Teddy Wilson. When *Duffy's*

Tavern premiered in 1941, the successful comedy series featured Eddie Green as a waiter, and music for the show was provided by John Kirby and his Orchestra.

Black characters were boldly enacted in several of the distinguished radio plays written and directed by Norman Corwin during the war years. In April 1943, director-producer William N. Robson, on his award-winning *Man Behind the Gun* series, dramatized the true story of an all-black Coast Guard cutter, the U.S.S. *Campbell,* which had sunk six enemy submarines.

History was made in June 1944, when Canada Lee was selected to narrate an NBC program, *Unofficial Ambassadors.* What was striking about the selection was that Lee was black and the program was neither about blacks nor demanded an Afro-American narrator. Accounting for this significant decision, a spokesman for the Young Men's Christian Association, sponsors of the program, asserted that Lee was chosen "solely for his acting abilities."[28] The following month, the appearance of black actor Maurice Ellis in the role of a white forest ranger on the top-ranked *Mr. District Attorney* was such a departure from tradition that it was reported in *Variety* as a news story.[29]

Bigotry of the past was particularly challenged in the many special broadcasts which featured prominent white Americans in appeals for tolerance and brotherhood. The most memorable of these programs was *An Open Letter on Race Hatred,* written and directed by William N. Robson, and featuring an appearance by former Republican candidate for President Wendell Willkie. The program was broadcast on CBS on the evening of Saturday, July 24, 1943, one month after a race riot in Detroit had resulted in thirty-five deaths. In documentary fashion, Robson's program sought the causes of that riot. But from the beginning of the broadcast, listeners knew that the implications of that battle were even more ominous for, as the announcer declared:

> Dear Fellow Americans: What you are about to hear may anger you. What you are about to hear may sound incredible to you. You may doubt that such things can hap-

pen today in this supposedly united nation. But we assure you, everything you are about to hear is true. And
so we ask you to spend thirty minutes with us, facing
quietly and without passion or prejudice, a danger which
threatens all of us. A danger so great that if it is not met
and conquered now, even though we win this war, we
shall be defeated in victory; and the peace which follows
will for us be a horror of chaos, lawlessness, and blood-
shed. This danger is race hatred.

The program was uncompromising with the rioters, showing how their action cost the war effort one million man-hours
of production in Detroit armament plants; how the riots
played into the hands of propagandists in Japan and Germany
who offered the world alternatives to the failing American system; and how the Detroit riots had caused "democracy to go
up in smoke and trickle away in the bloody gutters." At the
end of the broadcast, when Willkie spoke his own postscript,
the seriousness of the broadcast was fully understood.

The race problem in America was openly discussed in
many wartime special programs. *Too Long, America* in
March 1945, starred Edward G. Robinson and Rex Ingram,
and spoke of the progress being made in employment of
blacks. Fiorello LaGuardia also added his prestige as mayor of
New York City by appearing on the program. Rex Stout,
literary creator of the noted detective, Nero Wolfe, was an
outspoken radio critic of racial prejudice. During the war he
was head of the War Writers Board and hosted several series,
including *Council for Democracy* in 1941, and *Our Secret
Weapon* in 1942, in which he attacked discrimination. In May
1944, Stout carried his message directly to members of the
Radio Writers Guild, scoring them for the persistence of the
"white Protestant Anglo-Saxon myth" in their scripts.[30]

In December 1944, the prestigious CBS series, *People's
Platform,* presented a forthright discussion on the subject, "Is
the South Solving Its Race Problem?" Further, on several occasions the Blue network on *America's Town Meeting of the
Air* discussed racial problems. Here, on May 28, 1942, the participants were all blacks; and on July 15, 1943, and February
17, 1944, the integrated panels included authorities such as

author and editor, Carey McWilliams, and the black poet and
author, Langston Hughes.

One of the strongest and most impressive individual de-
nunciations of racism came from Kate Smith, perhaps the
most influential woman in the history of radio. Speaking on
We, the People in early 1945, Smith talked poignantly about
the future of a postwar world still plagued by racial intolerance:

> It seems to me that faith in the decency of human beings
> is what we *must* have *more* of, if there is to be a future
> for all of us in this world. We read in the papers every
> day about conferences on the best way to keep the peace.
> Well, I'm not an expert on foreign affairs—and I don't
> pretend to know all the complex things that will have to
> be done for a lasting peace. But I am a human being—
> and I do know something about people. I know that our
> statesmen—our armies of occupation—our military strate-
> gists—may all fail if the peoples of the world don't learn
> to *understand* and *tolerate* each other. Race hatreds—so-
> cial prejudices—religious bigotry—they are all the diseases
> that eat away the fibres of peace. Unless they are exter-
> minated it's inevitable that we will have another war.
> And where are they going to be exterminated? At a con-
> ference table in Geneva? Not by a long shot. In your own
> city—your church—your children's school—perhaps in your
> own home. You and I must do it—every father and
> mother in the world, every teacher, everyone who can
> rightfully call himself a human being. Yes, it seems to me
> that the one thing the peoples of the world have got to
> learn if we are ever to have a lasting peace, is—tolerance.
> Of what use will it be if the lights go on again all over
> the world—if they don't go on . . . in our hearts.[31]

Importantly, the sponsors of the program received over twenty
thousand requests for a reprint of the statement.

Of all the innovations to emerge in the war years, the
most impressive series treating the condition of blacks in a
prejudiced environment was *New World A-Coming*. This
weekly sustaining series premiered in March 1944 on WMCA.
It remained on that station until it was canceled in 1957. *New
World A-Coming* began as a dramatization of the book of the
same title written by Roi Ottley. It sought to reveal the inner
meaning of black life in America. With Canada Lee as nar-

rator, and with integrated casts that included personalities such as Leigh Whipper, Josh White, Mary Lou Williams, Alexander Scourby, and Mercedes McCambridge, *New World A-Coming* soon moved beyond the scope of Ottley's book and took up the general theme of racial inequality in America.

In its premier broadcast for the 1945–1946 season, for example, it dramatized Wendell Willkie's controversial treatise, *One World.* In October 1946, is presented Will Geer in a scathing indictment of the racist Senator Theodore G. Bilbo of Mississippi. Although the series always maintained its original commitment to dramatizing injustices against black citizens, by the 1950s it was probing discrimination against Puerto Ricans in New York City, the plight of war refugees still living in European camps, the nature of apartheid in South Africa, and the techniques of torture used on American military prisoners by the Communist Chinese and North Koreans.

During the first half of the 1940s, the situation of blacks in American broadcasting underwent a serious reappraisal. Caused primarily by World War II and the efforts of black servicemen fighting against international racists, radio in the United States consistently began portraying blacks as it had never attempted to do in the past. Special programs and series extolled black culture, achievement, and heroism. They pointed at injustice and demanded freedom of opportunity. These programs used words that were alien to prewar radio: brotherhood, integration, equality, prejudice. Spurred by the courage and conviction of individual entertainers, moreover, black actors protested employment policies and called for a more realistic portrayal of their race.

Certainly, this period did not produce a revolution in radio or the popular arts. Patterns from the past continued and the Toms, Coons, and Mammies from minstrelsy survived. Nevertheless, the significance of this era was twofold. On the one hand, new roles and new images of Afro-Americans entered radio to stay. For every comic type, intelligent, mature characterizations could be found. For every program that slurred blacks, there were programs now that rightfully praised their contributions to American civilization. On the other hand, the issues and tensions of World War II precipitated a general liberalization within society that would be felt in all forms of the popular arts. Film, literature, pop music, and radio explored new styles and objectives. The probe—questioning, re-evaluating, searching—became an operative motif in much of popular culture. Within radio, this was observable as a continuation, and even acceleration, of the liberalism fostered during the war. Although these developments did not issue forth a Golden Age in terms of America's treatment of its ethnic minorities, a significant stride toward freedom had been achieved. It was a first step, and it shifted the black social cause to a new plateau upon which later civil libertarians and reformers could build.

Postwar Radio

There can be no doubt that prejudice in broadcasting had been seriously challenged in wartime radio. Nevertheless, radio was slow to abandon older patterns. In the postwar period, this would create a climate of controversy as liberalizing forces sought to maintain the momentum of the early 1940s, and traditionalists acted to preserve much of the past.

Progressive spokesmen were not willing to forget the developments that had occurred during World War II. As early as May 1946, at the prestigious annual meeting of the Institute for Education by Radio at Ohio State University, several speakers enunciated a new militancy. In what *Variety* termed "one of the frankest meetings held here," several black and white critics attacked radio for failing to give a balanced picture of Afro-Americans as human beings. Speakers, such as Sidney Williams of the Cleveland Urban League, Gertrude Broderick of the U.S. Office of Education, and Walter N. Ridley of the American Teachers' Association, assailed the networks for continually placing blacks in menial positions in their programs. Specifically, they cited series such as *The Great Gildersleeve, When a Girl Marries, Amos 'n' Andy,* and the *Jack Benny Program,* all long-lasting and popular programs in which blacks appeared as maids, buffoons, or any

of the other minstrel stereotypes. Beyond programming, however, the conferees assailed other forms of segregation within
the industry, including the practice of trade unions and crafts
in restricting black membership, and the inability of black
technicians to find employment in radio.[32] In all, it was a
devastating critique of American broadcasting that placed the
blame squarely on the networks, stations, and unions.

It was not without reason that reformers attacked national radio. Despite the lessons of the war, most networks and
large advertising agencies, which produced many of the programs, persisted in airing shows that were demeaning to
blacks. Networks and agencies explained their attitude as
being dictated by economic realities. According to their
spokesmen, sponsors were reluctant to finance all-black or
racially-mixed programs if white listeners, the bulk of the
audience and the potential customers for the sponsor's product, would be alienated. This was especially true in the
southern region of the nation where for several generations
whites had maintained effective control of a segregated society.
In the South, network broadcasts from New York City or
Hollywood that did not conform to "acceptable" standards,
tended to offend white supremists. Thus, a program like
Night Life, a CBS summer series in 1946 which featured
black comedian Willie Bryant and a racially-mixed cast, was
dropped early because southern affiliates objected.[33] According to Frank Silvera, the failure of blacks to mature in network programming was a "touchy question," the answer to
which lay in the fear by advertising agencies and network
officials of offending the "Southern markets."[34]

Where there was a sympathy for the plight of black actors,
as well as an understanding of the economic imperatives of
broadcasting, some suggested segregation as the inevitable
answer. In 1950, for example, John Asher, research director for
CBS in Los Angeles, told an interviewer that the problem of
Afro-Americans in radio emanated from a lack of purchasing
power. "Once the sponsors realize the Negro's purchasing
power is great," he asserted, "programs will be designed to appeal to Negroes."[35] Although such "separate but equal" status

might have been preferable to exclusion, most reformers desired an integrated situation in which not only were blacks
portrayed with dignity, but mixed casts performed, and Afro-
American actors were not necessarily assigned only to black
roles.

During the struggle for equality by black actors in the
late 1940s, the slightest defeat brought forth stinging rebuke
by the proponents of change. To those entertainers, the
thought of retreat to traditional stereotypes meant a loss for
all blacks. No one better epitomized the bitterness born of
desperation than Canada Lee when in 1949 he attacked the
"giggling maids, Rochesters, Aunt Jemimas, and shiftless, lazy
individuals" usually portrayed by blacks. According to Lee:

> A virtual Iron Curtain exists against the entire Negro
> people as far as radio is concerned. Where is the story of
> our lives in terms of the ghetto slums in which we must
> live? Where is the story in terms of jobs not available?
> Who would know us only by listening to Amos and Andy,
> Beulah, Rochester, and minstrel shows?[36]

Quick to defend the stereotyping of racial characters were
several of the steadily-employed black actors in radio. Ernestine Wade felt that the black artists were actually broadening
the way for future actors. She maintained that the stereotypes
were nothing more than type-casting roles with as much meaning as that of a villain or miser. She contended, furthermore,
that cliché-ridden characters had no real effect upon blacks.
To Lillian Randolph, the traditional roles allotted to Afro-
Americans did not affect the past, present, or future of blacks.
Often a delegate to the conventions of the American Federation of Television and Radio Artists, Randolph always spoke
and voted against reformist resolutions condemning stereotypes. She argued that whites proposing such resolutions were
trying to stop blacks from playing these parts, not trying to
stop the roles themselves. Since white listeners would always
demand such characterizations, she argued, white actors would
inevitably fill the roles. Most defensive, however, was Eddie
Anderson. To justify his character, Rochester, he basically denied that there was discrimination in radio, contending, "I be-

lieve those who have shown they have something to offer have been given an equal opportunity." According to Anderson:

> I haven't seen anything objectionable. I don't see why certain characters are called stereotypes. . . . The Negro characters being presented are not labelling the Negro race any more than "Luigi" is labelling the Italian people as a whole. The same goes for "Beulah" who is not playing the part of thousands of Negroes, but only the part of one person, "Beulah." They're not saying here is the portrait of the Negro, but here is Beulah.[37]

Despite the controversy, there were important improvements for blacks in postwar radio. Established talent, like the spiritual group, Wings Over Jordan, returned to CBS in 1946 after a hiatus of several years. The same year *King Cole Trio Time,* sponsored by Wildroot hair tonic, introduced Nat "King" Cole to a national audience on NBC. Other black musical talents with new programs in this period included Louis Jordan and His Tympany Five, Duke Ellington, and singer Una Mae Carlisle. In late 1948, Jackie Robinson began his first radio series on the local station, WMCA; and in little more than a year he was hosting *The Jackie Robinson Show* before a national audience on ABC. Yet, in searching for programming which was more in line with the progressive thrust of radio during the war, one must turn to the many special broadcasts aired at this time.

The year 1948 was proclaimed, nationally, as the "Year of Rededication" in which citizens were asked to recommit themselves to American ideals. Throughout that year radio carried special programs and series on racial tolerance that met this request. One of the most controversial presentations occurred in March, 1948, when Mutual presented a four-part series, *To Secure These Rights,* which dramatized the findings of the President's Committee on Civil Rights. Even before the first program, southern politicians and station owners cautioned the network about possible reactions in their region. Though Mutual modified its original scripts, the series was received adversely in the South. During one broadcast, for example, the Mutual affiliate in Jackson, Mississippi, left the air and returned when the network transmission ended. The Conference of Southern Governors, and a group of twenty southern senators, led by Senator Richard D. Russell of Georgia, demanded from the network and received three half-hour periods in which to rebut the charges and implications of the series.

More indicative of postwar attitudes toward blacks in radio was a special series, *Freedom Theater,* produced in 1948 at WSM (Nashville). In this thirteen-part public service show, music was provided by a traditional country-western ensemble, Roy Acuff and His Smokey Mountain Boys, as well as by a black chorus, the Fisk University Choir. The series represented the first time racially-mixed programs had been broadcast from the same studio of that important southern station. If *Freedom Theater* was a breakthrough for racial change in radio, the appearance of an all-black dramatic theater series on WPWA (Chester, Pennsylvania) in April 1948, was another advancement for black actors. These were all small achievements, however. So, too, were the spot announcements for Brotherhood Week aired by Mutual in 1948. For example, listeners to *The Adventures of Sherlock Holmes* on February 29 were informed at the conclusion of that program:

> This is Brotherhood Week. Let's make it work. Judge every man by his individual worth, not by some label. Don't spread any rumor against any race or religion, and don't listen to them either. Speak up against prejudice, and for understanding.

Yet, as minor as these accomplishments may appear, they still represent an amazing change of attitude relative to prewar standards. While they certainly do not reveal a massive shift in national sentiment toward blacks, they do suggest that the liberalization realized during World War II was struggling to survive in peacetime.

There were many local programs in the postwar period which affected significantly the role of blacks in broadcasting. In 1945, WNEW (New York City) produced several musical programs featuring black entertainers such as Josh White,

Mary Lou Williams, Pat Flowers, and the popular trio, Day, Dawn, and Dusk. That same station also broadcast the prestigious *American Negro Theater.* This series was produced by Ted Cott, a respected white veteran of radio, and introduced black actors like James Earl Jones and Ruby Dee in legitimate dramas, adaptations of grand opera, and plays drawn from great fiction.

By the late 1940s, local black news and culture shows were aired for the Afro-American community. Notable in this regard were *Tales from Harlem* over WMCA, and *The Bon Bon Show,* hosted by George "Bon Bon" Tunnell on WDAS (Philadelphia). Other programs and series at this time took a more distinctively political orientation, exposing and attacking the root causes of injustice in American society. In 1945, for example, WIP broadcast for the Philadelphia Fellowship Commission a series that assailed anti-democratic institutions, and strongly advocated tolerance, unity, and racial harmony. In 1947, both WSB (Atlanta) through its series *The Harbor We Seek,* and WINX (Washington, D.C.) with its *Bright Tomorrow,* produced memorable attacks upon the Ku Klux Klan and its fanatical ideals. As an exposé of injustice in America, however, the most striking accomplishments occurred in Chicago.

Richard Durham was the most prolific and successful black writer in radio. Formerly an editor with the *Chicago Defender* newspaper and *Ebony* magazine, throughout the second half of the 1940s Durham wrote several distinctive series. *Democracy, U.S.A.* appeared in July 1946, as a local show on WBBM, the CBS-owned station in Chicago. This weekly fifteen-minute series for more than a year dramatized the lives of outstanding black citizens. In October 1947, Durham wrote and produced the first authentic serial on the life of an Afro-American family, *Here Comes Tomorrow.* This soap opera was aired three times weekly on WJJD, and it featured the tribulations of the Redmond family. In the series, however, Durham became more politically specific than he had been in his first program. Now, blending entertainment and indictment, he attacked prejudice. Thus, for example, he caused one character—a black veteran who had downed several enemy airplanes—to comment ironically, "I thought I could shoot down Jim Crow in the same way."

With the premier in June 1948 of *Destination Freedom*, Richard Durham wrote his most mature and sophisticated radio series. This weekly half-hour series was heard in Chicago on the NBC-owned station, WMAQ, for two years. Durham prepared more than one hundred scripts for it. The programs examined the careers of prominent black social achievers, focusing upon the manner in which they came to grips with American racism, and earned fame. Drawing from black history as well as contemporary events, Durham dramatized the accomplishments of historic figures such as Crispus Attucks, Denmark Vesey, and Sojourner Truth, as well as current celebrities like Dr. Ralph Bunche, Joe Louis, and Adam Clayton Powell. The series was given an award by the Institute for Education by Radio, and it received approval from leading state political officials in the late 1940s. Yet, the best commendation of the remarkable series came from Durham, himself, who, when dramatizing the life of Carter G. Woodson —the man largely responsible for Negro History Week— caused his principal character to say, "I am the historian who looked to uncover the treasure of Negro life, so that America's goal of equality and justice may be strengthened by the knowledge of their struggle for freedom in the past." Throughout the last half of the 1940s, then, Richard Durham wrote and produced what undoubtedly was the most consistent and prolonged protest against racial injustice by a single talent in all the popular arts.

The modest, liberal gains by blacks in radio were not anomalies. In the popular arts—and in films, particularly— mature images of blacks appeared with frequency in the immediate postwar years. In motion pictures such as *Lost Boundaries, Pinky,* and *No Way Out,* liberal writers and directors revealed the consequences of racism. In popular literature and even television at this time, black themes and entertainers also were noticeable.

Yet, by the end of the 1940s, the liberal movement was

stifled and proponents of further democratization were in retreat. Speaking in September 1950, before the metropolitan
New York Council of B'nai B'rith, Joseph Mankiewicz, the
noted film director and president of the Screen Directors
Guild, summarized the position of American liberals, "the
new minority," as they entered a new decade. According to
him:

> The American liberal—the new minority—is being
> hounded, persecuted, and annihilated today—deliberately
> destroyed by an organized enemy as evil in practice and
> purpose—and indistinguishable from—the Communist
> menace that fosters and encourages that destruction....
> Remember that it is the hope of this new minority, too,
> that this world will someday become a world of human
> beings and for human beings who live together in decency
> and dignity. Let this new minority be destroyed—and this
> hope will die with it.[38]

The threat which Mankiewicz denounced came from the
American political right. Even before World War II, the
House Committee on Un-American Activities chaired by
Martin Dies had been investigating alleged Communist infil-
tration in the motion picture industry. When the war ended,
that committee, now headed by J. Parnell Thomas, plus other
governmental committees and bureaucracies, resumed with
greater purpose the anti-Communist crusade. In the process,
many prominent radio personalities had their careers thwarted
because of allegations and rumors of membership in the Communist Party. Two prominent black spokesmen for change in
radio, Paul Robeson and Canada Lee, were among those so
affected. What was more significant, however, was that the
Congressional probes effectively arrested the liberal reform
movement. In the early 1950s, as the anti-Communist mentality gained increasing momentum, fear replaced confidence in
many who desired progressive social change.

By 1950, a person as prestigious as Eleanor Roosevelt felt
compelled to cancel an appearance by Robeson on her television panel show. And several months later, even the unity of
black performers was shaken when Josh White appeared be-

fore the House committee as a voluntary witness to denounce
Paul Robeson and those "groups fixed up to look like noble
causes which later were found to be subversive." White
apparently welcomed the investigation of his fellow entertainers, as he told the committee how he regretted that "an
effective exposure of Communistic activities in the theatrical
and musical fields had not been made long before now."[39]

In spite of the policies of anti-Communism and its deleterious effects upon American liberalism, the condition of
blacks in radio continued to make gains in the 1950s. Impressive in this regard were the efforts of NBC to improve its relationship with the Afro-American community. In 1950 the
network hired Joseph V. Baker Associates, a public relations
agency from Philadelphia that specialized in relations with
black society. By October of the same year, top executives of
NBC and the Radio Corporation of America were meeting
with black social leaders—including representatives of the
NAACP and the National Urban League—to explain their
new efforts in hiring black personnel and in carefully guarding
against stereotyping in program content. Three months later
a second meeting was held in Chicago, this one attended by
three NBC vice-presidents. Following a third meeting in early
1951, NBC released a new code of standards and practices
which stated that:

> All program materials present with dignity and objec-
> tivity the varying aspects of race, creed, color, and na-
> tional origin. The history, institutions and citizens of all
> nations are fairly represented. . . . Defamatory statements
> or derogatory references expressed or implied, toward an
> individual, nationality, race, group, trade, profession, in-
> dustry, or institution are not permitted.[40]

NBC moved to implement its new posture in January
1952, when Jackie Robinson was appointed director of community activities at WNBC, the network's key station in New
York City. The network also instituted a policy of "integration without identification" in its programming. This meant
the regular use of black talent in non-black roles, an example
being Meredith Howard, who in her regular role in *Pete*

Kelly's Blues neither played a black nor was identified as one. By the end of 1952, NBC officials were able to announce the results of their new policy: 1) a 200 percent increase in the use of black talent over the figure for 1951; 2) including musicians and members of performing groups, a total of 1,540 performances in radio by Afro-Americans.[41]

The positive changes produced by new policies at NBC and other networks were partially the result of the education of American society by black and white critics of biased broadcasting. Just as surely, the changes were influenced by meaningful economic changes that emerged within Afro-American society. The development by the late 1940s of a sizable black consumer market made black society commercially attractive to radio. As early as October 1949, *Sponsor Magazine* editorialized about the forgotten fifteen million black consumers in America, urging radio business concerns to consider servicing them. The burgeoning Afro-American market was especially important in New York City where several independent stations—among them, WLIB, WWRL, WNEW, and WMCA —by 1950 were locating their studios in Harlem and broadcasting as many as twenty-two hours each week of black-oriented programming. In the South, the new awareness of black consumers was noticeable in the number of radio stations in which black businessmen owned stock. According to one study, until 1949 there were no stations in which shares were owned by blacks; but by 1954, there were several such stations in the South—these being WEDR (Birmingham), WDIA (Memphis), WNOE (New Orleans), WSOK (Nashville), WERD (Atlanta), and WBCO (Birmingham/Bessemer).[42]

The development of black consumer potential was impressive to radio executives. In New York City by early 1952, for instance, a survey conducted by station WLIB called that potential a "billion dollar plus" market. This was made possible, in part, because the black population in New York City had risen 63.1 percent during the preceding decade. National figures, however, suggested that the economic strength of blacks was not localized. Between 1940 and the date of the WLIB survey, the average income of Afro-American families

in the United States had tripled, compared to an increase of
only 100 percent among the general population. Figures
showed a high percentage of employable blacks were working,
and high school and college enrollments were at record
levels.[43]

In this light, local stations moved rapidly to attract black
listeners. In New York City, this was noticeable in the new
dimensions in programming being offered. WNEW presented
Kitchen Kapers and a sports series aimed directly at black consumers. Station WLIB directed its efforts toward black political issues, offering such programs as *The Negro World* (a
weekly news round-up), *The Walter White Show* (hosted by
the national secretary of the NAACP), and *The Editors Speak*
(a panel discussion series featuring editors of black newspapers). New talent like Nipsey Russell was brought into
radio, and many established black stars, like Herb Jeffries and
Juanita Hall, also became radio personalities.

The competition for black listeners had become so intense
that WLIB in June 1954 was broadcasting sixty-eight hours
of black-oriented programs each week. While in 1943 only four
stations throughout the country were programming specifically for blacks, ten years later, 260 such stations were attracting national and local sponsors to their broadcasts. And
throughout the country many stations that traditionally had
been directed toward white consumers now switched their formats and became all-black outlets. Among these stations were
WMRY (New Orleans) in 1950, WEFC (Miami) in 1952,
WCIN (Cincinnati) in 1953, and WNJR (Newark/New York
City) in 1954.

By early 1954, radio executives were estimating the black
marketplace to be worth $15 billion. Even network stations
were attracted to this resource and by the mid-1950s had developed black announcers—such as Wallace Roy at KNBC
(San Francisco) and William H. Luke at KECA (Los Angeles), an ABC outlet—as well as new programming, and
technical assistants. In March 1955, for instance, when ABC
introduced its first all-black network series, *Rhythm & Blues
on Parade,* it not only had a black host, Willie Bryant, introduc-

ing black acts and conducting interviews, but, *Variety* reported, the network converted one of its TV cameramen into an audio engineer in order to keep the program totally black.[44]

Black entrepreneurs also tried to appeal to the new consumer demands. In January 1954, the National Negro Network commenced its service to radio with the premier of *The Story of Ruby Valentine,* a soap opera starring Juanita Hall and sponsored by Pet Milk and Phillip Morris. This network also set up several other short-lived series, including *It's a Mystery, Man,* featuring Cab Calloway; *The Life of Anna Lewis,* starring Hilda Simms; and it planned for a fourth serial to star Ethel Waters. Two other companies were formed at this time also seeking to appeal to Afro-Americans. Negro Radio Stories planned to introduce four new all-black soap operas: *My Man, Ada Grant's Neighbors, The Romance of Julia Davis,* and *Rebeccah Turner's Front Porch Stories.* And Broadcast Productions, a Chicago-based organization, sought to introduce Jesse Owens in a radio series.

Clearly, blacks had experienced by 1955 a tremendous alteration in their relationship to American radio. The combination of liberal politics, a declining radio audience, and the lure of the multi-billion dollar black economy after World War II had produced a significant change of attitude on all levels of broadcasting. Yet, in terms of program impact the most significant development was the appearance in the mid-1950s of rhythm and blues as a national musical phenomenon relying upon radio for its mass dissemination through scores of radio disk jockeys.

Rhythm and blues was nothing more than the most recent emergence of race music—the name applied since the 1920s to the blues and jazz recordings performed by, and produced for, black consumers—that had developed following the war. The music was based primarily upon blues structures, offering simple variations and interpretations. Yet, the emotionalism of the music, in terms of the pulsing rhythms and the manner in which singers and instrumentalists performed it, proved irresistible with younger black listeners and soon with a generation of white urban youth.

The importance of rhythm and blues music on radio was that it was heard by integrated audiences. While the increase in black programming was impressive in the 1950s, it still represented segregated radio. Black radio was a form of exclusion of Afro-Americans from the mainstream of American popular culture. But rhythm and blues was a black-and-white enterprise. Until white singers began to copy their hit recordings, all rhythm and blues artists were blacks, and their records were primarily distributed in Afro-American communities. The small independent companies for which most recorded, however, were owned primarily by whites. And white teenagers who purchased these records helped to change the course of American cultural and social development.

Between 1948 and 1955, dozens of radio stations in the metropolitan areas of the United States developed a new breed of disk jockey to play and promote this new black music. Typical of the new breed was Hunter Hancock on KFVD (Los Angeles) who aired the records, answered requests, read the commercials, and carried on a running conversation with his audience, all in an animated, fast-paced, and informal manner. By the 1950s rhythm and blues music was being purveyed by "deejays" like Phil "Dr. Jive" Gordon on WLIB and WWRL; Al Benson on WAAF, WGES, and WJJD (all Chicago); Zenas "Daddy" Sears on WOK (Atlanta); Alan Freed on WJW (Cleveland) and later WINS (New York City). The music they broadcast—until in the second half of the decade it was toned down, performed by white entertainers, and renamed "rock and roll"—was the first consistent glimpse of black culture that many white youngsters had ever experienced. Even after the more commercialized rock and roll music appeared on radio, listeners could not escape the fact that the new popular music was a product of Afro-American society.

This was a crucial development for it occurred simultaneously with the first victories of black civic leaders in their fight against school segregation and racial injustice. Legal achievements, such as the case of *Brown versus the Board of Education* in which the Supreme Court struck down the notion of separate-but-equal education, and the use of federal troops to insure the integration of Central High School in Little Rock, would have been milestones in the history of the civil rights struggle in America. But coming as they did during the radio-produced era of rhythm and blues and rock and roll, they were received by young people with more understanding than might have been expected. As early as 1955, Howard Lewis, a promoter of teenage dances throughout the Southwest, reported that rhythm and blues "has become a potent force in breaking down racial barriers."[45]

Through the new black music that was introduced almost totally through radio, a generation of white youngsters, protected from black realities by a tradition of segregation and bigotry, learned to appreciate Afro-American attitudes and realities. Dancing, working, relaxing, and singing to rhythm and blues, white listeners of radio in the 1950s came to know better than their parents the illogical nature of racism. Within a few years it would be this generation that would join with youthful blacks to form the idealistic vanguard of the civil rights movement of the 1960s.

By the 1960s, with the diminishing importance of radio in American society, the issue of blacks in the popular arts shifted to television. Yet, during the course of the three decades since 1930, important achievements in equality had occurred in radio. There remained many areas from which blacks were excluded in broadcasting. But relative to the rank stereotyping and the obvious discrimination that abounded in early radio, the patterns of prejudice by 1960 were not debilitating to black talent. Also, by the latter date the weight of federal law was being applied throughout the society to effect equitable treatment of Afro-Americans. That law would become a strong weapon for change within radio and television.

The posture of blacks in radio—whether it be the image of blacks, the issue of race discrimination, or the employment picture for actors and technicians—improved throughout the postwar period. By the early 1950s, however, success was actu-

ally leading to segregation in broadcasting as all-black programs and stations lost sight of the more idealistic integrated
possibilities. Yet, with the emergence of black music through
rhythm and blues and, eventually, rock and roll, a healthier
balance was achieved. Certainly there was a need for all-black
programming, just as there was a demand for other ethnic
groups to have their own broadcasts. The problem was to prevent such esoteric broadcasting from becoming irretrievably
segregated. But by 1960, the potential for a balance between
integrated and all-black programming, free from the open
bigotry of the past, had been achieved in radio.

Notes

Chapter 1
The History of Broadcasting, 1920-1960

1. Westinghouse Broadcasting Company, *The First Fifty Years of Radio* (LP album), 1970.
2. Samuel L. Rothafel and Raymond Francis Yates, *Broadcasting, Its New Day* (New York, 1925), p. 53.
3. Woodrow Wilson had broadcast his voice on at least two occasions before 1920, but such transmission had only been on naval equipment. See *New York Times*, February 10, 1924; and Erik Barnouw, *A Tower in Babel. A History of Broadcasting in the United States to 1933* (New York, 1966), p. 51.
4. *New York Times*, November 1, 1921.
5. Gleason L. Archer, *History of Radio to 1926* (New York, 1938), pp. 346–47.
6. *New York Times*, July 12, 1925.
7. Ibid., June 29, 1924.
8. Paul Schubert, *The Electric Word: The Rise of Radio* (New York, 1928), pp. 213–14.
9. *New York Times*, February 3, 1924.
10. For interesting descriptions of *The Eveready Hour* and other radio programs, see John Dunning, *Tune in Yesterday: The Ultimate Encyclopedia of Old-Time Radio 1925–1976* (Englewood Cliffs, 1976); and Frank Buxton and Bill Owen, *The Big Broadcast, 1920–1950* (New York, 1972).
11. See *New York Times*, July 14, 1925; March 2, 1924.
12. On the subject of popular songs about radio, see the article by musicologist Jim Walsh in *Variety*, July 29, 1953, p. 45.
13. "*Notes on the Air.*" *The Radio Year Book* (Chicago, 1925), p. 1.
14. Barnouw, pp. 33–35.
15. *The Electrical Experimenter*, December, 1917, p. 534.
16. Archer, p. 346.
17. Rothafel and Yates, pp. 153–54.
18. *New York Times*, August 23, 1925.
19. Barnouw, p. 94.
20. Paul Sann, *Fads, Follies and Delusions of the American People* (New York, 1967), p. 1.

21. Foster Rhea Dulles, *America Learns to Play* (New York, 1940), p. 211.

22. *New York Times,* January 25, 1925.

23. Hadley Cantril and Gordon W. Allport, *The Psychology of Radio* (New York, 1935), p. 99.

24. Joseph Gurman and Myron Slager, *Radio Round-Ups, Intimate Glimpses of the Radio Stars* (Boston, 1932), p. 44.

25. Arthur Frank Wertheim, "Relieving Social Tension: Radio Comedy and the Great Depression," *Journal of Popular Culture,* Winter, 1976, p. 513.

26. Barnouw, p. 273.

27. *New York Times,* April 8, 1924.

28. Edgar A. Grunwald, "Program-Production History, 1929–1937," *Variety Radio Directory, 1937–1938* (New York, 1937), p. 19.

29. *Variety,* February 21, 1933, p. 37.

30. The C.A.B. ratings received their second name because the statistics were gathered and assessed by the Archibald M. Crossley research house. For a good, cursory discussion of the rating services, see Judith M. Waller, *Radio: The Fifth Estate* (Boston, 1946), pp. 299–310.

31. Charles A. Siepmann, *Radio, Television and Society* (New York, 1950), pp. 48–49, 49n.

32. Charles A. Siepmann, *Radio's Second Chance* (Boston, 1946), pp. 186–87.

33. *New York Post,* April 12, 1947, as cited in *Variety,* April 16, 1947, p. 23.

34. Ibid., January 5, 1949, p. 97.

35. Ibid., July 20, 1938, p. 1.

36. A poll conducted in November 1945 revealed that more than any other institution—including the Church—the American people felt radio was doing an excellent job; see Paul F. Lazarsfeld, *The People Look at Radio* (Chapel Hill, 1946), p. 6.

37. W. F. Ogburn, "The Influence of Invention and Discovery," in President's Research Committee on Social Trends, *Recent Social Trends in the United States* (Washington, 1933), pp. 152–57.

38. Siepmann, pp. 82–83. That radio listening was primarily a middle-class habit, see Cantril and Allport, p. 87n.

39. The validity of this story and the name of the offender have been topics of much discussion. The latest publication to treat this matter (Dunning, pp. 622–23) is correct to argue that Uncle Don, much maligned with this rumor, did not utter the infamous profanity. The event seems to have been real, as *Variety* reported (April 23, 1930, p. 71) that a Philadelphia announcer lost his job earlier that month when he ended a bedtime story with the remark, "I hope that pleases the little b . . . [bastards]." As for the character who did utter the profanity, an article

twenty years later identified him as "Uncle Wip," a host of a local children's show on station WIP in Philadelphia; see Llewellyn Miller, "Radio's Own Life Story," *Radio and Television Mirror,* February, 1950, p. 93.

40. *Variety,* June 28, 1939, p. 26.
41. Ibid., April 5, 1939, p. 24; *Variety Radio Directory, 1939–1940* (New York, 1939), p. 559.
42. Robert J. Landry, *This Fascinating Radio Business* (Indianapolis, 1946), pp. 150–51; *Variety Radio Directory, 1937–1938* (New York, 1937), p. 723.
43. John Edwards, "Roxy Says: 'Take the Amateurs Off the Air!'" *Radio Mirror,* May, 1935, p. 21.
44. For a thorough analysis of the *War of the Worlds* broadcast, see Hadley Cantril, *The Invasion from Mars: A Study in the Psychology of Panic* (Princeton, 1940). The broadcast also had an immediate effect upon the popular arts. In radio, the old *Buck Rogers* series was revived and placed back on the air. Universal Studios quickly released the Buck Rogers movie serial that had been in preparation. Military authorities even welcomed the broadcast for it illustrated the state of unpreparedness for war among the American people; witness the front page headline carried in *Variety* on November 2, 1938—"RADIO DOES U.S. A FAVOR."
45. *Variety Radio Directory, 1939–1940,* pp. 254–62.
46. *Variety,* January 15, 1941, p. 30.
47. Ibid., January 22, 1941, pp. 34–35; January 29, 1941, p. 37.
48. *The Billboard,* November 26, 1938, p. 10.
49. *Variety,* January 9, 1946, p. 121.
50. Ibid., January 7, 1948, p. 95.
51. Ibid., May 16, 1945, p. 24.
52. Erik Barnouw, *The Golden Web. A History of Broadcasting in the United States, 1933–1953* (New York, 1968) pp. 241–42.
53. *Variety,* November 13, 1940, p. 3.
54. Ibid., September 13, 1939, p. 20.
55. Ibid., July 10, 1940, p. 24.
56. Ibid., May 27, 1942, p. 29; June 10, 1942, p. 32.
57. Ibid., May 6, 1942, p. 29; Landry, p. 249.
58. *Variety,* April 1, 1942, p. 34.
59. Ibid., June 2, 1943, p. 30; May 6, 1942, p. 28.
60. Ibid., January 25, 1939, p. 121.
61. Ibid., January 21, 1942, p. 25.
62. Landry, pp. 247–48.
63. *Variety,* January 21, 1942, p. 25.
64. Raymond Gram Swing, *"Good Evening!" A Professional Memoir* (New York, 1964), pp. 225–26.
65. *Variety,* June 13, 1945, p. 44.

66. Ibid., June 27, 1945, p. 30.
67. Ibid., October 23, 1946, p. 1.
68. Ibid., May 15, 1946, p. 32.
69. Ibid., January 9, 1946, p. 111.
70. Ibid.
71. Ibid., p. 184.
72. *New York Times,* September 13, 1925.
73. *Radio and Television Mirror,* September, 1939, p. 22.
74. *Variety,* March 15, 1944, p. 1.
75. Ibid., October 23, 1946, p. 91. The notion of TV as a monster
    appears to have persisted in the radio industry (see ibid., Sep-
    tember 29, 1948, p. 1).
76. Ibid., July 28, 1948, p. 41.
77. Ibid., December 21, 1955, p. 20; May 11, 1955, p. 29. A clue to
    the importance of radio was suggested two years earlier in a
    report prepared by Alfred Politz Research, Inc. According to the
    study, radio enjoyed a universal listenership, and that despite
    falling Nielsen ratings, two out of three adults listened to radio
    sometime during an average day. See ibid., December 16, 1953,
    p. 28.
78. Ibid., January 9, 1946, p. 120.
79. Barnouw, *The Golden Web,* p. 228.
80. *Variety,* February 12, 1958, p. 49.
81. Ibid., January 3, 1945, p. 71.
82. Ibid., p. 73.

Chapter 2
The Great Escape—The Story of Radio Comedy

1. Charles Martel, "It's Tough to Be a Comedian, Says Jack
   Pearl." *Tower Radio.* July, 1934, p. 76.
2. *Variety,* May 7, 1930, p. 72.
3. "The Editor's Opinion," *Radioland,* November, 1933, p. 11.
4. Charles Martel, "Never Try to Be Funny," *Tower Radio,* September, 1934, p. 21.
5. Paul F. Lazarsfeld, *The People Look at Radio* (Chapel Hill,
   1946), pp. 45, 135. See also Paul F. Lazarsfeld and Patricia L.
   Kendall, *Radio Listening in America* (New York, 1948), pp.
   136–39.
6. Milton Berle, "It's My Business to Be Funny," *Radio Varieties,*
   March, 1940, p. 9.
7. Fred Allen, *Treadmill to Oblivion* (Boston, 1954), p. 180.
8. Constance Rourke, *American Humor: A Study of the National
   Character* (Garden City, 1953), p. 109; Sir Harry Lauder, *Between You and Me* (New York, 1950), pp. 66–67.
9. *Variety,* February 8, 1939, p. 19.
10. Ibid., April 18, 1945.

11. Ibid., June 21, 1932, p. 55.
12. Ibid., June 4, 1947, p. 27.
13. Ibid., April 5, 1939, p. 24.
14. Ibid., May 22, 1935, p. 37.
15. Ibid., November 13, 1946, p. 38; April 23, 1947, p. 1.
16. Ibid., March 24, 1937, pp. 1, 78.
17. Arthur Frank Wertheim, "Relieving Social Tensions: Radio Comedy and the Great Depression," *Journal of Popular Culture*, Winter, 1976, pp. 501–19.
18. *Variety*, January 14, 1942, p. 22.
19. Ibid., April 23, 1930, p. 43.
20. *Variety Radio Directory, 1937–1938* (New York, 1937), p. 20.
21. Tom Carskadon, "Gagging Their Way Through Life," *Radioland*, September, 1933, p. 41.
22. Hadley Cantril and Gordon Allport, *The Psychology of Radio* (New York, 1935), p. 224.
23. *Variety*, August 14, 1934, p. 31.
24. Ibid., July 18, 1945, p. 1.
25. Carskadon, p. 41.
26. *Radioland*, January, 1935, p. 7; see also *Variety*, May 16, 1933, p. 43.
27. John Seymour, "Mirth with a Mission," *Tower Radio*, April, 1934, p. 13.
28. Jerald Mason, "Smart Alex Woollcott," *Radioland*, February, 1935, p. 16.
29. P. J. O'Brien, *Will Rogers, Ambassador of Good Will and Prince of Wit and Wisdom* (Philadelphia, 1935), pp. 148, 151.
30. Jack Benny, "Gags Have Grown Up," *Tune In*, April, 1945, p. 11.
31. Ibid., p. 10.
32. *Variety*, October 5, 1938, p. 30.
33. *Variety Radio Directory, 1939–1940* (New York, 1939), pp. 92–98; *Variety Radio Directory, 1940–1941* (New York, 1940), p. 95.
34. *Radio Guide*, November 28, 1936, p. 3.
35. Harrison B. Summers (editor), *A Thirty-Year History of Programs Carried on National Radio Networks in the United States, 1926–1956* (Columbus, Ohio, 1958), p. 115; *Variety*, April 19, 1944, pp. 22–23.
36. *Variety*, May 14, 1947, pp. 32, 36.
37. Gladys Hall, "Are Comedians Through on the Air?" *Radio Stars*, February, 1936, p. 73.
38. Jack Sher, "Television a Reality!" *Radio Mirror*, February, 1939, p. 64.
39. *Variety*, March 30, 1949, p. 53.
40. Ibid.,
41. Ibid., January 9, 1946, p. 7.

42. Ibid., March 30, 1949, p. 2.
43. Harriet van Horn, "Unrest in the Air," *Radio and Television Mirror,* March, 1949, p. 104.
44. *Variety,* September 8, 1948, p. 1.
45. Ibid., July 20, 1949, p. 1.
46. Ibid., July 28, 1948, p. 41.
47. Arthur Shulman and Roger Youman, *How Sweet It Was: Television, A Pictorial Commentary* (New York, 1966), p. 8.
48. Van Horn, p. 103.
49. *Variety,* February 2, 1949, p. 24.

Chapter 3
Detective Programming and the Search for Law and Order

1. Ken Crossen, "There's Murder in the Air," in Howard Haycraft (editor), *The Art of the Mystery Story* (New York, 1946), p. 304.
2. *Variety,* February 8, 1950, p. 29.
3. Ibid., June 28, 1950, p. 25.
4. Orrin E. Klapp, "Heroes, Villains and Fools as Agents of Social Control," *American Sociological Review,* February, 1954, p. 57.
5. Charles J. Rolo, "Simenon and Spillane: The Metaphysics of Murder for the Millions," in Bernard Rosenberg and David M. White (editors), *Mass Culture: The Popular Arts in America* (New York, 1957), pp. 174–75.
6. Tom Carskadon, "Crime Does Pay," *Tower Radio,* April, 1934, p. 35.
7. Basil Rathbone, "On Playing Sherlock Holmes," *Radio Varieties,* March, 1940, p. 6.
8. See appropriate listings in Harrison B. Summers (editor), *A Thirty-Year History of Programs Carried on National Radio Networks in the United States, 1926–1956* (Columbus, Ohio, 1958).
9. *Variety,* April 27, 1949, p. 1.
10. Dorothy Herzog, "Radio Enters the Fight on Crime," *Radioland,* January, 1935, p. 15.
11. *Radio Mirror,* May, 1939, p. 3.
12. *Radio Varieties,* February, 1940, p. 12.
13. John G. Cawelti, *Adventure, Mystery and Romance: Formula Stories as Art and Popular Culture* (Chicago, 1976), p. 155.
14. Crossen, p. 306.
15. *Variety,* April 30, 1947, p. 37.

Chapter 4
Westerns: From Shoot-'em-ups to Realism

1. *Variety,* March 23, 1938, p. 1.
2. William K. Everson, *A Pictorial History of the Western Film* (Secaucus, N.J., 1969), p. 131.

3. *Variety*, September 27, 1939, p. 28.
4. Ibid., October 21, 1942, p. 34.
5. Ibid., February 7, 1933, p. 40
6. Ibid., July 19, 1950, p. 30.
7. *Tune In*, April, 1945, p. 42.
8. Gene Autry, "Gene Autry's Prize Round-up," *Radio Television Mirror*, July, 1951, pp. 46, 86; see also Gene Autry, "Introduction," *Who's Who in TV & Radio*, v. I, n. 3 (1953), pp. 90–91.
9. *Variety*, April 20, 1949.
10. Ibid., January 19, 1955, p. 33.
11. Ibid., April 6, 1938, p. 29.
12. Robert J. Landry, *This Fascinating Radio Business* (Indianapolis, 1946), p. 178.
13. *TV-Radio Mirror*, May, 1957, p. 91.
14. *Variety*, April 30, 1952, p. 28.
15. Gordon Budge, "Gunsmoke!," *TV-Radio Mirror*, May, 1958, p. 86.
16. *TV-Radio Mirror*, May, 1957, pp. 65, 90.

Chapter 5
Soap Operas as a Social Force

1. George A. Willey, "End of an Era: The Daytime Radio Serial," *Journal of Broadcasting*, Spring, 1961, pp. 97–115.
2. *Variety*, August 31, 1948, p. 1.
3. Ibid., February 23, 1944, p. 28.
4. Ibid., December 13, 1944, p. 21.
5. James Thurber, "Onward and Upward with the Arts," *New Yorker*, May 15, 1948, p. 34.
6. Raymond William Stedman, *The Serials: Suspense and Drama by Installment* (Norman, Oklahoma, 1971), p. 341; *Variety*, May 25, 1942, p. 31.
7. Ibid., March 13, 1946, p. 45.
8. *Science News Letter*, July 3, 1943, p. 13.
9. *Variety*, January 19, 1944, p. 47.
10. Ibid., December 3, 1947, p. 25.
11. *Billboard*, February 18, 1939, pp. 2, 7.
12. Tom Carskadon, "Restoring Cinderella," *Radioland*, February, 1935, p. 64.
13. Harrison B. Summers (editor), *A Thirty-Year History of Programs Carried on National Radio Networks in the United States, 1926–1956* (Columbus, Ohio, 1958).
14. *Variety*, December 19, 1933, p. 40.
15. Ibid., June 26, 1940, p. 41.
16. Ibid., July 23, 1941, p. 46.
17. *Supra*, note 14.
18. Stedman, p. 235.

19. *Variety,* January 25, 1939, p. 26.
20. Ibid., May 11, 1938, p. 27; and December 30, 1936, p. 33.
21. Madeleine Edmondson and David Rounds, *The Soaps: Daytime Serials of Radio and TV* (New York, 1973), p. 55.
22. *Variety,* May 29, 1940, p. 26; and August 22, 1945, p. 37.
23. Mary Jane Higby, *Tune-In Tomorrow* (New York, 1968), p. 124.
24. *Variety,* May 8, 1940, p. 38.
25. Edmondson and Rounds, pp. 92–93.
26. *Radio and Television Mirror,* December, 1942, p. 24.
27. George A. Willey, "The Soap Operas and the War," *Journal of Broadcasting,* Fall, 1963, pp. 341–42.
28. In his article, "The Soap Operas and the War," Professor Willey erroneously stated that the OWI adaptation of *Our Gal Sunday* was postponed for several weeks. According to reviews in *Variety,* the CBS feature on *Our Gal Sunday* not only was broadcast on schedule, on October 13, 1942, but was actually aired fifteen minutes ahead of the *Stella Dallas* program. Compare *ibid.,* p. 347, and *Variety,* October 21, 1942, p. 34.
29. *Variety,* April 19, 1944, p. 24.
30. Ibid., May 19, 1943, p. 1.
31. Summers, pp. 96ff.
32. *Variety,* November 10, 1943, p. 47.
33. *New York Times,* November 26, 1960, p. 43.

Chapter 6
The Development of Broadcast Journalism

1. Sammy R. Danna, "The Rise of Radio News," in Lawrence W. Lichty and Malachi C. Topping, *American Broadcasting. A Source Book on the History of Radio and Television.* (New York, 1975), p. 343.
2. Samuel L. Rothafel and Raymond Francis Yates, *Broadcasting, Its New Day* (New York, 1925), p. 80.
3. David G. Clark, "Radio Presidential Campaigns: The Early Years (1924–1932)," *Journal of Broadcasting,* Summer, 1962, p. 232.
4. Ibid., p. 233.
5. *Variety Radio Directory, 1940–1941* (New York, 1941), pp. 107–9.
6. Ned Midgley, *The Advertising and Business Side of Radio* (New York, 1948), pp. 19–20.
7. That Winchell's commercial appeal was potent was noted by a biographer who mentioned an NBC survey showing that 19.8 percent of those listening to Winchell once a month used Jergen's Lotion; 30.3 percent of those listening two or three times

a month used the product; and 51.2 percent of those listening weekly used the product. See Bob Thomas, *Winchell* (New York, 1971), pp. 123–24.

8. David G. Clark, "H. V. Kaltenborn and His Sponsors: Controversial Broadcasting and the Sponsor's Role," *Journal of Broadcasting,* Fall, 1968, pp. 311–15.

9. *Variety,* July 25, 1945, pp. 26, 30. For a more recent and fuller study of the leading commentators in radio, see Irving E. Fang, *Those Radio Commentators!* (Ames, Iowa, 1977).

10. *Variety,* November 14, 1945, p. 27.

11. Robert Eichberg, "The Battle for News!," *Radio Stars,* January, 1934, p. 86.

12. *Radio Stars,* June, 1933, p. 51.

13. *Variety,* September 27, 1939, p. 24.

14. Norton Russell, "The Personal History of Floyd Gibbons, Adventurer," *Radio Mirror,* May, 1937, p. 67.

15. Mildred Luber, "His Life is News!" *Radio and Television Mirror,* August, 1939, p. 28.

16. Herman Klurfeld, *Winchell, His Life and Times* (New York, 1976), p. 21.

17. Edwin C. Hill, "Radio's New Destiny," *Radio Stars,* June, 1933, p. 7.

18. *Radioland,* September, 1933, p. 11.

19. Don Rockwell (editor), *Radio Personalities: A Pictorial and Biographical Annual* (New York, 1935), p. 84.

20. Paul Weber, "Coughlin Justifies Attack on Roosevelt!" *Radio Stars,* March, 1936, p. 15.

21. *Radio and Television Mirror,* January, 1940, p. 69.

22. *Tune In,* August, 1945, p. 40.

23. Robert D. Heinl, "Radio and the Next War," *Radioland,* September, 1933, pp. 12–15.

24. *Variety,* July 29, 1942, p. 25.

25. Ibid., November 24, 1943, p. 47.

26. Erik Barnouw, *The Golden Web* (New York, 1968), p. 156.

27. *Variety,* May 5, 1943, p. 52.

28. Ibid., February 17, 1943, p. 28.

29. Roger Burlingame, *Don't Let Them Scare You. The Life and Times of Elmer Davis* (Philadelphia, 1961), p. 200. For an interesting discussion in which wartime correspondents strongly criticized this type of governmental censorship, see *Variety,* May 5, 1943, p. 32.

30. *Variety,* October 6, 1943, p. 27.

31. Ibid., October 13, 1943, p. 33.

32. Ibid., October 6, 1943, p. 27.

33. Ibid., December 15, 1943, p. 27.
34. Ibid., December 27, 1944, p. 1.
35. Ibid., September 19, 1945, p. 38.
36. Ibid.
37. Ibid., January 28, 1948, p. 40.
38. Bryce Oliver, "Thought Control—American Style," *New Republic,* January 13, 1947, pp. 12–13.
39. Alexander Kendrick, *Prime Time: The Life of Edward R. Murrow* (Boston, 1969), p. 297.
40. Klurfeld, p. 131.
41. *Variety,* September 12, 1945, p. 30.
42. Ibid., November 7, 1945, p. 40.
43. Ibid., November 14, 1945, p. 27.
44. Ibid., January 16, 1952, p. 36.
45. Ibid., December 20, 1950, p. 22.
46. Ibid., June 30, 1954, p. 26; Kendrick, p. 374; Fred W. Friendly, *Due to Circumstances Beyond Our Control* (New York, 1967), p. 65.
47. David Holbrook Culbert, *News for Everyman: Radio and Foreign Affairs in Thirties America* (Westport, Conn., 1976), p. 110.
48. Burlingame, p. 336.
49. The wording of this statement is transcribed from a sound recording of that momentous telecast. It is interesting to note that this portion of Murrow's remarks is often misquoted. See Kendrick, p. 53; Friendly, p. 41.
50. *Variety,* May 26, 1954, p. 48.

Chapter 7
Stride Toward Freedom—Blacks in Radio Programming

1. Estelle Edmerson, "A Descriptive Study of the American Negro in United States Professional Radio, 1922–1953" (master's thesis, University of California at Los Angeles, 1954), p. 205.
2. Paul F. Lazarsfeld, *Radio and the Printed Page* (New York, 1940), p. 57.
3. *Variety,* March 27, 1946, p. 44.
4. Erik Barnouw, *The Golden Web* (New York, 1968), p. 110; see also the words of black comic, Johnny Lee, in Edmerson, p. 31.
5. Ibid., p. 100.
6. *Variety,* August 9, 1932, p. 44.
7. Hadley Cantril and Gordon W. Allport, *The Psychology of Radio* (New York, 1935), p. 76.
8. Edmerson, pp. 28–30, 39.
9. Hilda Cole, "Voodoo in the Air," *Radio Stars,* June, 1933, p. 49.

10. *Variety,* October 2, 1935, p. 3.
11. Figures cited in *The Chicago Daily News Almanac and Yearbook for 1934* (Chicago, 1934), p. 306. For an interesting discussion of this situation, especially in the rural areas, see Malcolm M. Willey and Stuart A. Rice, "The Agencies of Communication," in President's Research Committee on Recent Social Trends, *Recent Social Trends in the United States* (New York, 1933), p. 212.
12. Edmerson, p. 354.
13. Ibid., p. 108.
14. Arthur Frank Wertheim, "Relieving Social Tensions: Radio Comedy and the Great Depression," *Journal of Popular Culture.* Winter, 1976, p. 516.
15. *Variety,* January 3, 1940, p. 121.
16. Interview with Houston Stackhouse, *Living Blues,* no. 17, Summer, 1974, p. 26.
17. Wilson Brown, "How Long Will They Last...?" *Radio Stars,* May, 1933, pp. 42, 45.
18. Edmerson, pp. 192–93.
19. Erik Barnouw, *A Tower in Babel* (New York, 1966), pp. 229–30.
20. Freeman F. Gosden and Charles J. Correll, *All About Amos 'n' Andy* (New York, 1929), pp. 43–44.
21. Monroe N. Work (editor), *Negro Year Book, An Annual Encyclopedia of the Negro, 1931–1932* (Tuskegee, Alabama, 1931), pp. 17–18.
22. *Variety,* August 26, 1942, p. 2.
23. Ibid., October 25, 1944, p. 1.
24. Ibid., March 7, 1945, p. 38.
25. Barnouw, *Golden Web,* p. 162.
26. Jesse Parkhurst Guzman (editor), *Negro Yearbook, A Review of Events Affecting Negro Life, 1941–1946* (Tuskegee, Alabama, 1946), p. 449.
27. Paul Denis, "The Negro in Show Business," *Negro Digest,* February, 1943, p. 36.
28. *Variety,* July 26, 1944, p. 22.
29. Ibid., July 19, 1944, p. 27.
30. Ibid., May 24, 1944, p. 23.
31. *Tune In,* May, 1945, p. 41.
32. *Variety,* May 8, 1946, p. 27.
33. Ibid., November 13, 1946, p. 25; and June 19, 1946, p. 23.
34. Edmerson, p. 354.
35. Ibid., p. 349.
36. *Variety,* July 13, 1949, p. 35.
37. Edmerson, pp. 76–78.

38. *Variety,* September 20, 1950, p. 22.
39. Ibid., September 6, 1950, p. 2.
40. Ibid., July 18, 1951, p. 1.
41. Ibid., March 18, 1953, p. 1.
42. Edmerson, p. 325.
43. *Variety,* January 9, 1952, p. 32.
44. Ibid., March 30, 1955, p. 28.
45. Ibid., July 6, 1955, p. 43.

Bibliography

Unpublished Sources

Edmerson, Estelle. "A Descriptive Study of the American Negro in United States Professional Radio, 1922–1953". Master's thesis, University of California at Los Angeles, 1954.

Westinghouse Broadcasting Company. *The First Fifty Years of Radio.* (LP Album) 1970.

Newspapers, Magazines

Billboard. New York, weekly. 1938–1940.

The Electrical Experimenter. New York, monthly. 1917.

The New York Times. New York, daily. 1920–1960.

Radio and Television Mirror. (See *Radio Mirror.*)

Radio Guide. Chicago, weekly. 1936–1940.

Radioland. Louisville, monthly. 1933–1935.

Radio Mirror. New York, monthly. 1934–1961.

Radio News. Chicago, monthly. 1938–1939.

Radio Stars. New York, monthly. 1933–1938.

Radio Television Mirror. (See *Radio Mirror.*)

Radio-TV Mirror. (See *Radio Mirror.*)

Radio Varieties. Chicago, monthly. 1939–1940.

Science News Letter. Washington, weekly. 1943.

Tower Radio. Chicago, monthly. 1934–1935.

Tune In. New York, monthly. 1943–1945.

TV Radio Mirror. (See *Radio Mirror.*)

Variety. New York, weekly. 1930–1960.

Yearbooks, Almanacs

Chicago Daily News Almanac and Yearbook for 1934. Chicago, 1934.

Guzman Jesse Parkhurst (editor), *Negro Yearbook, A Review of Events Affecting Negro Life, 1941–1946.* Tuskegee: Tuskegee Institute, 1946.

Rockwell, Don (editor), *Radio Personalities. A Pictorial and Biographical Annual.* New York, Press Bureau Incorporated, 1935.

Summers, Harrison B. (editor), *A Thirty Year History of Programs Carried on National Radio Networks in the United States, 1926–1956.* Columbus, Ohio State University, 1958.

Variety Radio Directory, 1937–1938. New York, Variety, 1937.
Variety Radio Directory, 1939–1940. New York, Variety, 1939.
Variety Radio Directory, 1940–1941. New York, Variety, 1940.
Work, Monroe N. (editor), *Negro Year Book. An Annual Encyclo-
    pedia of the Negro, 1931–1932.* Tuskegee: Tuskegee Institute,
    1931.

Memoirs, Interviews

Allen, Fred. *Treadmill to Oblivion.* Boston: Little, Brown, 1954.
Benny, Jack. "Gags Have Grown Up," *Tune In,* April, 1945, pp.
    9–11.
Berle, Milton. "It's My Business to Be Funny," *Radio Varieties,*
    March, 1940, p. 9.
Friendly, Fred W., *Due to Circumstances Beyond Our Control.* New
    York: Random House, 1967.
Gosden, Freeman F. and Charles J. Correll, *All About Amos 'n'
    Andy.* New York: Rand McNally, 1929.
Higby, Mary Jane, *Tune In Tomorrow.* New York: Ace, 1968.
"Interview with Houston Stackhouse," *Living Blues,* no. 17. Summer,
    1974, pp. 20–36.
Rathbone, Basil, "On Playing Sherlock Holmes," *Radio Varieties.*
    March, 1940, p. 6.
Swing, Raymond Gram, *"Good Evening!" A Professional Memoir.*
    New York: Harcourt, Brace, 1964.

Secondary Materials—Books

Barnouw, Erik. *The Golden Web. A History of Broadcasting in the
    United States 1933–1953.* New York: Oxford University Press,
    1968.
Barnouw, Erik. *A Tower in Babel. A History of Broadcasting in the
    United States to 1933.* New York: Oxford University Press, 1966.
Burlingame, Roger. *Don't Let Them Scare You: The Life and Times
    of Elmer Davis.* Philadelphia: Lippincott, 1961.
Buxton, Frank, and Bill Owen. *The Big Broadcast, 1920–1950.* New
    York: Viking, 1972.
Cantril, Hadley. *The Invasion from Mars: A Study in the Psychol-
    ogy of Panic.* Princeton: Princeton University Press, 1940.
Cantril, Hadley, and Gordon Allport. *The Psychology of Radio.* New
    York: Harper, 1935.
Cawelti, John G., *Adventure, Mystery and Romance: Formula
    Studies as Art and Popular Culture.* Chicago: University of
    Chicago Press, 1976.
Culbert, David Holbrook. *News For Everyman: Radio and Foreign
    Affairs in Thirties America.* Westport, Conn.: Greenwood Press,
    1976.

Dulles, Foster Rhea. *America Learns to Play*. New York, Appleton-Century, 1940.

Dunning, John. *Tune-In Yesterday. The Ultimate Encyclopedia of Old-Time Radio, 1925–1976*. Englewood Cliffs, N.J.: Prentice-Hall, 1976.

Edmondson, Madeleine, and David Rounds. *The Soaps: Daytime Serials of Radio and TV*. New York: Stein and Day, 1973.

Everson, William K. *A Pictorial History of the Western Film*. Secaucus, N.J.: Citadel, 1969.

Fang, Irving E. *Those Radio Commentators!* Ames: Iowa State University Press, 1977.

Gurman, Joseph, and Myron Slager. *Radio Round-ups: Intimate Glimpses of the Radio Stars*. Boston: Lathrop, Lee & Shepard, 1932.

Kendrick, Alexander. *Prime Time: The Life of Edward R. Murrow*. Boston: Little, Brown, 1969.

Klurfeld, Herman. *Winchell: His Life and Times*. New York: Praeger, 1976.

Landry, Robert J. *This Fascinating Radio Business*. Indianapolis: Bobbs-Merrill, 1946.

Lauder, Sir Harry. *Between You and Me*. New York: James A. McCann Company, 1950.

Lazarsfeld, Paul F. *The People Look at Radio*. Chapel Hill: University of North Carolina Press, 1946.

Lazarsfeld, Paul F. *Radio and the Printed Page*. New York: Duell, Sloan & Pearce, 1940.

Lazarsfeld, Paul F., and Patricia L. Kendall. *Radio Listening in America: The People Look at Radio—Again*. New York: Prentice-Hall, 1948.

Midgley, Ned. *The Advertising and Business Side of Radio*. New York: Prentice-Hall, 1948.

"Notes on the Air": The Radio Year Book. Chicago: Radio Year Book Publishing Company, 1925.

O'Brien, P. J. *Will Rogers: Ambassador of Good Will and Prince of Wit and Wisdom*. Philadelphia: John C. Winston Company, 1935.

Rothafel, Samuel L., and Raymond Francis Yates. *Broadcasting: Its New Day*. New York: Century, 1925.

Rourke, Constance. *American Humor: A Study of the National Character*. New York: Doubleday Anchor Books, 1953.

Sann, Paul. *Fads, Follies and Delusions of the American People*. New York: Bonanza Books, 1967.

Schubert, Paul. *The Electric Word: The Rise of Radio*. New York: Macmillan, 1928.

Shulman, Arthur, and Roger Youman. *How Sweet It Was: Television, *A Pictorial Commentary*. New York: Bonanza Books, 1966.

Siepmann, Charles A. *Radio, Television and Society*. New York: Oxford University Press, 1950.

Siepmann, Charles A. *Radio's Second Chance*. Boston: Little, Brown, 1946.

Stedman, Raymond William. *The Serials: Suspense and Drama by Installment*. Norman: University of Oklahoma Press, 1971.

Thomas, Bob. *Winchell*. New York: Doubleday, 1971.

Waller, Judith C. *Radio: The Fifth Estate*. Boston: Houghton, Mifflin, 1950.

Secondary Materials—Articles

Autry, Gene. "Gene Autry's Prize Round-up," *Radio Television Mirror*, July, 1951, pp. 46, 86.

Autry, Gene. "Introduction," *Who's Who in TV & Radio*, v. I, no. 3 (1953), pp. 90–91.

Brown, Wilson. "How Long Will They Last . . . ?," *Radio Stars*, May, 1933, pp. 10–11, 42, 45.

Budge, Gordon. "Gunsmoke!" *TV-Radio Mirror*, May, 1958, pp. 50–51, 86.

Carskadon, Tom. "Crime Does Pay," *Tower Radio*, April, 1934, pp. 34, 59, 74.

Carskadon, Tom. "Gagging Their Way Through Life," *Radioland*, September, 1933, pp. 40–42, 84.

Carskadon, Tom. "Restoring Cinderella," *Radioland*, February, 1935, pp. 64–65, 68.

Clark, David G. "H. V. Kaltenborn and His Sponsors: Controversial Broadcasting and the Sponsor's Role," *Journal of Broadcasting*, Fall, 1968, pp. 309–321.

Clark, David G. "Radio Presidential Campaigns: The Early Years (1924–1932)," *Journal of Broadcasting*, Summer, 1962, pp. 229–38.

Cole, Hilda. "Voodoo in the Air," *Radio Stars*, June, 1933, pp. 33, 49.

Crossen, Ken. "There's Murder in the Air," in Howard Haycraft (editor), *The Art of the Mystery Story*. New York: Simon & Schuster, 1946, pp. 304–307.

Danna, Sammy R. "The Rise of Radio News," in Lawrence W. Lichty and Malachi C. Topping, *American Broadcasting: A Source Book on the History of Radio and Television*, pp. 338–44. New York: Hastings House, 1975.

Denis, Paul. "The Negro in Show Business," *Negro Digest*, February, 1943, pp. 22–24.

"The Editor's Opinion," *Radioland*, November, 1933, pp. 11–12.

Edwards, John. "Roxy Says: 'Take the Amateurs Off the Air!'" *Radio Mirror*, May, 1935, pp. 20–21, 85, 87.

Eichberg, Robert. "The Battle for News!" *Radio Stars*, January, 1934, pp. 48–49, 84, 86.

Grunwald, Edgar A. "Program-Production History, 1929–1937," in *Variety Radio Directory, 1937–1938*, pp. 17–28. New York: Variety, 1937.

Hall, Gladys. "Are Comedians Through on the Air?" *Radio Stars*, February, 1936, pp. 44–45, 70–73.

Heinl, Robert D. "Radio and the Next War," *Radioland*, September, 1933, pp. 12–15, 94–95.

Herzog, Dorothy. "Radio Enters the Fight on Crime," *Radioland*, January, 1935, pp. 15, 47, 50.

Hill, Edwin C. "Radio's New Destiny," *Radio Stars*, June, 1933, pp. 7, 43.

Klapp, Orrin E. "Heroes, Villains and Fools as Agents of Social Control," *American Sociological Review*, February, 1954, pp. 56–62.

Luber, Mildred. "His Life Is News!" *Radio and Television Mirror*, August, 1939, pp. 28–29, 74–75.

Martel, Charles, "It's Tough to Be a Comedian, Says Jack Pearl," *Tower Radio*, July, 1934, pp. 20–21, 74–76.

Martel, Charles, "Never Try to Be Funny," *Tower Radio*, September, 1934, pp. 20–21, 96–97.

Mason, Jerald. "Smart Alex Woollcott," *Radioland*, February, 1935, pp. 16, 50–51.

Miller, Llewellyn. "Radio's Own Life Story," *Radio and Television Mirror*, February, 1950, pp. 38–39, 91–94.

Ogburn, W. F., with the assistance of S. C. Gilfillan. "The Influence of Invention and Discovery," in President's Research Committee on Social Trends, *Recent Social Trends in the United States*, pp. 122–66. Washington: McGraw-Hill, 1933.

Oliver, Bryce. "Thought Control—American Style," *New Republic*, January 13, 1947, pp. 12–13.

Rolo, Charles J. "Simenon and Spillane: The Metaphysics of Murder for the Millions," in Bernard Rosenberg and David M. White (editors), *Mass Culture: The Popular Arts in America*, pp. 165–75. Glencoe, Ill.: The Free Press, 1957.

Russell, Norton. "The Personal History of Floyd Gibbons, Adventurer," *Radio Mirror*, May, 1937, pp. 56, 66–67.

Seymour, John. "Mirth with a Mission." *Tower Radio*, April, 1934, pp. 12–13, 77, 79.

Sher, Jack. "Television a Reality!" *Radio Mirror*, February, 1939, pp. 22–23, 64–65.

Thurber, James A. "Onward and Upward with the Arts," *New Yorker*, May 15, 1948, pp. 34–38, 40, 42, 44, 46–47.

van Horn, Harriet. "Unrest in the Air," *Radio and Television Mirror*, March, 1949, pp. 14–15, 103–4.

Weber, Paul. "Coughlin Justifies Attack on Roosevelt!" *Radio Stars*, March, 1936, pp. 14–15, 96–99.

Wertheim, Arthur Frank. "Relieving Social Tensions: Radio Comedy and the Great Depression," *Journal of Popular Culture*, Winter, 1976, pp. 501–19.

Willey, George A. "End of An Era: The Daytime Radio Serial," *Journal of Broadcasting*, Spring, 1961, pp. 97–115.

Willey, George A. "The Soap Operas and the War," *Journal of Broadcasting*, Fall, 1963, pp. 339–52.

Willey, Malcolm M., and Stuart A. Rice. "The Agencies of Communication," in President's Research Committee on Social Trends, *Recent Social Trends in the United States*, pp. 167–217. Washington: McGraw-Hill, 1933.

Index of Radio Programs

Index